*Facts, Valu*

Our values shape our lives – what we do and think, what we feel, even what we see or notice. Our norms, too, shape our lives – how we speak and act, what we feel is correct or out of line, what we treat as evidence, what we expect of ourselves and others. Since it seems neither desirable nor possible to remove values and norms from our lives, the question whether values and norms can be other than subjective, relative, or arbitrary becomes pressing. We do sometimes speak of *learning* what really matters, or how best to do things, from our choices and experiences. We speak, too, of "lessons of history" in ethics and politics and of "the test of time" in aesthetics and the practical sciences. Can any of this be understood as learning about values and norms themselves? A philosophical account of values and norms should help us to answer this question, and yet as we delve deeper, we encounter a host of difficulties in developing a credible picture of learning and objectivity about values and norms.

In this collection of essays, Peter Railton develops some of the elements needed for such a picture. He suggests ways of understanding the nature of value, and its relation to judgment, that would permit ordinary human experience to be a source of genuine understanding and objectivity. Using realistic examples and an accessible style of analysis, he presents a unified approach to such questions as: What is the meaning or function of evaluative and normative language? What role do consequences play in assessing moral rightness or wrongness? Is a moral perspective inherently alienating? Can there be genuine moral dilemmas? What is "normative guidance," and how does it emerge in individual and social practice? Does ideology exclude objectivity? To what extent, and in what ways, can we subject our moral, evaluative, or aesthetic judgments to criticism and revision?

The essays in this book are addressed to professionals and students in philosophy and also to those in other fields who seek an engaging but rigorous discussion of some basic philosophical questions about ethics, values, norms, and objectivity.

Peter Railton is the John Stephenson Perrin Professor of Philosophy at the University of Michigan.

CAMBRIDGE STUDIES IN PHILOSOPHY

*General editor* ERNEST SOSA (Brown University)

*Advisory editors:*
JONATHAN DANCY (University of Reading)
JOHN HALDANE (University of St. Andrews)
GILBERT HARMAN (Princeton University)
FRANK JACKSON (Australian National University)
WILLIAM G. LYCAN (University of North Carolina at Chapel Hill)
SYDNEY SHOEMAKER (Cornell University)
JUDITH J. THOMSON (Massachusetts Institute of Technology)

Recent Titles:
MARK LANCE and JOHN O'LEARY-HAWTHORNE *The Grammar of Meaning*
D. M. ARMSTRONG *A World of States of Affairs*
PIERRE JACOB *What Minds Can Do*
ANDRE GALLOIS *The World Without the Mind Within*
FRED FELDMAN *Utilitarianism, Hedonism, and Desert*
LAURENCE BONJOUR *In Defense of Pure Reason*
DAVID LEWIS *Papers in Philosophical Logic*
WAYNE DAVIS *Implicature*
DAVID COCKBURN *Other Times*
DAVID LEWIS *Papers on Metaphysics and Epistemology*
RAYMOND MARTIN *Self-Concern*
ANNETTE BARNES *Seeing Through Self-Deception*
MICHAEL BRATMAN *Faces of Intention*
AMIE THOMASSON *Fiction and Metaphysics*
DAVID LEWIS *Papers on Ethics and Social Philosophy*
FRED DRETSKE *Perception, Knowledge, and Belief*
LYNNE RUDDER BAKER *Persons and Bodies*
JOHN GRECO *Putting Skeptics in Their Place*
RUTH GARRETT MILLIKAN *On Clear and Confused Ideas*
DERK PEREBOOM *Living Without Free Will*
BRIAN ELLIS *Scientific Essentialism*
ALAN H. GOLDMAN *Practical Rules: When We Need Them and When We Don't*
CHRISTOPHER HILL *Thought and World*
ANDREW NEWMAN *The Correspondence Theory of Truth*
ISHTIYAQUE HAJI *Deontic Morality and Control*
WAYNE A. DAVIS *Meaning, Expression and Thought*

# Facts, Values, and Norms

## ESSAYS TOWARD A MORALITY OF CONSEQUENCE

PETER RAILTON

*University of Michigan*

CAMBRIDGE
UNIVERSITY PRESS

PUBLISHED BY THE PRESS SYNDICATE OF THE UNIVERSITY OF CAMBRIDGE
The Pitt Building, Trumpington Street, Cambridge, United Kingdom

CAMBRIDGE UNIVERSITY PRESS
The Edinburgh Building, Cambridge CB2 2RU, UK
40 West 20th Street, New York, NY 10011-4211, USA
477 Williamstown Road, Port Melbourne, VIC 3207, Australia
Ruiz de Alarcón 13, 28014 Madrid, Spain
Dock House, The Waterfront, Cape Town 8001, South Africa

http://www.cambridge.org

First published 2003

Printed in the United States of America

*Typeface* Bembo 10.5/13 pt. *System* LATEX 2$_\varepsilon$ [TB]

*A catalog record for this book is available from the British Library.*

*Library of Congress Cataloging in Publication Data*
Railton, Peter Albert.
Facts, Values, and Norms : essays toward a morality
of consequence / Peter Railton.
p. cm. – (Cambridge studies in philosophy)
Includes bibliographical references and index.
ISBN 0-521-41697-3 – ISBN 0-521-42693-6 (pbk.)
1. Ethics. I. Title. II. Series.
BJ1012 .R33 2003
170–dc21 2002066522

ISBN 0 521 41697 3 hardback
ISBN 0 521 42693 6 paperback

*For John and Thomas*

# Contents

# *Foreword*

"Oh. . . . Philosophy. Well, what *sort* of philosophy do you do?"
"Mostly ethics."
"Ethics? Do you think there really is any such thing?"

A fair question. Indeed, a host of fair questions. For there are many ways to be puzzled about ethics, and few easy answers. Some examples:

Moral claims are often made as if they possessed a kind of *objectivity* – as something more than personal or partisan preferences.[1] But where in the world can we find anything like objective values or principles to back this up? Even when we *disagree* morally, we typically act as if there were something at stake, something to be right or wrong about. And those who argue that moral principles are "cultural" or "relative" typically are on their way to making a case for tolerance, understanding, cooperation, fairness – but this itself looks like a moral view. What is the *meaning* of moral terms, and what sort of objectivity, if any, does it commit us to? And, if there is such a commitment, can we identify properties of moral practice, or values in the world, that would vindicate it? This is one family of questions.

The objectivity of ethics, it seems, would have to be different from the objectivity of science. Morality gives *practical guidance* – it purports to say not how things *are*, but how they *ought* to be, or how it would be *good* for them to be. This guidance, moreover, claims to be *rational* – moral concerns present themselves as good reasons for action, reasons serious enough to outweigh or even cancel certain other pressing concerns or interests. But what is this idea of "practical guidance"? And if morality has "rational force," where does this force come from — inside us? outside? nowhere? How is rational force weighed, and how is such a force to make itself felt among the real forces driving action? A second family of questions.

And what might this practical guidance be? It is one thing to say that there are objective, rational principles, and another thing to say what they are, and how one tells. Is morality based on goods and values, or on rules, commandments, and duties? And does moral evaluation reach into every corner of our lives, or is it sometimes out of place? Is it partial or impartial, local or global, general or particular? A third family.

Lastly, one might ask: Whether or not morality *should* matter, *does* it? Does all our moral talk have any real force in the world — apart from escalating the rhetoric of agreements and disagreements in attitudes and interests? Morality is not supposed to be empty words, mere froth upon the surface of real life. Moral *opinions* of course influence how people act and feel, but then so do opinions about ghosts, gods, and astral influences. Could real moral considerations ever *explain* anything, in a way that would give us some confidence we are not simply making the whole thing up? A fourth family.

There are more questions besides, but this is enough for now. One can become impatient with all these questions, and begin to wonder whether high-sounding doubts about "the reality of ethics" express genuine doubts, or simply mask the real concerns and discomforts people have when moral issues are raised. Hume, for one, felt there was something "disingenuous" about certain disputatious souls, who fluently express doubts about morality, but who show none of the real anxiety one might expect such doubts to bestir, and who invariably fall back into unreflective moralizing as soon as the subject changes or someone else's ox is gored. Moreover, this commonsense assurance about ethics might be very much stronger than our confidence in any argument contrived by a philosopher. So perhaps moral *philosophy* is beside the point — even when the doubts about morality are sincere, philosophical maneuvers cannot resolve them.

Certainly commonsense ethics seems unlikely to collapse without moral philosophy to underwrite it, but it does seem to me that commonsense moral life regularly leads people into quandaries of a philosophical nature. Far from being disingenuous, these quandaries are often most sharply felt by the very people who take moral concerns most seriously in everyday life. One would be hard put, I think, to understand the shape of religion, or its importance in people's lives, without taking into account the deeply felt need to say *something* about the basis of morality. Many do not find religious answers convincing, or find that the philosophical quandaries simply re-arise *within* religion. Philosophy should be able to help.

In that spirit, I offer this collection of essays. They were written over a span of twenty-five years, presenting, developing, and defending some ideas about how one might respond philosophically to the previously mentioned questions. The essays are just that – *essais*, trials, attempts. They exhibit a sense – a faith? – that ethics can find a solid place within the natural and human world, without mysterious faculties or supplementary metaphysics.

The more I read the great figures of moral philosophy in the past – Hume, certainly, but also Aristotle, Rousseau, Kant, Mill, and many others – the more I think that the ideas I seem to have come up with could have been unearthed by more careful attention on my part to what *they* were trying to get across. Serious historians of ethics will wink at this remark. It is the vice of every amateur to find in The Greats admirable statements of whatever it is that he or she already believes. Now that I discover I have this vice, I feel that the essays reprinted in the following chapters largely pay inadequate tribute to philosophical ancestors, or worse, sometimes saddle these writers with views – "Humean," "Kantian," "Aristotelian" – that a closer or more thorough acquaintance would show The Greats did not themselves hold. I hope this is forgivable.

Less forgivable would be a failure to acknowledge the influence of my contemporaries, especially those who struggled hard to talk some sense into me. They include many colleagues, here at Michigan and elsewhere, and also many who do not think of themselves as philosophers, but who taught me much philosophy. I would be very pleased if the footnotes acknowledging the help of colleagues and others in the reprinted essays could be set in boldface – that might give a fairer idea of these good people's importance in shaping my thought.

I have organized the essays into three groups.


PART I: REALISM ABOUT VALUE AND MORALITY

I've put the word 'value' ahead of 'morality' because it seems to me that the most credible entry into questions about the reality of ethics is through

xiii

the theory of value. A domain could have objectivity, principles, rules, practices, and even norms without taking what makes life worth living as its touchstone – witness mathematics or linguistics. But it wouldn't be ethics.

Now, some forms of value or worth themselves depend upon moral considerations, and so could not serve as entry points into ethics. Thus, the morally deserved happiness of someone whose generosity over the years has at last come back to her in friendship and gratitude has a *moral value* that the morally undeserved happiness of someone who has just become rich through cunning or accident does not. But the *intrinsic value* of subjective well-being is present in both cases, and explains why we think of happiness as an appropriate *reward* for past sacrifice.

Because subjective well-being has intrinsic value, it can serve as one of the entry points into morality. Which still leaves the question: Just what sort of thing is intrinsic value, and what explains why happiness, say, has it? This is not in the first instance a question about the *concept* of intrinsic value as such, which may be normative to its toes – as Moore in effect pointed out using the "open question argument." It is a question about the *property* of being intrinsically valuable – what does it consist in, and how can it be judged? This property is held to "supervene" – as Moore also observed – on natural features, in the sense that value differences are always explained or justified by other kinds of difference. But *what* does value supervene upon, what features of the world and our relationship to it might constitute value?

Intrinsic value, as I understand it, intriguingly straddles the objective and the subjective. On the one hand, our opinions don't determine the matter – Mill mentions the miser, who wrongly thinks money has intrinsic value because he has come to see it that way. On the other hand, intrinsic value does always seem to be related to, and realized by, subjects. Intrinsic value, for example, is thought to be related to *intrinsic motivation* – to questions of what is actually sought for its own sake. And we appeal to value when *deliberating*, and to explain and justify *choices*. If intrinsic value is to be considered an objective phenomenon, then we will have to explain the peculiar blending of objective features and subjective interests that gives rise to it. And if *value inquiry* is to make sense, we will have to explain how learning about value is possible. I attempt to develop a "naturalistic" approach to intrinsic value (including intrinsic aesthetic value) that would enable us to see how claims about objectivity could be well-founded and could support a critical evaluative practice.

If anything like the approach I suggest to intrinsic value is viable, then we have an entry point: ethics has something real to work with, something that answers to important human concerns and might provide an infrastructure to support some moral practices. This in itself could mitigate certain worries about "the reality of ethics," but we would still need to connect intrinsic value to the rest of ethics – for example, to judgments of what is right or wrong, obligatory or permitted, virtuous or vicious. How to make the connection? Philosophers in the twentieth century developed the idea of a *moral point of view*, a standpoint of assessment that is distinctive not just because it is concerned with the realization of intrinsic value – after all, the prudential point of view is as well – but because it asks us to see ourselves as but one among others, whose good has no different *intrinsic* weight than theirs. Assessments of acts or states of affairs from this "non-personal" point of view might be worthy of the name *moral evaluations* if we can link them suitably to our moral practices. To do this requires analyzing the place of moral judgment, and the distinctive roles of the different moral categories, in our lives. It also involves capturing enough of the substantive *content* of commonsense moral judgment – including its practices of criticism and justification – to give us some confidence that we are deepening our understanding of our actual moral life, rather than attempting to replace it. If this were possible, then these categories of moral judgment could inherit whatever objectivity was possessed by the original moral evaluations themselves. Ethics proper might to that extent be seen to be more real.

## PART II: NORMATIVE MORAL THEORY

Actual moral life at any time is not a systematic body of precepts or set of fixed procedures for resolving disputes. Moral agreement and moral disagreement are both part of the stuff of daily life, although the points of agreement and disagreement have not been constant across societies or times. All this might make ethics look very different from areas of inquiry such as natural or social science, and cause one to think that the ambition of finding some systematic or theoretical order in it is vain at best, dangerous at worst.

This contrast is readily overdrawn. Shifting patterns of agreement and disagreement can be found in the history of natural and social thought, or across the contemporary world once one looks beyond the groves of academe. Even within the groves at a given time, one can find great and impassioned disagreement over matters of substance and method in empirical inquiry. The fundamental differences between ethical inquiry and inquiry into the natural and social world do not really lie in this dimension.

Moreover, both morality and empirical inquiry contain *norms of practice* as well as substantive claims. In the first respect, they show remarkable parallels, as I try to argue in some of the essays included here. Where they most differ, I would guess, is that ethics gives a special place to substantive claims that are themselves of a normative character, and could not play the role it does in our lives if it did not. Given a substantive empirical theory, I can attempt to predict what I will be doing a day or a year from now, much as I might predict what someone else will be doing. But predicting this is not deciding it – and I can defy my own predictions on principled grounds as much as I might defy yours. A theory suited to the predictive task can greatly aid deciding, but will not suffice for it. Ethics is not alone in offering normative claims as part of its substantive core – so do prudence, jurisprudence, military strategy, engineering standards, pedagogical manuals, and so on. And it would be a reckless discipline that offered normative guidance without consulting a substantive body of empirical knowledge – prudent people and good doctors try to learn the facts, anticipate consequences, measure effects. But it would be no practical discipline at all that could only describe actions or explain outcomes, without ever advising us to seek some and shun others.

To be sure, prudent people and good doctors typically do not consult elaborate, systematic *normative theories* in acting. They act on personal experience; acquired skills and knowledge; and advice and consultation. We should not expect anything different to be typical in ethical decision making. So we would do well not to think of normative moral theories as specifying a "decision procedure" to be internalized and applied, but as schemes that enable us to *assess* the motives, strategies, skills, habits, practices, rules, etc. that people might defer to, act on, consult, and encourage. Such a scheme of assessment gives us critical purchase on practices that prudence, medicine, and moral choice *as actually practiced* badly need if they are to be done well.

Some such schemes afford greater critical purchase than others, and one of the pressing questions in contemporary ethics is whether moral theory has been given *too much* leverage in moral philosophy. The resistance of actual moral thought and practice to ready systematization might be trying to tell us something deep. I try to diagnose some of these forms of resistance, and learn from them how better to do moral theory. But my optimism on this score is not, I know, widely shared – doubt about the continuing usefulness of theory in normative ethics is rife.

Within normative ethics, philosophers have long disputed the relative priority of notions of right versus notions of value, or notions of principle versus notions of virtue. I believe that a coherent picture of normative ethics as a whole can emerge from a value-based, broadly consequentialist standpoint. This picture has the virtue (or vice, in some eyes) of bringing a great deal of empirical science to bear on normative conclusions. However *a priori* normative concepts might be, their guidance in conduct becomes very *a posteriori*. This is unsettling to many moral philosophers, but it does throw into relief those features we are most likely to cite, I suspect, for explaining why morality matters as much as it does – the ways we can affect one another and the values at stake as we live together.

PART III: THE AUTHORITY OF ETHICS AND VALUE –
THE PROBLEM OF NORMATIVITY

I first encountered "the problem of normativity" in trying to respond to critics of naturalism. A naturalistic theory of value, I was told, could not account for the *normative force* of value judgments. My first effort in this direction was a talk entitled "Naturalism and Normativity," but I was advised that "Naturalism and Prescriptivity" made a better title for publication, since the latter term was much more familiar. There is no danger of unfamiliarity nowadays. But despite heavy use, the term 'normativity' remains shrouded in a certain mystery. Thus far in the Foreword, I have used 'normative' freely, even to make important distinctions, without saying much of anything to explain it. We do have a sense of the ways in which notions of what *is* differ from notions of what *ought to be*, or of the gap between a generalization describing actual usage and a principle of *correct* usage. Can we add anything to illuminate this? A useful phrase seems to be 'direction of fit': an *is*-statement or descriptive generalization is supposed to fit the way things are, while the way things are is supposed to fit – or to be made to fit – *ought*-statements or principles of correctness. But 'supposed to fit' is itself a normative phrase. So it would seem we must begin a step further back.

We should not be too hard on ourselves. It is unsurprising that a very basic contrast, like that between normative and descriptive, is hard to characterize at any deeper level. Just try saying what 'true' and 'false' mean in an informative way without simply using near-synonyms. So let's not try that straight off. We *can* say a good deal that is informative about "what truth conditions are" or "what it is for a language to have a truth predicate." So let's talk of "what it is to be normative" or "what it is for a practice to have a norm." That is, let's talk in terms of *functions* or *roles* rather than *meanings* or *concepts* proper. Or so I suggest. We could demystify somewhat the question of what it would be for ethics to be real if we could see how a real property or state could come to have a normative function or role in a practice, and why. This I begin to do in the essays grouped in Part III, which I hope suggest a way beyond the "circle of synonyms."

Is any progress possible *within* the circle? Unless "normative guidance" and "rule following" are primitive concepts, then it should be possible to do a bit of anatomy. When we do, I think, we find two quite different components, roughly the "norm"-part and the "guided"-part, or the "rule"-part and the "following"-part. The first part must be in some sense *external* to the agent, a norm or rule that encodes a standard in some way independent of her will but with which she ordinarily can comply through some sort of voluntary activity (*ought* implies *can*, in some sense). The second part must be in some sense *internal*, a deference that *is* a will or *volonté* of hers, but itself a feeling rather than a product of will (lest regress follow). This is, I argue in the following text, a point of agreement between Hume and Kant – who have been thought to differ so deeply on normativity. Much later, Wittgenstein reaffirmed the point. Indeed, I find this idea present in Durkheim's analysis of religion. That at least this much of a shared conception of normativity can be found in these thinkers, despite their differences, gives me some hope (what else, with my amateur's vice?) that we can make progress in demystifying the concept of normativity, thereby removing another obstacle to seeing how there might "really be such a thing as ethics."

Finally, some will think I cannot be a serious person if I do not recognize the *ideological* role of moral discourse throughout history. They are right. I try to make a case that this recognition can strengthen, rather than weaken, our sense that ethics – real ethics – can be a force in the world. Moralities and mores come and go, ideologies rise and fall. But human suffering and well-being, exclusion and empathy, denial and recognition, struggle and solidarity, are realities that help explain why. And ethics can be as real as they are.

I subtitle this collection "Essays *Toward* a Morality of Consequence" because we aren't there yet.

I gladly dedicate this volume to my children, John and Thomas, because of what they have taught me about facts, values, and norms, and because an old and good saying has it that the only real way to thank one's parents is to give what one can to one's children in turn.

There are a dozen others, teachers and friends, to whom I would dearly love to dedicate a volume to tell them how much they have helped me along the way. Some are no longer alive for me to put it in their hands. And there are many others who deserve special thanks for thoughts, criticisms, and encouragement. Any dedication or expression of debts will also be an omission, but I would be remiss not to set down at least these names: Elizabeth Anderson, Nomy Arpaly, Kent Berridge, Paul Boghossian, Richard Boyd, Richard Brandt, Michael Bratman, Monique Canto-Sperber, Stephen Darwall, Jean-Pierre Dupuy, William Frankena, Allan Gibbard, Alan Goldman, Gilbert Harman, C.G. Hempel, David Hills, Octaaf Holbrecht, Thomas Holt, Frank Jackson, Richard Jeffrey, Mark Johnston, James Joyce, Shelly Kagan, Jaegwon Kim, David Lewis, Burns Lloyd, Harry Lloyd, Louis Loeb, Richard Miller, Thomas Nagel, Randolf Nesse, Richard Nisbett, Derek Parfit, Philip Petit, Gideon Rosen, T.M. Scanlon, Samuel Scheffler, Andrew Scott, Anne Scott, Rebecca Scott, Holly Smith, Michael Smith, Daniel Sperber, Nicholas Sturgeon, David Velleman, Peter Vranas, Kendall Walton, David Wiggins, and Susan Wolf.

Institutions that support our work and the many people who fund them deserve thanks, too. I am particularly grateful to the American Council of Learned Societies, the Centre de Recherche en Epistemologie Appliquée (Ecole Polytechnique, Paris), the Guggenheim Foundation, the Humanities Centers at Stanford University and Cornell University, the National Endowment for the Humanities, the James and Grace Nelson Endowment, and, above all, the University of Michigan and its Department of Philosophy, Institute for the Humanities, and Society of Fellows.

Finally, thanks are due to those who let our work see the light of day: Cambridge University Press and the editors of this volume, Terence Moore and Ernest Sosa, have been patiently supportive throughout; numerous other editors, journals, and presses gave the essays in this volume their first chance, and gave permission for them to reappear together here.

Peter Railton
Ann Arbor, Michigan

1. I will be using 'morality' and 'ethics' (and 'moral' and 'ethical') interchangeably. Some philosophers wish to mark a worthwhile distinction by distinguishing them – for example, Bernard Williams, in *Ethics and the Limits of Philosophy* (Cambridge: Harvard, 1985). But the roots *mores* and *ethos* are close, and usage seldom differentiates the modern terms.

# Part I

*Realism about Value and Morality*

# 1

## *Moral Realism*

Among contemporary philosophers, even those who have not found skepticism about empirical science at all compelling have tended to find skepticism about morality irresistible. For various reasons, among them an understandable suspicion of moral absolutism, it has been thought a mark of good sense to explain away any appearance of objectivity in moral discourse. So common has it become in secular intellectual culture to treat morality as subjective or conventional that most of us now have difficulty imagining what it might be like for there to be facts to which moral judgments answer.

Undaunted, some philosophers have attempted to establish the objectivity of morality by arguing that reason, or science, affords a foundation for ethics. The history of such attempts hardly inspires confidence. Although rationalism in ethics has retained adherents long after other rationalisms have been abandoned, the powerful philosophical currents that have worn away at the idea that unaided reason might afford a standpoint from which to derive substantive conclusions show no signs of slackening. And ethical naturalism has yet to find a plausible synthesis of the empirical and the normative: the more it has given itself over to descriptive accounts of the origin of norms, the less has it retained recognizably moral force; the more it has undertaken to provide a recognizable basis for moral criticism or reconstruction, the less has it retained a firm connection with descriptive social or psychological theory.[1]

In what follows, I will present in a programmatic way a form of ethical naturalism that owes much to earlier theorists, but that seeks to effect a more satisfactory linkage of the normative to the empirical. The link cannot, I believe, be effected by proof. It is no more my aim to refute moral skepticism than it is the aim of contemporary epistemic naturalists

3

to refute Cartesian skepticism. The naturalist in either case has more modest aspirations. First, he seeks to provide an analysis of epistemology or ethics that permits us to see how the central evaluative functions of this domain could be carried out within existing (or prospective) empirical theories. Second, he attempts to show how traditional nonnaturalist accounts rely upon assumptions that are in some way incoherent, or that fit ill with existing science. And third, he presents to the skeptic a certain challenge, namely, to show how a skeptical account of our epistemic or moral practices could be as plausible, useful, or interesting as the account the naturalist offers, and how a skeptical reconstruction of such practices – should the skeptic, as often he does, attempt one – could succeed in preserving their distinctive place and function in human affairs. I will primarily be occupied with the first of these three aspirations.

One thing should be said at the outset. Some may be drawn to, or repelled by, moral realism out of a sense that it is the view of ethics that best expresses high moral earnestness. Yet one can be serious about morality, even to a fault, without being a moral realist. Indeed, a possible objection to the sort of moral realism I will defend here is that it may not make morality serious enough.

### I. SPECIES OF MORAL REALISM

Such diverse views have claimed to be – or have been accused of being – realist about morality, that an initial characterization of the position I will defend is needed before proceeding further. Claims – and accusations – of moral realism typically extend along some or all of the following dimensions. Roughly put: (1) Cognitivism – Are moral judgments capable of truth and falsity? (2) Theories of truth – If moral judgments do have truth values, in what sense? (3) Objectivity – In what ways, if any, does the existence of moral properties depend upon the actual or possible states of mind of intelligent beings? (4) Reductionism – Are moral properties reducible to, or do they in some weaker sense supervene upon, nonmoral properties? (5) Naturalism – Are moral properties natural properties? (6) Empiricism – Do we come to know moral facts in the same way we come to know the facts of empirical science, or are they revealed by reason or by some special mode of apprehension? (7) Bivalence – Does the principle of the excluded middle apply to moral judgments? (8) Determinateness – Given whatever procedures we have for assessing moral judgments, how much of morality is likely to be determinable? (9) Categoricity – Do all rational agents necessarily have some reason to

4

obey moral imperatives? (10) Universality – Are moral imperatives applicable to all rational agents, even (should such exist) those who lack a reason to comply with them? (11) Assessment of existing moralities – Are present moral beliefs approximately true, or do prevailing moral intuitions in some other sense constitute privileged data? (12) Relativism – Does the truth or warrant of moral judgments depend directly upon individually or socially adopted norms or practices? (13) Pluralism – Is there a uniquely good form of life or a uniquely right moral code, or could different forms of life or moral codes be appropriate in different circumstances?

Here, then, are the approximate coordinates of my own view in this multidimensional conceptual space. I will argue for a form of moral realism that holds that moral judgments can bear truth values in a fundamentally nonepistemic sense of truth; that moral properties are objective, though relational; that moral properties supervene upon natural properties, and may be reducible to them; that moral inquiry is of a piece with empirical inquiry; that it cannot be known *a priori* whether bivalence holds for moral judgments or how determinately such judgments can be assessed; that there is reason to think we know a fair amount about morality, but also reason to think that current moralities are wrong in certain ways and could be wrong in quite general ways; that a rational agent may fail to have a reason for obeying moral imperatives, although they may nonetheless be applicable to him; and that, while there are perfectly general criteria of moral assessment, nonetheless, by the nature of these criteria no one kind of life is likely to be appropriate for all individuals and no one set of norms appropriate for all societies and all times. The position thus described might well be called 'stark, raving moral realism,' but for the sake of syntax, I will colorlessly call it 'moral realism.' This usage is not proprietary. Other positions, occupying more or less different coordinates, may have equal claim to either name.

## II. THE FACT/VALUE DISTINCTION

Any attempt to argue for a naturalistic moral realism runs headlong into the fact/value distinction. Philosophers have given various accounts of this distinction, and of the arguments for it, but for present purposes I will focus upon several issues concerning the epistemic and ontological status of judgments of value as opposed to judgments of fact.

Perhaps the most frequently heard argument for the fact/value distinction is epistemic: it is claimed that disputes over questions of value can persist even after all rational or scientific means of adjudication have been deployed; hence, value judgments cannot be cognitive in the sense that factual or logical judgments are. This claim is defended in part by appeal to the instrumental (hypothetical) character of reason, which prevents reason from dictating ultimate values. In principle, the argument runs, two individuals who differ in ultimate values could, without manifesting any rational defect, hold fast to their conflicting values in the face of any amount of argumentation or evidence. As Ayer puts it, "We find that argument is possible on moral questions only if some system of values is presupposed."[2]

One might attempt to block this conclusion by challenging the instrumental conception of rationality. But for all its faults and for all that it needs to be developed, the instrumental conception seems to me the clearest notion we have of what it is for an agent to have reasons to act. Moreover, it captures a central normative feature of reason giving, since we can readily see the commending force for an agent of the claim that a given act would advance his ends. It would be hard to make much sense of someone who sincerely claimed to have certain ends and yet at the same time insisted that they could not provide him even *prima facie* grounds for action. (Of course, he might also believe that he has other, perhaps countervailing, grounds.)

Yet this version of the epistemic argument for the fact/value distinction is in difficulty even granting the instrumental conception of rationality. From the standpoint of instrumental reason, belief-formation is but one activity among others: to the extent that we have reasons for engaging in it, or for doing it one way rather than another, these are at bottom a matter of its contribution to our ends.[3] What it would be rational for an individual to believe on the basis of a given experience will vary not only with respect to his other beliefs, but also with respect to what he desires.[4] From this it follows that no amount of mere argumentation or experience could force one on pain of irrationality to accept even the factual claims of empirical science. The long-running debate over inductive logic well illustrates that rational choice among competing hypotheses requires much richer and more controversial criteria of theory choice than can be squeezed from instrumental reason alone. Unfortunately for the contrast Ayer wished to make, we find that argument is possible on scientific questions only if some system of values is presupposed.

However, Hume had much earlier found a way of marking the distinction between facts and values without appeal to the idea that induction – or even deduction – could require a rational agent to adopt certain beliefs rather than others when this would conflict with his contingent ends.[5] For

Hume held the thesis that morality is practical, by which he meant that if moral facts existed, they would necessarily provide a reason (although perhaps not an overriding reason) for moral action to all rational beings, regardless of their particular desires. Given this thesis as a premise, the instrumental conception of rationality can clinch the argument after all, for it excludes the possibility of categorical reasons of this kind. By contrast, Hume did not suppose it to be constitutive of logic or science that the facts revealed by these forms of inquiry have categorical force for rational agents, so the existence of logical and scientific facts, unlike the existence of moral facts, is compatible with the instrumental character of reason.

Yet this way of drawing the fact/value distinction is only as compelling as the claim that morality is essentially practical in Hume's sense.[6] Hume is surely right in claiming there to be an intrinsic connection, no doubt complex, between valuing something and having some sort of positive attitude toward it that provides one with an instrumental reason for action. We simply would disbelieve someone who claimed to value honesty and yet never showed the slightest urge to act honestly when given an easy opportunity. But this is a fact about the connection between the values *embraced by* an individual and his reasons for action, not a fact showing a connection between moral evaluation and rational motivation.

Suppose for example that we accept Hume's characterization of justice as an artificial virtue directed at the general welfare. This is in a recognizable sense an evaluative or normative notion – "a value" in the loose sense in which this term is used in such debates – yet it certainly does not follow from its definition that every rational being, no matter what his desires, who believes that some or other act is just in this sense will have an instrumental reason to perform it. A rational individual may fail to value justice for its own sake, and may have ends contrary to it. In Hume's discussion of our "interested obligation" to be just, he seems to recognize that in the end it may not be possible to show that a "sensible knave" has a reason to be just. Of course, Hume held that the rest of us – whose hearts rebel at Sensible Knave's attitude that he may break his word, cheat, or steal whenever it suits his purposes – have reason to be just, to deem Knave's attitude unjust, and to try to protect ourselves from his predations.[7]

Yet Knave himself could say, perhaps because he accepts Hume's analysis of justice, "Yes, my attitude is unjust." And by Hume's own account of the relation of reason and passion, Knave could add "But what is that to me?" without failing to grasp the content of his previous assertion. Knave, let us suppose, has no doubts about the intelligibility or reality of "the general welfare," and thinks it quite comprehensible that people attach great significance in public life to the associated notion of justice. He also realizes that for the bulk of mankind, whose passions differ from his, being just is a source and a condition of much that is most worthwhile in life. He thus understands that appeals to justice typically have motivating force. Moreover, he himself uses the category of justice in analyzing the social world, and he recognizes – indeed, his knavish calculations take into account – the distinction between those individuals and institutions that truly are just, and those that merely appear just or are commonly regarded as just. Knave does view a number of concepts with wide currency – religious ones, for example – as mere fictions that prey on weak minds, but he does not view justice in this way. Weak minds and moralists have, he thinks, surrounded justice with certain myths – that justice is its own reward, that once one sees what is just one will automatically have a reason to do it, and so on. But then, he thinks that weak minds and moralists have likewise surrounded wealth and power with myths – that the wealthy are not truly happy, that the powerful inevitably ride for a fall, and so on – and he does not on this account doubt whether there are such things as wealth and power. Knave is glad to be free of prevailing myths about wealth, power, and justice; glad, too that he is free in his own mind to pay as much or as little attention to any of these attributes as his desires and circumstances warrant. He might, for example, find Mae West's advice convincing: diamonds are very much worth acquiring, and "goodness ha[s] nothing to do with it."

We therefore must distinguish the business of saying what an individual values from the business of saying what it is for him to make measurements against the criteria of a species of evaluation that he recognizes to be genuine.[8]

To deny Hume's thesis of the practicality of moral judgment, and so remove the ground of his contrast between facts and values, is not to deny that morality has an action-guiding character. Morality surely can remain prescriptive within an instrumental framework, and can recommend itself to us in much the same way that, say, epistemology does: various significant and enduring – though perhaps not universal – human ends can be advanced if we apply certain evaluative criteria to our actions. That may be enough to justify to ourselves our abiding concern with the epistemic or moral status of what we do.[9]

By arguing that reason does not compel us to adopt particular beliefs or practices apart from our contingent, and variable, ends, I may seem to have failed to negotiate my way past epistemic relativism, and thus to have wrecked the argument for moral realism before it has even left port. Rationality does go relative when it goes instrumental, but epistemology need not follow. The epistemic warrant of an individual's belief may be disentangled from the rationality of his holding it, for epistemic warrant may be tied to an external criterion – as it is for example by causal or reliabilist theories of knowledge.[10] It is part of the naturalistic realism that informs this essay to adopt such a criterion of warrant. We should not confuse the obvious fact that in general our ends are well served by reliable causal mechanisms of belief-formation with an internalist claim to the effect that reason requires us to adopt such means. Reliable mechanisms have costs as well as benefits, and successful pursuit of some ends – Knave would point to religious ones, and to those of certain moralists – may in some respects be incompatible with adoption of reliable means of inquiry.

This rebuttal of the charge of relativism invites the defender of the fact/value distinction to shift to ontological grounds. Perhaps facts and values cannot be placed on opposite sides of an epistemological divide marked off by what reason and experience can compel us to accept. Still, the idea of reliable causal mechanisms for moral learning, and of moral facts "in the world" upon which they operate, is arguably so bizarre that I may have done no more than increase my difficulties.

### III. VALUE REALISM

The idea of causal interaction with moral reality certainly would be intolerably odd if moral facts were held to be *sui generis*;[11] but there need be nothing odd about causal mechanisms for learning moral facts if these facts are constituted by natural facts, and that is the view under consideration. This response will remain unconvincing, however, until some positive argument for realism about moral facts is given. So let us turn to that task.

What might be called 'the generic stratagem of naturalistic realism' is to postulate a realm of facts in virtue of the contribution they would make to the *a posteriori* explanation of certain features of our experience. For example, an external world is posited to explain the coherence, stability, and intersubjectivity of sense-experience. A moral realist who would avail himself of this stratagem must show that the postulation of moral facts similarly can have an explanatory function. The stratagem can succeed in either case only if the reality postulated has these two characteristics:

(1) *independence*: it exists and has certain determinate features independent of whether we think it exists or has those features, independent, even, of whether we have good reason to think this;

(2) *feedback:* it is such – and we are such – that we are able to interact with it, and this interaction exerts the relevant sort of shaping influence or control upon our perceptions, thought, and action.

These two characteristics enable the realist's posit to play a role in the explanation of our experience that cannot be replaced without loss by our mere *conception* of ourselves or our world. For although our conceptual scheme mediates even our most basic perceptual experiences, an experience-transcendent reality has ways of making itself felt without the permission of our conceptual scheme – causally. The success or failure of our plans and projects famously is not determined by expectation alone. By resisting or yielding to our worldly efforts in ways not anticipated by our going conceptual scheme, an external reality that is never directly revealed in perception may nonetheless significantly influence the subsequent evolution of that scheme.

The realist's use of an external world to explain sensory experience has often been criticized as no more than a picture. But do we even have a picture of what a realist explanation might look like in the case of values?[12] I will try to sketch one, filling in first a realist account of non-moral value – the notion of something being desirable for someone, or good for him.[13]

Consider first the notion of someone's *subjective interests* – his wants or desires, conscious or unconscious. Subjective interest can be seen as a secondary quality, akin to taste. For me to take a subjective interest in something is to say that it has a positive *valence* for me, that is, that in ordinary circumstances it excites a positive attitude or inclination (not necessarily conscious) in me. Similarly, for me to say that I find sugar sweet is to say that in ordinary circumstances sugar excites a certain gustatory sensation in me. As secondary qualities, subjective interest and perceived sweetness supervene upon primary qualities of the perceiver, the object (or other phenomenon) perceived, and the surrounding context: the perceiver is so constituted that this sort of object in this sort of context will excite that sort of sensation. Call this complex set of relational, dispositional, primary qualities the *reduction basis* of the secondary quality.

We have in this reduction basis an objective notion that corresponds to, and helps explain, subjective interests. But it is not a plausible foundation for the notion of non-moral goodness, since the subjective interests it grounds have insufficient normative force to capture the idea of desirableness. My subjective interests frequently reflect ignorance, confusion, or lack of consideration, as hindsight attests. The fact that I am now so constituted that I desire something that, had I better knowledge of it, I would wish I had never sought, does not seem to recommend it to me as part of my good.

To remedy this defect, let us introduce the notion of an *objectified subjective interest* for an individual *A*, as follows.[14] Give to an actual individual *A* unqualified cognitive and imaginative powers, and full factual and nomological information about his physical and psychological constitution, capacities, circumstances, history, and so on. *A* will have become *A+*, who has complete and vivid knowledge of himself and his environment, and whose instrumental rationality is in no way defective. We now ask *A+* to tell us not what *he* currently wants, but what he would want his nonidealized self *A* to want – or, more generally, to seek – were he to find himself in the actual condition and circumstances of *A*.[15] Just as we assumed there to be a reduction basis for an individual *A*'s actual subjective interests, we may assume there to be a reduction basis for his objectified subjective interests, namely, those facts about *A* and his circumstances that *A+* would combine with his general knowledge in arriving at his views about what he would want to want were he to step into *A*'s shoes.

For example, Lonnie, a traveler in a foreign country, is feeling miserable. He very much wishes to overcome his malaise and to settle his stomach, and finds he has a craving for the familiar: a tall glass of milk. The milk is desired by Lonnie, but is it also desirable for him? Lonnie-Plus can see that what is wrong with Lonnie, in addition to homesickness, is dehydration, a common affliction of tourists, but one often not detectable from introspective evidence. The effect of drinking hard-to-digest milk would be to further unsettle Lonnie's stomach and worsen his dehydration. By contrast, Lonnie-Plus can see that abundant clear fluids would quickly improve Lonnie's physical condition – which, incidentally, would help with his homesickness as well. Lonnie-Plus can also see just how distasteful Lonnie would find it to drink clear liquids, just what would happen were Lonnie to continue to suffer dehydration, and so on. As a result of this information, Lonnie-Plus might then come to desire that were he to assume Lonnie's place, he would want to drink clear liquids rather than milk, or at least want to act in such a way that a want of this kind would be satisfied. The reduction basis of this objectified interest includes facts about Lonnie's circumstances and constitution, which determine, among other things, his existing tastes and his ability to acquire certain new tastes, the consequences of continued dehydration, the effects and availability of various sorts of liquids, and so on.

Let us say that this reduction basis is the constellation of primary qualities that make it be the case that Lonnie has a certain *objective interest*.[16]

That is, we will say that Lonnie has an objective interest in drinking clear liquids in virtue of this complex, relational, dispositional set of facts. Put another way, we can say that the reduction basis, not the fact that Lonnie-Plus would have certain wants, is the truth-maker for the claim that this is an objective interest of Lonnie's. The objective interest thus explains why there is a certain objectified interest, not the other way around.[17]

Let us now say that X is *non-morally good for A* if and only if X would satisfy an objective interest of A.[18] We may think of A+'s views about what he would want to want were he in A's place as generating a ranking of potential objective interests of A, a ranking that will reflect what is better or worse for A and will allow us to speak of A's actual wants as better or worse approximations of what is best for him. We may also decompose A+'s views into *prima facie* as opposed to "on balance" objective interests of A, the former yielding the notion of "*a* good for A," the latter, of "*the* good for A."[19] This seems to me an intuitively plausible account of what someone's non-moral good consists in: roughly, what he would want himself to seek if he knew what he were doing.[20]

Moreover, this account preserves what seems to me an appropriate link between non-moral value and motivation. Suppose that one desires X, but wonders whether X really is part of one's good. This puzzlement typically arises because one feels that one knows too little about X, oneself, or one's world, or because one senses that one is not being adequately rational or reflective in assessing the information one has – perhaps one suspects that one has been captivated by a few salient features of X (or repelled by a few salient features of its alternatives). If one were to learn that one would still want oneself to want X in the circumstances were one to view things with full information and rationality, this presumably would reduce the force of the original worry. By contrast, were one to learn that when fully informed and rational one would want oneself *not* to want X in the circumstances, this presumably would add force to it. Desires being what they are, a reinforced worry might not be sufficient to remove the desire for X. But if one were to become genuinely and vividly convinced that one's desire for X is in this sense not supported by full reflection upon the facts, one presumably would feel this to be a count against acting upon the desire. This adjustment of desire to belief might not in a given case be required by reason or logic; it might be "merely psychological." But it is precisely such psychological phenomena that naturalistic theories of value take as basic.

In what follows, we will need the notion of intrinsic goodness, so let us say that X is *intrinsically non-morally good for A* just in case X is in A's objective interest without reference to any other objective interest of $A$. We can in an obvious way use the notion of objective intrinsic interest to account for all other objective interests. Since individuals and their environments differ in many respects, we need not assume that everyone has the same objective intrinsic interests. *A fortiori*, we need not assume that they have the same objective instrumental interests. We should, however, expect that when personal and situational similarities exist across individuals – that is, when there are similarities in reduction bases – there will to that extent be corresponding similarities in their interests.

It is now possible to see how the notion of non-moral goodness can have explanatory uses. For a start, it can explain why one's actual desires have certain counterfactual features, for example, why one would have certain hypothetical desires rather than others were one to become fully informed and aware. Yet this sort of explanatory use – following as it does directly from the definition of objective interest – might well be thought unimpressive unless some other explanatory functions can be found.

Consider, then, the difference between Lonnie and Tad, another traveler in the same straits, but one who, unlike Lonnie, wants to drink clear liquids, and proceeds to do so. Tad will perk up while Lonnie remains listless. We can explain this difference by noting that although both Lonnie and Tad acted upon their wants, Tad's wants better reflected his interests. The congruence of Tad's wants with his interests may be fortuitous, or it may be that Tad knows he is dehydrated and knows the standard treatment. In the latter case we would ordinarily say that the explanation of the difference in their condition is that Tad, but not Lonnie, "knew what was good for him."

Generally, we can expect that what $A+$ would want were he in $A$'s place will correlate well with what would permit $A$ to experience physical or psychological well-being or to escape physical or psychological ill-being. Surely our well- or ill-being are among the things that matter to us most, and most reliably, even on reflection.[21] Appeal to degrees of congruence between $A$'s wants and his interests thus will often help to explain facts about how satisfactory he finds his life. Explanation would not be preserved were we to substitute 'believed to be congruent' for 'are (to such-and-such a degree) congruent,' since, as cases like Lonnie's show, even if one were to convince oneself that one's wants accurately reflected one's interests, acting on these wants might fail to yield much satisfaction.

In virtue of the correlation to be expected between acting upon motives that congrue with one's interests and achieving a degree of satisfaction or avoiding a degree of distress, one's objective interests may also play an explanatory role in the *evolution* of one's desires. Consider what I will call the *wants/interests mechanism*, which permits individuals to achieve self-conscious and un-self-conscious learning about their interests through experience. In the simplest sorts of cases, trial and error leads to the selective retention of wants that are satisfiable and lead to satisfactory results for the agent.

For example, suppose that Lonnie gives in to his craving and drinks the milk. Soon afterward, he feels much worse. Still unable to identify the source of his malaise and still in the grips of a desire for the familiar, his attention is caught by a green-and-red sign in the window of a small shop he is moping past: "7-Up," it says. He rushes inside and buys a bottle. Although it is lukewarm, he drinks it eagerly. "Mmm," he thinks, "I'll have another." He buys a second bottle, and drains it to the bottom. By now he has had his fill of tepid soda, and carries on. Within a few hours, his mood is improving. When he passes the store again on the way back to his hotel, his pleasant association with drinking 7-Up leads him to buy some more and carry it along with him. That night, in the dim solitude of his room, he finds the soda's reassuringly familiar taste consoling, and so downs another few bottles before finally finding sleep. When he wakes up the next morning, he feels very much better. To make a dull story short: the next time Lonnie is laid low abroad, he may have some conscious or unconscious, reasoned or superstitious, tendency to seek out 7-Up. Unable to find that, he might seek something quite like it, say, a local lime-flavored soda, or perhaps even the *agua mineral con gaz* he had previously scorned. Over time, as Lonnie travels more and suffers similar malaise, he regularly drinks clearish liquids and regularly feels better, eventually developing an actual desire for such liquids – and an aversion to other drinks, such as milk – in such circumstances.

Thus have Lonnie's desires evolved through experience to conform more closely to what is good for him, in the naturalistic sense intended here. The process was not one of an ideally rational response to the receipt of ideal information, but rather of largely unreflective experimentation, accompanied by positive and negative associations and reinforcements. There is no guarantee that the desires "learned" through such feedback will accurately or completely reflect an individual's good. Still less is there any guarantee that, even when an appropriate adjustment in desire occurs, the agent will comprehend the origin of his new desires or be able to represent to himself the nature of the interests they reflect. But then, it is a quite general feature of the various means by which we learn about the world that they may fail to provide accurate or comprehending representations of it. My ability to perceive and understand my surroundings coexists with, indeed draws upon the same mechanisms as, my liability to deception by illusion, expectation, or surface appearance.

There are some broad theoretical grounds for thinking that something like the wants/interests mechanism exists and has an important role in desire-formation. Humans are creatures motivated primarily by wants rather than instincts. If such creatures were unable through experience to conform their wants at all closely to their essential interests – perhaps because they were no more likely to experience positive internal states when their essential interests are met than when they are not – we could not expect long or fruitful futures for them. Thus, if humans in general did not come to want to eat the kinds of food necessary to maintain some degree of physical well-being, or to engage in the sorts of activities or relations necessary to maintain their sanity, we would not be around today to worry whether we can know what is good for us. Since creatures as sophisticated and complex as humans have evolved through encounters with a variety of environments, and indeed have made it their habit to modify their environments, we should expect considerable flexibility in our capacity through experience to adapt our wants to our interests. However, this very flexibility makes the mechanism unreliable: our wants may at any time differ arbitrarily much from our interests; moreover, we may fail to have experiences that would cause us to notice this, or to undergo sufficient feedback to have much chance of developing new wants that more nearly approximate our interests. It is entirely possible, and hardly infrequent, that an individual live out the course of a normal life without ever recognizing or adjusting to some of his most fundamental interests. Individual limitations are partly remedied by cultural want-acquiring mechanisms, which permit learning and even theorizing over multiple lives and life spans, but these same mechanisms also create a vast potential for the inculcation of wants at variance with interests.

The argument for the wants/interests mechanism has about the same status, and the same breezy plausibility, as the more narrowly biological argument that we should expect the human eye to be capable of detecting objects the size and shape of our predators or prey. It is not necessary to assume anything approaching infallibility, only enough functional success to hold our own in an often inhospitable world.[22]

Thus far the argument has concerned only those objective interests that might be classified as needs, but the wants/interests mechanism can operate with respect to any interest – even interests related to an individual's particular aptitudes or social role – whose frustration is attended even indirectly by consciously or unconsciously unsatisfactory results for him. (To be sure, the more indirect the association the more unlikely that the mechanism will be reliable.) For example, the experience of taking courses in both mathematics and philosophy may lead an undergraduate who thought himself cut out to be a mathematician to come to prefer a career in philosophy, which would in fact better suit his aptitudes and attitudes. And a worker recently promoted to management from the shop floor may find himself less inclined to respond to employee grievances than he had previously wanted managers to be, while his former co-workers may find themselves less inclined to confide in him than before.

If a wants/interests mechanism is postulated, and if what is non-morally good for someone is a matter of what is in his objective interest, then we can say that objective value is able to play a role in the explanation of subjective value of the sort the naturalistic realist about value needs. These explanations even support some qualified predictions: for example, that, other things equal, individuals will ordinarily be better judges of their own interests than third parties; that knowledge of one's interests will tend to increase with increased experience and general knowledge; that people with similar personal and social characteristics will tend to have similar values; and that there will be greater general consensus upon what is desirable in those areas of life where individuals are most alike in other regards (for example, at the level of basic motives), and where trial-and-error mechanisms can be expected to work well (for example, where esoteric knowledge is not required). I am in no position to pronounce these predictions correct, but it may be to their credit that they accord with widely held views.

It should perhaps be emphasized that although I speak of the objectivity of value, the value in question is human value, and exists only because humans do. In the sense of old-fashioned theory of value, this is a relational rather than absolute notion of goodness. Although relational, the relevant facts about humans and their world are objective in the same sense that such nonrelational entities as stones are: they do not depend for their existence or nature merely upon our conception of them.[23]

Thus understood, objective interests are supervenient upon natural and social facts. Does this mean that they cannot contribute to explanation after all, since it should always be possible in principle to account for any particular fact that they purport to explain by reference to the supervenience basis alone? If mere supervenience were grounds for denying an explanatory role to a given set of concepts, then we would have to say that

16

chemistry, biology, and electrical engineering, which clearly supervene upon physics, lack explanatory power. Indeed, even outright reducibility is no ground for doubting explanatoriness. To establish a relation of reduction between, for example, a chemical phenomenon such as valence and a physical model of the atom does nothing to suggest that there is no such thing as valence, or that generalizations involving valence cannot support explanations. There can be no issue here of ontological economy or eschewing unnecessary entities, as might be the case if valence were held to be something *sui generis*, over and above any constellation of physical properties. The facts described in principles of chemical valence are genuine, and permit a powerful and explanatory systematization of chemical combination; the existence of a successful reduction to atomic physics only bolsters these claims.

We are confident that the notion of chemical valence is explanatory because proffered explanations in terms of chemical valence insert explananda into a distinctive and well-articulated nomic nexus, in an obvious way increasing our understanding of them. But what comparably powerful and illuminating theory exists concerning the notion of objective interest to give us reason to think – whether or not strict reduction is possible – that proffered explanations using this notion are genuinely informative?

I would find the sort of value realism sketched here uninteresting if it seemed to me that no theory of any consequence could be developed using the category of objective value. But in describing the wants/interests mechanism I have already tried to indicate that such a theory may be possible. When we seek to explain why people act as they do, why they have certain values or desires, and why sometimes they are led into conflict and other times into cooperation, it comes naturally to common sense and social science alike to talk in terms of people's interests. Such explanations will be incomplete and superficial if we remain wholly at the level of subjective interests, since these, too, must be accounted for.[24]

## IV. NORMATIVE REALISM

Suppose everything said thus far to have been granted generously. Still, I would as yet have no right to speak of *moral* realism, for I have done no more than to exhibit the possibility of a kind of realism with regard to non-moral goodness, a notion that perfect moral skeptics can admit. To be entitled to speak of moral realism I would have to show realism to be possible about distinctively moral value, or moral norms. I will concentrate on moral norms – that is, matters of moral rightness and wrongness – although the argument I give may, by extension, be applied to moral value. In part, my reason is that normative realism seems much less plausible intuitively than value realism. It therefore is not surprising that many current proposals for moral realism focus essentially upon value – and sometimes only upon what is in effect non-moral value. Yet on virtually any conception of morality, a moral theory must yield an account of rightness.

Normative moral realism is implausible on various grounds, but within the framework of this essay, the most relevant is that it seems impossible to extend the generic strategy of naturalistic realism to moral norms. Where is the place in explanation for facts about what *ought* to be the case – don't facts about the way things *are* do all the explaining there is to be done? Of course they do. But then, my naturalistic moral realism commits me to the view that facts about what ought to be the case are facts of a special kind about the way things are. As a result, it may be possible for them to have a function within an explanatory theory. To see how this could be, let me first give some examples of explanations outside the realm of morality that involve naturalized norms.

"Why did the roof collapse? – For a house that gets the sort of snow loads that one did, the rafters ought to have been 2 × 8s at least, not 2 × 6s." This explanation is quite acceptable, as far as it goes, yet it contains an 'ought.' Of course, we can remove this 'ought' as follows: "If a roof of that design is to withstand the snow load that one bore, then it must be framed with rafters at least 2 × 8 in cross-section." An architectural 'ought' is replaced by an engineering 'if . . . then . . .'. This is possible because the 'ought' clearly is hypothetical, reflecting the universal architectural goal of making roofs strong enough not to collapse. Because the goal is contextually fixed, and because there are more or less definite answers to the question of how to meet it, and moreover because the explanandum phenomenon is the result of a process that selects against instances that do not attain that goal, the 'ought'-containing account conveys explanatory information.[25] I will call this sort of explanation *criterial*: we explain why something happened by reference to a relevant criterion, given the existence of a process that in effect selects for (or against) phenomena that more (or less) closely approximate this criterion. Although the criterion is defined naturalistically, it may at the same time be of a kind to have a regulative role in human practice – in this case, in house building.

A more familiar sort of criterial explanation involves norms of individual rationality. Consider the use of an instrumental theory of rationality

18

to explain an individual's behavior in light of his beliefs and desires, or to account for the way an individual's beliefs change with experience.[26] Bobby Shaftoe went to sea because he believed it was the best way to make his fortune, and he wanted above all to make his fortune. Crewmate Reuben Ramsoe came to believe that he wasn't liked by the other deckhands because he saw that they taunted him and greeted his frequent lashings at the hands of the First Mate with unconcealed pleasure. These explanations work because the action or belief in question was quite rational for the agent in the circumstances, and because we correctly suppose both Shaftoe and Ramsoe to have been quite rational.

Facts about degrees of instrumental rationality enter into explanations in other ways as well. First, consider the question why Bobby Shaftoe has had more success than most like-minded individuals in achieving his goals. We may lay his success to the fact that Shaftoe is more instrumentally rational than most – perhaps he has greater-than-average acumen in estimating the probabilities of outcomes, or is more-reliable-than-average at deductive inference, or is more-imaginative-than-average in surveying alternatives.

Second, although we are all imperfect deliberators, our behavior may come to embody habits or strategies that enable us to approximate optimal rationality more closely than our deliberative defects would lead one to expect. The mechanism is simple. Patterns of beliefs and behaviors that do not exhibit much instrumental rationality will tend to be to some degree self-defeating, an incentive to change them, whereas patterns that exhibit greater instrumental rationality will tend to be to some degree rewarding, an incentive to continue them. These incentives may affect our beliefs and behaviors even though the drawbacks or advantages of the patterns in question do not receive conscious deliberation. In such cases we may be said to acquire these habits or strategies because they *are* more rational, without the intermediation of any *belief* on our part that they are. Thus, cognitive psychologists have mapped some of the unconscious strategies or heuristics we employ to enable our limited intellects to sift more data and make quicker and more consistent judgments than would be possible using more standard forms of explicit reasoning.[27] We unwittingly come to rely upon heuristics in part because they are selectively reinforced as a result of their instrumental advantages over standard, explicit reasoning, that is, in part because of their greater rationality. Similarly, we may, without realizing it or even being able to admit it to ourselves, develop patterns of behavior that encourage or discourage specific behaviors in others, such as the unconscious means by which we cause those whose company we do not enjoy not to enjoy our company. Finally, as children we may have been virtually incapable of making rational assessments when a distant gain required a proximate loss. Yet somehow over time we managed in largely nondeliberative ways to acquire various interesting habits, such as putting certain vivid thoughts about the immediate future at the periphery of our attention, which enable us as adults to march ourselves off to the dentist without a push from behind. Criterial explanation in terms of individual rationality thus extends to behaviors beyond the realm of deliberate action. And, as with the wants/interests mechanism, it is possible to see in the emergence of such behaviors something we can without distortion call learning.

Indeed, our tendency through experience to develop rational habits and strategies may cooperate with the wants/interests mechanism to provide the basis for an *extended* form of criterial explanation, in which an individual's rationality is assessed not relative to his occurrent beliefs and desires, but relative to his objective interests. The examples considered earlier of the wants/interests mechanism in fact involved elements of this sort of explanation, for they showed not only wants being adjusted to interests, but also behavior being adjusted to newly adjusted wants. Without appropriate alteration of behavior to reflect changing wants, the feedback necessary for learning about wants would not occur. With such alteration, the behavior itself may become more rational in the extended sense. An individual who is instrumentally rational is disposed to adjust means to ends; but one result of his undertaking a means – electing a course of study, or accepting a new job – may be a more informed assessment, and perhaps a reconsideration, of his ends.

The theory of individual rationality – in either its simple or its extended form – thus affords an instance of the sort needed to provide an example of normative realism. Evaluations of degrees of instrumental rationality play a prominent role in our explanations of individual behavior, but they simultaneously have normative force for the agent. Whatever other concerns an agent might have, it surely counts for him as a positive feature of an action that it is efficient relative to his beliefs and desires or, in the extended sense, efficient relative to beliefs and desires that would appropriately reflect his condition and circumstances.

The normative force of these theories of individual rationality does not, however, merely derive from their explanatory use. One can employ a theory of instrumental rationality to explain behavior while rejecting it as a normative theory of reasons, just as one can explain an action as due to irrationality without thereby endorsing unreason.[28] Instead, the connection between the normative and explanatory roles of the instrumental conception of rationality is traceable to their common ground: the human motivational system. It is a fact about us that we have ends and have the capacity for both deliberate action relative to our ends and nondeliberate adjustment of behavior to our ends. As a result, we face options among pathways across a landscape of possibilities variously valenced for us. Both when we explain the reasons for people's choices and the causes of their behavior and when we appeal to their intuitions about what it would be rational to decide or to do, we work this territory, for we make what use we can of facts about what does-in-fact or can-in-principle motivate agents.

Thus emerges the possibility of saying that facts exist about what individuals have reason to do, facts that may be substantially independent of, and more normatively compelling than, an agent's occurrent conception of his reasons. The argument for such realism about individual rationality is no stronger than the arguments for the double claim that the relevant conception of instrumental individual rationality has both explanatory power and the sort of commendatory force a theory of *reasons* must possess, but (although I will not discuss them further here) these arguments seem to me quite strong.

Passing now beyond the theory of individual rationality, let us ask what criterial explanations involving distinctively moral norms might look like. To ask this, we need to know what distinguishes moral norms from other criteria of assessment. Moral evaluation seems to be concerned most centrally with the assessment of conduct or character where the interests of more than one individual are at stake. Further, moral evaluation assesses actions or outcomes in a peculiar way: the interests of the strongest or most prestigious party do not always prevail, purely prudential reasons may be subordinated, and so on. More generally, moral resolutions are thought to be determined by criteria of choice that are *nonindexical* and in some sense *comprehensive*. This has led a number of philosophers to seek to capture the special character of moral evaluation by identifying a *moral point of view* that is impartial, but equally concerned with all those potentially affected. Other ethical theorists have come to a similar conclusion by investigating the sorts of reasons we characteristically treat as relevant or irrelevant in moral discourse. Let us follow these leads. We thus may say that moral norms reflect a certain kind of rationality, rationality not from the point of view of any particular individual, but from what might be called a social point of view.[29]

By itself, the equation of moral rightness with rationality from a social point of view is not terribly restrictive, for, depending upon what one takes rationality to be, this equation could be made by a utilitarian, a Kantian, or even a noncognitivist. That is as it should be, for if it is to capture what is distinctive about moral norms, it should be compatible with the broadest possible range of recognized moral theories. However, once one opts for a particular conception of rationality – such as the conception of rationality as efficient pursuit of the non-morally good, or as autonomous and universal self-legislation, or as a noncognitive expression of hypothetical endorsement – this schematic characterization begins to assume particular moral content. Here I have adopted an instrumentalist conception of rationality, and this – along with the account given of non-moral goodness – means that the argument for moral realism given in the following text is an argument that presupposes and purports to defend a particular substantive moral theory.[30]

What is this theory? Let me introduce an idealization of the notion of social rationality by considering what would be rationally approved of were the interests of all potentially affected individuals counted equally under circumstances of full and vivid information.[31] Because of the assumption of full and vivid information, the interests in question will be objective interests. Given the account of goodness proposed in Section III, this idealization is equivalent to what is rational from a social point of view with regard to the realization of intrinsic non-moral goodness. This seems to me to be a recognizable and intuitively plausible – if hardly uncontroversial – criterion of moral rightness. Relative moral rightness is a matter of relative degree of approximation to this criterion.

The question that now arises is whether the notion of degrees of moral rightness could participate in explanations of behavior or in processes of moral learning that parallel explanatory uses of the notion of degrees of individual rationality – especially, in the extended sense. I will try to suggest several ways in which it might.

Just as an individual who significantly discounts some of his interests will be liable to certain sorts of dissatisfaction, so will a social arrangement – for example, a form of production, a social or political hierarchy, and so forth – that departs from social rationality by significantly discounting the interests of a particular group have a potential for dissatisfaction and unrest. Whether or not this potential will be realized depends upon a great many circumstances. Owing to socialization, or to other limitations on the experience or knowledge of members of this group, the wants/interests mechanism may not have operated in such a way that the

22

wants of its members reflect their interests. As a result they may experience no direct frustration of their desires despite the discounting of their interests. Or, the group may be too scattered or too weak to mobilize effectively. Or, it may face overawing repression. On the other hand, certain social and historical circumstances favor the realization of this potential for unrest, for example, by providing members of this group with experiences that make them more likely to develop interest-congruent wants, by weakening the existing repressive apparatus, by giving them new access to resources or new opportunities for mobilization, or merely by dispelling the illusion that change is impossible. In such circumstances, one can expect the potential for unrest to manifest itself.

Just as explanations involving assessments of individual rationality were not always replaceable by explanations involving individual *beliefs about* what would be rational, so, too, explanations involving assessments of social rationality cannot be replaced by explanations involving *beliefs about* what would be morally right. For example, discontent may arise because a society departs from social rationality, but not as a result of a belief that this is the case. Suppose that a given society is believed by all constituents to be just. This belief may help to stabilize it, but if in fact the interests of certain groups are being discounted, there will be a potential for unrest that may manifest itself in various ways – in alienation, loss of morale, decline in the effectiveness of authority, and so on – well before any changes in belief about the society's justness occur, and that will help explain why members of certain groups come to believe it to be unjust, if in fact they do.

In addition to possessing a certain sort of potential for unrest, societies that fail to approximate social rationality may share other features as well: they may exhibit a tendency toward certain religious or ideological doctrines, or toward certain sorts of repressive apparatus; they may be less productive in some ways (for example, by failing to develop certain human resources) and more productive in others (for example, by extracting greater labor from some groups at less cost), and thus may be differentially economically successful depending upon the conditions of production they face, and so on.

If a notion of social rationality is to be a legitimate part of empirical explanations of such phenomena, an informative characterization of the circumstances under which departures from, or approximations to, social rationality could be expected to lead to particular social outcomes – especially, of the conditions under which groups whose interests are sacrificed could be expected to exhibit or mobilize discontent – must be available. Although it cannot be known *a priori* whether an account of this kind is possible, one can see emerging in some recent work in social history and historical sociology various elements of a theory of when, and how, a persisting potential for social discontent due to persistently sacrificed interests comes to be manifested.[32]

An individual whose wants do not reflect his interests or who fails to be instrumentally rational may, I argued, experience feedback of a kind that promotes learning about his good and development of more rational strategies. Similarly, the discontent produced by departures from social rationality may produce feedback that, at a social level, promotes the development of norms that better approximate social rationality. The potential for unrest that exists when the interests of a group are discounted is potential for pressure from that group – and its allies – to accord fuller recognition to their interests in social decision making and in the socially instilled norms that govern individual decision making. It therefore is pressure to push the resolution of conflicts further in the direction required by social rationality, since it is pressure to give fuller weight to the interests of more of those affected. Such pressure may of course be more or less forceful or coherent; it may find the most diverse ideological expression; and it may produce outcomes more or less advantageous in the end to those exerting it.[33] Striking historical examples of the mobilization of excluded groups to promote greater representation of their interests include the rebellions against the system of feudal estates, and more recent social movements against restrictions on religious practices, on suffrage and other civil rights, and on collective bargaining.[34]

Of course, other mechanisms have been at work influencing the evolution of social practices and norms at the same time, some with the reverse effect.[35] Whether mechanisms working on behalf of the inclusion of excluded interests will predominate depends upon a complex array of social and historical factors. It would be silly to think either that the norms of any actual society will at any given stage of history closely approximate social rationality, or that there will be a univocal trend toward greater social rationality. Like the mechanisms of biological evolution or market economics, the mechanisms described here operate in an "open system" alongside other mechanisms, and do not guarantee optimality or even a monotonic approach to equilibrium. Human societies do not appear to have begun at or near equilibrium in the relevant sense, and so the strongest available claim might be that in the long haul, barring certain exogenous effects, one could expect an uneven secular trend toward the inclusion of the interests of (or interests represented by) social groups that are capable of some degree of mobilization. But under other circumstances, even in the long run, one could expect the opposite. New World plantation slavery, surely one of the most brutally exclusionary social arrangements ever to have existed, emerged late in world history and lasted for hundreds of years. Other brutally exclusionary social arrangements of ancient or recent vintage persist yet.

One need not, therefore, embrace a theory of moral progress in order to see that the feedback mechanism just described can give an explanatory role to the notion of social rationality. Among the most puzzling, yet most common, objections to moral realism is that there has not been uniform historical progress toward worldwide consensus on moral norms. But it has not to my knowledge been advanced as an argument against *scientific* realism that, for example, some contemporary cultures and subcultures do not accept, and do not seem to be moving in the direction of accepting, the scientific world view. Surely realists are in both cases entitled to say that only certain practices in certain circumstances will tend to produce theories more congruent with reality, especially when the subject matter is so complex and so far removed from anything like direct inspection. They need not subscribe to the quaint idea that "the truth will out" come what may. The extended theory of individual rationality, for example, leads us to expect that in societies where there are large conflicts of interest people will develop large normative disagreements, and that, when (as they usually do) these large conflicts of interest parallel large differences in power, the dominant normative views are unlikely to embody social rationality. What is at issue here, and in criterial explanations generally, is the explanation of certain patterns among others, not necessarily the existence of a single overall trend. We may, however, point to the existence of the feedback mechanisms described here as grounds for belief that we can make qualified use of historical experience as something like experimental evidence about what kinds of practices in what ranges of circumstances might better satisfy a criterion of social rationality. That is, we may assign this mechanism a role in a qualified process of moral learning.

The mechanisms of learning about individual rationality, weak or extended, involved similar qualifications. For although we expect that, under favorable circumstances, individuals may become better at acting in an instrumentally rational fashion as their experience grows, we are also painfully aware that there are powerful mechanisms promoting the opposite result. We certainly do not think that an individual must display exceptionless rationality, or even show ever-increasing rationality over his lifetime, in order to apply reason-giving explanations to many of his

25

actions. Nor do we think that the inevitable persistence of areas of irrationality in individuals is grounds for denying that they can, through
experience, acquire areas of greater rationality.

The comparison with individual rationality should not, however, be
overdrawn. First, while the inclusion-generating mechanisms for social
rationality operate through the behavior of individuals, interpersonal dynamics enter ineliminably in such a way that the criteria selected for
are not reducible to those of disaggregated individual rationality. Both
social and biological evolution involve selection mechanisms that favor
behaviors satisfying criteria of relative optimality that are collective (as in
prisoner's dilemma cases) or genotypic (which may also be collective, as
in kin selection) as well as individual or phenotypic. Were this not so, it
is hardly possible that moral norms could ever have emerged or come to
have the hold upon us they do.

Second, there are rather extreme differences of degree between the individual and the social cases. Most strikingly, the mechanisms whereby
individual wants and behaviors are brought into some congruence with
individual interests and reasons operate in more direct and reliable ways
than comparable mechanisms nudging social practices or norms in the direction of what is socially rational. Not only are the information demands
less formidable in the individual case – that is the least of it, one might
say – but the ways in which feedback is achieved are more likely in the
individual case to serve as a prod for change and less likely to be distorted
by social asymmetries.

Nonetheless, we do have the skeleton of an explanatory theory that
uses the notion of what is more or less rational from a social point of
view and that parallels in an obvious way uses of assessments of rationality from the agent's point of view in explanations of individual
beliefs and behaviors. Like the individual theory, it suggests prediction-
and counterfactual-supporting generalizations of the following kind: over
time, and in some circumstances more than others, we should expect
pressure to be exerted on behalf of practices that more adequately satisfy
a criterion of rationality.

Well, if this is a potentially predictive and explanatory theory, how good
is it? That is a very large question, one beyond my competence to answer.
But let me note briefly three patterns in the evolution of moral norms
that seem to me to bear out the predictions of this theory, subject to the
sorts of qualifications that the existence of imperfections and competing
mechanisms would lead one to expect. I do so with trepidation, however,
for although the patterns I will discuss are gross historical trends, it is not

26

essential to the theory that history show such trends, and it certainly is not part of the theory to endorse a set of practices or norms merely because it is a result of them.

### Generality

It is a commonplace of anthropology that tribal peoples often have only one word to name both their tribe and "the people" or "humanity." Those beyond the tribe are not deemed full-fledged people, and the sorts of obligations one has toward people do not apply fully with regard to outsiders. Over the span of history, through processes that have involved numerous reversals, people have accumulated into larger social units – from the familial band to the tribe to the "people" to the nation-state – and the scope of moral categories has enlarged to follow these expanding boundaries. Needless to say, this has not been a matter of the contagious spread of enlightenment. Expanding social entities frequently subjugate those incorporated within their new boundaries, and the means by which those thus oppressed have secured greater recognition of their interests have been highly conflictual, and remain – perhaps, will always remain – incomplete. Nonetheless, contemporary moral theory, and to a surprising degree contemporary moral discourse, have come to reject any limitation short of the species.[36]

### Humanization

Moral principles have been assigned various origins and natures: as commandments of supernatural origin, grounded in the will or character of a deity, to be interpreted by a priesthood; as formalistic demands of a caste-based code of honor; as cosmic principles of order; as dictates of reason or conscience that make no appeal to human inclinations or well-being; and so on. While vestiges of these views survive in contemporary moral theory, it is typical of almost the entire range of such theory, and of much of contemporary moral discourse, to make some sort of intrinsic connection between normative principles and effects on human interests. Indeed, the very emergence of morality as a distinctive subject matter apart from religion is an instance of this pattern.

### Patterns of Variation

In addition to seeing patterns that reflect some pressure toward the approximation of social rationality, we should expect to see greater approximation in those areas of normative regulation where the mechanisms postulated here work best, for example, in areas where almost everyone has importantly similar or mutually satisfiable interests, where almost everyone has some substantial potential to infringe upon the interests of others, where the advantages of certain forms of constraint or cooperation are highly salient even in the dynamics of small groups, and where individuals can significantly influence the likelihood of norm-following behavior on the part of others by themselves following norms. The clearest examples have to do with prohibitions of aggression and theft, and of the violation of promises.[37] By contrast, moral questions that concern matters where there are no solutions compatible with protecting the most basic interests of all, where there exist very large asymmetries in the capacity to infringe upon interests, where the gains or losses from particular forms of cooperation or constraint are difficult to perceive, and where individual compliance will little affect general compliance, are less likely to achieve early or stable approximation to social rationality. Clear examples here have to do with such matters as social hierarchy – for example, the permissibility of slavery, of authoritarian government, of caste or gender inequalities – and social responsibility – for example, what is the nature of our individual or collective obligation to promote the well-being of unrelated others?

Given a suitable characterization of the conditions that prevailed during the processes of normative evolution described by these patterns, the present theory claims not only that these changes could have been expected, but that an essential part of the explanation of their occurrence is a mechanism whereby individuals whose interests are denied are led to form common values and make common cause along lines of shared interests, thereby placing pressure on social practices to approximate more closely to social rationality.

These descriptions and explanations of certain prominent features of the evolution of moral norms will no doubt strike some as naive at best, plainly – perhaps even dangerously – false at worst. I thoroughly understand this. I have given impossibly sketchy, one-sided, simple-minded accounts of a very complex reality.[38] I can only hope that these accounts will seem as believable as one could expect sketchy, one-sided, simple-minded accounts to be, and that this will make the story I have tried to tell about mechanisms and explanation more plausible.

Needless to say, the upshot is not a complacent functionalism or an overall endorsement of current moral practice or norms. Instead, the account of morality sketched here emphasizes conflict rather than equilibrium, and provides means for criticizing certain contemporary moral practices and intuitions by asking about their historical genesis. For example, if we come to think that the explanation of a common moral intuition assigns no significant role to mechanisms that could be expected to exert pressure toward socially rational outcomes, then this is grounds for questioning the intuition, however firmly we may hold it. In the spirit of a naturalized moral epistemology, we may ask whether the explanation of why we make certain moral judgments is an example of a reliable process for discovering moral facts.

Thus far I have spoken of what is morally best as a matter of what is instrumentally rational from a social point of view. But I have also characterized a genuinely moral point of view as one impartial with respect to the interests of all potentially affected, and that is not a socially bounded notion. In fact, I have claimed that a trend away from social specificity is among the patterns visible in the evolution of moral norms. Part of the explanation of this pattern – and part, therefore, of the explanatory role of degrees of impartial rationality – is that the mechanisms appealed to in the preceding text are not socially bounded, either. Societies, and individuals on opposite sides of social boundaries, constrain one another in various ways, much as groups and individuals constrain one another within societies: they can threaten aggression, mobilize resistance to external control, withhold cooperation, and obstruct one another's plans; and they are prone to resort to such constraining activities when their interests are denied or at risk. As with intrasocial morality, so in intersocial morality, the best-established and most nearly impartially rational elements are those where the mechanisms we have discussed work most reliably: prohibitions on aggression are stronger and more widely accepted than principles of equity or redistribution. Of course, many factors make intersocietal dynamics unlike intrasocietal ones.... But the reader will for once be spared more armchair social science. Still, what results is a form of moral realism that is essentially tied to a limited point of view, an impartial yet human one. Is this too limited for genuine moral realism?

A teacher of mine once remarked that the question of moral realism seemed to him to be the question whether the universe cares what we do. Since we have long since given up believing that the cosmos pays us any mind, he thought we should long since have given up moral realism. I can only agree that if this were what moral realism involved, it should – with relief rather than sorrow – be let go. However, the account offered here gives us a way of understanding how moral values or imperatives might be objective without being cosmic. They need be grounded in nothing more transcendental than facts about man and his environment, facts about what sorts of things matter to us, and how the ways we live affect these things.

Yet the present account is limited in another way, which may be of greater concern from the standpoint of contemporary moral theory: it does not yield moral imperatives that are categorical in the sense of providing a reason for action to all rational agents regardless of their contingent desires. Although troubling, this limitation is not tantamount to relativism, since on the present account rational motivation is not a precondition of moral obligation. For example, it could truthfully be said that I ought to be more generous even though greater generosity would not help me to promote my existing ends, or even to satisfy my objective interests. This could be so because what it would be morally right for me to do depends upon what is rational from a point of view that includes, but is not exhausted by, my own.

In a similar way, it could be said that I logically ought not to believe both a proposition $p$ and a proposition that implies not-$p$. However, it may not be the case that every rational agent will have an instrumental reason to purge all logical contradictions from his thought. It would require vast amounts of cogitation for anyone to test all of his existing beliefs for consistency, and to insure that every newly acquired belief preserves it. Suppose someone to be so fortunate that the only contradictions among his beliefs lie deep in the much-sedimented swamp of factual trivia. Perhaps his memories of two past acquaintances have become confused in such a way that somewhere in the muck there are separate beliefs which, taken together, attribute to one individual logically incompatible properties. Until such a contradiction rears its head in practice, he may have no more reason to lay down his present concerns and wade in after it than he has to leave his home in suburban New Jersey to hunt alligators in the Okefenokee on the off chance that he might one day find himself stranded and unarmed in the backwaters of southeast Georgia.[39] What an individual rationally ought to do thus may differ from what logic requires of him. Still, we may say that logical evaluation is not subjective or arbitrary, and that good grounds of a perfectly general kind are available for being logical, namely, that logical contradictions are necessarily false and logical inferences are truth preserving. Since in public discourse and private reflection we are often concerned with whether our thinking is warranted in a sense that is more intimately connected with its truth conduciveness than with its instrumentality to our peculiar personal goals, it therefore is far from arbitrary that we attach so much importance to logic as a standard of criticism and self-criticism.

By parallel, if we adopt the account of moral rightness proposed we may say that moral evaluation is not subjective or arbitrary, and that good, general grounds are available for following moral 'oughts,' namely, that moral conduct is rational from an impartial point of view. Since in public discourse and private reflection we are often concerned with whether our conduct is justifiable from a general rather than merely personal standpoint, it therefore is far from arbitrary that we attach so much importance to morality as a standard of criticism and self-criticism.

The existence of such phenomena as religion and ideology is evidence for the pervasiveness and seriousness of our concern for impartial justification. Throughout history individuals have sacrificed their interests, even their lives, to meet the demands of religions or ideologies that were compelling for them in part because they purported to express a universal − *the* universal − justificatory standpoint. La Rochefoucauld wrote that hypocrisy is the tribute vice pays to virtue,[40] but 'hypocrisy' suggests cynicism. We might better say that ideology is the respect partisans show to impartiality. Morality, then, is not ideology made sincere and general − ideology is intrinsically given to heartfelt generalization. Morality is ideology that has faced the facts.

I suspect the idea that moral evaluations must have categorical force for rational agents owes some of its support to a fear that were this to be denied, the authority of morality would be lost. That would be so if one held onto the claim that moral imperatives cannot exist for someone who would not have a reason to obey them, for then an individual could escape moral duties by the simple expedient of having knavish desires. But if we give up this claim about the applicability of moral judgment, then variations in personal desires cannot license exemption from moral obligation.[41]

Thus, while it certainly is a limitation of the argument made here that it does not yield a conception of moral imperatives as categorical, that may be a limitation we can live with and still accord morality the scope and dignity it traditionally has enjoyed. Moreover, it may be a limitation we must live with. For how many among us can convince ourselves that reason is other than hypothetical? Need it also be asked: How many of us would find our sense of the significance of morality or the importance of moral conduct enhanced by a demonstration that even a person with the most thoroughly repugnant ends would find that moral conduct advanced them?

31

One implication of what has been said is that if we want morality to be taken seriously and to have an important place in people's lives – and not merely as the result of illusion or the threat of repression – we should be vitally concerned with the ways in which social arrangements produce conflicts of interest and asymmetries of power that affect the nature and size of the gap between what is individually and socially rational. Rather than attempt to portray morality as something that it cannot be, as "rationally compelling no matter what one's ends," we should ask how we might change the ways we live so that moral conduct would more regularly be rational given the ends we actually will have.

### VI. SUMMARY AND CONCLUSION

I have outlined a form of moral realism, and given some indication of how it might be defended against certain objections. Neither a full characterization of this view, nor full answers to the many objections it faces, can be given within the present essay. Perhaps then I should stop trying to say just a bit more, and close by indicating roughly what I have, and have not, attempted to show.

I have proposed what are in effect reforming naturalistic definitions of non-moral goodness and moral rightness. It is possible to respond: "Yes, I can see that such-and-such an end is an objective interest of the agent in your sense, or that such-and-such a practice is rational from an impartial point of view, but can't I still ask whether the end is good for him or the practice right?" Such "open questions" cannot by their nature be closed, since definitions are not subject to proof or disproof. But open questions may be more or less disturbing, for although definitional proposals cannot be demonstrated, they can fare better or worse at meeting various desiderata.

I have assumed throughout that the drawing up of definitions is part of theory-construction, and so is to be assessed by asking (1) whether the analyses given satisfy appropriate constraints of intelligibility and function, and (2) whether the terms as analyzed contribute to the formulation and testing of worthwhile theories. How do my proposals fit with these criteria?

(1) Beyond constraints of intelligibility, such as clarity and non-circularity, specifically naturalistic definitions of evaluative terms should satisfy two further analytic constraints arising from their intended function. (a) They should insofar as possible capture the normative force of these terms by providing analyses that permit these terms to play their

central evaluative roles. In the present setting, this involves showing that although the definitions proposed may not fit with all of our linguistic or moral intuitions, they nonetheless express recognizable notions of goodness and rightness. Further, it involves showing that the definitions permit plausible connections to be drawn between, on the one hand, what is good or right and, on the other, what characteristically would motivate individuals who are prepared to submit themselves to relevant sorts of scrutiny. (b) The naturalistic definitions should permit the evaluative concepts to participate in their own right in genuinely empirical theories. Part of this consists in showing that we have appropriate epistemic access to these concepts. Part, too (and a related part), consists in showing that generalizations employing these concepts, among others, can figure in potentially explanatory accounts. I have tried to offer reasonably clear definitions and to show in a preliminary way how they might meet constraints (a) and (b).

(2) However, a good deal more must be done, for it remains to show that the empirical theories constructed with the help of these definitions are reasonably good theories, that is, theories for which we have substantial evidence and which provide plausible explanations. I have tried in the most preliminary way imaginable to suggest this. If I have been wholly unpersuasive on empirical matters, then I can expect that the definitions I have offered will be equally unpersuasive.

It is an attraction for me of naturalism in ethics and epistemology alike that it thus is constrained in several significant dimensions at once. One has such ample opportunities to be shown wrong or found unconvincing if one's account must be responsive to empirical demands as well as normative intuitions. Theorizing in general is more productive when suitably constrained; in ethics especially, constraints are needed if we are to have a clearer idea of how we might make progress toward the resolution of theoretical disputes. Of course, not just any constraints will do. A proposed set of constraints must present itself as both appropriate and useful. Let me say something about (1) the utility of the constraints adopted here, and then a final word about (2) their appropriateness.

(1) Consider three classes of competitors to the substantive moral theory endorsed previously, and notice how criticisms of them *naturally* intertwine concerns about normative justification and empirical explanation. *Kantian* conceptions of morality are widely viewed as having captured certain intuitively compelling normative characteristics of such notions as rationality and moral rightness, but it seems they have done so partly at

the expense of affording a plausible way of integrating these notions into an empirical account of our reasons and motives in action. Moreover, this descriptive difficulty finds direct expression on the normative side. Not only must any normative 'ought' be within the scope of an empirical 'can,' but a normatively compelling 'ought' must – as recent criticisms of Kantianism have stressed – reach to the real springs of human action and concern. *Intuitionist* moral theories also enjoyed some success in capturing normative features of morality, but they have largely been abandoned for want of a credible account of the nature or operation of a faculty of moral intuition. It is too easy for us to give a non-justifying psychological explanation of the existence in certain English gentlemen of something that they identified upon introspection as a faculty of moral insight, an explanation that ties this purported faculty more closely to the rigidity of prevailing social conventions than to anything that looks as if it could be a source of universal truth. *Social choice theories* that take occurrent subjective interests or revealed preferences as given fit more readily than Kantian or intuitionist theories with empirical accounts of behavior, and, unlike them, have found a place in contemporary social science. But they suffer well-known limitations as normative theories, some of which turn out to be bound up with their limitations as explanatory theories: they lack an account of the origin or evolution of preferences, and partly for that reason are unable to capture the ways in which we evaluate purportedly rational or moral conduct by criticizing ends as well as means.

(2) However, the issues at stake when we evaluate competing approaches to morality involve not only this sort of assessment of largish theories, but also questions about which criteria of assessment appropriately apply to definitions and theories in ethics, and about whether definitional systematization and largish theorizing are even appropriate for ethics. I am drawn to the view that the development of theory in ethics is not an artificial contrivance of philosophers but an organic result of the personal and social uses of moral evaluation: time and again individuals and groups have faced difficult questions to which common sense gave conflicting or otherwise unsatisfactory answers, and so they have pressed their questions further and pursued their inquiry more systematically. The felt need for theory in ethics thus parallels the felt need for theory in natural or social science.[42] It does not follow from this alone that ethical theorizing must run parallel to or be integrable with theorizing in the natural and social sciences. Ethics might be deeply different. Although initially plausible and ultimately irrefutable, the view that ethics

34

stands thus apart is one that in the end I reject. We are natural and social creatures, and I know of nowhere else to look for ethics than in this rich conjunction of facts. I have tried to suggest that we might indeed find it there.[43]

NOTES

*The Philosophical Review*, XCV, No. 2 (April 1986).

1. Nineteenth-century evolutionary naturalism affords an example of the former, Dewey – and, on at least one reading, perhaps Mill as well – an example of the latter.
2. A. J. Ayer, *Language, Truth, and Logic* (New York: Dover, 1952) 111.
3. In saying this, I am insisting that questions about what it would be rational to believe belong to practical rather than theoretical reason. While results of theoretical reason – for example, conclusions of deductive inferences – are in general relevant to questions about rational belief, they are not determinative apart from the agent's practical reasons.
4. Of course, individual belief-formation is not typically governed by explicit means-end reasoning, but rather by habits of belief-formation and tendencies to invest varying degrees of confidence in particular kinds of beliefs. If we accept an instrumental account of rationality, then we can call such habits rational from the standpoint of the individual to the extent that they fit into a constellation of attitudes and tendencies that promote his ends. This matter will arise again in Section IV.
5. Neither these remarks, nor those in subsequent paragraphs, are meant to be a serious exegesis of Hume's arguments, which admit of interpretations other than the one suggested here. I mean only to capture certain features of what I take Hume's arguments to be, for example, in bk. III, pt. I, sec. I of *A Treatise of Human Nature*, L. A. Selby-Bigge, ed. (Oxford: Clarendon, 1973) esp. 465–6, and in Appendix I of *An Inquiry Concerning the Principles of Morals*, C. W. Hendel, ed. (Indianapolis: Bobbs-Merrill, 1957) esp. 111–12.
6. Philippa Foot has questioned this thesis, although her way of posing and arguing the question differs enough from mine that I cannot judge whether she would be in agreement with the argument that follows. See her *Virtues and Vices* (Berkeley: University of California Press, 1978) esp. Essay XI. The presentation of the issues here owes its main inspiration to William K. Frankena's distinction between the rational and the moral points of view.
7. See the *Inquiry Concerning the Principles of Morals*, pt. II, sec. IX, 102–3.
8. The ancient criticism of noncognitivism, that it has difficulty accounting for the difference between moral value and other sorts of desirability (so that Hume can speak in one breath of our approval of a man's "good offices" and his "well-contrived apartment"), gains some vitality in the present context. To account for such differences it is necessary to have a contentful way of characterizing criteria of moral assessment so that moral approval does not reduce to "is valued by the agent." (Such a characterization will be offered in Section IV.) Value *sans phrase* is a generic, and not necessarily moral, notion. One sometimes hears it said that generic value becomes moral in character when we reach that which the agent

prizes above all else. But this would invest pets and mementos with moral value, and have the peculiar effect of making amoralism a virtual conceptual impossibility. It seems more plausible to say that not all value is moral value, and that the highest values for an individual need not be, nor need they even seem to him to be, moral values. Once we turn to questions of duty, the situation should be clearer still: moral theorists have proposed quite different relations among the categories of moral rightness, moral goodness, and non-moral goodness, and it seems implausible to say that deeming an act or class of actions morally right is necessarily equivalent to viewing it personally as valuable *sans phrase*.

9. The character of moral imperatives receives further discussion in Section V.

10. Such theories are suitably externalist when, in characterizing the notions of *reliability* or *warrant-conferring causal process*, they employ an account of truth that does not resolve truth into that which we have reason to believe – for example, a nontrivial correspondence theory.

11. Or if moral facts were supposed to be things of a kind to provide categorical reasons for action. However, this supposition is simply Hume's thesis of practicality in ontological garb.

12. J. L. Mackie, in *Ethics: Inventing Right and Wrong* (Harmondsworth, Middlesex: Penguin, 1977), and Gilbert Harman, in *The Nature of Morality: An Introduction to Ethics* (New York: Oxford University Press, 1977), both challenge moral realism in part by questioning its capacity to explain. Nicholas L. Sturgeon, in "Moral Explanations," David Copp and David Zimmerman, eds., *Morality, Reason and Truth: New Essays in the Foundations of Ethics* (Totowa, NJ: Rowman and Allanhead, 1984), takes the opposite side, using arguments different from those offered in the following text.

13. A full-scale theory of value would, I think, show the concept of someone's good to be slightly different from the concept of what is desirable for him. However, this difference will not affect the argument made here.

14. It was some work by Richard C. Jeffrey on epistemic probability that originally suggested to me the idea of objectifying subjective interests. See note 17. I have since benefited from Richard B. Brandt's work on "rational desire," although I fear that what I will say contains much that he would regard as wrong-headed. See *A Theory of the Good and the Right* (Oxford: Clarendon, 1979) pt. I.

15. We ask this question of $A+$, rather than what $A+$ wants for himself, because we are seeking the objectified subjective interests of $A$, and the interests of $A+$ might be quite different owing to the changes involved in the idealization of $A$. For example, $A+$ presumably does not want any more information for himself – there is no more to be had and he knows this. Yet it might still be true that $A+$ would want to want more knowledge were he to be put in the place of his less well-informed self, $A$. It may as a psychological matter be impossible for $A+$ to set aside entirely his desires *in his present circumstances* with regard to himself or to $A$ in considering what he would want to want were he to be put *in the place of* his less-than-ideal self. This reveals a measurement problem for objective interests: giving an individual the information and capacities necessary to "objectify" his interests may perturb his psychology in ways that alter the phenomenon we wish to observe. Such difficulties attend even the measurement of subjective interests, since instruments for sampling preferences (indeed, mere

acts of reflection upon one's preferences) tend to affect the preferences expressed. For obvious reasons, interference effects come with the territory. Though not in themselves sufficient ground for skepticism about subjective or objective interests, these measurement problems show the need for a "perturbation theory," and for caution about attributions of interests that are inattentive to interference effects.

16. 'Interest' is not quite the word wanted here, for in ordinary language we may speak of a want where we would not speak of a corresponding interest. See Brian Barry, *Political Argument* (London: Routledge and Kegan Paul, 1965) esp. ch. X, for discussion. A more accurate, but overly cumbersome, expression would be 'positive-valence-making characteristic.'

17. Suppose for a moment, contrary to what was urged in the preceding text, that there is a workable notion of epistemic probability that determines rational degrees of belief independent of the contingent goals of the epistemic agent. Perhaps then the following analogy will be helpful. Consider a physically random process, such as alpha-decay. We can ask an individual what subjective probability he would assign to an event consisting in a certain rate of decay for a given sample of uranium; we can also ask what rational degree of belief the individual would assign to this event were he to become ideally informed about the laws of physics and the relevant initial conditions. Call the latter rational degree of belief the *objectified subjective probability* of the event, and suppose it to be equal to one fifth. (Compare Richard C. Jeffrey, *The Logic of Decision* [New York: McGraw-Hill, 1964] 190–6.) But now consider the physical facts that, in conjunction with the laws of quantum mechanics, ground the idealized individual's judgment. Call these the *reduction basis* of that judgment. This reduction basis is a complex set of primary qualities that can be said to bring it about that the event in question has an *objective probability* of one fifth. (It should be said that it is not part of Jeffrey's approach to posit such objective probabilities.) The existence of this objective probability can explain why an ideally informed individual would select an objectified subjective probability equal to one fifth, but the probability judgment of an ideally informed individual cannot explain why the objective probability is one fifth – that is a matter of the laws of physics. Similarly, the existence of an individual's objective interest can explain why his ideally informed self would pick out for his less-informed self a given objectified subjective interest, but not *vice versa*.

18. More precisely, we may say that $X$ is non-morally good for $A$ at time $t$ if and only if $X$ would satisfy an objective interest of $A$ the reduction basis of which exists at $t$. Considerations about the evolution of interests over time raise a number of issues that cannot be entered into here.

19. $A+$, putting himself in $A$'s place, may find several different sets of wants equally appealing, so that several alternatives could be equal-best for $A$ in this sense. This would not make the notion of 'the good for $A$' problematic, just pluralistic. However, a more serious question looms. Is there sufficient determinacy in the specification of $A+$'s condition, or in the psychology of desire, to make the notion of objective interest definite enough for my purposes? Without trying to say how definite *that* might be, let me suggest two ways in which an answer to the worry about definiteness might begin. (1) It seems that we do think that there are rather definite answers to questions about how an individual $A$'s desires would change were his beliefs to change in certain limited ways. If Lonnie were to learn the

37

consequences of drinking milk, he would no longer want his desire for milk to be effective. But a large change in belief can be accomplished piecemeal, by a sequence of limited changes in belief. Thus, if (admittedly, a big 'if') *order* of change is not in the end significant, then the facts and generalizations that support counterfactuals about limited changes might support an extrapolation all the way to $A+$. (2) Beliefs and desires appear to covary systematically. Typically, we find that individuals who differ markedly in their desires – for example, about careers or style of life – differ markedly, and characteristically, in their beliefs; as individuals become more similar in their beliefs, they tend to become more similar in their desires. This suggests that if (another big 'if') the characterization given of $A+$ fixes the entire content of his beliefs in a definite way (at least, given a choice of language), then his desires may be quite comprehensively fixed as well. If we had in hand a general theory of the covariation of beliefs and desires, then we could appeal directly to this theory – plus facts about $A$ – to ground the counterfactuals needed to characterize $A$'s objectified interests, eliminating any essential reference to the imaginary individual $A+$.

20. The account may, however, yield some counterintuitive results. Depending upon the nature and circumstances of given individuals, they might have objective interests in things we find wrong or repulsive, and that do not seem to us part of a good life. We can explain a good deal of our objection to certain desires – for example, those involving cruelty – by saying that they are not *morally* good; others – for example, those of a philistine nature – by saying that they are not *aesthetically* valuable; and so on. It seems to me preferable to express our distaste for certain ends in terms of specific categories of value, rather than resort to the device of saying that such ends could under no circumstances be part of anyone's non-moral good. People, or at least some people, might be put together in a way that makes some not-very-appetizing things essential to their flourishing, and we do not want to be guilty of wishful thinking on this score. (There will be wishful thinking enough before we are through.)

21. To put the matter in more strictly naturalistic terms, we can expect that evolution will have favored organisms so constituted that those behaviors requisite to their survival and flourishing are associated with positive internal states (such as pleasure) and those opposed to survival or flourishing with negative states (such as pain). 'Flourishing' here, even if understood as mere reproductive fitness, is not a narrow notion. In order for beings such as humans to be reproductively succesful, they must as phenotypes have lives that are psychologically sustainable, internally motivating, and effectively social; lives, moreover, that normally would engage in a wide range of their peculiarly human capacities. Humankind could hardly have been a success story even at the reproductive level were not pursuit of the sorts of things that characteristically have moved humans to action associated with existences of this kind. However, it must be kept in mind that most human evolution occurred under circumstances different in important ways from the present. It therefore is quite possible that the interaction of evolved human motivational potentials with existing circumstances will produce incongruities between what we tend to aim at, or to be driven by, and what would produce the greatest pleasure for us. That is one reason for doubting hedonism as a theory of motivation.

22. 'Functional success' rather than 'representational accuracy' for the following reason. Selection favors organisms that have some-or-other feature that happens in their particular environment to contribute to getting their needs met. Whether that feature will be an accurate representational capacity cannot be settled by an argument of this kind. Of course, it would be a very great coincidence if beings who rely as heavily upon representations as we do were able to construct only grossly inaccurate representations while at the same time managing successfully in a range of environments over a long period of time. But such coincidences cannot be ruled out.

23. Although some elements of their reduction basis depend upon our past choices, our objective interests are not therefore subjective in a sense damaging to the present argument. After all, such unproblematically objective facts about us as our weight, income, and spatial location depend in the same way upon past choices. The point is not that our subjective interests have no role in shaping the reduction basis of our objective interests, but rather that they can affect our objective interests only in virtue of their actual (rather than merely desired) effects upon this reduction basis, just as they can affect our weight, income, or spatial location only in virtue of actual (rather than merely desired) effects upon our displacement, employment, or movement.

24. In a similar way, it would be incomplete and superficial to explain why, once large-scale production became possible, the world's consumption of refined sugar underwent such explosive development, by mentioning only the fact that people liked its taste. Why, despite wide differences in traditional diet and acquired tastes, has sugar made such inroads into human consumption? Why haven't the appearance and promotion of other equally cheap foodstuffs produced such remarkable shifts in consumption? Why, even in societies where sugar is recognized as a health hazard, does consumption of sugars, often in concealed forms, continue to climb? Facts about the way we are constituted, about the rather singular ways sugar therefore affects us, and about the ways forms of production and patterns of consumption coevolved to generate both a growing demand and an expanding supply, must supplement a theory that stops at the level of subjective preferences. See Sidney W. Mintz, *Sweetness and Power: The Place of Sugar in Modern History* (New York: Viking, 1985) for relevant discussion.

25. For a discussion of how informally expressed accounts may nonetheless convey explanatory information, see sec. II of my "Probability, Explanation, and Information," *Synthese* 48 (1981) 233–56.

26. Such explanation uses a naturalized criterion when rationality is defined in terms of relative efficiency given the agent's beliefs and desires. A (more or less) rational agent is thus someone disposed to act in (more or less) efficient ways. There is a deep difficulty about calling such explanation naturalistic, for the constraints placed upon attributions of beliefs and desires by a "principle of charity" may compromise the claim that rational-agent explanations are empirical. Although I believe this difficulty can be overcome, this is hardly the place to start *that* argument.

27. For a survey of the literature, see Richard Nisbett and Lee Ross, *Human Inference: Strategies and Shortcomings of Social Judgment* (Englewood Cliffs: Prentice-Hall, 1980), where one unsurprisingly finds greater attention paid to drawbacks than advantages.

28. To recall a point from Section II: one may make assessments relative to particular evaluative criteria without thereby valuing that which satisfies them.

29. I realize that it is misleading to call a point of view that is "impartial, but equally concerned with all those potentially affected" a *social* point of view – some of those potentially affected may lie on the other side of an intersocial boundary. This complication will be set aside until Section V.

30. It also means that the relation of moral criteria to criteria of individual rationality has become problematic, since there can be no guarantee that what would be instrumentally rational from any given individual's point of view will coincide with what would be instrumentally rational from a social point of view.

31. A rather strong thesis of interpersonal comparison is needed here for purposes of social aggregation. I am not assuming the existence of some single good, such as happiness, underlying such comparisons. Thus the moral theory in question, although consequentialist, aggregative, and maximizing, is not equivalent to classical utilitarianism. I *am* assuming that when a choice is faced between satisfying interest $X$ of $A$ versus satisfying interest $Y$ of $B$, answers to the question "All else equal, would it matter more to me if I were $A$ to have $X$ satisfied than if I were $B$ to have $Y$ satisfied?" will be relatively determinate and stable across individuals under conditions of full and vivid information. A similar, though somewhat weaker, form of comparability-across-difference is presupposed when we make choices from among alternative courses of action that would lead us to have different desires in the future.

32. See, for example, Barrington Moore, Jr., *The Social Origins of Dictatorship and Democracy: Lord and Peasant in the Making of the Modern World* (Boston: Beacon, 1966) and *Injustice: The Social Bases of Obedience and Revolt* (White Plains, NY: M. E. Sharpe, 1978); E. P. Thompson, *The Making of the English Working Class* (New York: Pantheon, 1963); William B. Taylor, *Drinking, Homicide, and Rebellion in Colonial Mexican Villages* (Stanford: Stanford University Press, 1979); Charles Tilly, *From Mobilization to Revolution* (Reading, MA: Addison-Wesley, 1978); and Charles Tilly, et al., *The Rebellious Century, 1830–1930* (Cambridge: Harvard University Press, 1975).

33. A common theme in the works cited in note 32 is that much social unrest is revindicative rather than revolutionary, since the discontent of long-suffering groups often is galvanized into action only when customary entitlements are threatened or denied. The overt ideologies of such groups thus frequently are particularistic and conservative, even as their unrest contributes to the emergence of new social forms that concede greater weight to previously discounted interests. In a similar way, individuals often fail to notice irrationalities in their customary behavior until they are led by it into uncustomary difficulties, which then arouse a sense that something has gone wrong. For familiar reasons, a typical initial individual response is to attempt to retrieve the *status quo ante*, although genuine change may result from these restorative efforts.

34. It should be emphasized that these mechanisms do not presuppose a background of democratic institutions. They have extracted concessions even within societies that remained very hierarchical. See, for example, Taylor, *Drinking, Homicide, and Rebellion*.

35. Indeed, the mechanism just described may push in several directions at once: toward the inclusion of some previously excluded interests, and toward the exclusion of some previously included interests. To be sure, if interests come to be excluded even though their social and material basis remains more or less intact, a new potential for unrest is created. Some groups present a special problem, owing to their inherent inability to mobilize effectively, for example, children and future generations. To account for the pressures that have been exerted on behalf of these groups it is necessary to see how individuals come to include other individuals within their own interests. (Compare the way in which one's future selves, which can exert no pressure on their own behalf, come to be taken into account by one's present self in virtue of one's identification with them.) Unless one takes account of such processes of incorporation and identification, morality (or even prudence) will appear quite mysterious, but I will have little to say about them here. For some preliminary remarks, see sec. IX of my "Alienation, Consequentialism, and the Demands of Morality," *Philosophy and Public Affairs* 13 (1984) 134–71. Reprinted here as Chapter 6.
36. Here and elsewhere, I mean by 'contemporary moral theory' to refer to dominant views in the academies, and by 'contemporary moral discourse' to refer to widespread practices of public moral argumentation, in those societies that have achieved the highest levels of development of empirical science generally. Again, the moral realist, like the scientific realist, is not committed to worldwide consensus.
37. However, such prohibitions historically have shown limitations of scope that are no longer recognized as valid. The trend against such limitations is an instance of the first sort of pattern, toward increased generality.
38. Moreover, the accounts are highly general in character, operating at a level of description incapable of discriminating between hypotheses based upon the particular account of moral rightness proposed here and others rather close to it. (Roughly, those characterizing moral rightness in terms of instrumental rationality relative to the non-moral good of those affected, but differing on details regarding instrumental rationality – for example, is it straightforwardly maximizing or partly distributive? – or regarding non-moral goodness – for example, is it reducible to pleasure? For a discussion of not-very-close competitors, see Section VI.) If the method I have employed is to be used to make choices from among close competitors, the empirical analysis must be much more fine-grained. Similar remarks apply to the weak and extended theories of individual rationality appealed to in the preceding text.
39. It is of no importance whether we say that he has *no* reason to do this or simply a vanishingly small one. I suppose we could say that a person has a vanishingly small reason to do anything – even to expend enormous effort to purge minor contradictions from his beliefs or to purge alligators from distant swamps – that might *conceivably* turn out to be to his benefit. But then we would have no trouble guaranteeing the existence of vanishingly small reasons for moral conduct. This would allow naturalized moral rightness to satisfy a Humean thesis of practicality after all, but in a way that would rob the thesis of its interest.
40. François (duc de) la Rochefoucauld, *Reflexions, ou sentences et maximes morales suivi des reflexions diverses*, Jean Lafond, ed. (Paris: Gallimard, 1976) 79.

La Rochefoucauld apparently borrowed the phrase from the cleric Du Moulin. I am grateful to a remark of Barrington Moore, Jr. for reminding me of it. See his *Injustice*, 508.

41. Contrast Harman's relativism about 'ought' in *The Nature of Morality*. Harman adopts the first of the two courses just mentioned, preserving the connection between an individual's moral obligations and what he has (instrumental) reason to do. He defends his approach in part by arguing that, if we suppose that Hitler was engaged in rational pursuit of his ends, an "internal" judgment like 'Hitler (morally) ought not to have killed six million Jews' would be "weak" and "odd" compared to an "external" judgment like 'Hitler was evil' (see 107 ff). I would have thought the opposite, namely, that it is too "weak" and "odd" to give an account of morality such that Hitler can be judged to be consummately evil (which Harman claims, without explanation, his brand of relativism *can* do) but in which 'Hitler (morally) ought not to have acted as he did' is false.

42. This felt need is also reflected in the codification of laws, and in the development of legal theories. However contrived the law may at times seem, surely the general social conditions and needs that have driven its development are real enough. Indeed, the elaborate artifice of law and its language is in part an indication of how pressing the need to go beyond pretheoretic common sense has been.

43. I am indebted to a great many people, including Peter Achinstein, Robert Audi, Annette Baier, Michael Bratman, Stephen Darwall, Allan Gibbard, Thomas Nagel, Samuel Scheffler, Rebecca Scott, Nicholas Sturgeon, Nicholas White, and the editors at *The Philosophical Review*, who have kindly provided comments on previous drafts or presentations of this paper.

# 2

# *Facts and Values**

I

The fact/value distinction, in league with such equally grand and obscure distinctions as those between objectivity and subjectivity and between reason and emotion, has been vastly influential. Yet it appears on inspection to rest upon surprisingly insecure foundations. Thus I believe we should feel a certain unease about the weight it is asked to bear when we use it to support claims of the utmost importance about the nature of knowledge and the limits of inquiry. Perhaps it is time to consider what might happen were we to stop viewing these two realms as categorically distinct. A pair of alternatives immediately suggests itself: we might soften up facts, or harden up values. I propose to follow the latter course, but only after questioning an assumption about what the hardness of facts is supposed to consist in.

The sort of value I will be concerned with here is generic or non-moral goodness, often simply called intrinsic value. This is the sort of value that ordinarily is at issue when disputes occur about what an individual's or group's good consists in, about what kinds of lives are good to lead, or about what is desirable as an end in itself. Other species of value – such as moral or aesthetic value – I propose to leave aside for now.[1]

II

No doubt the fact/value distinction owes its prevalence to a great diversity of causes. However, it seems to me that among the arguments that have been most important to the *philosophical* defense of the fact/value distinction are these three: the argument from rational determinability,

43

the argument from internalism, and the argument from ontological "queerness." Let us take them up in turn.

## Rational Determinability

Genuinely factual disputes, it has been thought, can be resolved by appeal to reason and experience. If two individuals differ over a question of fact, yet each is wholly rational in the formation and assessment of his beliefs, then it should always be possible in principle for experience and logical argument to bring them into accord. By contrast, it is claimed, two entirely rational individuals who differ in their values may be able to confront all possible experience and argumentation and still find their normative disagreement intact.

This defense of the fact/value distinction appears to presuppose that there are canons of induction so powerful that experience would, in the limit, produce convergence on matters of fact among all epistemic agents, no matter what their starting points. There is considerable room for doubt on this score. The history of efforts to discover a "logic of induction" has convinced many philosophers that no such canons exist: our beliefs about the world are underdetermined even by all possible evidence.[2]

However, suppose for the moment that there were an uncontroversial logic of induction that assigned a univocal degree of epistemic probability to any given proposition on the basis of any given bit of evidence. Surprisingly, this would not rescue the argument from rational determinability.

To see why, consider deductive logic. Does deductive logic tell us what it is rational to believe? No, it tells us only which propositions follow from other propositions (or, in the case of logical truths, from no propositions at all). The following inference, for example, is manifestly not logically valid:

(1) I believe that $p$.
(2) $p$ implies $q$.
_____
(3) I rationally ought to believe that $q$.

The conclusion would follow were we to add the premise:

(0) One always rationally ought to believe the logical implications of one's current beliefs.

But (0) is not a principle of *logic* at all.[3] Moreover, (0) is not a very plausible principle, for it would require that we believe infinitely many things, and, indeed, if there happened to be any contradictions among our

44

beliefs, it would require us to believe every proposition and its negation. Principles of deductive logic – and of inductive logic, should such things exist – are undoubtedly relevant to the question "What rationally ought one to believe?", but only because obeying these principles, or knowing their import, sometimes serves the purposes of practical reason. The fact that deductive inferences are truth preserving makes deduction very handy, but, as the absurd consequences of (0) show, rational agents need not always go where the application of logic would lead them. So, if facts are supposed to be distinguished from values in virtue of what reason requires us to believe, then even the existence of an inductive logic would not secure the distinction. The question "What rationally ought one to believe?" will always belong to practical rather than theoretical reason.

Facts are hard, I believe, but not because reason and experience force them upon us. They are hard because they are part of a world that is causally responsible for our experience, a world most of whose features do not depend upon our conception of it or our aspirations in it. Reason, then, does not make facts hard; it finds them hard.

## Internalism

Some proponents of the fact/value distinction have sought to draw the line between facts and values in a different way. Consider a claim on my part that I value something. This claim is undoubtedly a factual assertion. It may reflect a value judgment, but it is not itself such a judgment – others may accept my claim without sharing my value. But now consider a claim on my part that something is *valuable*. This remark does express a value judgment, and its normative character is revealed by the fact that a person who did not share my value would not in full knowledge and sincerity accept this statement. How are we to characterize the normative force of such a remark? One answer is that when I claim that something is valuable, I am claiming that it is in some sense an appropriate object of valuation or pursuit. It is this notion of appropriateness – and perhaps an associated commendatory force – that stands between my remark and its acceptance by someone with different values.

Now it has been held by contemporary Humeans and Kantians alike that in order for a normative judgment to apply to an individual, he must have some reason – not necessarily overriding – to comply with it. This thesis makes use of the notion of having a reason, and thus it takes various forms depending upon the conception of rationality presupposed.

45

A Kantian might require that the normative judgment be a maxim of the rational will of the individual. A Humean might require that the individual have some desire or end relative to which there is instrumental reason for complying with the judgment.

Suppose, for example, that I claim that the contemplation of beauty is intrinsically valuable. Certainly, I am not just preaching to the converted. The normative scope of my remark includes not only those who happen already to go for the contemplation of beauty, but also those who do not, saying that it would be a good thing if they did. One common, if rather dramatic, way of putting this is to say that the normative scope of my remark encompasses all rational beings as such.

If this were what value judgments involved, then, given the instrumental conception of rationality (and here contemporary Humeans and Kantians part company), it would follow at once that value-judgments could not be factual. For according to instrumentalism, there are no substantive ends or activities – such as the contemplation of beauty – that all rational beings as such have a reason to pursue regardless of their contingent desires. But then, necessarily, my remark's normative reach would exceed its grasp, so that the truth-conditions of 'The contemplation of beauty is intrinsically valuable' could never be satisfied. A common response to this conclusion has been to recommend abandonment of the idea that value judgments have truth-conditions, for it would be hard to explain their role in actual discourse on the assumption that they are factual assertions, but always – and necessarily – false ones.

By contrast, although values may be involved in deliberation about which factual statements to believe or assert, no normative commitments figure in the truth-conditions proper to them. For example, the statement that 'People value the contemplation of beauty' does not involve any ideas about the desirability of such contemplation, or even about the desirability of believing or asserting this statement. So the combination of internalism with the instrumental conception of rationality does not give rise to any difficulty about the truth-conditions of factual statements being met.

Of course, an individual could as a contingent matter have a positive attitude toward the contemplation of beauty, and could recommend to all rational beings that they share this attitude. There would be nothing odd about his choosing the phrase 'The contemplation of beauty is intrinsically valuable' to make public his view. This phrase might even carry some descriptive content. But thus employed it would not be a mere statement of fact, for it would partake of the realm of expression or commendation, and so mere facts could not make it true.

The argument may be summarized: internalism plus instrumentalism yields the fact/value distinction.

Can this argument be stopped? One might join the Kantians in challenging the premise of instrumentalism, and attempt to argue that some substantive ends or actions are indeed mandated by rationality. Such challenges have a noble history, and even a noble representation in the present, but I find the ignoble instrumentalist view the clearest idea we have of what it is, at a minimum, to have a reason for acting.[4]

The remaining premise is internalism. Is it true that all normative judgments must find an internal resonance in those to whom they are applied? While I do not find this thesis convincing as a claim about all species of normative assessment, it does seem to me to capture an important feature of the concept of intrinsic value to say that what is intrinsically valuable for a person must have a connection with what he would find in some degree compelling or attractive, at least if he were rational and aware. It would be an intolerably alienated conception of someone's good to imagine that it might fail in any such way to engage him. What I do not see, however, is a justification for the further claim that in order for something to be intrinsically valuable *for a particular person*, that something must induce a resonance in any arbitrarily different rational being. Let us call this further claim the thesis of *value absolutism*. The argument for the fact/value distinction under consideration can now be seen to have three premises rather than two: internalism plus instrumentalism plus value absolutism. Some form of the first two premises I am prepared to grant; the third premise I doubt.

I doubt it because I doubt that it is essential to the concept of *intrinsic* value that such value be absolute as well. Let me suggest a view of the nature of value that leads to a conception of intrinsic value, but not through any notion of absoluteness.

It seems to me that notions like good and bad have a place in the scheme of things only in virtue of facts about what matters, or could matter, to beings for whom it is possible that something matter. Good and bad would have no place within a universe consisting only of stones, for nothing matters to stones. Introduce some people, and you will have introduced the possibility of value as well. It *will* matter to people how things go in their rock-strewn world. Of course, what in particular will matter, or could matter, to these people will depend upon what they are like. Are they, for example, capable of the same range of beliefs and desires as we?

Humans are persons, but they are much else besides: they are made up of carbon-based stuff rather than silicon-based stuff, they are the result of a particular evolutionary history, they have various individual developmental histories, and so on. What matters to them, even when they are fully rational, need not matter to all rational beings. If certain sociobiologists are right, humans typically are capable of intrinsic motivation by beliefs about the well-being of those toward whom they have feelings of commonality, such as kinship. Had the mechanisms of genetic replication and natural selection been different, and had rational beings nonetheless emerged, they might have been virtually incapable of intrinsically desiring the well-being of others.

In a naturalistic spirit, we might think of goodness as akin to nutritiveness. All organisms require nutrition, but not the same nutrients. Which nutrients a given organism or type of organism requires will depend upon its nature. Cow's milk nourishes calves and many humans, but it won't nourish those organisms, including some humans, who cannot produce the enzymes needed to digest it; and some elements essential to human nutrition are toxic to other organisms. There is, then, no such thing as an *absolute* nutrient, that is, something that would be nutritious for all possible organisms. There is only *relational* nutritiveness: substance $S$ is a nutrient for organisms of type $T$. Is there, therefore, no *intrinsic* nutritiveness, either? In a sense, yes: nothing is a nutrient in and of itself, irrespective of whom or what it might nourish. But in another sense, no: we may distinguish among the things that nourish an organism those that do so *directly* and those that do so *mediately*. Some substances are, for a given organism, in themselves nutritious – they are ultimate dietary requirements. Some substances (and not always different ones) are a source of nutrition in virtue of their contribution to the production or consumption of that which is an ultimate nutrient. Calcium is itself, intrinsically, a nutrient for humans – it is essential that we get it, but not essential how. Cakes and ale, on the other hand, are nutritious only insofar as they are vehicles for ultimate nutrients.

Similarly, we might say that although there is no such thing as absolute goodness – that which is good in and of itself, irrespective of what or whom it might be good *for* or the good *of* – there may be relational goodness. Moreover, among the relational goods for a given being, some may be intrinsic and others instrumental. To call a good intrinsic in this sense is to say something about why or how it matters to that being: Is it the sort of thing that matters – or would matter, under suitable circumstances – for its own sake, or merely as a means to other things? Here internalism comes naturally into play, directing us to look at the being's motivational system: Is it capable of intrinsic motivation by a given consideration, and, if so, under what circumstances?

It is important to see that relationalism of this sort is distinct from relativism. Heaviness, for example, is a relational concept; nothing is absolutely heavy. But the two-place predicate '$X$ is heavier than $Y$' has an objectively deteminate extension. Similarly, although a relational conception of value denies the existence of absolute good, it may yield an objectively determinate two-place predicate '$X$ is part of $Y$'s good.'

Perhaps the simplest relational theory of goodness is that of Hobbes, who held that to call something good is always to speak of someone's good, and that the only sense in which something can be good for someone is that he desires it.[5] To call something part of someone's *intrinsic* good, on this view, would presumably be to say that he desires it for its own sake. This theory has many virtues: it is uncomplicated, nonpaternalistic, and epistemically as straightforward as the idea of desire. Moreover, it easily meets at least one version of the internalist requirement, since according to the simpler forms of instrumentalism, the fact that one desires $X$ is *ipso facto* a reason for pursuing it.

Yet this theory is deeply unsatisfactory, since it seems incapable of capturing important elements of the critical and self-critical character of value judgments. On this theory one can, of course, criticize any particular current desire on the grounds that it ill fits with other, more numerous or more powerful current desires on one's part, or (if it is an instrumental desire) on the grounds that it is the result of a miscalculation with the information one has. But this hardly exhausts the range of assessment. Sometimes we wish to raise questions about the intrinsic desirability of the things that now are the main focus of our desires, even after any mistakes in calculation have been corrected.[6] This appears to be a specific function of the vocabulary of goodness and badness, as distint from the vocabulary of desire and aversion. But what could be the grounds for such potentially radical reassessment? Once one has accepted an instrumental conception of rationality, one cannot ask that reason by itself accomplish the criticism of ends. And once one has accepted internalism as well, one must find the grounds of criticism somewhere in the realm of things that actually or possibly find some internal resonance in the agent. Let us consider how such criticism might proceed.

Sheila is a journalist who has made something of a name for herself covering business and agriculture for a major newspaper in the Northwest. Word of her work spreads and, as a result, in from the East comes a job offer from *The Daily Planet*, a great metropolitan newspaper. It would not have occurred to her to seek out such an offer, but immediately upon receiving it she feels a powerful urge to accept. Although it has made a significant contribution to her success, Sheila's small-town, Western background has always made her a bit apologetic. And she has never liked having to explain to people outside her profession that her paper "really is quite well regarded."

Yet when she thinks through the choice, she cannot escape noticing that a great many of the things that have made her life in recent years so enjoyable and productive – reportorial freedom, ready access to nature, and integration of family life with work – seem to count in favor of keeping her present job. Indeed, Sheila is a bit surprised at herself when these considerations seem to move her so little once she faces the lure of the big time. She wonders whether she has made an uncomfortable discovery about herself or whether she simply is so impressed by the thought of her byline on the front page of the *Planet* that she has lost sight of what fundamentally matters to her. She worries whether what she most desires really corresponds to what would be the best sort of life for her.

The connection between this normative concern and her desires – as required by internalism – is indirect. Her sense that she is being less attentive to the actual prospects of the options she faces than to their immediate impact upon her self-image does not by itself so weaken her attraction to the *Planet* job that this desire no longer predominates. Like the rest of us, Sheila is concerned with her future well-being, but for her, like the rest of us, this concern is sometimes dim in comparison to more vivid goods. Still, a plausible version of internalism should allow the normative worry to stand, for it clearly has an internal grip on Sheila – it is a worry of *hers*.

There are other important classes of cases in which we question whether our good coincides with what we most desire. Consider Beth, a successful and happy accountant, who nonetheless wants above all to quit and devote herself full time to writing. Beth's desire, let us suppose, does not depend upon any failure to envisage vividly her best-warranted expectations about the future, nor does it involve any failure to calculate accurately with the information she has at hand. Unfortunately, however, although she has no convincing evidence to show it – after all, some of the short stories she wrote as an undergraduate were admired by her friends and teachers – Beth does not have the skill or temperament to be a writer. So, when the accumulation from her earnings enables her to give up ledgerbooks for copybooks, things go badly. She finds it enormously difficult to bring herself to write with any regularity, and what work she does produce fails to gain acceptance. Another sort of person might return more or less quickly to accounting, closing the episode, and putting it down to experience. But Beth has never been one who knew when to cut her losses. She feels she must keep at it and make a success of it, so year in and year out she putters around her house while trying to spend time at the desk, traipses off to writers' workshops, takes part-time jobs, and sends off unsolicited manuscripts. Yet success does not arrive, and she becomes increasingly bitter, unproductive, and indebted. Looking back, she concludes that she paid too high a price in lost well-being and self-confidence for the information that she is not suited to writing. Knowing what she now knows, she thinks it would have been better had she fended off her desire to be a writer and remained an accountant with a few shelves of good current fiction.

This judgment distinguishes her good at a time from what she most desired at that time. Moreover, it distinguishes her good at a time from what was, given her beliefs and desires, instrumentally rational at that time. It may even so be said to assert a connection between her good and her all-things-considered desires, namely, between the all-things-considered desires of the sadder-but-wiser Beth and the good of her earlier self. Should internalism allow this sort of internal connection to support a judgment recommending against the writer's life for Beth at the time of her decision? There is an internal grip: Beth herself feels all too poignantly the evaluative force of her later, better-informed views.

Yet it is the later Beth who feels this force, for it is she who has the information.[7] What force would the views of the later Beth have for the earlier Beth, were they somehow to become known to her? It might have the effect of quickly dulling the earlier Beth's desire to write. But we can also imagine that her earlier self's desire to become a writer would remain quite strong, perhaps stronger than any competing desire. Yet even in this latter case, it is natural to expect that her desire *that this desire be effective* will become more tentative, and that some contrary desires will emerge.

Why is this natural? Partly because it is natural to care about whether one is happy and whether one's desires are satisfied. The earlier Beth has every reason to believe that her later self takes these concerns to heart, since the later Beth is contemplating what she would want to pursue were she actually to relive the intervening years. Moreover, the earlier Beth also has reason to believe that her later self is better situated than she to know what would most satisfy Beth's desires during those years.

These observations tend in a certain direction. Presumably, the earlier Beth would find the views of the later Beth still more compelling had the later Beth knowledge not only of the outcome of attempting a career in writing, but of the outcome of alternative pursuits as well. What, for example, would it really have been like for Beth to have remained in accounting? To have a desire is, among other things, to care whether or not it is satisfied. Although fuller information about how one's actual desires will fare in the world may not always contribute to the satisfaction of those desires – one may know too much – the advice of someone who has this fuller information, and also has the deepest sort of identification with one's fate, is bound to have some commending force.

To learn of a reassessment that would arise from full information (and vividness, rationality, and so on) may have force for another reason as well. The ground for this force is also – as it must be on the present account – in the contingent concerns of the actual individual. In this case, however, the concerns are immediately directed not at the satisfaction of desires, but at their defense.

Let us say that one *embraces* a desire, or accepts it as *goal setting*, when one desires that it be effective in regulating one's life. This is not to say one desires that it be overriding; rather one desires that it influence the course of one's life – insofar as this is within one's power – in rough proportion to its strength. In the examples given, Sheila worries whether to embrace her desire to take the *Planet* job and the later Beth, reflecting upon the circumstances of her earlier self, no longer embraces the desire to be a writer. At least one of the features that distinguishes those among our desires that we call our goals is that we normally do not – at least, not without qualm – call a desire that we are not prepared upon reflection to embrace a goal. For an individual to deem something a goal or value of his own involves the idea on his part that it is an appropriate object of desire or pursuit.[8] The notion of appropriateness at work is internal, but may concern the desires he would want to be effective in his actual life were he to contemplate that life with full awareness of the facts and full rationality in deliberation.

These counterfactual circumstances concern the defensibility of the desires themselves against certain sorts of criticism, although 'criticism' here has a special meaning. There is no logical contradiction involved in embracing wholeheartedly a desire that one knows one would want not to be effective in one's actual life were one fully informed and rational. The sort of conflict that is basic to the criticism of desires is psychological rather than logical. One might call this conflict "cognitive dissonance" were it merely cognitive. But what perhaps is most striking about it is that it involves a linkage between the cognitive and the conative. We should expect this sort of linkage in the psychology of value, since valuing is an *attitude*, and an attitude is neither merely a desire nor merely a belief: it involves a collection of desires and an associated *outlook* or characteristic way of seeing things, an outlook that is partly constituted by characteristic beliefs about what one is seeing, and by a tendency to interpret or explain things in certain ways rather than others. That is why, when crucial beliefs are altered or challenged, the agent's outlook itself shifts, with the result that the landscape he previously perceived changes and his desires, which had felt at home in that terrain, become unsettled.

If taking an attitude or embracing a desire involves certain beliefs, it also involves an assumption that these beliefs are not merely false, that one's outlook is not largely a matter of, or psychologically dependent upon, error or ignorance. What is it about the possibility of error or ignorance that creates a potential threat to one's outlook itself? The beginning of an answer may be this. We call upon our basic goals, as distinct from our mere (though perhaps insistent) desires, to explain to ourselves and to others the *worthwhileness* and *point* of our choices – indeed, of our lives. The price we pay for using our values in this way is a commitment to their defensibility. If our values are to support us, we must support them. And we defend our attitudes by appeal to facts psychologically congenial to them. Hence, if someone raises convincing doubts about our understanding of the facts, he causes us unease in our values. We could, of course, always in such circumstances insist that the absence of a logical connection between beliefs and desires permits us to keep our values intact, no matter how wrong or uninformed we discover ourselves to have been on the facts. It is interesting that we so seldom do this. One reason might be that such a response seems to be a shrinking from the task of explaining the worthwhileness and point of what we do. That is, it seems to involve something akin to an admission of defeat – an admission to others and to ourselves that there is less to our lives than had seemed to be the case.

Unless the idea that we must support those values that support us is to involve a mere conjuring trick, we must find somewhere outside our ends, seen as personal desires, to gain a toehold. Historically, this has been done by appeal to such things as gods, ancestors, and the order of nature. The existentialists were quite right in saying that if, as moderns, we reject these props, and if we further conclude that valuation and choice are a mere matter of fixing on something by fiat, then values cannot confer meaning and life becomes absurd. But there *are* fixed points beyond the self. When we defend our values by appeal to facts, facts whose truth-values do not fluctuate with our particular desires or decisions, we are seeking such a toehold. Importantly, too, these truth-values do not fluctuate with the decisions or desires of others, so that this toehold can support us even when we find ourselves in a world with people whose beliefs or ends differ from our own. If we discover that our values are psychologically dependent upon ignorance or error, we lose this source of support.

Of course, our first-order desires may press upon us willy-nilly, and may be remarkably insensitive to discovery that we were wrong on the facts. But for this very reason it does not do much to explain to myself or others the worthwhileness or point of what I have done with my life to say that I have simply acted upon whatever desire happened to be most urgent at the moment. Higher-order desires of the sort that are involved in embracing a desire are more responsive to changes in belief, and so not only do they become more closely tied to our identity, they become the basis of the idea of value.

The proposal I would make, then, is the following: an individual's good consists in what he would want himself to want, or to pursue, were he to contemplate his present situation from a standpoint fully and vividly informed about himself and his circumstances, and entirely free of cognitive error or lapses of instrumental rationality. The wants in question, then, are wants regarding what he would seek were he to assume the place of his actual, incompletely informed and imperfectly rational self, taking into account the changes that self is capable of, the costs of those changes, and so on.[9] A fully informed and rational individual would, for example, have no use or desire for psychological strategies suited to circumstances of limited knowledge and rationality; but he no doubt would want his incompletely informed and imperfectly rational actual self to develop and deploy such strategies.

My claim is that this notion of someone's good affords an explanation of the normative force of judgments of one's good, for it gives expression to an idea of appropriateness or *fitness* of an end for an agent. Fitness consists in a certain match between an agent's motivational system, on the one hand, and his capacities and circumstances, on the other, when all are accurately represented and adequately appreciated. Moreover, this notion of someone's good also satisfies an appropriate internalist constraint: we can see in the psychology of value, as discussed previously, the ways in which the views we would have were we to become free of present defects in knowledge or rationality would induce an internal resonance in us as we now are.

Let us then say that an individual's *intrinsic* good consists in attainment of what he would in idealized circumstances want to want for its own sake – or, more accurately, to pursue for its own sake (for wanting is only one way of pursuing) – were he to assume the place of his actual self. This account leaves open the possibility that the intrinsic good of different persons may differ, and thus splits internalism from value absolutism. It therefore removes an essential premise from the argument from instrumentalism and internalism to the fact/value distinction. If the intrinsic good of a rational being can depend upon its contingent features, in particular, upon those features that determine the being's idealized hypothetical wants, then the fact that no substantive ends would necessarily exist for all instrumentally rational beings does not stand in the way of the facticity of value judgments.

It now is possible to deal with the remaining defense[10] of the fact/value distinction – the argument from "queerness" – rather more rapidly.

### Queerness

The usual sort of objection to the facticity of values on grounds of ontological queerness is parasitic upon the two arguments already considered. It *would* be peculiar, to say the least, if there were features of the world that evoked in all rational beings, no matter what their contingent nature, a sense of "to-be-pursuedness" (to use Mackie's phrase[11]). But we need not believe in the reality of such things in order to believe that there are facts about values. We need only believe in those properties of the world, most conspicuously, of human motivational systems and the situations in which they find themselves, that support the counterfactuals concerning idealized desires used previously to characterize intrinsic goodness.

The argument from queerness concerns the nature of reality, and so some Hegelian reflections may not be out of place. The aboriginal objectivist view of value is perhaps the idea of an end that commands our allegiance, no matter what we are severally like. The commanding in question might be done by a deity, or, in the more sophisticated versions, by rationality itself. A good of this kind would be absolute, and of it one could say that it is not valuable because we desire it, but rather, we desire it (at least, when we know what we're about) because it is valuable. But the idea of an end that commands our allegiance from without drops altogether from view once the world is seen from a secular, nonteleological, instrumentalist standpoint. This may tempt us to negate the objectivity of value and assert instead its subjectivity. We carry out the same sort of inversion of the concept of objective value that Hume accomplished in the case of causal necessity or Feuerbach in the case of the Holy

Family – the concept of objective good is held to be a projection, a reification of a subjective human response as if it were a self-subsistent reality. The slogan becomes: we do not desire things because they are valuable, we deem them valuable because we desire them.

But now for the Hegelian point: the negation of this negation is not far off in dialectical space, and when we reach it, we are able to transcend the antithesis of objectivity and subjectivity that both the aboriginal objectivist conception of value and the subsequent subjectivist negation of it presuppose.

As suggested previously, the notions of good or bad have a place in the scheme of things only in virtue of facts about what matters or could matter to beings for whom it is possible that something matter. A being for whom something can matter is a being with a point of view, a subjectivity. In a universe without subjectivity, there is no value either. But all actual subjective beings are at the same time objective beings. They have determinate properties that are not merely constituted by their conception of themselves, and these properties determine what sorts of things do, or can, matter to them. Their self-conception may be more or less objective, that is, may more or less accurately reflect what they really are like, how they actually are situated, and so on. According to the sketch of the psychology of value and of the nature of intrinsic good given previously, that which is genuinely valuable is constituted by what matters to subjective beings whose conception of themselves and their world is in this sense objective. Value, then, is not a merely objective or merely subjective matter. It is in virtue of our subjectivity that valence can exist, but it is in virtue of our objective nature that we possess a subjectivity, and moreover a subjectivity of a kind that valences some things rather than others and that finds a special valence, called 'value,' in those things that would be subjectively compelling were our consciousness objectified. The notion of subjectivity objectified affords a convenient way of expressing a point made previously, that in our attempts to defend our values we look beyond mere subjective identification with them, seeking to show that this identification can withstand full rational appropriation, and appreciation, of the real.

III

We are hardly through with objections, however. Even if one were to succeed in turning back familiar arguments for the fact/value distinction, few would likely be convinced that value judgments can be factual in the absence of a plausible factualist theory of value. I have tried to sketch what I take to be such an account, yet it in turn faces a number of serious difficulties that now must be addressed. Within the confines of this paper, I can consider only two such difficulties, both of which have figured in recent criticisms of naturalistic theories of value. One difficulty concerns the determinateness of value, as characterized here; the other concerns its naturalness. Let us now turn to the first of these.

### *Determinateness*

It might be questioned whether what has been said thus far suffices to show that judgments of non-moral value might be factual, since there are grounds for skepticism about whether there is such a thing as "what one would, if fully and vividly informed and fully instrumentally rational, want oneself to seek were one to assume one's actual place."[12] Surely, the idealization involved is severe. As finite beings, we may be incapable of being fully informed about ourselves and our world, or of assessing in an appropriate way the relevance of so many considerations. How, then, are we to evaluate counterfactuals about what one would desire if one were fully informed and rational?[13]

It seems to me that the only answer possible is that the notion of idealized desires is an unabashedly theoretical one. While we have no direct epistemic access to such desires, a theory-assisted extrapolation may nonetheless be available from the present state of an individual's cognitive and conative systems. For part of any comprehensive psychological theory will be an account of the factors that influence which desires we form and how these desires evolve in response to various sorts of changes, including changes in belief. We saw an instance of such a process in the case of Beth. As her beliefs about her aptitude and prospects changed, so did her desire to be a writer. Although she might continue to *wish* that she could become a writer, she no longer wants this wish to be effective for her as she is. The changes in her desires precipitated by her realizations are, we noted, of an entirely familiar kind.

More generally, it is a familiar fact about people that their desires – especially, their values – and their beliefs show a certain coherence. For example, we typically do not find two individuals who agree about the likely effects upon an individual of participation in contact sports or homosexual relations, one of whom thinks that such activities are part of individual flourishing while the other thinks they could not be. Of course, not all differences in desire are caused by differences in belief – sometimes it is the other way around, as in wishful thinking. Thus what we should say is simply that differences in desire are generally *associated with* differences in belief of characteristic kinds, so that individuals who differ in their beliefs tend to differ predictably in their desires, and individuals who are in close agreement in their beliefs tend to resemble one another in their desires as well. So the idealization I have described, which in the limit fixes the full content of an individual's beliefs, may leave rather restricted scope for variation in desires. This claim is all the more plausible in light of the fact that, insofar as possible, the idealization holds fixed the individual's non-belief properties, so that the contribution of these features to desire-formation would remain largely the same.

We are not ourselves fully informed, and thus do not know the answer to the question where an extrapolation of our desires would lead. We may, however, gain greater confidence that there is a relatively determinate answer to this question by considering a series of much smaller and more manageable questions. Begin with an individual who believes, wrongly, that $p$. Then ask how his desires would change were he to believe instead that not-$p$, but to remain the same in every other property (except those that could not coexist with believing that not-$p$). Given nothing more powerful than commonsense psychological theory, we may feel reasonably confident that there is an answer. We then imagine this process repeated until all of the individual's erroneous beliefs have been set right, and his system of beliefs has been enlarged to accommodate as much of the truth as possible. No doubt the extrapolation becomes more tenuous the further it is carried, and the larger the interactive effects of accumulated changes in belief, but thus far the idea of extrapolation does not seem to have become ungrounded.

However, the possible effects upon the individual of the *order* and *mode* of presentation of the information he receives create serious difficulties for this picture of determinate, piecemeal change.

The way an individual's desires evolve upon receipt of information may depend in part upon which illusions he is disabused of first. To specify that full information be supplied but make no reference to order of presentation may thus be too indefinite. Yet it would seem arbitrary to fix upon one order of presentation, for this would build any effects peculiar to that ordering into the idealization itself. What is needed, then, is some way to avoid both indefiniteness and arbitrary definiteness.

Now some of the effects of order of presentation can be expected to become very dilute as the total volume of information grows. Moreover, with greater information second-order mechanisms of neutralization will come into play. For the information an individual receives will include knowledge of psychological theory in general, and of its application to his psychology in particular. He therefore will become aware of the differential effects upon him of various orderings of the same information, and it is well known that awareness of such effects tends to reduce their impact. In the limit, we can imagine that full awareness of effects of sheer order will leave them without significant net impact.

An experiment in cognitive psychology reveals that when subjects observe two individuals taking a test, one of whom answers a high percentage of the early questions correctly but then falters, while the other does poorly initially but then answers a high percentage of the later questions correctly, the first is usually viewed as more able, even though in the end each answers the same number of questions correctly in all.[14] If the subjects had been asked which test-taker they would prefer as a math tutor, they likely would have answered "The first," and perhaps they would also have been willing to pay a premium to secure his services. But if they were to become convinced of the influence of sheer order on their evaluations of relative ability, they presumably would no longer want their initial preference for the first test-taker to influence their choices – or willingness to pay – in this way.[15]

A similar response may be made to the worry about mode of presentation. Part of the idealization described is that the information an individual receives be vivid as well as complete. But it is not hard to imagine that two modes of presentation of a given body of information might be equally vivid, but different in effect. A story vividly recounted by Dickens might evoke a different response in us than the same story vividly told by Mailer. Of course, it is difficult in such cases to say when we have the same story twice rather than two stories about the same subject: information may be conveyed by mode of representation. Moreover, the information conveyed by a story is a function of both message and receiver. A certain word and its dictionary equivalent may awaken in some hearers, but not others, quite different trains of images. In a related way, vividness, too, depends upon receptivity – purple prose may be vivid to some, deadening to others.[16]

It is difficult or impossible, then, to characterize mode of presentation in a way entirely unrelated to content. But that merely allows us to put the worry about mode of presentation in another way. For if there are an infinite number of ways of representing a given state of affairs, and if some of these might have evocations that others do not – even when vividness is equal – then it becomes doubtful whether full information could have a determinate effect. In response it can be said that as one's information becomes more complete, one learns more about the possible range of modes of presentation and their specific effects upon one. Moreover, although language and other forms of representation may be infinitely expressive, our conative systems are not infinitely fine-grained: for any given individual, vast classes of modes of presentation would have essentially the same effect. Effects peculiar to a given class of presentations may be dampened precisely by exposing oneself to an array of effect-producing presentations and to the facts about how these various sorts of presentation differentially affect one. We may not be able to remove such effects, but we may be able self-consciously to play them against one another to weaken the hold of any specific sort of presentation upon our choices,[17] thereby achieving greater independence from mode of presentation.

Yet, even when purified, extended, and compensated as far as possible for effects of order and mode of presentation, an *actual* individual's beliefs will always fall well short of embodying full information. We must then begin to ask: Of the things we cannot cram into his head, are there any that are of a kind that our psychological theory indicates would change the desires of someone like him, and, if so, *how* would they change them? We may for example be unable to get a given individual to absorb the whole truth about the behavior of subatomic particles. Yet we may be able to attain reasonable confidence that none of the facts in this subject inaccessible to him would alter his present desires in any significant way. By contrast, we may also be unable to get him to absorb the whole truth about social psychology, but may be reasonably confident that these further facts would quite undermine some of his present attitudes toward his co-workers.

Slowly, we move away from the picture of trying to cram information into a person's head, and instead look at a given individual as something like a *personality*, a collection of properties that ground dispositions to react in various ways to exposure to certain facts. Just as there is a *reduction basis* for an individual's current desires – those features of his psychology, physiology, and circumstances in virtue of which he now has these desires – there is a reduction basis for his idealized hypothetical desires. When we ask how his desires would change upon the impact of further information, we appeal to this basis. We, in effect, hold this basis as nearly constant as possible when asking what someone like *him* would come to desire – or, more precisely, would come to want that he pursue were he to assume the place of his original self.

It is an open matter how determinate our answers to such questions can be. There are, however, two sorts of indeterminateness, only one of which would be genuinely troubling for the present account. It might turn out that, given what a particular individual is like, more than one set of hypothetical desires is compatible with full information. This sort of "tie for first place" need not be upsetting. Why should we suppose that there could not be several possible lives that would be equally valuable for an individual to lead? Beth was ill suited to be a writer, but a life as an accountant with a strong avocational interest in wildlife preservation might be as good for her as a life as a wildlife foundation administrator with a strong avocational interest in contract bridge. Either would suit. Indeed, the same might be true of basic values. A life for a given individual in which the value of autonomy plays an important organizing role might tie with a life characterized by less autonomy and more accomplishment. Of course, once certain choices have been made and acted upon, some options may cease to be equal-best. But new equal-best options are bound to emerge.

A second sort of indeterminacy would be more troubling. Suppose that we cannot formulate a psychological theory powerful enough to yield anything like the general principles previously appealed to regarding the interrelation of beliefs and desires. Then we might have no grounds for confidence in any extrapolation beyond what we can *actually* accomplish by way of fixing an individual's desires through fixing his beliefs. There are two cases to consider. In the first, the facts about what an individual's desires would be might be determinate, but we would be unable to extrapolate to them because no general theory of an appropriate kind capable of subsuming these changes is available. Presumably, those who recently have argued against the possibility of a general theory of human action that would establish a system of psychological and psychophysical laws, but who believe that our behavior is law governed under other descriptions, might hold such a view. This would permit us to think that there are facts that determine how an individual's desires would evolve under ever more ideal information, and thus not undermine the present account of intrinsic value, but it would deny us access to these desires – and thus to facts about intrinsic value – through psychological theory.

In the second case, even the idea that there is determinacy about what someone would desire under ideal conditions would be dropped. One might, for example, hold that there are no facts or principles at any level of description that fix the way an individual's desires would evolve under full information. For example, one might say that since it is *nomologically* impossible for individuals to become fully informed, one cannot treat the acquisition of full information as a limit process within psychological theory.

In general, it is not an objection to a counterfactual that it involves hypothesizing circumstances that are, in the actual course of things, nomologically impossible. It would be excessively skeptical to insist that there is no fact of the matter about how our lives would be changed were our natural life span to be increased two-fold, or our unassisted memory tenfold, yet such hypothetical circumstances would involve violation of laws of physiology. Indeed, if we suppose the world to be deterministic, then no contrary-to-fact circumstance could obtain except as the result of the violation of a law.

The objection must be that the case at hand is really quite extreme: the rupture effected in psychological theory by the supposition of equipping otherwise normal people with full information would leave too little of the fabric of that theory intact to support the relevant counterfactuals. But this, too, seems excessively skeptical. It is for theoretically deep reasons that matter cannot achieve frictionlessness or perfect elasticity or absolute zero, yet we may – with the aid of physical theory – see matter as possessing properties in virtue of which it would be disposed to behave in a certain way in such idealized conditions, and different kinds of matter, to behave differently. Similarly, it might be said that owing to the psychological properties of actual people, it is impossible to bring them to a state of full and vivid information, yet we may see them as possessing properties in virtue of which they would be disposed to respond in certain ways to ever more complete and vivid information (supposing a capacity to absorb it), and different kinds of people, to respond differently.[18]

### Naturalness

One consequence of this discussion is to suggest that, if a psychological theory of the sort I have in mind is possible, then appeal to the hypothetical desires of an idealized individual has an essentially *heuristic* function. The work is being done by the lawful regularities linking desires, beliefs, and other features of individuals, and by the relevant "initial conditions," that is, the facts about a given individual's psychology, physiology, and circumstances that are the reduction basis of his dispositions to desire.

Indeed, I propose to say that what makes some or other end or activity be part of an individual's good is not the fact that he would, were he ideally informed (and so on), desire that his actual self pursue it, but rather the existence of the reduction basis for that counterfactual, namely, the particular constellation of law-governed features of the actual individual and his circumstances in virtue of which these claims about idealized hypothetical desires hold. Thus, the truth-condition of the claim that such-and-such is good for a given individual is directly given by the existence of this constellation of features, without detour through idealized desires. We may then take an individual's desires, as they approach idealization in the limit, to be *indicators* of his good, of the presence of the sort of fit discussed previously between an individual and an end or activity.

This has the advantage of demystifying claims about one's good, and also of suggesting a possible response to an important objection to naturalism about value.[19] According to a view that has wide currency among epistemic naturalists, purportedly factual claims earn their place in our going theory of the world by making some contribution to explanation. But claims about what is valuable have no obvious explanatory role. It would seem always to be possible to explain people's behavior in terms of their actual beliefs and desires without making any reference to whether what they desire really is good. Of course, we might have to make reference to their *beliefs* about what is good, but that would be just one more piece of descriptive sociology.

How, then, is the naturalist about value to satisfy the demands of epistemic naturalism? Or more generally, can it be said there are natural facts about value if these alleged facts – unlike other natural facts with which we are familiar – can make no contribution to explanation?

Consider again Beth, the erstwhile accountant. She desired to become a writer, and that desire forms part of the core of the explanation of her decision to leave accounting to try her hand at other sorts of fiction. Recall that, although she could not have known it at the time, she lacked the talent or personality to be a writer. We may suppose that this lack derives from some underlying facts about her psychology, which in turn derive from some deeper underlying facts about her physiology, circumstances, and so on. These facts help to explain why she fails as a writer, and moreover why her experience as a writer eventually undermines her commitment to writing. Yet on the present account, it is these self-same facts that constitute the fact that a life of writing is not part of her good. Thus, facts about what is or is not part of Beth's good can play a role in explaining her decision to give up writing.

Note that this role is prior to any change in Beth's beliefs about whether the writer's life is a good one for her. For though her loss of the desire to be a writer may explain most immediately why she ultimately abandoned that career, the further and prior fact that writing is not a good career for her explains why she came to lose this desire. Thus, the features of her in virtue of which she lacked the ability to write compelling prose help to explain why her writing did not win the approval of editors or readers; the features of her in virtue of which she lacked the patience and discipline necessary for long periods of unstructured and unrewarded work help to explain why she became so frustrated and unproductive; and so on. During the entire initial portion of the saga of her editorial rejection, personal frustration, and professional unproductivity, Beth wanted to be a writer, and firmly believed that being a writer was part of her good. This belief and associated desires only came to change as her experience, in which facts about what was or was not good for her played a causal role, grew. This fits a general schema for learning that eventuates in naturalistically justified belief: the fact that $p$ helps to explain why one comes to believe that $p$.

Note, too, that one's good can play a role in the evolution of one's behavior even though one never comes to form an accurate idea of it. Consider Henry, another successful and happy accountant (this is, after all, the 80s) who also desires above all to be a writer, and who also lacks the ability or personality for it. But Henry, alas, has an additional property: he is not very perceptive, especially when it comes to noticing anything at odds with his rather generous view of himself. So when he quits accounting and takes up writing, he attributes his subsequent misery and failure to the idiocy of editors, the torment of true genius, and the decline of the West. There never comes a time when, in retrospect, Henry questions his decision. Let us suppose, however, that were Henry to have surveyed his options with full information and rationality at the time of his choice, he would have wanted that he stay on in accounting rather than attempt writing. Although there are some interesting problems here about whether someone can be gotten to believe unpleasant truths, it may be supposed that were Henry to see vividly the tortuousness, lack of accomplishment, and clumsy self-deception of the life he would lead as a writer, and set this against the pleasant, productive, and sociable existence available to him as an accountant, he would form a firm desire that his passion for writing not be effective. The reduction basis for this desire – which would include Henry's ability, personality, and circumstances – constitutes the fact that a life as a writer would not be a good life for him. Idiomatically, we would say that "He was not cut out to be a writer." We may point to this fact to explain why Henry's life, which as an accountant had been reasonably happy and successful, became such a mess.

Now let us amend the story somewhat. Suppose that, to ease the financial strain of writing, Henry took a part-time job doing accounts for the business of one of his few remaining friends. As he took the job, he promised himself that he would continue to write, and would return to full-time writing as soon as possible. He believed as strongly as ever that working as an accountant was not part of a life in which he could flourish. However, after several weeks at the new job, during which the necessity of learning the ropes meant that he was quite fully engaged in accounting and was prevented from doing any serious writing, he found his mood improving, and others found his company more bearable. This he took to be evidence that he was all the more ready to write as soon as the accounting work was behind him. He decided to work full time at accounting in order to speed his return to writing. He found he had greater energy and concentration than before, and that the pleasure he had taken in many of the small things in life, which had left him, was beginning to come back. From this he inferred that he was ready at last to begin his novel. But he decided that he needed to stay on a bit longer at accounting, and to take on a few more accounts, in order to earn enough to tide him over the long span of time such an ambitious work would take. And so on. Slowly the papers on Henry's writing desk yellowed, and his urge to sit down at that desk, or to chastise himself for not doing so, departed. He spent the next thirty years in accounting, always ready to tell you over a drink of his plans to return to writing in his retirement. He in fact spent his retirement in a lucrative second career in real estate. One fall he sold his suburban house and bought a condominium in Florida, and, feeling strangely unmoved, he left for the housecleaners the dusty folders containing his unfinished writing projects to discard, stacked alongside a pile of back issues of *The New Yorker* and some bundled-up newspapers he had meant to recycle. We cannot explain Henry's trajectory in terms of his belief that he is fit for a career in accounting, but not writing. He did not believe this. Yet we may be able to explain his trajectory in terms of the suitability for him of the accountant's life, but not the writer's. Here, then, is another important kind of learning, in which the fact that $p$ helps to explain why someone acts "in accord with" $p$, even though he does not come to believe that $p$.

We can be pictured as beings who form many and varied desires, and in effect try them out by acting upon them, for we tend to keep acting upon those that bring with them some reinforcement. In this process, the sorts of facts about us that constitute our good – in the naturalistic sense in which that notion is understood here – may have considerable opportunity to influence our behavior. Of course, many other processes affect behavior, and as individuals our experimentation, flexibility, and sensitivity are limited. So we cannot expect to have very full knowledge of our good, or to act as we would if we did. Especially, we cannot expect this once we notice how much information would be necessary to arrive at reliable views about what is good for complex and interactive organisms like us.

Still, we can expect that people may do a reasonable job over a certain range of goods. This would help to explain two widely held views. First, on a number of matters where technical expertise is not required, individuals are held to be the best judges of their own good. We ordinarily think that their choices are more likely in the long run to reflect their good than the choices a third party, however well-meaning, would make for them. That would make sense on the present view, for it is the individual himself who has the most intimate and sustained exposure to experience of a kind to promote learning about his good using the mechanisms just described. And a second truism would make sense as well: we in general think that an individual's judgment of his own good – or the likelihood that his choices will reflect his good – improves with greater, and especially broader, experience.

I won't pretend to argue here that these value-involving explanations are well warranted. I can at best put them forward as potential counterexamples to the complaint often voiced against naturalism about value that we cannot even begin to imagine how facts about what is good for us might enter into a scheme explaining what we do, and why.

NOTES

*Philosophical Topics,* XIV, No. 2 (Fall 1986).
* I would like to thank Richard Brandt, Michael Bratman, Stephen Darwall, William Frankena, Allan Gibbard, Donald Regan, Michael Smith, and David Velleman for helpful discussion of some of the material contained in this paper.
1. It is controversial whether one can discuss intrinsic value without also discussing moral value. For an account of moral evaluation that dovetails with the account to be offered in the text of non-moral goodness, and that is not prior to it, see my "Moral Realism," *The Philosophical Review* 95 (April 1986), 163–207. Reprinted here as Chapter 1.
2. The chief difficulties encountered were the impossibility of associating individual hypotheses with particular experiences, owing to the holistic character of theory testing, and the impossibility of motivating a unique choice or weighting among various criteria of theory assessment: empirical adequacy, conservatism, simplicity, generality, falsifiability, and explanatory unity are only some of the possible candidates, and each admits of diverse formulations.
3. One can, to be sure, incorporate logical principles into principles about what one rationally ought to believe, as in the principle 'One ought not to believe both $p$ and not-$p$,' or in principle (0). Informally, we may say that these are "principles concerning what we logically ought to believe," although this is elliptical for

"principles concerning what we ought to believe, on the assumption that we seek to bring our beliefs (construed as a system of propositions) and inferences into conformity with logical standards."

4. I therefore will assume in what follows a version of the doctrine of internalism according to which normative judgments must be linked to the promotion of the ends of those to whom the judgments are applied, in particular, to the satisfaction of their actual or idealized desires.

5. Thomas Hobbes, *Leviathan*, C.B. MacPherson, ed. (Harmondsworth, Middlesex: Penguin, 1981) 120.

6. It may be worth saying again that my concern in this essay is with non-moral value. We, of course, also sometimes wish to raise questions about the moral worth of our ends, or, for that matter, about their aesthetic merit. While I believe that these other dimensions of assessment exhibit important relations to intrinsic value, I also believe that clarity is served by recognizing the differences as well as the similarities in their evaluative bases and normative roles.

7. In Brandt's account of "rational desire," that which is good for someone is tied to the best available information at the time. On such a view, it might turn out that writing *was* good for Beth at the time she chose it, since the best information at that time may not have presaged what Beth later, to her regret, discovered. I find it much more natural to say that writing merely *appeared* good at the time. See Richard C. Brandt, *A Theory of the Good and the Right* (Oxford: Clarendon, 1979) 111f.

8. Hypocrisy arises when an individual who says he values *X* nevertheless does not really want this value to be effective (whether or not he admits this to himself). (Sheila may be in the midst of asking herself whether her earlier – and not infrequent – pronouncements on the value of freedom of action, nature, and family were to a degree hypocritical.) Weakness of the will arises when the desire for *X* to be effective *is* present, but some other desire, a desire that one does not upon reflection want to be effective in proportion to its strength, prevails. (Sheila may in the end come to want that her desire to stay put be effective, but then disover that the allure of Metropolis is stronger.) Obviously, these descriptions are very gross. Cf. Harry Frankfurt, "Freedom of the Will and the Concept of a Person," *The Journal of Philosophy* 68 (January 1971), 5–20.

9. This notion is not the same as that of an individual's welfare, for it may turn out that an ideally informed and rational individual would want to seek as an end in itself (were he to step into the place of his present self) the well-being of others as well as himself.

10. Remaining, that is, from among the three mentioned at the opening of the present section.

11. J.L. Mackie, *Ethics: Inventing Right and Wrong* (Harmondsworth, Middlesex: Penguin, 1977) 40. The argument from queerness goes back at least as far as Hume. See the *Treatise of Human Nature*, bk. Three, pt. I, sec. i, 464f in the Selby-Bigge edition (Oxford: Oxford University Press, 1888).

12. See, for example, David Velleman, "Brandt's Definition of 'Good'," *Philosophical Review* 97 (1988), 353–71.

13. In what follows, I will focus on the problems of full information rather than full rationality. I am assuming that we tend to think ourselves in a better position

to judge how our wants would differ were we fully rational (but had the same information we now have) than were we fully informed (but were about as rational as we now are). Perhaps we think – not altogether without cause – that the gap between our actual condition (at least, in our saner moments) and full instrumental rationality is smaller than the gap between our current beliefs and full information. Of course, it is one thing to be fully rational relative to existing information, and another to be fully rational relative to complete information. What will be said is partly addressed to worries about assessing the instrumental relevance of bits of information when one has such an abundance of them.

14. The experiment is reported in Richard Nisbett and Lee Ross, *Human Inference: Strategies and Shortcomings* (Englewood Cliffs: Prentice-Hall, 1980) 174. Nisbett and Ross emphasize both the difficulty of overcoming some primacy effects and the effectiveness of information in offsetting others.

15. The example might be thought an unfair one, since, intuitively, it is uncontroversial that order of correct response is simply irrelevant to mathematical ability, and since the judgments in the example seem to direct us precisely to the question of assessing mathematical ability. However, I have been unable to find a convincing example in which both (i) sheer order of receipt of information would have an effect upon the net impact of a given body of information and (ii) there are some intuitive grounds for thinking that this effect might be relevant to the judgment at hand.

16. Receptivity, in turn, will depend upon an individual's personal history. This gives rise to the observation that it may make a great difference to the motivational effect of a bit of information whether the individual has had some experience that would serve to give it life. The later Beth's hard-won realization that writing did not suit her can be expected to have greater force for her than the earlier Beth's mere receipt of the news about the preferences of her later self. When, in the present idealization, it is required that information be fully vivid, it is in effect required that the individual have undergone whatever experience or education would be necessary for this. Fortunately, as fiction and drama show, not every fact need be directly experienced in order to make a profound impression upon us. A well-told or well-acted or well-filmed tale, perhaps one that connects with whatever kinds of experience one already has had, may do the job.

17. There is evidence in the psychological literature that we develop strategies of image-balancing even as children. See W. Mischel and B. Moore, "The Role of Ideation in Voluntary Delay for Symbolically-Presented Rewards," *Cognitive Therapy and Research* 4 (1980), 211–21.

18. It *would* have quite drastic effects upon psychological theory to suppose that humans had come onto the evolutionary scene without cognitive limitations. Much of what we are now like reflects the fact that our cognitive means have been in various ways limited. But in assessing counterfactuals about how full information would affect us as we *now* are, we should not let our imagination wander off into rewriting history. Ordinary usage shows that counterfactuals do not "backtrack" in this way. See the discussion in David Lewis, "Counterfactual Dependence and Time's Arrow," *Collected Papers*, vol. II (New York: Oxford University Press, 1986).

19. For a parallel criticism of naturalism about moral value, see Mackie, *Ethics*, and especially Gilbert Harman, *The Nature of Morality* (New York: Oxford University Press, 1977).

# 3

# Noncognitivism about Rationality: Benefits, Costs, and an Alternative

Where might norms be found in a world of facts? We can observe social practices, express personal ideals, criticize behavior, enforce laws, and consult rule books. But in the process, we never seem to encounter *normative facts*, whatever they would be.

Perhaps philosophers should not look for normative facts behind these social phenomena. Given the natural facts, and facts about language and meaning, there may already be facts enough to sustain our *normative practices* – and searching for normative facts would be hunting a red herring. That attractive idea motivates a diverse collection of philosophical approaches to domains of human discourse and practice known as *noncognitivism*. Allan Gibbard's *Wise Choices, Apt Feelings* represents the splendid flowering of this idea into a powerful and instructive contribution not only to philosophy, but also to the broad enterprise of coming to grips with human life. No one interested in such questions will want to miss it.

Philosophers frequently talk of the need to give "philosophical explanations," but it is rare to come across work that is genuinely explanatory and at the same time fully alive to philosophical questions. Gibbard's discussion of rationality and ethics affords an astonishing amount of insight into such diverse phenomena as linguistic representation, evolutionary rationales for various human emotions, and discursive conceptions of objectivity. In this paper, I will take shameless advantage of Gibbard's hard work to make some remarks about the difficulties I see in noncognitivism. Regrettably, this will mean focusing narrowly on but a few aspects of a very ambitious book, and passing over much that I agree with in it.

A note on terminology. The term 'noncognitivism' has been used by philosophers with various meanings, though a canonical idea emerged by the mid-twentieth century: a noncognitivist about a domain of discourse held that, literally interpreted, the declarative sentences in that discourse did not function to express propositions, and were incapable of being strictly speaking true or false. Noncognitivists were at pains to insist that such sentences might nonetheless express some *other* ("emotive," "commending," etc.) sort of meaning. Moreover, the sentences might be subject to rigorous conditions of justification, and might play a significant role in regulating human activity. The domain in question need not lack what a *psychologist* would call "cognitivity" – serious involvement of such mental faculties as perception, inference, expectation, association, or intention. Indeed, one of Gibbard's chief contributions is to show with fresh ingenuity how this sort of cognitivity might be possible even for sentences that do not express propositions. So the term 'nonfactualism' has been introduced more recently, with something like the following standard sense: a given domain of language may behave on its surface as if it were attributing properties, expressing propositions, denoting facts, capable of truth or falsity, and so on, but it is best interpreted as doing something else.[1] For Gibbard, that something else is the expression of attitudes of norm acceptance.

Why opt for nonfactualism? Like earlier ethical noncognitivisms, Gibbard's norm-expressivism affords a plausible and straightforward account of two distinctive features of moral discourse: the apparent internal link of judgment to motivation, noted by Hume, and the possibility of a serious open-question argument for substantive "analyses," noted by Moore.[2] Interpretations of moral discourse that seek to capture these two features and while accepting at face value its property–attributing form may end up associating with normative terms some rather unusual properties, and will tend – even if the view of property and truth in play is pleonastic – either toward mystery or toward error theories. By contrast, noncognitivist interpretations promise to effect an unmysterious tie between judgment and motivation, to explain why substantive analyses fail, and to avoid imputation of systematic error.

Gibbard's noncognitivism has special interest because of its broadly naturalistic framework and its very thorough development. Moreover, unlike earlier noncognitivisms, Gibbard's account involves no asymmetry between the moral and the rational, or between practical and theoretical reason – all alike are normative, and thus he treats all alike in terms of a norm-expressivist model. On this view, morality emerges as a domain of reasons, and in this, as well as in deploying a nonmetaphysical conception of objectivity for normative judgment, Gibbard's account emerges as an heir not only to much that is best in Hume the naturalist, but also much that is best in Kant the nonnaturalist.

Like all nonfactualisms, Gibbard's noncognitivism spares itself the difficulty of trying to find a place for normative facts within the natural order. Since it is none too easy to find such place, this must be seen as a significant economy. Yet nonfactualism is at the same time a very dramatic philosophical response, and its costs need to be reckoned alongside its benefits. Consider:

(1) The nonfactualist who would capture ordinary normative discourse must provide a nonstandard semantic theory that shows how all the surface features of cognitive discourse – including logic, complex embedding, etc. – can be sustained without the discourse being (strictly speaking) apt for truth evaluation. Moreover, anyone who wishes to preserve (something like) the standard, factualist view of non-normative discourse while treating normative discourse nonfactually must have two semantic theories, one for each side of the fact/value distinction. These two theories must not only each preserve surface cognitive grammar and logic for their respective domain of discourse, but also must show: first, how there could be a worthwhile distinction in the way that truth or predication function in the two domains, and, second, how these two semantically distinct areas of discourse could nonetheless exist side-by-side, seamlessly, even in individual embedded clauses. Moreover, other strong and interesting relations between these two domains of discourse must be sustained, notably, inferential and justificatory links and the supervenience of the normative upon the non-normative.[3]

(2) In addition to this semantic dualism, Gibbard's nonfactualism must be dualistic in another way as well. For there are substantive (as well as grammatical or logical) uses of normative concepts that appear to presuppose there to be a fact of the matter. I have in mind here particularly *explanatory* uses. Take rationality, for instance. We have a well-established folk and social-scientific practice of explaining human action in terms of rational agency, beliefs, and desires. As we ordinarily deploy it, such "rationalizing" explanation appears to depend upon finding explanatorily relevant reasons-for-action that are also reasons in a normative (though

perhaps minimal) sense. Indeed, the particular sort of understanding rational-agent explanations convey involves a normative idea of "making sense" that Gibbard's view assigns to the nonfactual side of rationality.

One influential approach to rational-agent explanation attempts to reconcile these two elements by claiming that the phenomena of belief and desire picked out in normative attribution of reasons to agents can, under different descriptions, be seen to play the right sort of causal role to producing action.[4] On such an approach, norms play a constitutive role in the framing of rational-agent explanations while causal role functions to select which reasons really were the agent's. But if, as on Gibbard's account, judgments about reasons and rationality are nonfactual, then there are no such things as the phenomena "picked out by" such judgments, no "referents" which, under some other, nomological description, are found to be causal-explanatory.

The nonfactualist may reply dualistically: there are, in our language, really two notions of rationality – a normative one, judgments of which are beholden to an essential element of endorsement and go nonfactual, and another, descriptive one, judgments of which are beholden to different, causal/explanatory norms but nonetheless factual.[5]

This bifurcating reply may be the most sensible thing anyone can say about the matter. Certainly, the Janus-faced explanatory/justificatory character of judgments of rationality raises a host of philosophical questions. But, as noted, intimate linkages between the two "senses" appear to underwrite rational-agent explanation. Indeed, attribution of some degree of rationality with evaluative heft has been thought by many to be a condition on the attribution of beliefs and desires at all.[6]

If the wedding of explanatory and justificatory functions within one term is an error, it is an error of common sense, and so divorce would involve a non-trivial revision of our ordinary discourse. Ironically, it has been one of the chief arguments against naturalistic cognitivist rivals to noncognitivism that they involve some revision of natural language. The sort of nonfactualism under consideration here also seems open to the charge.[7]

(3) Once we stand back and watch language for a bit, we realize how extensively it is suffused with normativity. This is evident not only in the multiplicity of specialized "thin" evaluative vocabularies – of ethics, prudence, epistemology, aesthetics, etc. – but also in the vast number of "thick" concepts that seem to combine some measure of essential

description with some measure of essential commendation.[8] But suffusion is more pervasive still, for even humdrum assertoric uses of "nonevaluative" language involve claims of authority and licensings of belief. Gibbard goes much further than previous noncognitivists in appreciating normative suffusion and the large challenge it poses to views that find a significant linguistic joint between the factual and the evaluative. We have already mentioned his commendable way of pushing his nonfactualism "upstairs" to the domain of rationality itself, and his clarity about the way epistemic assessment must be brought within the nonfactual ambit. Gibbard's grand strategy is to make do with a brass-tacks Galilean core of descriptive language and an all-purpose normative term, roughly, 'is rational.'[9] A number of points might be raised at this juncture, none of which am I able here to sharpen, much less press.

Let me mention four.

First, to make good his distinction between representative and nonrepresentative discourse, Gibbard develops a natural-selectionist theory of representation that distinguishes bits of talk that represent naturally from bits that don't. However, selection certainly wasn't for the theory-saturated kind of talk that inhabits today's Galilean core. Can we build out from natural representation to capture the right amount of artificial representation and the right amount of fine graining to have a language adequate to physics? If not, then the account that yields the fact/value distinction may not yield all of the Galilean core on the factual side. Can we be sure that certain substantive properties will not turn out to have been explanatorily relevant in the evolution of discourse about morality or rationality? – If not, then some of morality or rationality may end up on the factual side.[10] Finally, can a suitably discriminatory test of "essential evolutionary/explanatory role" be formulated to exclude moral facts without also excluding (say) everything except basic physics? – If not, then chemistry, geology, biology, and psychology may end up on the nonfactual side.[11] These ways of posing such questions are peculiar to Gibbard's use of a natural-selectionist theory of representation, but any nonfactualist will face similar issues.[12]

Second, while one may find nothing unintelligible in the idea that there could be elements of language whose allegiance to action-guidingness is pure, it is by now fairly obvious that the earliest noncognitivists were wrong in identifying *moral* language as such an element, and it may for somewhat similar reasons seem that attributions of *rationality* are not such an element, either.

73

Certain substantive judgments seem so central to the discourse of rationality that we might legitimately wonder whether we are discussing a common subject matter with someone who denied all or most of them. Rationality at a minimum seems truistically to involve certain forms of internal coherence and of the adjustment of means to ends and to risks. Gibbard, moreover, finds it "self-evident" that the fact that I would enjoy something affords a reason (defeasible, certainly) in favor of my doing it (177).

Now even this much substance permits us to formulate something like an open-question argument with respect to 'rational' and the guiding of action. Maybe Weber and others are onto something in contrasting rationalizing cultures with (say) honor-based cultures. Might not rationality, like morality, have its Nietzsche? Nietzsche himself wrote: "Man does not seek happiness; only the Englishman does that." Mightn't another Nietzsche take some inspiration from this – perhaps in part owing to the "conceptual" tie just mentioned between rationality and enjoyment – and write "Man does not seek rationality; only the Englishman [who else!] does that"? And certainly some people have been inclined to raise a banner that says "Theirs not to reason why/Theirs but to do and die" (Tennyson's Light Brigade) or "*L'audace, toujours l'audace!*" and to use nondeliberative means to rally others to it.[13] So if there is an element of language that is purely action guiding, I suspect it is closer to "the thing to do" than to "the rational thing to do," or to "the thing it makes most sense to do." This casts doubt not upon Gibbard's general idea of seeking a nonfactualist account of the *purely* normative, but upon the idea that such an account would yield a *direct* answer to the question with which Gibbard begins his book: viz., "what the term 'rational' means" (vii).

Third, one might wonder whether the project of trying to make language live up to a fact/value distinction, if it is possible, is best approached at the level of vocabulary. Just as holists about descriptive meaning have argued that individual terms or sentences are units too small for translation, so might one argue that normative meaning is holistic – individual elements of vocabulary do not have normative "implications" to call their own.[14] Indeed, classical doctrines of meaning holism bundled together norms of inference and theory choice all along.

What sort of difference might a holistic perspective make to the discussion of normativity? Consider an expression like 'morally good,' and contrast an interpretation that imputes to it an intrinsic, categorical normative force with an interpretation that sees its normative role contextually, as the upshot of the operation various internalized, culturally privileged beliefs and motivations along with the special place which that culture as it stands by and large assigns to the things to which the term is characteristically applied. In this sense, a large number of terms may function normatively, though some more uniformly so than others (at least as things now stand). This opens up the possibility of seeing the sort of "judgment internalism" characteristic of noncognitivism as resting upon a reification of sorts: a web of beliefs and commitments that is central to our going scheme (though always subject to revision) and within which a term now characteristically functions normatively is hypostatized as a situation in which a particular term bears an intrinsic, categorical normative force.

Fourth, it has recently been argued that we should add meaning itself to the list of normative notions.[15] Now this claim is more than a bit unclear, and some philosophers are certainly not convinced. Indeed, the arguments for the normativity of meaning may trade on something like holism or normative suffusion – perhaps the contexts of assertion and belief assessment bring into play norms that entail *oughts* and that assign a special place for the content of assertions or beliefs, creating an illusion that categorical normativity "resides in" content when only hypothetical normativity is at work. But let us suppose that the arguments are fine as they stand and that their implication is that meaning attribution is normative in much the same way as Gibbard views judgments of rationality.

If the thesis that meaning is normative is combined with Gibbard's nonfactualist account of normativity, then the framework of Gibbard's book, mentioned previously, will need some rethinking. The original trio of normative facts, natural facts, and facts of meaning is reduced in the book to a duo, as normative facts go by the board. Now meaning facts would have to be asked to join them. At least, to this extent: just as we bifurcated the notion of rationality into a pair of notions, one descriptive/explanatory and the other normative, so could we bifurcate meaning.[16] The worries expressed about such a bifurcation of rationality, and about accommodating or otherwise accounting for the intimate relations of descriptive/explanatory and normative uses, would now arise in connection with meaning itself.

But a further worry would accompany these. For the very intelligibility of denying there to be facts about meaning is not clear. Especially, this may not be clear if one wishes to sustain a fact/value distinction. For such a distinction appears to call for a robustness to meaning attribution that nonfactualism would preclude.[17] If meaning attribution goes nonfactual, so, it would seem, must the fact/value distinction.[18] We might, that is, end up having to ask whether a nonfactualist construal of meaning talk pulls the rug from under itself, by destabilizing the very notion of meaning needed to frame the fact/nonfact contrast. Note that the threat of destabilization comes not from seeing meaning as essentially normative as such, nor from nonfactualism about the normative as such, but from their combination. A full development of Gibbard's project would treat discourse as nonfactual *wherever* there is essential normativity. Not having shrunk from taking on rationality and epistemology, nonfactualism should not (if meaning indeed is normative) shrink from meaning. It is a marvelous philosophical project to explore where this challenge might lead, but it would take someone more familiar with nonfactualist ways than I to have a firm opinion on whether this leads us into *terra incognita* or *terra utopia*. Gibbard, at least, accepts the challenge in his recent work. This is not the place, I think, for speedy dismissiveness. Let us see what can be learned from trying. But let us also note that having to try – at least, if meaning is normative – is a cost of all-purpose nonfactualism about the normative.

## II

So much, then, for some of the possible costs of nonfactualism. Nothing I have said, however, gives us a fair estimate of the size of these costs. For that, at least two things would be necessary. First, the nature of the alleged problems of nonfactualism and the range of possible nonfactualist responses would have to be made clearer. And second, but equally important, factualist alternatives would have to be explored to determine whether they are not much more expensive in their own ways. The magnitude of costs and benefits relevant to choice among philosophical hypotheses is always a relative matter – without competitors and *their* costs in view, we cannot sensibly ask whether the cost of a philosophical position is high, much less too high.

What might a factualist alternative look like? We must be careful here. Finding relevant facts to *ground* normative judgments would not be enough – for Gibbard's view is a view about *meanings*, and the would-be factualist competitor must either show that she doesn't need the notion of meaning or that she can give an appropriately factualist account of meaning. The second course promises to be difficult, since Moorean open-question arguments can be used – albeit only with some care, as Gibbard notes (11–22) – against treating any of the best-known substantive conceptions of rationality as accounts of the meaning of the term. Yet the first course may be more difficult still – for how do the relevant facts get picked out by language if not through something like a meaning?[19]

76

In my previous writings I have shied away from meaning claims, primarily because I find the subject of meanings so daunting. If I ask why this is so, at least two reasons are salient to me. First, it has always struck me that meanings must be very complex, given everything they are asked to do. Second – for reasons that may help explain how Quine's critique of the analytic/synthetic has managed to outlive some of his original arguments for it – many of the elements that would constitute these complex meanings are empirical and "distributed" (i.e., would involve systemic features of our cognitive and affective dispositions, actual conditions in the natural world we inhabit, actual social and causal/historical relationships, and so on). This not only renders problematic the most straightforward ways of thinking about the units and stability of meaning, but also raises methodological concerns about access to meanings, for such empirical and "distributed" elements would not, except formalistically, be within the scope of the sort of *a priori* inquiry typical of "conceptual analysis." This, in turn (which circles back to the first reason), makes it harder to see how meanings could play the sort of role they are asked to perform in accounting for linguistic competence, acquisition, and communication. And so on.

Nonetheless, it may be possible to make some progress talking about the meanings of individual terms in a rather structural or formalistic manner, so let us consider one such possible approach to the task of sketching a natural-factual meaning for 'rational.' Here is the general strategy. For any term, normative or non-normative, develop a "job description" corresponding to the many roles – some inferential, some not – a term plays in discourse, deliberation, and the regulation of affect and action. Call this job description the meaning of the term. Owing to what we previously called normative suffusion, many terms will turn out to have normative elements somewhere in their job description; in the case of 'rational,' we can be sure of this. Now, let us grant without discussion that unreduced normative predicates are *prima facie* problematic from a natural-factual perspective. Nonetheless, work of Ramsey, Carnap, and Lewis on the definition of theoretical terms in science suggests how one might proceed to develop natural-factual job descriptions from our "mixed" job descriptions.[20] Let us suppose that the job description for 'rational' is generated by taking our going theory of the world as a whole, including all the roles, action-guiding and explanatory, we ask rationality to play, and all the theoretical and nontheoretical, normative and non-normative, notions with which rationality is hooked up, everything that is hooked up with those notions in turn, and so on. Make all this into one big,

conjunctive sentence. This sentence will include empirical generalizations, theoretical and practical truisms, and paradigm cases. Ramsify this
sentence by replacing all normative predicates with second-order variables, bound by existential quantifiers.[21] Then make a Russellian definite
description out of the Ramsey sentence by placing the inverted iota opera-
tor before the second-order variable that uniformly replaced occurrences
of 'rational,' bringing it out in front. The resulting job description for
'rational' would thus contain only naturalistic predicate constants, and
would function, as a meaning should, to pick out the property, if there is
a unique such, that fills the bill for rationality.

A number of difficulties arise at once for such an approach. In the first
place, it seems bound to make an error theorist of our natural factualist.
For the roles we ask 'rational' to play, and the truisms we associate with
it, and the paradigm cases we point to, are unlikely all to cohere, or to
be satisfied by any property instantiated in *this* world, at least.[22] Indeed,
rationality apart, there surely will be errors somewhere in the Ramsey
sentence.

In the second place, this sort of definition would seem to have just the
weakness that Gibbard repeatedly emphasizes when discussing naturalistic
accounts of the meaning of normative terms (12–22). The definition
would appear to settle much too much as a matter of sheer linguistic
convention, and would not afford us a term that could be used – except
as a result of linguistic ignorance – to express the issues in contention
among various competing accounts of rationality. Either these accounts
would accord with the job description, or they would not.[23]

Fortunately, both of these difficulties can be remedied by a modification
that, in any event, the definition needed if it was to be plausible in other
ways.[24] Among the clauses that state the job description should be some
that have the effect of introducing slack, so that the definite description
reads something like: "Rationality is whatever unified (or almost unified)
property plays all (or most) of these roles (or the most central among them)
fully (or most fully)...." Without such a clause, the definition would
badly overcommit, and not only about rationality. With such a clause, we
can see how error theory might be avoided: some fairly unified natural
property might, at least in the population of *Homo sapiens*, satisfy almost all
of the clauses pretty well, or most of the central ones quite well, and that
could be enough for us. For example, a structured and tolerably unified
but complex constellation of psychological properties might be found that
both fills the explanatory bill and affords the right sort of engagement with
motivation to make it clear why internalism holds (insofar as it does).[25]

We don't wish to represent our discourse or practices involving rationality as more definite than, in fact, they are.

Moreover, with such a clause, we can see how genuine debate is possible, while also gaining some insight into the particular nature of the dialectical constraints of that debate: advocates of competing substantive accounts of rationality are claiming on behalf of their account a better overall balance in meeting the job description. This would help us to understand the standard moves in debates over theories of rationality: Does a given account capture the paradigm cases? Does it preserve all (or most) of the truisms? Can it fit into a framework for the explanation and understanding of behavior? Does it enable us to understand the assumed normative or motivational "pull" rationality, or attributions thereof, has for us? And so on.[26]

Too, such an approach to the meaning of 'rational' would help us to explain why certain substantive views are beyond the pale: someone who simply wrote off large or central chunks of the job description would strike us as no longer interested in rationality, though he might, like the new Nietzsche or the members of Tennyson's Light Brigade mentioned in Section I, be interested in something fundamentally action guiding. Further, we could see, with this job description, how it would be intelligible to wonder about the place of rationality in one's life, and thus how some sort of open question remains with respect to action.

This very rough outline of the meaning of 'rational' faces a number of questions, among them:

(1) Would any particular clauses of the definition be strictly essential? This is a question one cannot answer without seeing such a proposal fully spelled out. It does not seem unimaginable, however, that any one of the clauses might fail to be satisfied by a sufficiently good overall candidate, especially if that candidate could satisfy a clause rather like the one missed.

(2) Would there be a bright line between changing the subject altogether and offering a revisionist account of rationality? No, just as it might be indistinct in a given case whether a dispute is over the rationality of a response, rather than some other, nearby feature. Gibbard makes room for this sort of flexibility in his own account of *morality*, for he distinguishes a wider and a narrower sense of the term (40–1). In the narrow sense, according to Gibbard, morality is tied essentially to norms licensing the feeling of guilt or resentment. But he recognizes the possibility of someone arguing wholesale against guilt and resentment on what certainly seem to be moral grounds – perhaps these sentiments are criticized as

inimical to human flourishing, self-respect, or respect for others. Using the broader sense, Gibbard is able to interpret this as a debate about the moral justifiability of guilt and resentment. He recognizes, that is, that sometimes the normative flavor of a discussion will best be captured if we see it as moral in the broad sense, whereas other times it will afford a better understanding to see a debate as taking place "on the outside" of morality, for example, a debate over the place of morality in its familiar form in our lives. Presumably, there will also be borderline cases, where our sense of the distinction between urging a new moral doctrine and urging that we take up a new subject weakens.

(3) Would the Ramsey-Lewis definite description involve rigidification in the manner of the job description one might write for 'water'? It seems likely in the case of 'rational' that the functional rather than substantival features will predominate, so that the definite description will not rigidify by fixing upon whatever neurophysiological phenomena *actually* fill the bill as the essence of the matter.

(4) Could this sort of meaning really play the role of a meaning? For example, of the sense that we grasp when we acquire competence with the term? That seems doubtful. And certainly this sort of meaning is unlikely to be transparent to competent speakers. But, then, as we've noted, we give meaning multiple roles. *Its* job description includes fixing reference, explaining communication, explaining language acquisition, meshing with epistemic practice, and underwriting patterns of linguistic authority, deference (such as the "linguistic division of labor"), and change. So why not treat the meaning of 'meaning' the same Ramsey-Lewis way just suggested for the meaning of 'rational' – and with the same slack? If there are meanings, then perhaps they need only do most of these jobs reasonably well. Thus meaning facts could turn out to be plain old facts after all, removing some of the worries – but also some of the excitement – of seeing whether one can sustain nonfactualism "all the way down."

A Ramsey-Lewis natural factualism would, if successful, provide a way of addressing – rather, of beginning to address – a number of the problems discussed in Section I in connection with nonfactualism. It would not require invention of an alternative, nonfactualist semantics capable of capturing cognitive surface behavior, since the account would itself be straightforwardly cognitive. Moreover, there would be no special question concerning how the semantics of normative language could "mesh with" familiar, factualist semantics – the semantics of discourse about 'rationality' would just be the familiar, factualist kind.[27] It would avoid bifurcation, building (some measure of fulfillment of) both evaluative and descriptive/explanatory roles of 'rationality' into the job description. The account would be suitably holistic, given the character and scope of the Ramsey sentence. Moreover, it would embody some substantive constraints, which would help explain the nature of debate over rationality. It might escape the potentially self-undermining effects of nonfactualism about meaning.[28] And finally, among its clauses would presumably be the (truistic) constraint of supervenience itself, thereby making the account both naturalistic and one for which supervenience is an *a priori* truth. With slack, of course.

Surely a conspicuous difficulty facing such an approach would be in finding some property that *could* jointly satisfy (some suitably strong version of) various elements of rationality's job description, for example, the normative and explanatory constraints. Meeting the normative constraint would involve a clause calling for an appropriately modal connection to motivation (on the part of either the judge or the agent); meeting the explanatory constraint would involve a clause attributing to the property picked out the right features for supporting rational agent explanations. But further exploration of a Ramsey-Lewis account is a task that must remain for another occasion.[29]

It would be absurdly premature to conclude that a natural-factualist account of meaning along these lines is a strong competitor to Gibbard's much more fully developed nonfactualism. So the costs ballyhooed in Section I might turn out to be nothing in comparison to the problems of natural factualism. But I hope to have suggested a line for investigating an alternative to Gibbard's account, the further development of which might enable us to learn more about where relevant costs and benefits of nonfactualism are to be found.

### NOTES

This paper is a (slightly edited) version of the original paper of the same title, which appeared in *Philosophical Issues* 4 (1993), 36–51. Section I of this paper also appeared, under the title "Nonfactualism about Normative Discourse," as part of a symposium in *Philosophy and Phenomenological Research* on Allan Gibbard's *Wise Choices, Apt Feelings* (Cambridge: Harvard University Press, 1990). Unless otherwise indicated, all page number references occurring in the present text are to that book.

1. I owe this useful term to Paul Boghossian. Certainly it suits my purposes here, since the term 'noncognitivism' has unfortunate associations both with emotivism in ethics and with a rather blank model of the state of mind expressed by "noncognitive sentences." Gibbard's view does seem to involve a kind of noncognitivism

about the emotions – they are not, as some have argued, to be understood as propositional attitudes on the model of beliefs. But he is very attentive to questions about the structure of states of mind, and gives a central role to the idea that a feeling can be more or less warranted.

2. For discussion, see Stephen Darwall, Allan Gibbard, and Peter Railton, "Toward *Fin de siècle* Ethics: Some Trends," *Philosophical Review* 101 (1992), 115–90, esp. 115–24 and 144–52.

3. Since I gather that other contributors to this symposium will be discussing Gibbard's ingenious approach to these problems – through a formal representation involving credal-normative worlds (83–102) – I will not comment further on this matter here, except to say: (1) I am concerned that the appeal to "consistency" made in Gibbard's account may amount to assuming away part of the problem; (2) relatedly, I think there may be an Achilles-and-the-Tortoise problem of regress in appealing to higher-order norms to account for the deliberative role of consistency; and (3) it is not obvious to me how Gibbard's scheme of the normatively permitted and forbidden can appropriately be extended to normative judgments of an axiological rather than deontological kind.

4. See Donald Davidson, "Actions, Reasons, and Causes," "Mental Events," and "Psychology as Philosophy," all reprinted in D. Davidson, *Essays on Actions and Events* (Oxford: Oxford University Press, 1980).

5. I draw here from a related discussion of meaning in Gibbard's Hempel Lectures (unpublished), Princeton University, March 1992. I do not know whether Gibbard would be happy with this line of thought. Gibbard is clear – in a way that many have not been – that being beholden to explanatory or epistemic norms does not preclude factual representation (122).

6. Gibbard does not contest this, for at least a minimal "core" of substantive rationality:

   ... we succeed in attributing a minimal substantive rationality to a person or we fail to interpret him (159).

7. Although some, including myself, are not inclined to view "revisionism" as a fatal flaw, it is quite relevant to assessing a claim that a given account supplies analytic truths about the meaning of terms as they occur in natural language. Compare:

   What does it mean to call an alternative rational, or another irrational? That is the puzzle of this book ... (4).

8. See Philippa Foot, "Moral Arguments," *Mind* 67 (1958), 502–13 and Bernard Williams, *Ethics and the Limits of Philosophy* (Cambridge: Harvard University Press, 1985). How well Gibbard's norm-expressivism can handle "thick concepts" deserves further discussion. I must pass over these important issues here.

9. Gibbard also suggests the somewhat more flavorless expression 'makes sense' (124). This seems to me a step in the right direction if an all-purpose action-guiding term is wanted. For a further step, see the following text. One might wonder whether all normativity is kindred enough to make do with one such term.

10. Gibbard recognizes this possibility, but finds it implausible:

   One might imagine a program of "normative realism" that proposes a kind of fact to do the job. If such a program is developed and a candidate is proposed, we shall have to examine it. I myself, though, have found no kind of fact that works: no substantive kind of fact, correspondence to which might plausibly, among our ancestors, have done the coordinating of normative judgments (116).

It seems entirely appropriate that, for Gibbard, the issue of the acceptability of "normative realism" turns out to be an empirical matter, though one about which he can (already) see some pretty impressive reasons for skepticism.

11. Gibbard sensibly seeks to avoid such overly narrow construals of "explanatory indispensability" tests, but then greater care is required in ruling out normative properties (123–5).
12. We will see in the following text that some questions of a different kind arise about the workability of a fact/value distinction within Gibbard's nonfactualism. (To foreshadow, we must here be taking the selectionist story as a story about meaning-in-the-explanatory-sense.)
13. Gibbard at one point remarks that "[p]art of having a normative conviction is to think one could win an argument over it" (198–9), but perhaps there are other, non-deliberative thoughts behind a normative conviction, for example, that the mere *display* or *experience* of a life would bowl others over. And there is always rhetoric: Tennyson writes of the "noble six hundred."
14. Compare W.V. Quine, "Two Dogmas of Empiricism," *Philosophical Review* 60 (1951), 177–97.
15. See Saul Kripke, *Wittgenstein on Rules and Private Language* (Cambridge: Harvard University Press, 1982) and Paul Boghossian, "The Rule-Following Considerations," *Mind* 98 (1989), 507–49.
16. See Gibbard's Hempel Lectures.
17. Cf. Boghossian, "The Status of Content," *Philosophical Review* 99 (1990), 157–84.
18. Gibbard experiments with this idea in the Hempel Lectures. I am also indebted to Gibbard, Paul Boghossian, and David Velleman for related discussions.
19. This is, of course, meant to include (say) causal theories, which can be seen as coming up with something like a meaning. Of course, this something might be a somewhat unfamiliar or miscellaneous complex. See Hilary Putnam, "The Meaning of 'Meaning'," in K. Gunderson, ed., *Language, Mind, and Knowledge* (Minneapolis: University of Minnesota Press, 1975).
20. F. P. Ramsey, "Theories," in *The Foundations of Mathematics*, R.B. Braithwaite, ed. (London: Routledge and Kegan Paul, 1931); R. Carnap, *Philosophical Foundations of Physics*, Martin Gardner, ed. (New York: Basic Books, 1963) ch. 28; and David Lewis, "How to Define Theoretical Terms," *The Journal of Philosophy* 67 (1970), 427–46.
21. This approach assumes that all the normative language involved can effectively be rewritten as predicates. That may be a problematic assumption.
22. Note, however, that if one accepts the remarks in Section I concerning the mutual dependence of the explanatory and normative roles, these roles will not stand in quite so much tension as some have held.
23. Actually, of course, things are not so straightforward. Since the definite description may involve as much as the whole of our going theory, it will be no easy matter to determine whether some property or other fulfills it. Certainly, it could turn out that no quick, purely aprioristic argument could settle the matter.

24. I have benefited here from discussions with David Lewis, Frank Jackson, and others who participated in a seminar I taught at Princeton University in the Spring Term, 1990.

25. For a very simple example of this sort of property and this sort of argument, using a job description for the normative property of intrinsic non-moral good, see Railton, "Naturalism and Prescriptivity," *Social Philosophy and Policy* 7 (1989), 151–74. Does discussion of *how well* a given property fills the bill introduce an undermining normativity into this allegedly naturalistic, factual proposal? This is not an easy question, though it does have some easy answers. Much of what is going on when one discusses the idea of a "best satisfier" is normative, but the norms are generic to all sophisticated empirical or semantic inquiry. All well-developed methodologies employ notions of relative degree of fit with various normative constraints or desiderata. If this alone were enough to render a subject matter nonfactual, then there certainly would be no contrast in this regard between theoretical physics and ethics, or between the analysis of normative and nonnormative language.

26. All this would not amount to "essential contestability" as yet – only a great deal of contestability. Perhaps as much as we really find plausible.

27. Now it might be protested that this way of treating 'meaning' shows it to be irreducibly normative – and therefore, if Gibbard is right about the normative, nonfactual – after all. For our definition seems to involve judgments of "what best fits . . ." or "what adequately fits. . . ." Of course, as we noted previously in connection with 'rationality,' one must distinguish involvement of norms in a domain of inquiry from the normativity of its subject matter. Still, difficult questions remain.

28. But see note 27.

29. Again, see Railton, "Naturalism and Prescriptivity." Also, Railton, "Facts and Values," *Philosophical Topics* 14 (1986), 5–31. Reprinted here as Chapter 7. These papers try to show how descriptive and explanatory constraints associated with the notion of intrinsic non-moral good might jointly be met by naturalistic properties.

# 4

## Aesthetic Value, Moral Value, and the Ambitions of Naturalism*

INTRODUCTION

Here's a story that Hume, I believe, would have liked.[1]

Someone I know once led a group of U.S. journalists on a tour of Germany. The tour was part of a public relations effort by a German company, so naturally the journalists were prone to be skeptical of what they saw and heard. One of the stops was a sort of clearinghouse where professional tasters made judgments about the quality, readiness, price, and so on of wines from various vineyards and regions. To display their skill to the journalists, the tasters performed blind tests – the journalists would pour wine from numbered bottles into unlabeled cups and then bring them to the tasters, who would attempt to identify the number of the wine. The tasters did so well that one of the journalists thought there must be a trick. He therefore surreptitiously contrived to pour wine from two different bottles into a single cup before submitting it to the tasters. He stood back to watch the reaction. The first taster washed the wine over his tongue, spat it out, and pronounced: "Hmmm ... Something's the matter here ... maybe you accidentally poured some wine into a cup that wasn't empty? I think I can taste some of number ten, but there's also a bit of something more like number seventeen or. . . ." After leaving the clearinghouse, the journalist later confessed the trick to his host. "You know," he said, "those guys are really onto something."

What they are onto, of course, is a set of complex perceptual qualities that make up the taste of wine. Does this show anything about whether they might also be onto the qualities that make up taste *in* wine? Evaluation, we all believe, is a profoundly subjective phenomenon. And yet we may ask, Mightn't it also be objective? Indeed, might value lie precisely

85

at the intersection of the subjective and objective? So I will claim. Such a claim, if it could be made out, might help us to get beyond a certain initial skepticism about evaluation, a dark unease over what sort of thing value is and how it might find a place in the world.[2]

Other, perhaps decisive, grounds for skepticism could still lie ahead. To be sure, evaluative talk is an important part of our daily lives – it seems impossible to imagine life without it. But that isn't much of an endorsement of any particular evaluative discourse. We can see that, over time, many forms of evaluative discourse have come and gone. (Think, for example, of evaluations in terms of nobility, or male and female honor.) Evaluative discourse is by its nature bound up with a great deal else in thought and culture, even as it aspires to something more. Thus, evaluative forms can have the rug pulled out from under them when our overall view of the world changes. (Think, for example, of evaluations in terms of piety.)

At present, moral and aesthetic evaluation – our chief concerns here – are, by and large, still standing. Indeed, one might say that they have come wholly into their own only within the modern period (a point to which we will return). But there unquestionably are insistent forces tugging at *their* rugs. The contemporary intellectual world is one in which cosmology is done by physicists rather than theologians, in which no guiding intelligence seems to have written value into the world. Perhaps a conception of value thoroughly acclimated to the contemporary world must view all evaluative talk – morality and aesthetics included – as a *projection*, much as Feuerbach held the secret of the Holy Family to be the human family. This thought naturally finds expression in the claim that value is subjective. The objective purport of evaluation rings out, but finds no echo.[3]

Evaluative talk is at risk in part because of its objective purport.[4] If evaluation were no more than the expression of preference, then its place in the world would be fairly secure. There is some, but not much, controversy over the reality of human desires and preferences. Evaluation is of course closely tied to preference – preference is surely the main point of entry into evaluation – but evaluation has further ambitions. A companion who says to us as we descend the steps on our way out of the Annual Young Artists show, "I don't know much about art, but I do know what I like – and I don't like *that*," is signaling that he does not pretend to be pronouncing an aesthetic judgment. One seemingly needs more than strong preferences if one is to claim authority on value. Indeed, we even speak of value as *explaining* preferences, as for example when we contrast a case in which we believe that the acclaim received by a work of art is attributable to mere fashion – and no doubt soon will pass – with a case in which we believe that a work's acceptance has been won over time by a growing recognition of its merit. The critical pretensions and explanatory ambitions of value discourse would come to nothing if talk of value were no more than the shadow of our preferences.

Coming to terms with these ambitions presents us with various philosophical challenges. We might seek to characterize the *concept* of value – to give an analysis that would capture the difference in meaning between unadorned claims of preference and attributions of value. But we might in a more explanatory spirit ask whether anything in the *characteristic functions and presuppositions* of value attribution – and, especially, of attributions of objective value – renders talk of objective value incompatible with a sober, naturalistic view of ourselves and our world. Answering this second question certainly presupposes some competence on our part in the language of value – else how would we know what to look for? Yet we might have sufficient competence to raise and answer questions about functions and presuppositions without being able to produce a satisfactory conceptual analysis. To show that the wherewithal exists within the natural world to sustain talk of objective value would not be tantamount to giving a naturalistic reduction of value. As G. E. Moore recognized, even if goodness is an unanalyzable, non-natural concept, the goodness of anything still supervenes upon its natural features.[5] In consequence, even a non-naturalist's claims about value cannot be vindicated unless the world contains natural properties capable of playing whatever roles our evaluative practices call for.[6]

In this essay I propose largely to set aside the first, conceptual question about value. I will assume that we have sufficient working understanding of the meaning of 'value' in general – and of 'moral value' and 'aesthetic value' in particular – to ask some central questions about how objectivity in value and valuation could be possible for creatures like us in a world like ours. This project is therefore largely independent of partisan debates within the metatheory of value.

I will pair moral and aesthetic value in part because I believe each can help us to understand the potential objectivity of the other. From moral value we will borrow a vertical-and-horizontal model of objectivity that arguably (surprisingly?) fits the aesthetic case. From aesthetic value we will borrow the idea that value can be objective and nonhypothetical without standing in a necessary relation with claims of obligation, an idea that arguably (surprisingly?) fits moral value. To begin, however, we will look somewhat generically at notions of subjectivity and objectivity in value.

In what sense is value subjective? A proper answer would be fairly complex and would force us to examine a number of central tendencies in "modern culture." It says a great deal about us that the man in the street (or the undergraduate in our classroom) is so ready to agree that value is "subjective" and so quick to elide this to "arbitrary." The task of the present essay is not, however, intellectual history. Instead, we need to ask whether we can locate a compelling case for saying that subjectivity is essential to value.

I believe the best case to be a highly abstract one. According to this case, value enters the picture when *mattering* does. (Nihilists thus have hit on an apt phrase when they say, "Nothing matters.") If we imagine a world without any locus of mattering or concern – say, a world composed entirely of oxygen molecules in random motion – no issues of value would arise internal to that world. Within that stark world it couldn't matter less what happens, because it doesn't matter at all. If to this world we add some beings to whom something matters, then questions of value might have a foothold. It matters quite a lot to us how we fare – for example, whether there is any oxygen in *our* vicinity. Some philosophers are drawn to the thought that ours is really, at bottom, a stark world: when viewed as the physicist sees it – viewed "objectively," according to some – it is no more than molecules in motion. But the "no more than" seems gratuitous. There is a striking difference between our world and the original oxygen world, for ours is one in which some of the molecular goings-on constitute mattering.

Of course, this mattering might just be desire – likes and dislikes, and their associated psychology. And this has seemed an inadequate ground for value in general or objective value in particular. As Bertrand Russell wrote:

I cannot see how to refute the arguments for the subjectivity of ethical values, but I find myself incapable of believing that all that is wrong with wanton cruelty is that I don't like it.[7]

It was natural for Russell to phrase the question of whether the objectivity of morality could be upheld in terms of whether good and evil also matter in some larger, more objective sense. He put it like this: "Are good and evil of importance to the universe, or only to man?"[8]

This formulation of the problem of "mattering in some objective sense" or "mattering objectively," however, makes a positive solution seem out of the question. For what could it possibly mean to say that good and evil matter *to the universe* – or anything remotely like that? If "mattering objectively" means something like "mattering from an objective standpoint" and if a standpoint is objective only if it is free of subjectivity, then we seem to have reached a dead end. For a standpoint without any subjectivity is a standpoint with no point of view – which is to say, no standpoint at all.

A genuine, nonmetaphorical standpoint or point of view is always a locus of experience, centered on a subject ("Archibald's standpoint" or "my cat's standpoint") or somehow composed of subjects ("the standpoint of Local 1099" or "the standpoint of future generations"). Fortunately, Russell's formulation is idiosyncratic: our forebears were far more likely to ask whether *God* cared than what the universe might think. This suggests an approach. If an ideal, divine subject were thought by its nature to occupy a standpoint that could underwrite "mattering objectively" and provide an appropriately nonsubjective standard of value, mightn't we mortal subjects accomplish something along the same lines by *achieving* a suitably similar standpoint? So, naturally, we are led to ask in what ways subjects can be objective.

## THE OBJECTIVITY OF SUBJECTS

Subjects can, we think, be more or less objective. Three notions of objectivity in particular seem important.

(1) We often speak of objectivity in belief or perception as a matter of whether one reliably cognizes an independently existing domain of objects and their properties.[9] Because of its worldly focus, let us call this the *objectual* sense of objectivity. A subject who, owing to preconceptions or other limitations, systematically distorts or misrepresents the world around him lacks this sort of objectivity. "Try to be objective," we admonish, "try to see things as they are rather than as you think they are, or wish they were." The representational efforts of subjects, such as reports, testimony, or even paintings, can also be more or less objective in this sense. Of course, perfect objectivity of this sort seems unattainable by beings like us, since our perceptual and cognitive processes involve mechanisms that could not function without some preconception or bias. But when all goes reasonably well, our preconceptions and biases can promote quite considerable objectual objectivity.

Although thinking of objectivity in this way orients us toward "the external world," it could hardly demand the banishment of subjectivity. On the contrary, objectivity in representation, belief, or assertion requires the real presence of a representer, believer, or asserter. An undetected stratum of ice in Antarctica may more accurately reflect the local magnetic field 55,000 years ago than any current believer's thinking, but the ice layer is in itself a mere object, not a locus of representations. Subjects, on the other hand, are such loci and can be more or less objective to the extent that they possess epistemic and semantic capacities that nonaccidentally result in representations that approximate features of the world around them.

(2) A second familiar way of conceiving the objectivity of subjects shifts the focus away from relations to the external world. A subject can be objective in virtue of reasoning in accord with rules or conditions that are either demonstrably valid or (in some other sense) deliberatively appropriate for subjects regardless of their individual variability. Let us call this *deliberative* objectivity.

In this case, too, subjectivity is not eliminated as a precondition for objectivity. Only subjects are capable of self-regulation through the self-imposition of rules or conditions on reasoning. Unconstrained subjectivity can of course undermine this sort of objectivity, because subjects are prone to mistaking their particular, contingent thoughts for something universally rational or valid. That is a kind of reifying illusion. But if subjects were *genuinely* to recognize a rule or condition as valid and to commit themselves to following it, this would implicate them in no reifying illusion at all. Since this second conception locates objectivity in rules or conditions for subjects rather than a relation to external metaphysics, it is (for want of a better term) a 'subjectual' rather than objectual conception.[10]

(3) The third familiar way in which subjects can be objective is often described as disinterestedness, though seldom without an also-familiar caveat: 'disinterested' means not "unengaged" but something more like "displaying a general, impartial regard combined with a serious – and not merely instrumental – engagement." What this comes to is not easy to say, but we can often (even in the face of substantive disagreements) reach consensus about what we are looking for in a suitably disinterested mediator, judge, referee, or adviser, or about how to go about identifying one. To avoid the unwanted associations of 'disinterested,' let us call this third conception the *impartialist* conception of objectivity.

This third notion has both objectual and subjectual affinities. On the one hand, impartiality in perspective is a way of overcoming incomplete or biased representation of the matters at stake; on the other hand, there certainly is no presumption in the idea of impartiality that the matters at stake are wholly objectual – wholly independent of us or our activities.

If value has its origin in subjects, and if subjects can in these three ways be more or less objective, do we therefore have in hand the requisites for capturing the notion of objective value? Hume begins his own account of aesthetic judgment by despairing of both objectualist and deliberative approaches. First, the objectualist:

There is a species of philosophy, which cuts off all hopes of success in such an attempt, and represents the impossibility of ever attaining any standard of taste (6).

This view, he goes on, treats judgments of taste on the model of judgments of independently existing properties of the object appreciated. Yet matters of taste are essentially tied to "the common sentiments of human nature," according to Hume (7).

Hume then argues that the linkage of value to sentiment equally implies that the standard of taste cannot be objective in the second sense:

It is evident that none of the rules of composition are fixed by reasonings *a priori*, or can be esteemed abstract conclusions of the understanding, from comparing those habitudes and relations of ideas, which are eternal or immutable (7).

Does the involvement of sentiment preclude altogether the possibility of a genuine objectivity in aesthetic judgment? Hume notes a certain tendency of common sense to embrace this thought, and he reflects upon the familiar proverb *de gustibus non disputandum est:*

... the proverb has ... determined it to be fruitless to dispute concerning tastes. ... [C]ommon sense, which is so often at variance with philosophy, especially with the sceptical kind, is found, in one instance at least, to agree in pronouncing the same decision (6).

And yet now it is Hume who wishes to play the antiskeptic. He notes that

... there is certainly [also] a species of common sense, which opposes [this proverb], or at least serves to modify and restrain it. Whoever would assert an equality of genius and elegance between Ogilby and Milton or Bunyan and Addison, would be thought to defend no less an extravagance, than if he had maintained a mole-hill to be as high as Tenerife, or a pond as extensive as the ocean. Though there may be such persons, who give the preference to the former authors; no one pays attention to such a taste; and we pronounce, without scruple, the sentiment of these pretended critics to be absurd and ridiculous (7).

If sentiment – rather than independent reality or pure reason – is at the core of taste, how are sentiments themselves to be thus evaluated?

[The real] foundation [of rules of composition] is the same with that of all the practical sciences, experience; nor are they any thing but general observations, concerning what has been universally found to please in all countries and ages (7).

This foundation can exist even if sentiment "only marks *a certain conformity or relation between the object and the organs or faculties of the mind*" (6, emphasis added). Here, then, is the sort of antiskeptical position on value that Hume will seek to make a place for: many questions of taste *are* justly disputable, for they are not proprietary matters to be referred only to one's own sentiments; rather, they are questions, at least in part, of *general* sentiment. We begin to see here a role for the third conception of objectivity – impartiality. Humean objectivity in aesthetic judgment has, one might say, a *horizontal* as well as *vertical* character: it is a matter not only of what now pleases us, but what would please us and others across time and space. I must "conside[r] myself as a man in general" (15). Of course, any actual aesthetic *experience* is individual and particular, and for that reason no single experience (or content thereof) affords the touchstone in aesthetic evaluation.

We shall be able to ascertain [beauty's] influence not so much from the operation of each particular beauty, as from the durable admiration which attends those works that have survived all the caprices of mode and fashion, all the mistakes of ignorance and envy (8–9).

As this way of framing things indicates, Hume's account of beauty gives it sufficient independence from particular reactions that it can be cited in the *explanation* of experience:

The same Homer who pleased at Athens or Rome two thousand years ago, is still admired at Paris and at London. All the changes of climate, religion, and language, have not been able to obscure his glory (9).

Because it is a general matter of whether "a certain conformity . . . really exist[s]" rather than a direct content of experience, beauty – or "glory" – can explain not only individual experiences, but also patterns of similarity in experience.

It emerges that, for Hume, although no questions of taste are resolvable *a priori*, many aesthetic judgments are as definite and determinable as "matters of fact" in the *a posteriori* objectualist sense. Let us call the relation of conformity between objects and general "organs or faculties of the mind," such that the objects are "by the structure of the mind . . . naturally calculated to give pleasure" (10), a *match*. Although this match may not itself be a content of direct experience, it is a frequent cause of experience, so that the "conformity or relation between the object and . . . the mind" is not for us simply an esoteric, speculative matter. Rather, our familiar experiences – especially as developed and shared across individuals and over time – suffice to give us reasonably secure knowledge of it.

Though in speculation we may readily avow a certain criterion in science, and deny it in sentiment, the matter is found in practice to be much more hard to ascertain in the former case than in the latter. . . . [N]othing has been more liable to the revolutions of chance and fashion than these pretended decisions of science. The case is not the same with the beauties of eloquence and poetry. Just expressions of passion and nature are sure, after a little time, to gain public applause, which they maintain for ever (18).

### VALUE'S INFRASTRUCTURE

This notion of a match needs considerable refinement. We must, for example, sharpen its characterization so that emphasis is placed upon attention to the object itself and to perceptually based experience of it (rather than some other means by which it might cause pleasure in us). Hume writes: "[A] critic . . . must . . . allow nothing to enter into his consideration, but the very object which is submitted to his examination" (14–15). But this is too strong. The meaning of a work, for example, will depend upon the context in which it was created. And Hume indeed immediately amends his exclusion:

. . . every work of art, in order to procure its due effect on the mind, must be surveyed from a certain point of view, and cannot be fully relished by persons whose situation, real or imaginary, is not conformable to that which is required by the performance (15).

We must, further, make sure our understanding of *pleasure* is broad enough to include a range of intrinsically sought-after experiences. And we must ask *which* humans Hume has in mind.

Hume speaks of what is "universally found to please," but that is for him a term of art. Human variability is surely enough, he admits, that nothing will meet universal approbation (17). Moreover, great delicacy is needed to form a just opinion of an object (13). Neither of these considerations will eliminate the prospect of a standard of taste, however, as long as there is sufficient underlying similarity among humans to permit the existence of (what I will call) the *infrastructure* for a suitable *field of value*.

The picture of Hume's approach I have been sketching here should be distinguished from another, perhaps more familiar way of characterizing his view. According to the present account, Hume is *not* offering a *definition* of 'beauty' (or necessary truth conditions for statements of the form "*x* is beautiful") in terms of the consensual responses of a particularly sensitive subgroup of humanity, the experts. Rather, he is giving an account of the features of human sensibility and the world we inhabit in virtue of which aesthetic value can exist and afford a domain of objective judgment, a domain in which expert opinion is possible. The "joint verdict" of expert opinion is offered by Hume as a solution to the problem of finding a *standard* of taste, not as a way of saying what constitutes aesthetic value. Delicacy of sentiment, freedom from prejudice, extensive practice, comparative knowledge, and so on are important so that the expert critic can discern matches, that is, can "discer[n] that very degree and kind of approbation or displeasure which each part is naturally fitted to produce"(13). To be a reliable detector of matches is no cinch:

... it must be allowed, that there are certain qualities in objects which are fitted by nature to produce those particular feelings [of beauty and deformity]. Now, as these qualities may be found in a small degree, or may be mixed and confounded with each other, it often happens that the taste is not affected by such minute qualities, or is not able to distinguish all the particular flavors, amidst the disorder in which they are presented (11).

Those of us with ordinary tastes will often miss these differences, even though the differences could be expected to manifest themselves in ordinary experience in the long run as experience extends across an increasingly large and diverse population of individuals in an increasing variety of contexts. The generalized "test of time" thus has great discriminatory power even with regard to subtle differences. Hume explains how individual experts can also possess this sort of discriminatory power:

Where the organs are so fine as to allow nothing to escape them, and at the same time so exact as to perceive every ingredient in the composition, this we call delicacy of taste (11).

An analogy may be useful. We might think of a much more literal sort of match, the fitting together of parts in a complex machine. Superficial inspection of a machine may show the parts to fit nicely, turn easily, work smoothly. But the long-run reliability of the machine depends upon much finer tolerances than superficial inspection can reveal, tolerances in the thousandths of inches detectable only by delicate measuring devices. These differences will tend to reveal themselves over time, as a machine (or type of machine) is subject to repeated use in various settings. Engineering and manufacturing standards for tolerances, materials, and so on are developed along these lines.

Hume himself is drawn to a mechanical analogue, borrowing Fontenelle's image of "a clock or watch":

[T]he most ordinary machine is sufficient to tell the hours; but the most elaborate alone can point out the minutes and seconds, and distinguish the smallest differences in time.[11]

A clock or watch can afford a more or less reliable standard of time. A perfectly precise timepiece could afford a true standard. In Hume's day, the most pressing need for high accuracy and reliability in timepieces was the famous "longitude problem" of navigation at sea. For a timepiece to be a true standard, its reading would have to remain – no matter where or how transported – in perfectly regular correspondence with solar time at a fixed location on the globe, say, Greenwich, England. Being a true standard of time in this sense is clearly not the same as constituting time. The connection between the reading of any particular clock and fixed-location solar time (an alignment between a point on the earth's surface and the position of the sun) is nomological, not definitional.[12]

Of course, unawareness of tiny differences is not the only way we misjudge matches. We can also be misled by "caprices of mode and fashion," by "ignorance and envy" (9), or by lack of experience and narrowness of understanding:

[A] true judge in the finer arts [possesses] strong sense, united to delicate sentiment, improved by practice, perfected by comparison, and cleared of all prejudice . . . (17).


THE THIRST FOR TASTE

True judges can exist because there is a *subject matter* with respect to which they can develop expertise, authority, and objectivity. This subject matter is afforded by the underlying sensory and cognitive structures that we share with other humans and, in particular, with such judges. If refinement on their part led to a fundamental alteration in their underlying sensory

95

and cognitive structures, they might be subtle judges, but their "joint verdict" would no longer represent expertise about *our* taste, or *human* taste. We differ from the experts not so much in what matches best and most durably the potentials of our underlying structures as in how well we can detect these matches. As a result, we accord greater authority to those with genuinely acute and experienced palates, and greater authority to ourselves as our palates become more acute and experienced.

This deference to more acute and experienced palates is not mere snobbery or acquiescence in a cultural hierarchy. Rather:

> Many men, when left to themselves, have but a faint and dubious perception of beauty, who yet are capable of relishing any fine stroke which is pointed out to them (19).

The enjoyments identifiable and accessible through heightened sensibility, we learn from experience, are very great, widely available, and little dependent upon "the good or ill accidents of life."[13] Thus,

> a delicate taste of wit or beauty must always be a desirable quality, because it is the source of all the finest and most innocent enjoyments of which human nature is susceptible (12).

Partly for this reason, and perhaps also partly for other, less instrumental reasons, Hume believes that we are moved to be concerned about whether we are good judges, and that a man cannot be satisfied with himself if he suspects that he is mistaking trendiness for beauty, or "suspects any excellence or blemish ... has passed him unobserved" (12).

This doctrine – of the fundamental similarity of underlying sensory and cognitive structures and resultant widespread availability of the special enjoyments attending real difference in excellence or beauty – helps us to explain various readily observable phenomena.

First, to return to the story with which we began, it helps us to see why, in purchasing wine wholesale (or in selecting tea or coffee for import, or blending whiskey, or preparing tobacco, or choosing the raw materials for perfume), businesses devoted to commercial success rather than to higher aesthetics nonetheless purchase the services of expert tasters, whose palates (or noses) are vastly more discerning than our own. Of course, such companies do seek the opinion of tasters of only typical sensitivity – they carry out "field trials" of products before release and in order to make continuing changes. But if I (and many others like me) can't tell the difference between two wines, why should the company that seeks to sell wine to me (and many others like me) employ people with expensive taste buds to select and blend wine? The answer is that the broad population *can* taste these differences or, perhaps more accurately, can *respond* to these differences in forming its preferences. Of course, we don't as individuals fully realize these potentials – any one of us might fail to respond to particular differences on particular occasions, and almost all of us would fail to identify them clearly or reliably. But even so seemingly straightforward a matter as maintaining the constancy of taste of a product to a broad population of consumers requires a taste-testing procedure of considerable refinement – available ingredients are seldom perfectly constant in character (or cost), and within broad populations over time there will be a nearly full representation of the various components of our sensory potentials. "You can fool all of us some of the time, and some of us all of the time, but you can't fool all of us all of the time," Lincoln once said in a different context.

Second, this doctrine of fundamental similarities helps us to understand our social practices of evaluation. We seek not only to have good taste, but to be taken as having good taste and to identify other possessors of good taste. We are relentless producers and consumers of opinions, advice, and guides. Our conversation often turns to the exchange of judgments, and we are eager to share our enthusiasms and to find confirmation of our judgments in the opinions or experiences of others. We hardly obey the maxim of not disputing matters of taste. And though such disputes may lead to an impasse, we have both familiar ways of mitigating difference – we can retreat to the language of expressed preference – and an inveterate tendency to continue to seek agreement. Shared judgment yields a gratifying confirmation and bond, as well as useful evidence that our taste and enjoyment are no fluke. If we were grossly unrealistic in continuing to seek out judgments shared among friends and companions, or shared with various critics, authorities, or wider circles, one would not expect the practice to have gone on so long and so vigorously.

The bustling commerce in aesthetic evaluations is, after all, almost entirely voluntary. No threat of an Aesthetic Judgment Day is needed to bring us to scrutinize our aesthetic evaluations, or to pay heed to them in choice. Bookstores bulge with guides, and newspapers and journals do a steady business in reviews. We readily pay for reliable restaurant ratings, travel great distances to view recognized natural wonders, and freely swap judgments on music or movies. Some people, of course, pay little attention to all this – they can't be bothered. Where, if anywhere, are they going wrong? We see them, I think, as *missing something*, as partly blind. It would not be uncommon for us to say that such people have a good reason to pay more attention to aesthetic matters – what they fail to appreciate is something very much worth having. It would be uncommon, I think, to speak of such people as exhibiting a necessary irrationality or incoherence. There are substantive goods out there of which they are unaware, but that is more like a deficit in knowledge than a kind of inconsistency. Its price is an impoverishment or truncation of their lives.

## THE COMMONALITY ASSUMPTION

All this is very breezy. Just how plausible is Hume's assumption of commonality in our underlying sensory and cognitive structures, sentiments, and so on? Rather than attempt to answer this directly, let us begin with the opposite hypothesis and see how things would look. Assume that variability in underlying human sensory and cognitive capacities and sentiments is very great and thoroughly unsystematic. Consider two scenarios.

### Scenario 1

Great knowledge and experience do not tend to produce any general similarity or stability in judgment. Objects that please some of us could not be expected to please others, even with increasing familiarity, and there would be little predictability from one person's likes and dislikes to another's or from one person's likes in one area to her likes in another. What would someone who does not know me intimately learn about what she might expect from a performance or a meal upon hearing that I thought it wonderful? What pleasure or reward could arise from sharing such judgments, or from "trying out" particular judgments of mine against the judgments of others and finding agreement? Discovering commonalities and differences would be rather more like discovering that others have the same or different birthdays, a curiosity perhaps, but not evidence of much else. As a society, we would lack not (the equivalent of) the chance coincidence of shared birthdays, but rather (the equivalent of) the institution of common holidays, special days publicly observed, capable of playing a collective role across a broad population. One of the more important sources of social solidarity would be missing, and it would be fairly bootless to ask whether someone was good-looking, to consult gastronomic guidebooks, to offer the opinion that a given morning is beautiful, to debate the excellence of films, or to discuss the charm of cities. There would be, in effect, no regular commerce in taste. Chefs, designers of public buildings, and film directors could not rely upon their own reactions,

98

or the reactions of those around them, to gauge "effect." If words such as 'beautiful' and 'delicious' were in use, they would have a social role and force much closer to expressions of mere preference, and the language of preference itself would lose much of its familiar predictive value.

## Scenario 2

As before, except that powerful cultural institutions are in place to attempt to regiment opinion on what is or is not excellent, or beautiful, or delicious. Natively, our sensations and sentiments are not much alike, but we are under strong social pressure to conform to established norms concerning which colors are harmonious, which natural phenomena are awe inspiring, which writers are moving, which mornings are beautiful. How successful might such cultural hegemony be expected to be in the absence of an infrastructure of shared faculties – how much like existing social practices and institutional pressures would this be? While it would be impossibly naive to deny that the authority of institutions or the desire to belong make important contributions to shaping our tastes, it would seem equally naive to imagine that all of the current spontaneous commerce in taste could be sustained by pressures or urges to conform. Indeed, in this scenario one would have to imagine, I think, that the exercise of taste would have a social character much more like etiquette or morality than it currently does: here is what is expected of you; from youth upward you are told that this is for your own good; you will lose your standing in the community if you depart from standards of taste; and so on. There is, indeed, an element of taste in society that has just this character – the cultivation of "good taste." And it does have its characteristic effects, among which are also a certain cynicism and resistance as well as deference. What is more difficult to imagine, however, is that the whole bustling, ungrudging world of taste – a world ranging from Best of Boston readership polls to oral sagas and folk melodies carefully passed along for generations in remote hills and islands – could be explained in this way.

How far we in the actual world are from the arbitrary variation from subject to subject in sensation and sentiment in these scenarios is measured by how different our world seems from either Scenario 1 or Scenario 2. This, along with the manifest similarity among *Homo sapiens* in respect to the physiology of sensation, seems ground for believing there to exist sufficient similarity to provide the infrastructure among us for a very large *field of aesthetic value*: there will be some things that excel in their match with our sensibilities, and that can become a source of durable pleasure or interest as familiarity grows, independently of otherwise large variations in personal experience, situation, or culture. If the cultivation of expert palates led to the outright replacement of common capacities and sensibilities by others, it would be difficult to explain why we heed the opinion of expert critics or why commercial enterprises rely so much upon expert tasters. Hard-to-detect failures of match can, of course, easily be masked by temporary enthusiasms, lack of familiarity, small variations in personal experience and sensitivity, or the distraction of other factors. The masking by such features of a failure of match cannot, however, be expected to last forever. Hume, at least, was sure it could not.

To reconnect with our notion of the objectivity of subjects, we can say that the judgments of Humean experts *combine* the three sorts of objectivity discussed previously: objectual (their strong sense allows them to detect minute but real differences in the things themselves), deliberative (they reason properly from experience and possess clear ideas),[14] and impartialist (they compare and are free of prejudice). What they must possess as well is a set of structures and capacities for sensation, cognition, and sentiment that are largely shared with the rest of us.

### A DIVISION OF LABOR

But surely, one can argue, when I judge a work of art to be excellent I am not making a complex descriptive claim about its capacity to match widespread human sensibilities. Such a claim would merely be a species of general causal judgment and would account for neither the *normative* character of aesthetic claims nor the *phenomenology* of aesthetic judgment. Moreover, is not Hume himself famous for insisting that value judgment be linked to the will, a view that has become the foundation of modern antidescriptivism? Would not G. E. Moore rush to point out that one can intelligibly say, "Yes, we can agree that this object matches widespread human sensory capacities and sentiments in such a way as to produce robust and lasting enjoyment, but can we not still intelligibly ask whether it is beautiful?" Have I so bungled the interpretation of Hume as to make him guilty of a "naturalistic fallacy" in aesthetics?

There is nothing in the present reading of Hume to set such worries in motion. We have not supposed that Hume's ambition was to give an account of the concept of Beauty, the meaning of 'beauty,' or the peculiar phenomenology of experience under aesthetic concepts. His main interest, we have suggested, lay elsewhere, in examining the worldly infrastructure of aesthetic evaluation and asking whether it would support a species of objective judgment or a standard of good judgment.

Is it anachronistic to imagine that Hume himself might have divided the questions in anything like that way? Is there evidence that he distinguished the task of giving a definition or conceptual analysis from giving an account of the function or infrastructure of a discourse? In fact, he seems to have just such a distinction in mind in the *Treatise*, when introducing his discussion of pride and humility:

> The passions of PRIDE and HUMILITY being simple and uniform impressions, 'tis impossible we can ever, by a multitude of words, give a just definition of them, or indeed of any of the passions. The utmost we can pretend to is a description of them, by an enumeration of such circumstances, as attend them.[15]

The "attending circumstances" he goes on to illuminate are the characteristic *objects, causes*, and *effects* of these passions (the section is subtitled "Of pride and humility; their objects and causes"). This gives, if you will, a partly functional characterization of the role played by pride and humility in our mental economy and collective lives. How is Hume able to discuss these features in detail without defining the relevant concepts?

> [A]s these words, *pride* and *humility*, are of general use, and the impressions they represent the most common of any, every one, of himself, will be able to form a just idea of them, without any danger of mistake.[16]

Let us, then, have a philosophical division of labor, and distinguish five elements in a Humean (or at least Hume-inspired) account of beauty.

(1) *The beautiful things* are those things (if any) genuinely possessing beauty. We know something of Hume's opinion on this matter – for example, he believed that Homer and Milton wrote beautiful things, vastly more beautiful than Ogilby did. Hume claims, not implausibly, that many judgments of what is beautiful are sufficiently uncontroversial that denying them outright would only earn one the name of a crank.

(2) *The beauty-making characteristics*, or "beauties," are those features of an object or performance in virtue of which it is beautiful. The works of Homer and Milton, for example, are made beautiful by their language, form, narrative structure, evocative power, insight, originality, and so on. These features engage our sensory and cognitive capacities and our sentiments in ways we find intrinsically enjoyable, and the more deeply and intensely so upon greater familiarity and broader experience.

Some examples:

In all the nobler productions of genius, there is a mutual relation and correspondence of the parts ... (16).

[This poet] charms by the force and clearness of his expression, by the readiness and variety of his inventions, and by his natural pictures of the passions ... (8).

These are general features, which works may possess in various degrees and combinations. Moreover, they may be found alongside other features – for example, lack of coherence and extreme improbabilities – that produce intrinsically "disagreeable" experiences, even disgust (7–8). The aesthetic value of a work depends upon the balance of its beauty-making characteristics and its ugly-making or indifferent features. In Ariosto's work, for example, ". . . the force of these beauties has been able to ... give the mind a satisfaction superior to the disgust arising from the blemishes" (7–8). Given the *general* character of the beauty-making features, Hume believes, there are *principles* concerning such relationships. Moreover, these principles may be somewhat genre specific. Poetry, Hume notes, cannot be held to the normal principle of discourse that we should aim to say what is true, since "[m]any of the beauties of poetry, and even eloquence, are founded on falsehood and fiction ..." (7). However, other principles are at work: "[Poetry] must be confined by rules of art, discovered to the author either by genius or observation" (7).

(3) *The functional characterization of beauty*, as suggested in Hume's account, has been our principal focus here. It is a characterization of the typical objects, causes, and consequences of the experience of beauty and of judgments of taste, including the roles played by such experiences and judgments in artistic creation and our thoughts and practices more generally. I have attributed to Hume a functional characterization of beauty as a particular sort of robust and general match between objects or performances and widespread human sensory capacities and sentiments – "[t]he relation, which nature has placed between the form and the sentiment" (9) – that permits these objects and events to bring about intrinsically sought, perceptually based experiences in those who become acquainted with them. Features that can play this role are beauty-making features; things that can play this role are the beautiful things. As Hume writes:

Did our pleasure really arise from those parts of [Ariosto's] poem, which we denominate faults, this would be no objection to criticism in general: it would only be an objection to those particular rules of criticism, which would establish such circumstances to be faults. . . . If they are found to please, they cannot be faults, let the pleasure which they produce be ever so unexpected and unaccountable (8).

Because this characterization of what makes for beauty is largely functional, it follows that were we humans significantly different in our sensory and cognitive capacities or our sentiments, different things would be beautiful and different features would be beauty-making characteristics (of which more later). Moreover, if we humans showed arbitrary individual or temporal variability in the relevant capacities and sentiments, there might be no identifiable group of objects and features that could fulfill the functional characterization robustly, stably, or generally enough to warrant uncontroversially (or perhaps at all) the name 'beautiful' or 'beauty making.' Indeed, in such circumstances, we would not see the familiar social commerce in taste, patterns of deference to expertise, and so on: ". . . all the general rules of art are founded only on experience, and on the observation of the common sentiments of human nature" (8).

(4) *A standard of taste or beauty* is a means for reliably detecting or measuring how well the functional characterization is met in particular cases. Though the standard does not itself constitute beauty, coming to see how such a standard could exist may nonetheless reveal a good deal about the nature of beauty. Hume's standard of taste – the "joint verdict" of those of greatest force and delicacy of sentiment, freedom from prejudice, and breadth of experience – points us both to the subjectuality of aesthetic value, the impossibility of removing sentiment from the equation to leave a purely objectual form of judgment, and to its sources of objectivity.

It is, of course, not always easy for us to make the sorts of discriminations that would enable us to discern whether certain objects please chiefly because they are in vogue or have certain salient but superficial characteristics, or because they genuinely possess beauty-making characteristics. The latter, were we to attend closely to them, would be a source of lasting pleasure even after fashions have changed or acquaintance grew. We wish to create and surround ourselves with objects that can be sources of rich, perceptually based pleasure, objects moreover that will provide the occasion for shared pleasures among family and friends, that will call forth the admiration of others, and that will afford deeper satisfaction the better we know them. A standard of taste, if it could be established, would help us make these choices. It would help us, too, to resist a too-ready dismissal of objectivity in taste in view of the diversity of actual opinion.

(5) *The concept of beauty* is something (in principle) different from either standard or functional characterization. Though we are all familiar with the word 'beauty,' it is no simple matter to say what this concept might be. Even if we suppose there to be a definite concept lying behind our use, philosophical opinion differs as to what in general a concept is or does. One fairly common view is that a concept is (*inter alia*) what we must internalize if we are to become competent speakers in a given area of discourse. On this view, the concept of beauty is what we must grasp in order to understand judgments of beauty and to make novel and appropriate judgments of beauty on our own. Grasp of this concept, further, may be seen as making it possible for us to have what we might call *distinctively aesthetic experience*. Distinctively aesthetic experience is different from the experience of perceptually based pleasure merely as a causal consequence of characteristics that would qualify as beauty making. A pleasurable awe at sunsets is something we seem to share with many beasts. Distinctively aesthetic experience is also different from the experience of those with an entirely intuitive grasp of various beauty-making characteristics – those who possess the practiced eye or hand of a skilled artisan, say, but who do not represent things to themselves in terms of (a general-purpose notion of) beauty. Wittgenstein offers as a model of "appreciation" a tailor or clothes cutter studying the length of a customer's suit with his practiced eye and saying "Too long" or "All right."[17] On a Humean account, this can be understood as a kind of sensitivity on the cutter's part to the beauty-making characteristics. A clothes designer, by contrast, might observe the same suit when the cutter's work is finished and pronounce, "A beautiful suit – just right in proportion and fit." Both make perceptually based judgments that are responsive to beauty, but perhaps only the designer is appropriately said to deploy the concept of beauty and to have a distinctively aesthetic experience. Full grasp of distinctively aesthetic concepts involves the higher-order idea that an object may *merit* certain responses on our part, thanks to its beauty. Mastering the concept beauty, as opposed to merely being able to appreciate or be responsive to beauty, involves a (perhaps tacit) understanding that beauty is *normative* for attitudes such as appreciation and for practices such as artistic and artisanal creation.[18] This, of course, is a commentary rather than a reductive analysis.

As far as I know, Hume does not attempt to give an analysis, reductive or otherwise, of the concept of beauty. Instead, he seems to assume (along the lines of his discussion of pride and humility) that we are familiar enough with this notion that he can without any such definition proceed to develop an account of what such judgments are founded upon and how there might be a standard for assessing them, even if actual opinion on matters of beauty seems remarkably diverse.

Hume proceeds by considering the objects of aesthetic assessment, the causes of perceptually based pleasure, the sources of stability and convergence in aesthetic judgment, and also familiar patterns of deference in judgment. From these he develops an idea both of what makes for beauty and of what, correspondingly, would make for a difference between true judges of beauty and those who can only pretend to possess genuine expertise. He believes we can, like the U.S. journalist at the German wine tasting, be led to see that some critics are "really onto something," such that their judgments can carry authority that extends beyond merely personal or arbitrary preferences. This acknowledgment that there *is* something there to be onto – rather than a "free-fire zone" of preference and undeserved prestige – is one expression of the idea that there is the requisite human infrastructure for a field of aesthetic value.

We began by thinking of value as essentially subjective, arising from *mattering*. In any nonmetaphorical case of mattering, we should be able to fill in the formula "*x* matters to *y* for G." Hume, in effect, fills in this formula in the case of taste by replacing *y* with humankind and G with reliable conduciveness to perceptually based, intrinsically desirable experience. Things of aesthetic value matter to us in virtue of the possibility of robust matches with our capacities and sentiments.

The match between Homer and our capacities is not altogether unlike the match of the chemical structure of sucrose with the physiology of the sweetness receptors on the human tongue, which enables us to explain why sugar tastes sweet. This is not an account of the phenomenology – it does not explain "why sugar tastes like *that*." Instead, it explains why sugar (and various similar substances) might reliably cause sensations of a kind that, when they occur, we want them to continue (at least up to some point of satiation). This match might, in the case of sugar as in the case of Homer, be independent of fashion, indoctrination, or particularities of "climate, religion, and language."[19] When a work of art or natural phenomenon is in this way a quite general match for our capacities and sentiments and, further, when the intrinsically desirable experiences it helps produce are such that they become more intense and ramified with further and more discriminating experience of the object (again, at least up to some point of satiation), we have arrived at "the catholic and universal beauty" (8). It will be complained that this is too broad and does not distinguish aesthetic experience from other forms of pleasurable, perceptually based experience. But for Hume's purposes, this is a virtue of the account. In particular, it helps us to see how beauty might have a noncircular explanatory use.

VALUE-BASED EXPLANATIONS

This sort of account, with its division of labor between the beautiful things, the beauty-making characteristics, the functional characterization of beauty, a standard of taste, and the concept of beauty, allows Hume to vindicate the explanatory ambition he exhibits when he seeks to attribute Homer's long-standing success to the "glory" of his work (9).

Consider the perennial question: "Do we like it because it is beautiful, or is it beautiful because we like it?" Both claims seem to have plausibility. Hume can explain why this is so – without circularity, and even for expert opinion.

*We like it because it is beautiful.* Beauty can substantively explain preference. There is, on Hume's account, a difference between preferences that arise in virtue of an object's possession of the right sort of match with our sensory and cognitive capacities and sentiments, on the one hand, and preferences that arise because an object is in fashion, or is recommended by prestigious individuals, or possesses superficial pleasingness, on the other. In the first sort of case, but not the second, the beauty of the object explains our liking it. For its beauty is *constituted by* its possession of the properties that make for the right sort of match – its "beauties," as Hume calls them, "which are naturally fitted to excite agreeable sentiments" (9). This sort of explanation is possible even for the "joint verdict" of expert judges – what makes them different, and what makes them tend to converge in judgment more than the rest of us, is their greater and more reliable sensitivity to the characteristics that make for a robust match. Consider a parallel: solubility is a match of sorts between the chemistry of the solute and the activity of the solvent. Is this just a matter of the former dissociating in the latter? Then solubility could not *explain* the dissociation. But now note the following contrast: a molecule of calcium carbonate (which is very sparingly soluble in water) that dissociates into ions the moment it is placed in water because it happens to be struck by a cosmic ray at that time versus a molecule of calcium chloride (which is readily water soluble) that breaks into parts at such a moment because of the normal electrochemical properties of interaction with water to produce dissociation of the molecule. Both the

106

calcium carbonate and calcium chloride molecules could in the circumstances be said to "dissociate when placed in water," but only one case is explicable in terms of solubility. The same distinction can be applied to preferences: I might come to prefer an object I experience – be I expert or layman – as the result of the operation of a match with common underlying perceptual and cognitive capacities on my part, or as the result of suggestibility, or faddishness, or (even) a chance cosmic ray's effects on my neurons.

*It is beautiful because we like it.* Beauty has been functionally characterized in terms of a capacity to produce (in a certain way) intrinsically desirable experiences in us. In this sense, if we did not possess certain perceptually based capacities for liking and disliking, nothing could be beautiful – the infrastructure for the field of aesthetic value would be absent.

The explanation Hume offers for why Homer still pleases, despite "changes of climate, religion, and language," is that such changes "have not been able to obscure his glory" (9). For Homer's glory to do its job of shining through, it has not been necessary that his readers possess the concept of "aesthetic value" or that they judge his work to be beautiful – it is enough that the work win their admiration as a result of those features in which its beauty consists. Suppose, for example, that scholars are correct in saying that the idea of the fine arts and associated distinctively aesthetic concepts – including the contemporary notion of aesthetic taste – did not emerge until the eighteenth century.[20] Equipped with these concepts, our appreciation of Homer might grow and ramify in various ways, but there will also remain a great deal that is common to the admiration won by Homer in ancient Athens and contemporary London. In particular, at least some of this admiration will be attributable to his work's possession of those features in virtue of which it is a robust match for our sensibilities. The "ground-level" experiences that underwrite aesthetic value thus need not possess a peculiar, aesthetically tinged phenomenology. The beauty of an object can therefore explain why it inspires singular interest or has achieved an enduring popularity, even if we imagine that many of those who have been drawn to it or moved by it do not deploy distinctively aesthetic concepts or enjoy distinctively aesthetic experiences. Moreover, the beauty of objects can help explain why humans have chosen to shape or decorate them just so, or to give these objects a conspicuous place in their lives, even before the emergence of a going practice of actively judging their aesthetic value as such. Indeed, one might go so far as to suggest that it is the existence and enjoyment of beautiful things that explain why aesthetic concepts emerged, seemed to make sense, and could form the basis of a coherent, enduring practice that yields judgments we find worth making and following.

Once aesthetic concepts have been introduced, we can readily be led into distinctively aesthetic appreciation and evaluation. The pleasure we feel on attending intrinsically to a given beautiful work can be accompanied or even enhanced by a judgment of its beauty; this sort of appreciative experience may have a special place in understanding the nature and value of art.[21] But whether a given object is such as to achieve a match that "by the structure of the mind be naturally calculated to give pleasure" (10) is a matter of its causal powers and their fit with our sensory and cognitive apparatus, and not a content of immediate appearance. We can become as accustomed to making this sort of causal inference in the case of value as any other, and so may find ourselves making almost immediate perceptual judgments. Works can strike us as beautiful, much as situations can strike us as dangerous or words can strike us as misspelled.

It is an empirical question whether there are beautiful objects – objects capable of playing the role of being beautiful – and so an empirical question whether there are any credible "aesthetic explanations." Perhaps Homer's long-lasting admiration is best explained by the prestige of cultural icons from ancient Greece. Hume might be able to convince us that he has identified a standard of taste, and yet we might find that no actual objects or performances meet it. This would be a very great surprise, perhaps, but if humans are much more diverse than Hume takes them to be, it would be comprehensible. I take it to be a strength of the Humean approach sketched here that it enables us to understand in a principled way why the observed diversity of human opinion is evidence for skepticism about beauty. This remains a strength of the approach even if we are inclined to agree with Hume that, in the actual world, the human diversity that would remain once variability in knowledge, experience, sensitivity, perspective, and partiality were taken into account, would not be sufficient to shake our confidence in aesthetic value.

This is not to say that all questions of aesthetic value permit determinate answers. Hume compares aesthetic judgment to the distinguishing of mountains from molehills, and there we find determinacy enough: Mozart really is superior to Lully. But it is well known that determinacy breaks down once we deal with smaller mountains and larger hills. We need to find an infrastructure of judgments of taste that affords as much, but no more, determinacy in these judgments than we believe there actually to be. It is important to be able to account for the perennial popularity of a Beethoven or an Ellington, and the entirely predictable charm of

108

fall foliage and Alpine meadows. But a theory of the infrastructure of aesthetic value need not yield a determinate ranking, or even much by way of comparability, in all cases. There is, for example, surprisingly little call for genre-unspecific aesthetic evaluations. Does anyone think that we cannot judge Beethoven and Shakespeare great until we can rank them? Indeed, an account of value's infrastructure should help us to understand why we do not think there is an answer to questions like "Who writes better, Dante or Milton?" or, for that matter, "Which tastes better, vanilla or chocolate ice cream?" A Humean account is able to suggest why this might be so: neither, really, is a better overall match for widespread human capacities and sentiments; whatever decisive preferences we do find across individuals on these choices seem attributable to differences in the individuals themselves, differences that greater experience, sensitivity, and so on reveal to be equally basic.

## MAD (NO, ECCENTRIC) AESTHETICS AND MARTIAN AESTHETICS

The Humean account of the functional characterization of beauty enables us to understand a number of familiar features of our value discourse, but also something a bit less familiar, yet nonetheless (I think) intuitively comprehensible.

Suppose we reflect upon the possibilities of genuinely alternative aesthetic communities – not alternative cultures of *Homo sapiens*, whom we might imagine we could bring (thanks to the underlying similarity in their perceptual and cognitive apparatus) to see things as we do, but communities possessing radically different physiologies and, therefore, a different aesthetic infrastructure.

Imagine Martians. Might there be something deserving the name 'Martian beauty' even if it were quite different from what we recognize to be beauty?[22] How would we understand this? How would we interpret "This image leaves us cold, but it possesses true Martian beauty"? Such a remark certainly need not mean that Martians find it to have the distinctive qualities *we* identify as beauty making – for example, particular structures, symmetries, harmonies, and palettes. For we can understand well enough that Martians might be sufficiently dissimilar from us that they would not find excitement or delight in the forms or palettes that please us. Martians might even have quite different senses. Yet don't we understand well enough what it would be for them to have a distinctively aesthetic practice of *evaluating beauty?* It would be (*inter alia*) for them to have a practice using distinctive terms, which they take to be normative, for those objects that have a general, robust match with *their* sensory and cognitive capacities for experiences *they* intrinsically desire.

Looked at from this perspective, we might say that it is very unsurprising that we humans find sensory delight in symmetry, given the world in which we evolved. In our world, the animals that have interested us and our ancestors (as prey, menace, or mate) are overwhelmingly symmetric along at least one axis. Indeed, the vast majority possess bilateral symmetry when confronted in the most salient way, head-on.[23] We should therefore expect that not all symmetries interest us equally. This expectation appears to be borne out in (for example) architecture, where bilateral symmetry in the front elevation of a building clearly has been a powerful organizing feature of admired buildings and monuments over time and across cultures, while symmetry along other axes and radial symmetry (viewed, say, from overhead) have played a much smaller role. Martians themselves might, along with their fellow Mars-bound creatures, possess radial symmetry, or perhaps no simple form of symmetry at all. They might find the front elevations of our great pyramids, cathedrals, totems, stately houses, tombs, and burial mounds to be disturbingly unbalanced ("bottom heavy," say) or unrelievedly dull.

Turning this thought back on ourselves, should we be unsettled in our aesthetic practices to learn that the matches we detect are distinctively human matches and might properly be said to constitute *human beauty* rather than a "catholic and universal beauty"? We are Earthlings, and we should not be embarrassed by the contingency and worldliness our tastes display. We seem to share with bees a high regard for showy flowers, with bears a taste for honey and berries, and with crows and gulls an attraction to sunsets. An austere Martian world of radially symmetric, intelligent subterranean life that drew its nutrition from minerals in the soil and absorbed solar energy from the soil's warmth might find none of these aspects of Earth the least aesthetically interesting, yet they could be rhapsodic about our hot mud springs and undersea manganese nodules. Does our aesthetic discourse depend for its interest and authority on a claim that Martian beauty is at best only Martian beauty, while human beauty is beauty itself?

Of course, there might be a substantive *universal aesthetic*. Perhaps every form of intelligent life capable of sensory experience would thrill to Bach's *Magnificat*, at least once the work and its conventions were familiar enough.[24] But this is vastly speculative, and in any event one wonders whether such a condition could possibly be necessary for our practices of attributing greater or lesser aesthetic value to be in good order. It would seem sufficient to meet the criticism that "mere" human beauty is "not sufficiently objective" to point out that the functional description of beauty *is* universal, and that it is an objective (though subjectual) matter what, if anything, meets that description for us.

There is, however, what might be seen as a much greater threat nearer home. We deceive ourselves, I suspect, if we think Mozart would please every human, even every human freed of prejudice and capable of fine discrimination. But if Mozart's music isn't "objectively beautiful," what is? How essential to our aesthetic practice is strictly universal *human* agreement? Hume himself concedes that human tastes are variable even when there is no prejudice, ignorance, or want of discrimination, for there seems to exist some degree of basic variation in the human physiology and condition.

... where there is such a diversity in the internal frame or external situation as is entirely [free of "prejudice, ... want of practice, or want of delicacy"], and leaves no room to give one the preference above the other; in that case a certain diversity in judgment is unavoidable, and we seek in vain for a standard, by which we can reconcile the contrary sentiments (19).

The process of aging, for example, is for Hume a ground for "blameless" diversity in taste. "A young man, whose passions are warm, will be more sensibly touched with amorous and tender images, than a man more advanced in years ..."(20). Yet for a field of value to exist and to function as the ground of aesthetic practice, we might think, there must be a *sufficiently extended* population showing *sufficient degrees* of similarity in the relevant respects. Something like this is not out of the question. Not only are young and old quite broad groups, but long-standing experience suggests that the young and old are enough alike to support a notion such as 'a beautiful sunset' or 'a beautiful person' or 'a magnificent building' without elaborate qualification.

The social role of the aesthetic vocabulary clearly depends upon some degrees of commonality, at least within broad groups. Beauty has vertical (intrapersonal) and horizontal (interpersonal) objectivity. But consider now the following sort of case. I have met a learned man who insists that, try as he might, he can find no beauty in music written after 1800 comparable to that of earlier music. Let us suppose that he is *not* disputing whether any music written after 1800 is such as to robustly match widespread human capacities and sentiments. And let us also suppose that his unusual preference is not attributable to lack of experience, errors in thought, or lack of acuity on his part. He and we can, I think, understand each other quite well. We can imagine how it could be that his capacities and sentiments are functioning well and sensitively, and yet the work of Beethoven, Stravinsky, and Monk will not speak to him. We have learned that he is different: an eccentric or unusual (perhaps in the way a colorblind person is unusual), but not irrational or foolish. He is even an authority of sorts, but mostly for those more like him than we seem to be. We don't feel much pressure to share all his tastes (just as we don't feel much pressure to share a colorblind person's relative lack of interest in the Venetian school of painting). The existence of blameless eccentrics (as Hume might call them) serves to remind us of the contingency of our tastes – they really do depend upon what we are like, and the principles of taste are "nearly, if not entirely, the same in all men" (17). But all this leaves the infrastructure of aesthetic judgment essentially unchanged. The unthreatening understanding we possess of just what sort of authority our eccentric possesses reveals our tacit recognition of the functional character of beauty.

### AN EXAMPLE?

In his political writings, Hume emphasized that in matters of morality one should not expect the sorts of radical new discoveries that have characterized natural science.[25] Social practices and norms have been hammered into shape by generations of conflict, compromise, and experience, he thought, and thus embody a kind of accumulated wisdom about the conditions under which men and women can live together with moderate calm and mutual advantage. To think that these could be radically challenged on speculative moral grounds he considered to be a mark of poor judgment.

We might balk at the extent of Hume's conservatism. After all, some of the very innovations that seemed terribly at odds with traditional practice in Hume's day have become part of current conventional wisdom about how best to live. But he has a point: there is a certain riskiness about claims of value unattached to long-evolved practices. And one might expect this point to apply equally to aesthetic judgment.

Consider a rather careless parallel. Historically, composers we regard as "serious" or "highbrow" have drawn deeply from rhythms, harmonies, melodies, and voices that evolved over centuries of folk musical practice: playing together, singing together, dancing together – sharing music and also shaping music and the instruments on which it was performed. The great composers before the emergence of distinctively modern music obviously did not simply reproduce these forms, and often pushed them in new directions. Yet they remained in many ways strongly attached to these forms, and their popular audience was surprisingly broad by contemporary standards.[26]

In this century, by contrast, we have seen in certain conspicuous strands of "serious" music the emergence of styles of composition and forms of instrumentation and performance that have deliberately separated themselves from this folk musical past and that do not lend themselves to informal, shared, rhythmic, and melodic appropriation – these were in effect left to the domain of more "popular" composers and performers. The widespread perception that, however excellent and interesting such "serious" composition as total serialization and concrete music might be in various respects, it is unlikely to achieve the widespread acceptance or the lasting greatness of (say) nineteenth-century "serious" music could be given a Humean diagnosis in terms of a loss of connection to musical traditions that had finely developed matches with widespread human sensibilities. Contemporary "serious" music certainly draws on various beauty-making features in ways that make it possible to form relative judgments of merit. No doubt, too, it has expanded our understanding of the possible sources of beauty. But we should not be surprised if much less of it survives the "test of time" or enters into the repertoire of works widely deemed great music and spontaneously demanded by audiences and informally performed by individuals and groups across broad populations. At the same time, the idea of a match with general human capacities is not hostage to any particular tradition. This idea helps us to understand why the music, visual arts, or cuisine of another culture might come to us as a real revelation, despite a lack of connection to our particular cultural history. And it holds out the prospect not only of pluralism and syncretism, but of genuine cultural innovation, the discovery of powerful matches previously unknown or undeveloped. Twentieth-century "serious" visual art has surely demonstrated this – and so has twentieth-century popular music, there being no reason to expect that successful aesthetic innovation must come from "high-" rather than "lowbrow" origins.

## SOME FEATURES OF AESTHETIC VALUE, ACCORDING TO THE PRESENT ACCOUNT

Thus we arrive at a view about the nature of aesthetic value with the following characteristics.

113

First, it is (in principle) *naturalistically grounded*; that is, nothing lying outside the domain of the natural seems required in order for the functional characterization to be met. Aesthetic judgment can be seen to call upon actual human sensation and its capacities, as qualified by familiar forms of knowledge and causal inference. However, a naturalistic ground is not, we have stressed, the same thing as a naturalistic reduction of the concept of aesthetic value.

Indeed, nonreductionists can recognize the importance of providing a naturalistic ground of some sort, for most nonreductionists hold that aesthetic value *supervenes* on nonaesthetic, natural features of the world. This Humean account could therefore answer to their purposes as well – if it is even roughly right about how aesthetic value is constituted, it would enable us to see how the natural world might provide the wherewithal to underwrite aesthetic judgment.

Second, because it involves a *functional characterization* of beauty, it enables us to understand how aesthetic value might be multiply realized in diverse populations. We can see the sort of role aesthetic evaluation would play for such populations, what kind of information about the world (and their relation to it) such talk would carry, and the conditions under which it might guide a useful, stable practice and discourse.

Third, it is *phenomenologically thin*. The experience of aesthetic value, on such a view, need not be an experience presenting itself under an aesthetic concept. Both in our own individual developmental histories and in human history in general, genuine experiences of beauty can exist and can shape our behavior before the emergence of distinctively aesthetic concepts. A young child's experience of pleasure in examining an autumn leaf or hearing a lullaby may be appropriately explained by the beauty of the leaf or song, even if she does not yet grasp the concept of beauty. Beauty, indeed, can explain why certain things come to be liked. The Humean account is entirely compatible with recognizing as well a special kind of experience that does involve perceiving an object "under an aesthetic concept"; it simply does not treat such experience as the fundamental response to examine if one is to see how the field of aesthetic value is underwritten.

Fourth, this account is (in principle) *critical*. That is, it can help us to understand how some judgments or tastes could be better based or more authoritative than others, and it points us to specific ways in which such authority or grounding can be gained. In matters of taste, we show some deference – in ourselves and in seeking the opinion of others – to preferences based upon greater knowledge, wider experience, and finer discrimination. This pattern of deference reflects the generalizing ambition of aesthetic value discourse, its claim to speak not for a momentary personal experience, but on behalf of beauty and excellence. At the same time, the existence of a practice with this ambition hardly ensures that the world is such as to vindicate the practice. This, too, shows critical potential: the account preserves the skeptical possibility that there is no such thing as genuine aesthetic value. However, the fact that some works of artistry or artisanship, folk tunes, scenic vistas, and foods do seem to have withstood the "test of time" is evidence that outright skepticism about aesthetic greatness is implausible.

Fifth, as we have seen, this account can help us to understand some of the *motivation* to take aesthetic judgment seriously. If, as Hume supposes, our underlying sentiments and sensory capacities are much more similar than they are different, then we learn what can robustly, durably please us when we learn what is genuinely beautiful or what meets the "joint verdict" of experts' standards. These pleasures are, Hume stresses, both powerful and widely available.

The good or ill accidents of life are very little at our disposal; but we are pretty much masters [of] what books we shall read, what diversions we shall partake of, and what company we shall keep.[27]

This observation stresses the contribution of a developed taste to individual enjoyment. The Humean account also possesses a sixth feature of note: it is *social*, drawing our attention to the extent to which our aesthetic practices depend upon a community of relevantly similar individuals and unite us with that community. An account of aesthetic value should help us to understand the importance in human society of the sharing of taste and of aesthetic experiences. Our enduring proclivity toward public spectacle, public monuments, the celebration of icons of beauty, the vigorous commerce in taste, the development of shared styles in dress and building – these are among the most impressive features of human existence. Archaeological evidence suggests that they emerged early across the globe, even in societies of modest surplus. It therefore makes sense that our aesthetic vocabulary, once it emerged, had terms of appraisal subject to a double objectification: not only what appeals as one grows more knowledgeable, broad-minded, and discriminating (vertical objectivity), but also what appeals widely across society and time (horizontal objectivity).

Is there any reason to expect extensive similarities across individuals in their perceptual and cognitive faculties? Speculative evolutionary thinking suggests that the similarities are bound to be very great indeed. The problem of trying to predict others' behavior, or to coordinate our behavior and expectations with theirs, would seem impossibly complex unless our own sensations, thoughts, and sentiments were reasonably good models for the sensations, thoughts, and sentiments of others. Moreover, in a species such as ours, which has gained its livelihood for nine-tenths of its time on this planet as communities of foragers who shared food among themselves and found mates exogamously, the benefits of having our tastes be close models of one another's – despite other differences – would be very significant.

All this is compatible with a good deal of slack or unspecificity in the infrastructure of aesthetic judgment. Cultural variations may fix ideas of aesthetic worth in cases where (what Hume might call) native faculties do not. A shared culture of judgment and exchanged opinion is part of how societies self-identify and distinguish themselves. This connects with some of the most powerful sources of human motivation – the need to belong, to have an identity, to know one's community. One knows one is at home by the look of things – the idea of a proper house, a proper way of dressing, a proper way of talking.

Seventh, this account is *incomplete*. Perceptually based pleasure might in itself be enough to secure the beginnings of a theory of aesthetic value, but it cannot be the whole story. Beauty – our principal focus here – is not the only dimension of aesthetic evaluation, which concerns itself also with other ways that works might intrigue us, challenge us, or instruct us. How, for example, are we to explain in terms of sensory pleasure the following remark, concerning the words of a plaintive traditional work song of Koreans mining in Japan?

This is not the sort of thing one calls a favorite poem. Not, that is, unless a favorite poem is one that has made its home in your mind, one that has permeated your very depths and refuses to be moved.[28]

We had better make room in a theory of aesthetic value for a favorite poem in this latter sense – poems that give us experiences that are almost too much to bear (and yet that we also cannot bear letting go of), not just poems that fill us with delight. Completing a Humean account requires at the least that we move from something like "pleasure" to something more like "intrinsically sought experience." Not all intrinsically sought experiences are pleasant. But this formulation is still too vague to be satisfactory.

Eighth, and last, this account makes aesthetic value remarkably similar in certain respects to *moral value*. Looking at the two together might help us see a bit more clearly how objectivity in evaluation is possible in either case. So let us turn briefly to morality.

## MORAL VALUE

Intrinsic moral value has not been the central category of philosophical attention in ethics in this century; that has been *moral obligation* or *the moral 'ought.'* In the words of P. H. Nowell-Smith's classic introduction, *Ethics*:

> Practical discourse ... consists of answers to practical questions, of which the most important are "What shall I do?" and "What ought I to do?"[29]

More recently, however, judgments of moral value – of what makes a life, a person, an act, a practice, a trait of character, and so on *morally good* – have begun to receive greater attention.

A number of conceptions of moral value, and of its place within moral assessment generally, exist side by side. An important distinction among them traces the line between accounts of "that which constitutes the intrinsic value (or source of intrinsic value) in distinctively moral actions or attitudes" – for example, conscientiousness, a good will – and accounts of "those features of acts, motives, outcomes, etc. which count favorably from a moral point of view."[30] The former conception is especially concerned to identify "distinctively moral actions or attitudes"; the latter is prepared to find moral value in actions and attitudes done for nonmoral reasons, for example, out of friendship, loyalty, or generosity. Because we have been concerned here with aesthetic value chiefly in the sense of "those features of objects or performances which count favorably from an aesthetic point of view" rather than "that which constitutes the intrinsic value (or source of intrinsic value) in distinctively aesthetic acts or attitudes," it is appropriate in the present context for us to consider a conception of moral value of the second sort in making our parallel.

The most influential conception of moral value of this second kind treats it as based upon two elements. First, there are the *intrinsic goods* humans are capable of realizing, the stuff of a good life. Classical hedonists recognize only one such good, happiness. Pluralists imagine that there might be many – happiness, aesthetic experience, accomplishment, autonomy, integrity, and so on. Perhaps the goods are all experiential, perhaps some are not. What is common to these views is that intrinsic good is in some sense *nonmoral.* That is, intrinsic goods do not depend for their desirability upon their moral character or contribution. Nor do they

117

depend for their recognition upon distinctively moral concepts. Thus, there is something desirable about experiencing happiness or avoiding pain, even prescinding from the question whether the experience is morally deserved or undeserved. The archetype of such an intrinsic nonmoral good is individual well-being, so let us use it as our example.

Perhaps the most widely held account of individual well-being understands it in terms of what is intrinsically desirable with regard to the course of one's life. What is this desirability? Mill famously remarked that the sole evidence it is possible to produce that something is desirable is that we actually desire it.[31] Actual desires concerning the course of one's life may, however, be based upon mistaken information, lack of experience, irrationality, inattention, and so on. Mill, acknowledging this, held that the true standard on the question is afforded by the settled views of those of wide experience.[32] Like Hume, Mill seems to have assumed considerable similarity across individuals, such that he could speak of "the permanent interests of a man as a progressive being."[33]

We can, I think, describe this notion of desirability in much the same terms as those used previously for the grounding of aesthetic value. Using the division of labor already suggested, we can distinguish a *functional characterization* of intrinsic human well-being in terms of those activities or states – if any – that afford a robust and general *match* with human capacities to produce the kinds of lives or experiences they intrinsically prefer. The hedonist, for example, argues that only happiness affords a robust and general intrinsic motivator, so that nothing matches – at least for humans – except owing to the happiness it affords. We test such hypotheses by examining how we might best explain the seemingly intrinsic preferences we possess. Thus, the hedonist defends his substantive account by appealing to a functional characterization. Desires arising from peer pressure, erroneous assumptions, imperfect acquaintance, or lack of sensitivity are explained away as not accurately reflecting such matches. Mill's discussion of desire as *evidence* of desirability thus makes sense, and his account of the settled preferences of experienced judges falls into place as a *standard* of desirability much like Hume's standard of taste. At least since Moore, there has been a tendency to construe Mill's view as a proposed analysis of the concept of desirability. But we need not see it in this light. Mill might more plausibly be seen as giving an account of what the sort of desirability relevant to well-being consists in, and suggesting, Hume-like, how there could be an infrastructure for a domain of objective judgment about well-being with respect to which experienced judges afford an appropriate standard.

This gives us a rough idea of individual well-being. But what of moral value? For this we need to introduce a form of generalization, such as the notion of a *moral point of view*. This point of view has been variously characterized. It is, however, largely agreed that it is at least in part an impartial point of view concerned with well-being – it is disinterested with respect to particular individuals or groups but positively engaged on behalf of the well-being of any and all individuals. From this point of view, we can ask to what extent various courses of action, or institutions, or states of character, and so on are conducive to the realization of human well-being.

Moral value, as understood by this approach, is parallel in a number of ways to aesthetic value as interpreted previously. Both possess intrapersonal and interpersonal components, and thus vertical and horizontal dimensions: the contribution made to an individual life as well as the extent to which this contribution extends to the lives of all potentially affected. Moreover, neither aesthetic nor moral value would itself possess a distinctive phenomenology. In both cases, general causal tendencies are in question, and in both cases this permits a kind of noncircular explanation: the reception of a work or a practice, and the convergence of expert opinion on a judgment of it, can be explained in terms of its beauty or its goodness. Finally, in both cases objectivity is obtained without banishing the subjectual.

Notoriously, the notion of a moral point of view presents problems of aggregation and balancing: if an act or institution would not be in all respects optimal for everyone alike, how are we to weigh the various gains or losses within and across individual lives in arriving at an overall assessment? Similar issues should, if the present Humean account is right, attend aesthetic evaluation as well. That we tend not to think of aesthetic judgment as involving aggregation and balancing might be in part the result of the way that paradigms – Beethoven, Milton, Homer – have tended to occupy the focus of attention in aesthetic discussion. Hume himself considers some cases of more middling value. Concerning the vertical (intrapersonal) dimension, Hume writes (as already noted) that Ariosto's poetry is able to "give the mind a satisfaction superior to the disgust arising from its blemishes" (7–8). Concerning the horizontal (interpersonal and intertemporal) dimension, Hume writes (also noted previously) that works of great aesthetic value will identify themselves by winning more sincere admiration "the longer [they] endure, and the more wide they are spread" (9), that is, the more nearly their match is universal in the human population, even though none can be expected to be fully universal (17). In both moral and aesthetic evaluation, then, assessment is disciplined by objectifying considerations in the vertical and the horizontal. Experienced judges are sensitive to the features that will manifest themselves in moral or aesthetic differences, and therefore often are able, like experienced physicians or mechanics, to grasp a situation and make a judgment that concerns complex causal tendencies "at a glance." But it is not the character of this refined experience that makes the judgments of moral or aesthetic value true.

## NONHYPOTHETICALNESS

The parallel structure of aesthetic and moral value may help us to see a familiar feature of moral evaluation in a somewhat different light.

Moral judgment is often said to be nonhypothetical in character. Wittgenstein gives a helpful example:

Supposing that I could play tennis and one of you saw me playing and said "Well, you play pretty badly" and suppose I answered "I know, I'm playing badly but I don't want to play any better," all the other man could say would be "Ah, then that's all right." But suppose I had told one of you a preposterous lie and he came up to me and said "You're behaving like a beast" and then I were to say "I know I behave badly, but then I don't want to behave any better," could he then say, "Ah, then that's all right"? Certainly not; he would say "Well, you *ought* to want to behave better."[34]

Note that in both cases an *evaluative judgment* is made ("you play pretty badly" and "you're behaving like a beast") and is followed by a *practical judgment* ("that's all right" and "you *ought* to want to behave better"). The practical judgments differ in kind: a judgment of permissibility versus a judgment of obligatoriness. A traditional way of explaining this difference is in terms of *reasons for action*. We have a hypothetical reason to play tennis well – if we care about tennis. But we have a categorical reason to eschew beastliness – whether we care or not. If Wittgenstein doesn't care about his tennis game, then he may have no reason to strive to play better; if he doesn't care about his honesty, then he is acting contrary to reason, showing a kind of practical irrationality or incoherence.

But Wittgenstein himself diagnoses this difference in other terms. He says of the second case: "Here you have an absolute judgment of value, whereas the first instance was one of a relative judgment."[35] Picking up on this use of the language of value – though not on his terms 'relative' and 'absolute'[36] – we might say that we are reading these cases in a particular

120

way. We tacitly assume that the only value really at stake in Wittgenstein's playing of poor tennis is his own enjoyment, and so he should suit himself. Suppose, instead, that Wittgenstein is playing against a friend, whom he knows to be facing an important upcoming match and to be secretly hoping that Wittgenstein will serve as a good training partner. Then Wittgenstein's cavalier attitude begins to seem beastly – insensitive to the values at stake. Note that it could still be true that Wittgenstein does not himself want to play any better; it simply no longer is true that the values at issue turn entirely on that fact. Now when we return to the second case, we can see that we are reading it in just this way. We are assuming that the values at stake in Wittgenstein's dishonesty do not turn entirely on his own interest. This manifests itself as a kind of nonhypotheticalness: because the agent's particular purposes in acting are not the complete infrastructure of the evaluative field within which he acts, there are grounds for assessing his act or character that are independent of his purposes. If those elements in the evaluative field to which the agent is insensitive are themselves within the purview of a moral point of view, then his insensitivity is morally evaluable.

Aesthetic evaluation exhibits a similar nonhypotheticalness. Suppose that I am building a house, and you observe that it is uninteresting in design, graceless, or incongruous. "You've designed it pretty badly," you observe. Would my reply, "I know, but I'm not concerned with how it looks" serve to render your evaluation irrelevant or inapplicable? On the contrary, the building will lack or possess beauty-making features whether I or anyone happens to notice or care, and I cannot make this "absolute" judgment inapplicable to me by my own indifference.

Now the question emerges: How natural would it be to describe my failing here as a kind of deliberative or practical incoherence? Do I collide with a categorical reason to care about aesthetics? Is it not more plausible to say that I exhibit a kind of obliviousness to a value (or disvalue) whose presence does not depend upon my particular concerns? One might seize on this difference to argue that moral value is fundamentally disanalogous with aesthetic value, but another reaction is possible: perhaps we moved too quickly from the "absolute" character of the value judgment in the moral case to a particular *explanation* of this absoluteness – perhaps non-hypothetical evaluation can have a grounding other than nonhypothetical imperatives.

As a builder I can, of course, ignore aesthetics. What I cannot do is either exempt my creation from aesthetic assessment or place it into the category of "aesthetic success" by limiting my aesthetic ambitions. As

121

we noted at the outset, aesthetic evaluation has an ambition that extends beyond gratifying personal preference.

I have tried in the preceding sections of this essay to suggest how ambition might be understood and underwritten by a suitable infrastructure. If there truly are beauty-making features – such that I am in principle able to make a building not only that pleases *me* or that I *think* beautiful, but also that is genuinely beautiful – then this is owing to an infrastructure that extends well beyond my current concerns. Indeed, we may not need to know anything about authorial intention in order to make aesthetic assessments, as when we judge the beauty of phenomena that have no author at all (rock formations, the morning light over an offshore island, a prairie storm) or objects not made for any distinctively aesthetic purpose (tools, artifacts, haphazardly evolved urban landscapes). As an ordinary individual, my sensory capacities and sentiments are part of the infrastructure for beauty, but only a part.

Return now to Wittgenstein's "outrageous lie." One might have supposed that the possibility of supporting a nonhypothetical negative judgment of this lie in the face of the liar's evident lack of concern would depend upon showing that the liar is mistaken – he somehow rationally *must* be concerned to avoid this particular dishonesty, whether or not he cares on other grounds. He is *rationally obliged* to do so. But we cannot assume that moral value – including judgments of "beastliness" – is always tied so closely to obligation. In the first place, much of what we assess in terms of moral value – emotions, traits of character, institutions, social practices – is not under an individual's voluntary control.[37] We cannot even infer from the judgment that a given practice or trait of character realizes greater moral value to a practical conclusion that we ought to do whatever is in our power to bring it about – sometimes striving to bring about an end will have quite the opposite effect. Nor can we infer from obligation to value. In a moral dilemma, any particular act one might take could be morally bad, even though one must (as a matter of practical necessity) act.

Attribution of moral value thus does not appear to be hypothetical on the reasons for action of the agent or the judge. We may account for this by noting that the ambition of an assessment of moral value need not be to tell us what is or is not rationally required. Judgments of moral value express a quite recognizable kind of moral concern, a humane concern with human weal and woe, with how institutions, practices, actions, and so on affect them. We can, I think, understand the role and infrastructure of such judgments without settling whether reason requires each of us always to follow them. Indeed, that is what enables us to ask intelligibly the question of how moral value and moral obligation, or reasons for action, are related. The infrastructure of moral value certainly will include the well-being of the agent or the judge. But, as in the case of aesthetic value, this represents only a part of a broader foundation.

What, then, is the ground of negative moral evaluation, if it is not that there is something incoherent about embodying, or pursuing, that which is morally bad? Well, what is the ground of negative aesthetic evaluation? We are more likely to say that someone is *missing something* by aesthetic indifference, or *impoverishing* himself and others by aesthetically bad creations. Impoverishment is not merely metaphorical here: it is a case of lost value. Perhaps other values compensate, but this one will be gone.

We need to convince ourselves that value can be objective without being tied to something like obligation. Why is it, after all, that the dedicated egoist or contented philistine has so little power to induce skepticism in us by announcing "I could care less" when we raise broader questions of value? Because he seems to us incoherent? Or because we can see so clearly just how there could exist real differences between weal and woe, or between beauty and ugliness, without their commanding *his* interest? Whatever we think of his reasoning, we can see that he is missing something.

Our response is quite different when a Nietzsche or a Marx comes along and provides powerful arguments meant to explode comfortable assumptions about where our values come from and what sustains them. We then are forced to ask whether what we took to be a solidly underwritten field of value is not instead a historically specific combination of prejudice, privilege, *ressentiment*, ignorance, and illusion. Our practices are portrayed by such critics as narrow-minded and in the service of particular interests, in just that area of life where we took them to be broad-minded and universal, sensitive to a wide and comprehensive field of value. This sort of critique mobilizes our own evaluative ambitions against ourselves in a way that the moral or aesthetic philistine professing personal indifference cannot. Our soaring objective purport is brought crashing down to earth, and we are forced to ask anew whether there could be anything that genuinely plays the role of moral or aesthetic value.[38]

CONCLUSION

If aesthetic and moral value are in these ways similar, how are they different? How, in particular, to avoid Bentham's error in assimilating all value to moral value?

The brief answer is that, although both aesthetic and moral value are grounded in intrinsically desired states, and both possess vertical and horizontal dimensions, the states need not be the same in character or cause, and the dimensions can evidently differ.

Even if we consider Benthamite theories of well-being that equate it with an experiential state, still such theories do not characteristically restrict attention to perceptually based experiential states or to the vehicles of sensation the way aesthetic evaluation does. Thus, two performances might possess the same moral value owing to their overall contribution to well-being, while one has much greater aesthetic value than the other. In the case of the former, a considerable component of the good it does may arise from its beauty-making characteristics; in the case of the latter, a lesser aesthetic value might be offset morally by other positive effects on well-being. Aesthetic evaluation thus may concern some features of the world that contribute to moral value, but not all such. Similarly, an act or institution may possess moral value in virtue of protecting people from various sorts of harm, without making any identifiable contribution to the aesthetic quality of their lives.

This is a difference in the *vertical* character of aesthetic versus moral value – the sorts of effects on individual lives that lie at the bottom of these two species of value. The two differ as well in the *horizontal* dimension, even if both moral and aesthetic points of view are held to be informed, unbiased, and so on. The existence of a field of aesthetic value that could underwrite an actual practice of aesthetic evaluation depends upon the existence of sufficient *similarity* in sensory capacities and sentiments in the relevant population. The existence of a field of moral value, by contrast, need not assume this sort of similarity. There will be moral questions about the decent treatment of others, for example, that do not depend upon shared sensibilities (though our ease and confidence in answering them might). Indeed, it is sometimes said that moral value has as its peculiar vocation helping us to fairly assess situations in which underlying sensibilities, interests, and so on are in conflict. Notice, however, that interests may conflict in part *because* sensibilities are shared: because the Mona Lisa is so widely admired, a moral question arises about how best to reconcile conflicting interests in having the work on public display and in protecting its security. Part of this question is aesthetic – for example, do security arrangements substantially obstruct the beauty-making features? But part concerns actual or likely *access* to the work – the possibility of a broad population experiencing the work's value. Here the horizontal dimension concerns actual or likely extent of effect on well-being, not simply the existence of a concentration of beauty-making characteristics that *could* be widely recognized.

These differences in moral and aesthetic evaluation help to explain what otherwise might be thought a puzzling feature of aesthetic evaluation, in contrast to moral or even prudential evaluation: the seeming absence in aesthetic evaluation of a category comparable to that of duty or obligation.[39] On a Humean scheme, property and its associated obligations have their origin in "the conditions of justice," where scarcity and conflicting interests are defining characteristics. If the world were one of perfect abundance, he speculates, we would not have a role for property and related notions of justice.[40] Aesthetic evaluation takes place in pleasant abstraction from questions of scarcity. In part, this is a feature of the nonexclusive character of aesthetic enjoyment. It has a loaves-and-fishes character that permits a single musical composition to yield aesthetic enjoyment, in principle, to the entire globe without diminishing its potential. Moreover, as we have noted, Hume sees us as much better able to control what we read or observe than other elements of our fate or fortune.[41]

Some aspects of moral evaluation have a similar abstraction from the nasty business of supply and demand: when we characterize our moral ideals we are free to ask (for example), "What would be the highest degree of excellence in moral character?" or "What are the best motives?" or "What would a perfect society be like?" These judgments, like aesthetic judgments, concern in-principle concentration, intensity, and extent. In principle, the whole world can derive moral satisfaction from the contemplation of morally singular persons or institutions. Here we reach that area of moral value closest to aesthetics (and furthest from obligation?). It concerns what we deem most admirable and is normative not in the first instance for action – we may think there is no reasonable prospect of achieving the most admirable character, say, and that aiming at this would not be wise – but rather for attitude.[42] Does that mean this species of moral evaluation is not the "business end" of ethics, that it is "mere aesthetics"?

Mere aesthetics! – as if discussing and deciding about what we truly admire or detest were not a central, shaping force in human life. Our views about what is excellent and what is poor, admirable or despicable, exert a dominion over our daily thought and conduct no less extensive than our views about what is right and what is wrong.

How plausible is this quasi-Humean picture of aesthetic and moral evaluation – of their infrastructure, their field of value, their subjectual origin, and their dimensions of objectivity? It has not been my ambition to answer that question here, and in any event, significantly more development of both views would be required before that question could be in good shape for answering. The present picture indicates how the groundwork might exist to support to a reasonable degree the objective and explanatory purport of value discourse, though arguably there are further aspirations in such discourse that it cannot accommodate. It can, for example, yield a quite general characterization of the functional role of beauty, but it cannot ensure that this role will be played by the same characteristics in all populations. In a grand scheme, then, the account of beauty is relational rather than absolute.

Relational is not, however, relativistic or arbitrary. The relational infrastructure might be as broad as a species, perhaps broader.[43] And it can be objective. There might, however, be a further aspiration of our concepts of beauty and well-being, an aspiration that resolutely transcends relationality. If so, then the quasi-Humean approach considered here threatens to unsettle rather than undergird our evaluative practices. For on such an approach, it is distinctly difficult to see how anything could play the role of beauty or well-being independently of any contingent features of our capacities or sentiments. If beauty or well-being must have a universal match – match not only for all actual sentient beings, but for any being that could count as sentient – then the spirit informing the quasi-Humean account would seem to lead us in a skeptical direction. Without sensation or sensibility, what would there be to match?

For my part, I think the aspirations of our talk of beauty and well-being are not so grandiose and empty. As far as I can see, we are well within our rights to say – to those who are listening – that the world is full of many beauties, that life can be good, and that aesthetic and moral value therefore matter.

NOTES

*Aesthetics and Ethics: Essays at the Intersection,* Jerrold Levinson, ed. (Cambridge: Cambridge University Press, 1998).
* I would like to thank Kendall Walton, David Hills, and Michael Smith for helpful conversation. Over the years, Allan Gibbard has much influenced my thinking about matters of value. Jerrold Levinson, David Hills, and Kendall Walton kindly provided comments on an earlier version of this essay, which I hope I have put to good use. I owe a special debt to Jerrold Levinson for his patience.
1. Cf. the famous anecdote Sancho Panza tells about his kinsmen, as recounted by Hume in "Of the Standard of Taste," reprinted in *Of the Standard of Taste and Other Essays, by David Hume,* John W. Lenz, ed. (Indianapolis: Bobbs-Merrill, 1965)

10–11. Hereinafter, unattributed page references in the text are to Hume's essay in this reprinting.

2. Belief, too, one might say, lies at this intersection. (For some discussion, see P. Railton, "Truth, Reason, and the Regulation of Belief," *Philosophical Issues* 5 [1994], 71–93.) The two claims characterize a shared aspect of the two key ingredients in a broadly Humean picture of agency: degrees of belief and degrees of value. This feature of straddling objective and subjective emerges as especially important in trying to develop a Humean account of *free, rational agency*. But all of that is a long story.

3. Cf. John Mackie's thesis of "the subjectivity of value" in his *Ethics: Inventing Right and Wrong* (Harmondsworth: Penguin, 1977). Mackie holds that were God *not* dead, objective value could have a place in the world (48, 203–8).

4. Do noncognitivist accounts of value avoid this risk? After all, they deny that evaluative talk attributes a distinctive class of properties to the world, and so need not be guilty of *that* sort of projection. However, since the aspiration to objectivity seems endemic to evaluative discourse (at least in the case of moral and aesthetic value), even the noncognitivist must give some account of whether and in what sense this aspiration can be made good. For an example of a norm-expressivist working toward a naturalistic understanding of how the objective purport of evaluative discourse might be vindicated, see Allan Gibbard, *Wise Choices, Apt Feelings* (Cambridge: Harvard University Press, 1990).

5. Moore wrote: "It is true, indeed, that I should never have thought of suggesting that goodness was 'non-natural,' unless I had supposed that it was 'derivative' in the sense that, if a thing is good (in my sense), then that it is *follows* from the fact that it possesses certain natural intrinsic properties. . . ." From G. E. Moore, "Reply to My Critics," in *The Philosophy of G. E. Moore*, Paul Schilpp, ed. (La Salle, IL: Open Court, 1968) 588.

6. Moore was, famously, a cognitivist about moral judgments and a Platonist about properties. Giving up these positions – embracing noncognitivism about moral language or minimalism about properties – would not, however, remove the challenge of exhibiting compatibility between the functions of value discourse and the nature of the nonevaluative world. For noncognitivists and minimalists do not abandon supervenience (indeed, they often take it to be a conceptual feature of moral value), and so do not avoid the challenge of asking whether the world contains the requisites for our evaluative practices to be sustained.

7. Bertrand Russell, "Notes on PHILOSOPHY, January 1960," *Philosophy* 35 (1960), 146–7. I owe this reference to David Wiggins's essay "A Sensible Subjectivism?" in his *Needs, Values, Truth* (Oxford: Basil Blackwell, 1987) 185.

8. B. Russell, *The Problems of Philosophy* (New York: Oxford University Press, 1969) 155.

9. Cf. Crispin Wright's idea of "correspondence to the facts": ". . . in our practice of the discourse, we interact in a cognitive-representational manner with matters that are independent of us." From his *Truth and Objectivity* (Cambridge: Harvard University Press, 1992) 175. Here he is speaking of objectivity in a realist's sense.

10. I once thought I had a better term in 'subject-ive.' I didn't. 'Subjectual' at least cures the chronic hiccough of that locution. See "Subject-ive and Objective," *Ratio* 8 (1995), 259–76.

11. David Hume, "Of the Delicacy of Taste and Passion," as reprinted in *Of the Standard of Taste*, Lenz, ed., 28.

12. The public visibility in his day of the longitude problem perhaps makes it unlikely that Hume was thinking of a timepiece as itself the *determinant* of true time, rather than as a more or less reliable standard. In the context of marine navigation, one could not even stipulate that the "convergence" reading of timepieces of a particular kind would by definition give the "true time" at a given location – the revolution of the earth would not be constrained to obey these timepieces, and so actual worldly location could not be guaranteed to correspond to differences between the "convergence" reading of such watches and local solar time. See Dava Sobel, *Longitude* (New York: Walker, 1995).

13. Hume, "Of the Delicacy of Taste and Passion," 26.

14. Hume writes, ". . . reason, if not an essential part of taste, is at least requisite to the operations of this latter faculty" (16). Of course care is needed here. Hume meant reason to include not only sound reasoning, but also a "sound understanding" of the empirical features and factual context of an object of judgment (16–17), which many nowadays would not ordinarily deem to be part of reason proper.

15. David Hume, *A Treatise of Human Nature*, A. Selby-Bigge, ed. (Oxford: Clarendon, 1888) 277. I am grateful to an unpublished paper by David Aman on Hume's account of pride, which cited this passage.

16. Ibid., 277.

17. He also notes, "That [someone] is an appreciator is not shown by the interjections he uses, but by the way he chooses, selects, etc." See Ludwig Wittgenstein, *Lectures and Conversations*, Cyril Barrett, ed. (Berkeley: University of California Press, 1966) 7.

18. For an example of an account of aesthetic value that, unlike the Humean account discussed here, makes essential use of higher-order aspects of aesthetic experience, see Kendall Walton, "How Marvelous! Toward a Theory of Aesthetic Value," *Journal of Aesthetics and Art Criticism* 51 (1993), 499–510.

19. Apparently, if a sugar-based mixture is injected into the amniotic sac, a human fetus will begin drinking the amniotic fluid. This has been used as a way of administering medicine directly to the fetus. Hume uses the analogy between "bodily taste" and sugar, on the one hand, and "mental taste" and beauty, on the other (11).

20. See Paul Oscar Kristeller, "The Modern System of the Arts," in his collection of essays, *Renaissance Thought and the Arts* (Princeton, NJ: Princeton University Press, 1964).

21. There certainly is room here for the idea of distinctively *aesthetic* pleasures, pleasures that are possible only thanks to the taking of an evaluative attitude toward a work – finding beauty in it, say – and perhaps also thanks to the special enjoyment or excitement one can have precisely from finding it so fine. On this point, see again Walton, "How Marvelous!"

22. I am plainly indebted here to David Lewis's discussion of pain in "Mad Pain and Martian Pain," reprinted in his *Philosophical Papers* (New York: Oxford University Press, 1983) 122–32.

23. Some fish apparently manifest a fear response or mating behavior if presented with schematic wire constructions that display bilateral symmetry but otherwise do not much resemble a fish.

24. Lewis Thomas once considered the proposal that the radio-frequency signals beamed into space in our search for intelligent extraterrestrial life take the form of Bach's compositions, though he worried it might be "bragging." See his *Lives of a Cell* (New York: Viking, 1974) 45.

25. David Hume, "Of the Original Contract," reprinted in his *Political Essays*, Charles W. Hendel, ed. (Indianapolis: Bobbs-Merrill, 1953) 60–1.

26. See Lawrence Levine, *High Brow and Low Brow: The Emergence of Cultural Hierarchy in America* (Cambridge: Harvard University Press, 1988). The importance of shared rhythmic and melodic performance is, like our taste for fruit, something we seem to have in common with a very wide swath of other species. No doubt it is connected to some very deep sources of social solidarity and identification.

27. Hume, "Of the Delicacy of Taste and Passion," 26.

28. Morisaki Kazue, from a passage in *My Imaginary Marriage to My Motherland*, Kazuko Fujimoto, trans., in "Singing Voices from the Bottom of the World: One of My Favorite Poems," *Concerned Theater Japan* 2 (1973), 165. I am indebted to an unpublished essay by Brett de Bary, " 'Two Languages, Two Souls': Morisaki Kazue and the Politics of the Speech Act," for bringing this passage to my attention.

29. P. H. Nowell-Smith, *Ethics* (Harmondsworth: Penguin, 1954) 11. More recently, Bernard Williams has diagnosed the preoccupation of contemporary moral philosophy with an obligation-based "moral system" as a chief defect. See B. Williams, *Ethics and the Limits of Philosophy* (Cambridge: Harvard University Press, 1985).

30. Sigrun Svavarsdottir emphasized a similar distinction in her Ph.D. dissertation, "Thinking in Moral Terms" (Ann Arbor: University Microfilms, 1993). I am grateful to her for enlightening discussion.

31. John Stuart Mill, *Utilitarianism*, George Sher, ed. (Indianapolis: Hackett, 1979) 34.

32. Ibid., 10–11.

33. "On Liberty," reprinted in *Utilitarianism and Other Essays by John Stuart Mill*, Mary Warnock, ed. (New York: New American Library, 1962) 136.

34. Ludwig Wittgenstein, "Lecture on Ethics," *Philosophical Review* 74 (1965), 5.

35. Ibid.

36. And setting aside his use of the term 'ought' for now. See note 37.

37. See, for example, Robert Adams, "Motive Utilitarianism," *Journal of Philosophy* 73 (1976), 467–81. What of Wittgenstein's remark tying 'beastliness' (seemingly) directly to a corresponding 'ought'? The transition will seem immediate and unproblematic as long as the 'ought' is taken in a moral sense; if we take it in a rational sense, we can see room for question. Beastliness may be conceptually linked to moral error, but is it so linked to rational defect?

38. A functional understanding of value can, it seems to me, enable us to see both why a Nietzschean or Marxist critique can be genuinely unsettling, and why it might also appropriately be viewed as itself an alternative aesthetic or moral position – to the extent, that is, that it seems to offer an alternative to play the functional role of value. How fully this claim could be sustained in either case is a matter requiring discussion in its own right.

39. In prudential evaluation, the principal source of conflict of interest occurs over *time* when, for example, one would gain from deferring the realization of an attractive benefit or be harmed in the long run by yielding to current temptation.

40. Hume, "Of the Origin of Justice and Property," in his *Political Essays*, Hendel, ed. Hume's thought here needs supplementation, presumably, by an account of scarcities that are not affected by material abundance, for example, human relationships that cannot simply be "replicated" owing to the abundance of alternative partners or the capacity to produce new offspring.

41. Hume, "Of the Delicacy of Taste and Sentiment," 26. We see here, too, the influence of the modern idea of Art or Fine Arts, and the carving out of a special evaluative space for taste as apart from other species of judgment of the usefulness or suitability of an object.

42. I am indebted to Elizabeth Anderson for framing questions about the nature of value in terms of its purporting to be normative for attitude.

43. As always, with allowances made for unusual individuals.

# 5

# *Red, Bitter, Good**

I

Valuing and evaluation are pervasive features of our lives, yet their purported object, value, has proven puzzling. Many philosophers have concluded that we do best to explain it away – to develop an understanding of valuing and evaluation without objectifying value. A principal motive for such "anti-reificationism" has been the belief that attributions of value are essentially expressions of subjective responses to the nonevaluative features of the world. No evaluative objects are needed to answer to these judgments: value is projected upon the world, not discovered in it.

Recently, however, interest has grown in philosophical approaches to value that seek to explain it as involving a subjective response without thereby explaining it away. Value might be akin to a secondary quality, such as color. Of course color attribution is linked to a sensibility on our part, but this need not in itself impugn our familiar ways of talking about color – that objects indeed are colored, that their colors can (and often do) guide our color judgments, and so on. Perhaps we could be led to question these familiar ways of talking about color if we could be convinced that color perception or color discourse somehow systematically misrepresents the world. But such claims would require substantial further argument and do not follow simply from the observation that rationally optional sensibilities are implicated in color perception.

How good is the analogy between color and value? An adequate answer would involve giving an account of both, and that clearly is too large a project for this paper. But there might nonetheless be room to discuss one important set of issues concerning the analogy, roughly, those connected with *relativism*. One line of objection to the analogy between color and value has been that color, precisely because of its involvement with subjectivity, is relativistic in a way that moral value in particular purportedly is not.[1] Simon Blackburn has written:

> It is not altogether simple to characterize the "mind-dependence" of secondary qualities. But it is plausible to say that these are relative to our perceptions of them in this way: if we were to change so that everything in the world which had appeared blue came to appear red to us, this is what it is for the world to cease to contain blue things, and come to contain only red things. The analogue with moral qualities fails dramatically: if everyone comes to think of it as permissible to maltreat animals, this does nothing at all to make it permissible: it just means that everybody has deteriorated.[2]

Other writers have, however, defended the analogy between value and color at just this point. They share Blackburn's anti-relativism about moral qualities, but take issue with what he says about the sense in which color is "relative to our perceptions." They argue as follows.

It is agreed on all sides that the extension of color terms is partly determined by reference to subjective human perceptual experience. Disagreement sets in when defenders of the analogy insist – against Blackburn – that the extension is *rigidly* fixed by *actual* human perceptual experience. That is, many philosophers would reject the following equation:

(1)  $x$ is red = $x$ is such as to elicit in normal humans (and in normal circumstances) the visual impression of redness.

Imagining a thought experiment similar to Blackburn's, these philosophers argue that changing human physiology in such a way as to make blue things look red to (then) normal humans would *not* change their color. As Sidney Shoemaker puts it:

> I don't think that if overnight massive surgery produces intrasubjective spectrum inversion in everyone, grass will have become red and daffodils will have become blue; instead, it will have become the case that green things look the way red things used to, yellow things look the way blue things used to, and so on. I think that our color concepts are, for good reasons, more "objective" [than certain other sensory qualities]. . . .[3]

Typically, intuitions such as Shoemaker's are captured by moving from an equivalence like (1), to something closer to (2):

(2)  $x$ is red = $x$ is such as to elicit in normal humans as they *actually* are (and in *actual* normal circumstances) the visual impression of redness.[4]

Let us grant that Shoemaker's intuition about color change is more plausible than Blackburn's, so that (2) is a better candidate for truth than (1). Color concepts, we will suppose, enjoy the sort of non-relativism or "objectivity" (which here means in part: independence from certain changes in our attitudes or sensibilities) that (2) confers.

The rigidification in (2) may remove the disanalogy Blackburn had in mind between color and value.[5] Might we even deploy this notion of "objectivity" to understand the purported non-relativism of moral value? Here is one approach to moral value, modeled on (2):

(3) $x$ is morally good = $x$ is such as to elicit in normal humans as they *actually* are (and in *actual* normal circumstances) a sentiment of moral approbation.

If (3) were correct, then the mere fact of humans changing their moral attitudes concerning the treatment of animals would not in itself alter the moral quality of gratuitously tormenting animals. *Actual* humans, we suppose, do in fact morally disapprove of this sort of thing.[6]

Equation (3) would secure a certain non-relativism or "objectivity" (again: independence from fluctuating attitudes or sensibilities) for moral value in a manner that closely parallels what we have said about color. Too closely, I will argue. For there are, I believe, serious obstacles to an approach to moral non-relativism through fixing reference by actual moral responses. An alternative explanation of moral non-relativism or "objectivity" – meant to account for intuitions like Blackburn's – will be suggested. As we will see, this alternative account may not spoil the analogy between moral value and secondary qualities, but it does suggest that the secondary qualities in question are not those of color, despite their paradigmatic status.

II

Consider the following science-fictive case, which may afford an analogy of sorts with Shoemaker's science fiction about color.

Let us suppose that a widespread change in human circumstances and ontogeny results in a decisive shift in our intrinsic, informed preferences or tendencies toward approbation. Actual normal humans, it is often claimed, take an *intrinsic* interest in kin relationships. For example, we are said to intrinsically prefer, other things equal, bestowing a benefit on a biological relative – a parent, offspring, next-of-kin – rather than on an unrelated individual whom we happen to know equally well and who is otherwise equally deserving. The preference in question is not only *that a relative be*

133

*benefited* (rather than a nonrelative), but also *that we do the bestowing*. Some measure of value would be lost were the benefit not bestowed in accord with the line of kin connection.

This preference is thought to be independent of whatever other values might be realized in conveying the benefit. For example, it does not depend on whether greater happiness is produced in aiding a relative – indeed, it does not depend on whether one is aware that the benefited individual is a relative. If one were approached for aid by two nearly identical individuals in nearly identical circumstances, *except* that one is long-lost (and no longer recognized) kin – say, a brother or parent from whom one had been separated at birth – then this particular value would be realized if one's aid went to the individual who happened to be kin, knowingly or not. Such an outcome would, on this view, simply be more fitting. Kinship, flesh and blood, is thought to matter in its own right, and not solely because of the extrinsic gains to welfare that would arise from such special connections.

Now for the science fiction. Imagine that advances in medical technology, combined with a growing sense of the inconveniences of caring for infants (not to mention the special challenges of living through adolescence!), lead adult humans to devise a form of reproduction through automated, full-scale replication of themselves. Happily, one might say, the process does not produce exact replicas. The replica individuals bear a strong resemblance to the originals, but, for reasons that are not well understood, they tend to look somewhat different from, and to lack the individual memories of, their "parents." They emerge from the automated process tongue-tied and awkward, but surprisingly soon most become fully fluent in word and motion. Indeed, their initial, confused condition and subsequent (usually rapid) progress are reminiscent of nothing so much as the recovery of young adults who have undergone strong shocks in accidents.

Imagine, too, that (again for reasons not well understood) replica individuals also lack a special, intrinsic interest in those from whom they are replicated or who are otherwise genetically close to them. Biological relatedness does not seem to matter in its own right to them, even after they have fully "matured" and are successfully integrated into the community, and even when they are well informed and reflective. In virtually all other respects, they are emotionally and affectively our replicas. They are, for example, perfectly capable of developing strong and lasting affections, and they, like us, tend to take an especially strong interest in those with whom they share interests and daily life. A new human who has been helped through the initial, postreplicative stages by his or her biological "parent" typically forms a special, long-term attachment to that individual. But this sort of attachment is only contingently related to actual kinship – replicas can be, and often are, "raised" by someone biologically unrelated to them. So this "filial affection" is more like the special gratitude and affection old humans would feel toward those who acted as one's parents during a challenging year as a foreign exchange student. For the new humans, it would not matter intrinsically whether their "host family," as we might call it, was in fact genetically related to them.

We may suppose that, although the two groups, old and new humans, mutually recognize their differences on this score, such recognition does not change either group's intrinsic preferences. Precisely because the preferences in question are intrinsic, neither group feels it can satisfactorily explain itself to the other. Older humans find it hard not to think that (in one respect, at least) new humans are missing something in life; new humans find it hard not to think that (in one respect, at least) old humans are incorrigibly prejudiced in thinking that biological relatedness, over and above the stuff of actual human interactions, is a special value-making feature.

Let us pursue a bit further our fictive narration. Despite the initial oddness of this reproductive arrangement – and some of its counterintuitive results in the eyes of old humans – it soon proves so satisfactory overall that it fully replaces other forms of reproduction. Diaper manufacturers and publishers of books with titles such as *Raise Your Newborn Right*, *The Two-Career Family: How to Win Back Your Life*, *Why Teens Won't Listen*, and *Juvenile Delinquency* (3 vols.) switch to other lines of business. Only new humans exist.

Suppose now that we actual humans are contemplating such a time. We are asked to imagine the following course of events. One new human, Ed, underwent replication some years ago to create another, Ethan, but became separated immediately afterward owing to a medical problem that required that Ed be taken to a distant city. Ethan thus was "raised" during the early months of life not by biological kin, but by unrelated new humans. This is not a rare or painful thing. Many replicas are raised by unrelated individuals, and sufficiently many new humans enjoy this process – which comes to be called "awakening" and to be mildly subsidized for related and unrelated host families alike – that there was, at the time of Ethan's arrival, a waiting list of those eager to host replicas. Social scientific research shows no interesting difference between individuals awakened by related versus nonrelated hosts.

As typical new humans, neither Ed nor Ethan has a special interest in biological relatedness as such. Ed undergoes a protracted recovery, and when he finally leaves the hospital his deep gratitude to his doctors and nurses is uppermost in his mind, not Ethan. He resettles in his new city, knowing there are excellent arrangements for the awakening of replicas in the absence of biological kin. Ethan, for his part, does not pine to meet or learn of his biological "parent." He has a relatively untroubled awakening, and forms a warm bond to his host family. He gives the idea of "reconnecting" with his biological "parent" no more thought than we old humans would give "reconnecting" with the attending physician present at our birth.

Years go by. Though Ethan and Ed plainly resemble one another, differences in eating habits, manner, grooming, accent, and dress give them fairly distinct appearances and personas. One might meet them both at a party and not immediately conclude that they are kin. Ed prospers in his new location; Ethan takes a job involving extensive travel. One day he travels to a city that happens to be the one to which Ed moved, though Ethan is unaware of that. We find Ethan boarding the airport limousine to travel to his hotel. He's normally chatty and sociable in this sort of setting, quick to strike up a conversation with whoever happens to be next to him. As it happens, the person who sits on his left is Ed himself; on his right, an unrelated stranger. Were Ethan to enter into a conversation with either, it would be somewhat enjoyable for both parties – Ethan really is pleasant to chat with for the span of a twenty- or thirty-minute ride, even if he does dwell a bit too much on himself. Let us suppose that the un-related stranger would enjoy such a conversation a bit more than Ed, and that Ed and Ethan wouldn't recognize one another as related in any event. It remains true that if Ethan were to engage Ed in conversation, then a biological "parent" would make a connection with his offspring. He'd meet his "son," and come to learn from Ethan himself something of what has become of him in life (though not, of course, under that description). Ethan seldom gets twenty minutes into a pick-up conversation without having touched on the high points of his professional life. Ed, we will suppose, would never otherwise "reconnect" with Ethan. Indeed, were Ethan instead to have initiated a conversation with the man seated on his right, Ed would simply have taken no notice of him. Ethan's conversation with the other man would also touch on life highlights, but they'd all escape Ed – he'd soon have donned his Walkman headset and absorbed himself in an airport news-shop novel. Ed would get off at his downtown office without so much as exchanging a word or a glance with Ethan.

An actual human contemplating these two possible scenarios among new humans might find an intrinsic preference that Ethan turn and talk to Ed, his "parent," rather than the man on the right. It is better or more fitting, we might think, that his own flesh and blood make this acquaintance and hear something of the story of his life. (We will assume that, from the standpoint of morality, there is no independent issue about the permissibility of his speaking to either.) From our old-human perspective, we would deem that some measure of value would be lost if the opportunity afforded by this chance re-encounter were altogether squandered and the two men were to remain utter strangers to each other. "Too bad," we'd think.

But would this response on our part really make sense? How would we justify the view that greater value would be realized if Ethan were to speak to Ed – or that this would be a morally better outcome? Extrinsically, more good would be done if Ethan were to speak to the stranger, who would enjoy his company more. And intrinsically, no one present in the limousine – or even alive at the time – prefers giving consideration to kin connections as such. Of course, we may find that we intrinsically prefer that Ethan talk to Ed – just as, in this world, we favor kin connections even when the agents involved are indifferent. But we and our ilk will be long gone by the time Ed and Ethan are seated side by side, and no more good could come to us. Could our intrinsic preference, which has no echo in their preferences or indeed any in anyone's preferences from then onward, be a ground for some good coming about through their actions, or for a moral directive as to how they should act?[7]

If the extension of 'intrinsic value' is *rigidified* in the manner of talk of color (recall equation (2), previous), then it seems we are committed to saying that there is indeed some intrinsic good in Ethan talking to Ed rather than the stranger, a good that could in principle offset the greater enjoyment of the stranger in Ethan's company. Recall that according to the rigidified view of color, a widespread shift in the human physiology of color perception would not change the color of grass – it would remain green even though it came to look red to humans, and humans who judged it red *tout simple* would be making a mistake. If we considered intrinsic value to be likewise rigidified, then the particular change in human intrinsic preferences imagined previously would not alter the intrinsic value of relations effected among biological kin – it would mean only that humans had become insensitive to this value. When we ask ourselves what is good in relations among new humans, on this view, we always advert to what is intrinsically motivating for actual humans in actual circumstances. That is, we would have to say that even if making a connection to one's genetic kin ceased to hold any intrinsic interest for humans, and even if humans did not seem to be suffering any sort of anomie or dysfunction as a result, still, such connections would make things intrinsically better – and perhaps also morally better.

Such an assessment does not seem terribly plausible. John Stuart Mill offers a famous (notorious?) principle that might help explain why:

(M) ... the sole evidence it is possible to produce that anything is desirable is that people do actually desire it.[8]

Mill's 'actually,' I would suggest, is not the rigidifying 'actually' – it can be replaced by a contextual 'in fact.' Indeed, he goes on to write:

If the end which the utilitarian doctrine proposes to itself were not, in theory and in practice, acknowledged to be an end, nothing could ever convince any person that it was so.[9]

Now once there are no more old humans, there is no longer anyone who is – in theory or in practice – intrinsically interested in kin relationships. So, just as it would not advance my good in the present to satisfy a desire I once had but have long since lost – to use an example of Richard Brandt's, a childhood desire to celebrate each and every birthday for the rest of my life with a ride on the Gravity Monster roller-coaster[10] – it would not advance anyone's good for kin connections to be made after intrinsic motivation in favor of such relations had disappeared from the planet.[11] And it is perhaps equally difficult to see any moral purpose advanced thereby.

III

If value – at least in the case of intrinsic, and perhaps also moral, value – is not rigidified in the manner of color, does this mean that there cannot be a useful analogy between value and secondary qualities? Perhaps not. For, as Sidney Shoemaker has argued, not all secondary quality predicates appear to be rigidified, either.

Consider Jonathan Bennett's example of phenol-thio-uria, which

tastes bitter to three-quarters of the population and is tasteless to the rest. If as the result of selective breeding, or surgical tampering, it becomes tasteless to everyone, I say it has become tasteless. And if more drastic surgical tampering makes it taste sweet to everyone, I say it has become sweet.[12]

138

Shoemaker's remark may not apply to the whole range of gustatory terms, but his intuition does seem quite plausible for 'sweet' and 'bitter.' And these terms, one might think, are very much closer to "Pleasing/not pleasing to the tongue" than 'red' or 'green' is to "pleasing/not pleasing to the eye."[13] That might help us to understand their lack of rigidification. Shoemaker writes:

> Our dominant interest in classifying things by flavor is our interest in having certain taste experiences and avoiding others, and not our interest in what such experiences tell us about other matters. With color it is the other way around. . . .[14]

It seems to me plausible that our vocabulary of intrinsic value is likewise primarily geared to the task of asking what to seek and what to avoid, depending upon whether it would be (in some sense) a positive or negative thing intrinsically to lead a given life.[15] It is, then, unsurprising that the domain of what is intrinsically good for humans is not rigidly fixed by actual human responses, but reflects instead potentially evolving or changing human responses.

Does this make judgments of intrinsic good relativistic? Not if that means something like "observer dependent." What matters is not who is making the judgment, but *of whom* the judgment is being made, which can be constant across differences in observers. It would be better to say that intrinsic good is *relational* – what is intrinsically good for an individual *I* of kind *K* depends upon the nature of *I* and *K*. Likewise, one might say, for sweetness. Phenol-thio-uria is "relationally sweet" – whether it is, for *x*, sweet does not depend upon the identity or nature of the person asking this question, but upon the identity and nature of *x*.[16]

Would this mean that there is no answer to the question "Is sugar sweet?", when asked not of some particular person but simply in general? No more than there is no answer to the question "Is Michael Jordan tall?" Sugar is sweet because it is a physiological *match* for the sweetness-sensing capacities of almost everyone; Michael Jordan is tall because he is taller than the vast majority of humans. Ordinary contexts assume ordinary comparison classes. But there are special contexts. We might be comparing Michael Jordan to other high-scoring greats in the history of basketball (among whom he is not particularly tall), and we might be talking about sugar and the gustatory propensities of those with damaged nerves in the tongue. "Sugar isn't *always* sweet," a researcher might tell us.[17]

The image of sugar as a match for normal human sweetness-sensing capacities can now be deployed in describing the fictive example of the old versus new human ways of life and reproduction. There is, we have assumed, a match between the realization of special connections with genetic kin and something in the intrinsic motivational structure of old, that is, actual, humans. Actual humans exhibit a fascination with ancestry and a commitment to progeny that go well beyond evident gains in other sorts of value. There would, however, be no corresponding match between the realization of such special connections and the intrinsic motivational structure of new humans. Genetic relatedness would persist, but no corresponding intrinsic motivation. It would therefore be quite unclear how realizing such special connections could be "more fitting" in a world exclusively populated by new humans, or how it could make their lives (or anyone's life) intrinsically better or more worthwhile.

IV

Hume argued that justice is an "artificial virtue," arising from conditions of moderate scarcity and confined sympathy. It depends, on his view, upon a contingent mutuality of interests, "education," and "human conventions."[18]

"Artifice" here is not the same thing as arbitrariness, he emphasizes, since the interests justice serves are of central importance to us as things now stand. Still, were scarcity much less, or generalized human sympathies much greater, then we would find no vice at all in the behavior of a hungry child who takes an apple – which otherwise would remain unpicked, fall to the ground, and rot – from a tree on the vast estate of a distant lord. Indeed, the very notion of an "estate" would seem to us without moral standing. Hume contrasts the artifice of justice and property with "natural virtue," such as special concern for one's genetic kin:

> In like manner we always consider the *natural* and *usual* force of the passions, when we determine concerning vice and virtue.... A man naturally loves his children better than his nephews, his nephews better than his cousins, his cousins better than strangers, where everything else is equal. Hence arise our common measures of duty, in preferring the one to the other. Our sense of duty always follows the common and natural course of our passions.[19]

But what if these "natural" passions themselves depend upon certain patterns of reproduction and child rearing? Evolution may well predispose us to form special attachments to those who raise us and whom we raise,[20] but new humans would not undergo the usual developmental period of prolonged infancy and they might frequently be "raised" primarily by biologically unrelated individuals. Special love of nephews and a preference for nephews over cousins may have seemed perfectly natural and virtuous in eighteenth-century Scotland, but may come to seem more of a social artifact even from the perspective of the highly mobile society of the United States in the twentieth century, where these "natural duties" and their distinctive emphases in concern seem attenuated.[21] The seeming intelligibility of the example of new humans, however, suggests that "human nature" could persist without this particular intrinsic motivator. New humans might lack altogether our current genetic preoccupations and base their recognizably human sympathies instead upon other forms of mutual interest and personal loyalty familiar to us. These concerns would occur "naturally" to them, and would help form the foundation for their individual and social flourishing. If taking up the moral point of view involves (at least) nonpartial, intrinsic concern for the well-being of those affected, it would seem untenable for us to insist that new humans would exhibit a moral deficiency in showing greater loyalty and devotion to friends, lovers, colleagues, and to their "hosts" and replicas they have "awakened" – those, in sum, with whom they share formative experiences – rather than those with whom they share DNA.

Moral thought is sometimes labeled *projective*, and there are disputes about the aptness of this characterization and about whether the label is in some way pejorative. Moral thought *would*, I think, be projective in a pejorative sense if by its very nature it committed us to referring moral judgments about a world of new humans and their norms to the responses of actual humans in actual circumstances. Before we project norms garnering the approbation of actual humans onto relations among non-actual humans we must ask whether the sorts of lives from which we and they derive meaning and intrinsic value are the same. In posing this question we need not appeal to a utilitarian principle as such. Rather, a much more general principle is at stake, one which (for example) Rawls has used to criticize utilitarianism: "the correct regulative principle for anything depends on the nature of that thing."[22]

V

Rigidification, then, seems to this extent inappropriate as a way of capturing the objectivity of moral assessment. In asking whether new humans would still bathe in water we may wish to keep the extension of water rigidly fixed by actual human usage and actual circumstances. In asking whether ripe bananas would still be yellow in the new-human world we may wish to rigidify on our actual color responses. But in asking whether it would be intrinsically or morally good for new humans to give special weight to kin connections we may not want the reference of 'intrinsically good' or 'morally good' to be fixed by what elicits the positive responses of actual humans in actual circumstances.[23]

Does giving up on this sort of rigidification lead to the moral relativism Blackburn decried? That would appear unacceptable. David Wiggins begins his own discussion of a rigidified subjectivism by invoking a remark of Bertrand Russell's:

I cannot see how to refute the arguments for the subjectivity of ethical values, but I find myself incapable of believing that all that is wrong with wanton cruelty is that I don't like it.[24]

Rigidified subjectivism – along the lines of equation (3), previous – does indeed yield the result that even if humans were to undergo some change that would make them approve wanton cruelty, this would not make it morally good. It is the moral approvals and disapprovals of actual humans – including their disapproval of wanton cruelty – that would fix the extension of 'morally good.'

In rejecting equation (3), it may seem that we have lost the capacity to respond to Russell's concern, or to accommodate Blackburn's telling intuition about the treatment of animals.[25] What if, for example, the new humans not only had decidedly different attitudes toward parent/child relations, but also no longer disapproved of wanton cruelty toward animals? Would such conduct thus become morally unobjectionable?

Relationalism about intrinsic value, along with the (relatively uncontroversial) view that moral evaluation is non-partial, has no such implication. Pain, we believe, is intrinsically bad for whoever – or whatever – experiences it. Wanton cruelty toward animals involves the unrestrained infliction of pain upon them without any commensurate benefit to their well-being, a condition that would not be changed if we were to change *our* attitude toward its permissibility. Human approbation of its torment would not in the least improve the experience of a dog being kicked or a horse being whipped. Russell is certainly correct in saying that what is wrong with wanton cruelty is not that we dislike it. Rather, it is the intrinsically unliked character of the torment such conduct would cause its recipients – a torment which is unaffected by our attitude – that makes the behavior wrong.

This is an alternative explanation of the "objectivity" – in the sense of "independence from our particular attitudes" – of our judgments about wanton cruelty or maltreating animals, an explanation that does not

142

involve either non-relational intrinsic value (it is enough if pain is a harm to the beings experiencing it) or rigidification of our moral response to kickings and whippings.

Is this a sufficient explanation of Russell's and Blackburn's observations about objectivity? How far can we appeal to such notions to capture other forms of objectivity in moral judgment? Might there be some higher-order level of evaluative or normative language at which rigidity re-emerges? These questions take us beyond the scope of the present paper.

## VI

The question whether intrinsic value or moral value is analogous to secondary qualities is overly broad. One might do better to ask: analogous to *which* secondary qualities and in *what* respects? Color has been the natural stand-in for 'secondary quality' in most philosophical discussions of the analogy, reflecting perhaps the predominance of vision in human sensory life. But perhaps taste – or rather, the gustatory vocabulary of bitterness and sweetness – is a more plausible candidate. To be sure, value talk is full of visual imagery, but perceptual models of value judgment are only partly convincing, and even there gustatory imagery is also common – one is, I suppose, about as likely to say that one "savors" value as that one "sees" it. But even this is too hasty. 'Intrinsic' value is indeed rather like 'sweet' and 'bitter' – and unlike 'red' and 'green' – in its relational, functional character and its relation to guiding choice toward the desirable and away from the undesirable. But moral value has a more complex character, which in certain cases leads it to mimic the rigidification of color. Intuitively, Shoemaker notes, we use color terms to assemble information about the world around us for input into deliberation, not to steer choice more directly. Thus, changing human color reception would not change colors. We would not want people to *misread* the change in the appearance of grass as a change in its physical constitution and environment. Similarly, changing human sensibilities toward animals would not change the moral badness of wanton cruelty toward them. We would not want people to misread the change in their own attitudes as a change in what happens to the beasts themselves. Thus color and moral value seem to run in parallel.

The parallel breaks down on the moral side, however, once we consider cases in which the sensibilities that change are those partially *constitutive* of a moral good, such as special concern for genetic kin. If these change, then what was held to be morally better – for example, a special connection

143

with kin – can become morally indifferent. The point here is that sub-jectivity can enter in various ways into the making and perceiving of value, some of which may have no parallel at all with the involvement of subjectivity in secondary qualities.

In thinking about value it is altogether too easy to project, conflat-ing the familiar and conventional with the natural and inevitable. One could write a pocket history of progress in moral sensibility in terms of the successive unmasking of such conflations – with respect to slavery, inherited rule, the status of women, and the borders of tribe, 'people,' or nation. Objectivity about intrinsic and moral good alike calls for us to gain critical perspective on our own actual responses, not to project their objects rigidly.

NOTES

*European Review of Philosophy*, Roberto Casati and Christine Tappolet, eds., 3: *Response-Dependence* (Stanford: CSLI Publications, 1998), 67–84.

* I am grateful to Alex Byrne, Jonathan Dancy, James Griffin, Alex Miller, James Pryor, Robert Stalnaker, and Stephen Yablo, among others, for helpful discussion. They are plainly not responsible for whatever confusions remain.

1. To say that moral value "purportedly" is not relativistic is to say that moral relativism is viewed by most as a strongly *revisionary* thesis in ethics.

2. Simon Blackburn, "Errors and the Phenomenology of Value," in Ted Honderich, ed., *Morality and Objectivity: A Tribute to J.L. Mackie* (London: Routledge and Kegan Paul, 1985) 14. Blackburn here speaks of moral permissibility, which is not itself a value term in the strict sense. Some slippage will be needed between deontic and evaluative categories if we are to weave together the words of various discussants into a single debate. I do not believe, however, that the point Blackburn wishes to make turns on whether we see him as speaking of moral permissibility or moral goodness.

3. Sidney Shoemaker, "Self-Knowledge and 'Inner Sense'," *Philosophy and Phenomeno-logical Research* 54 (1994), 249–314, 302.

4. See for example Mark Johnston, "Dispositional Theories of Value," *Proceedings of the Aristotelian Society*, suppl. vol. 63 (1989), 139–74, esp. 140–1. The orig-inal inspiration for this rigidification is found in Martin Davies and Lloyd Humberstone, "Two Notions of Necessity," *Philosophical Studies* 38 (1980), 1–30, esp. 22–5.

5. Blackburn lists five other "significant differences between secondary properties and those involved in value and obligation." See his "Errors and the Phenomenology of Value," 13–15.

6. Though equation (3) is consilient with Blackburn's intuition, it faces an immediate difficulty: the gap between any actual human response, even if normal and even if the response has the phenomenology of moral approbation, and any genuinely *normative* conclusion. It would appear that (3) – which presumably would be deemed *a priori* true – enables us to bridge the fact/value gap effortlessly.

What if, for example, actual human approbation settles upon a certain kind of act or practice owing in part to a *factual misunderstanding* on our part of its nature or consequences? One remedy might be to shift (3) into an idealized, subjunctive form: what actual humans *would* morally approve were they fully informed, vividly aware, and so on.

Yet there remains a logical gap (it seems) between idealized moral approbation (a psychological phenomenon) and moral goodness (which has normative purport).

Many advocates of the analogy between color and moral value therefore have insisted that (4), rather than (3), is the proper *a priori* equation:

(4) $x$ is morally good $= x$ is such as to *make appropriate* in normal humans as they actually are (and in actual normal circumstances) a sentiment of moral approbation.

Equation (4) preserves the rigidification that allowed (3) to escape relativism arising from changes in moral attitudes, but it is normative on both right- and left-hand side, and so bridges no fact/value gap.

This certainly removes one obstacle to the acceptance of (4) as an account of moral value. But the manifest disparity between our revised equation for color, (2), with its causal talk of eliciting a response, and our revised equation for moral value, (4), with its overtly normative talk of making a response appropriate, has disenchanted some philosophers with the claim that the analogy with color runs deep.

In what follows, I will attempt to take the analogy to color more nearly at face value, and thus will rely upon formulation (3).

7. This concern does not depend upon any premise to the effect that a person's good can only be advanced by something that makes a difference to the course of her experience. At least insofar as intrinsic preferences are concerned, reflection on examples involving experience machines, systematic deception, and the like may convince us that we have robust intrinsic preferences concerning the course of our *lives* that are not necessarily reflected in differences in our *experiences*.

8. J.S. Mill, "Utilitarianism," ch. 5; 288 as reprinted in Mary Warnock, ed., *John Stuart Mill: Utilitarianism [and other essays]* (New York: New American Library, 1962). Mill's point is about the *epistemology* of value judgments. But when I make a value judgment about the good of "new humans," can I do otherwise than rely upon my own, "old human" feelings with respect to the counterfactual case of being a "new human"? What else would explain the intuitive normative force *for me* of an example involving the desires of people different from myself? So don't actual human motivations determine my value judgments after all? Even if this were so, it would be of no particular use to the secondary-quality theorist who would defend the analogy with color. For this explanation of intuitive normative force is the favored account of his non-cognitivist semantic rival, according to whom value judgments are non-propositional and serve to *express* the motivational state of the speaker. Consider an actual but *atypical* human, who happens to be like the "new humans" in intrinsic motivational structure. Were she to gauge the appropriateness of her judgment concerning the good of "new humans" against *her* motivational structure rather than that of normal actual humans, she would be making a mistake, according to the color-based view – much like a color-blind person who took his own color-similarity experience as the gauge for rating the

similarity of red and brown rather than deferring to the color-similarity ratings made by the normal human population, but for which he has no "intuitive feel."

9. Ibid.
10. Richard B. Brandt, *A Theory of the Good and the Right* (Oxford: Oxford University Press, 1979) 249–50. The example has been slightly altered.
11. We are assuming that this intrinsic preference has disappeared not only from actual preferences, but even from reflective, informed preferences. It has lost its motivational ground in the human population altogether.
12. Shoemaker, "Self-Knowledge and 'Inner Sense'," 302. Shoemaker refers the reader to Jonathan Bennett's "Substance, Reality, and Primary Qualities," in C.B. Martin and D.M. Armstrong, eds., *Locke and Berkeley* (New York: Anchor Books, 1968). I am grateful to James Pryor for calling my attention to Shoemaker's claim and to Mark Crimmins for helping me to locate it.
13. My dictionary gives "Having or being of a taste that is sharp, acrid, and unpleasant" as the first definition of 'bitter'; and it gives "Pleasing to the senses, feelings, or the mind; gratifying" as the second definition of 'sweet.' Neither its definition of 'red' nor of 'green' makes any mention of such positive or negative experiential features. See *The American Heritage Dictionary of the English Language* (Boston: Houghton-Mifflin: 1979).
14. Shoemaker, "Self-Knowledge and 'Inner Sense'," 302–3.
15. We can, I think, expand Shoemaker's point to include our intrinsic concern that our lives possess certain non-experiential features as well.
16. A relational approach differs from a relativistic, indexical approach in much the same way that equation (1) (which makes explicit a relation to *normal human* responses) differs from (2) (which makes explicit an indexical *actually*). For a relativistic, indexical approach to statements of value that contrasts with the relationalism discussed here, see James Dreier, "Internalism and Speaker Relativism," *Ethics* 101 (1990), 6–26.
17. To my ear, "Sugar isn't *always* sweet" suggests initially something about changing sensation, while "Grass isn't *always* green" suggests initially something about changing grass (e.g., in the dry season). Context, of course, affects these initial readings.
18. *A Treatise of Human Nature*, bk. III, pt. II, sec. I. In the edition by L.A. Selby-Bigge (Oxford: Clarendon, 1888) 483. Hume elsewhere notes other factors, including the "ravishability" of many goods and the importance of rules.
19. *Treatise*, ibid., 483–4.
20. This might be "inclusively fit," since we cannot ordinarily identify genetic kin by observation, and since (we suppose) "those who raise us" has typically correlated well in the evolutionary past with those more closely genetically related than the human population at large.
21. Of course, an intrinsic interest in closer kin connections survives in this country even so. History affords another interesting example of a related sort of change. When political rule was personal or familial, it was typically thought appropriate for leaders to give special preference to kin. In the modern period, the rise of (in principle) impersonal forms of government has made favoritism toward family members a paradigmatic vice.

22. John Rawls, *A Theory of Justice* (Cambridge: Harvard University Press, 1971) 29. Rawls invokes this principle in arguing that utilitarianism is unacceptable because it does not take into account the separateness of persons.

23. Plainly, I do appeal to *some* principles of ours in asking how we'd assess the new human example: that morality is impartial and concerned with (perhaps among other things) the goodness of lives, that satisfying someone's intrinsic, reflective desires is *prima facie* a contribution to the goodness of her life, or that the proper regulative principle for a thing regulates in accord with the nature of that thing. These principles are, however, (something like) necessary or constitutive truths of the moral or evaluative domain rather than substantive moral or evaluative judgments. Holding these constant as we consider which more substantive judgments would be made concerning acts or persons in another world is thus akin to holding constant our notions of color or taste or water when asking what color grass has, or whether phenol-thio-uria is sweet, or whether XYZ is water, in another world.

24. Quoted in Wiggins' essay "A Sensible Subjectivism?", in his *Needs, Values, Truth* (Oxford: Blackwell, 1987) 185. Once again, we need to slide between the vocabulary of "ethical values" and the vocabulary of rightness and wrongness. I take it, however, that Russell's point could equally be expressed as: "I find myself incapable of believing that all that is morally bad about wanton cruelty is that I don't like it." To the extent that Russell has in mind *expressivism* as a subjectivist view, it can be replied that no clear-headed expressivist need regard his or her likes and dislikes as the right- and wrong-making features of the world.

25. There is at least one difficulty about both Russell's and Blackburn's examples that we will ignore here. One might argue that 'wanton cruelty' and 'maltreatment' are both *by definition prima facie* morally questionable. Substantive moral theory is not needed to show that we could not, by any possible change in attitude, make such conduct right – a dictionary would suffice. We must imagine that the examples have been stated in less tendentious language: for example, instead of 'wanton cruelty,' substitute 'the deliberate infliction of significant pain on others for the sole purpose of satisfying one's desire to do so.'

# Part II

*Normative Moral Theory*

# 6

# Alienation, Consequentialism, and the Demands of Morality*

## INTRODUCTION

Living up to the demands of morality may bring with it alienation – from one's personal commitments, from one's feelings or sentiments, from other people, or even from morality itself. In this article I will discuss several apparent instances of such alienation, and attempt a preliminary assessment of their bearing on questions about the acceptability of certain moral theories. Of special concern will be the question whether problems about alienation show consequentialist moral theories to be self-defeating.

I will not attempt a full or general characterization of alienation. Indeed, at a perfectly general level alienation can be characterized only very roughly as a kind of estrangement, distancing, or separateness (not necessarily consciously attended to) resulting in some sort of loss (not necessarily consciously noticed).[1] Rather than seek a general analysis I will rely upon examples to convey a sense of what is involved in the sorts of alienation with which I am concerned. There is nothing in a word, and the phenomena to be discussed in the following text could all be considered while avoiding the controversial term 'alienation.' My sense, however, is that there is some point in using this formidable term, if only to draw attention to commonalities among problems not always noticed. For example, in the final section of this article I will suggest that one important form of alienation in moral practice, the sense that morality confronts us as an alien set of demands, distant and disconnected from our actual concerns, can be mitigated by dealing with other sorts of alienation morality may induce. Finally, there are historical reasons, which will not be entered into here, for bringing these phenomena under a single label; part of the explanation of their existence lies in the conditions of modern "civil society," and in the philosophical traditions of empiricism and rationalism – which include a certain picture of the self's relation to the world – that have flourished in it.

Let us begin with two examples.

## i. JOHN AND ANNE AND LISA AND HELEN

To many, John has always seemed a model husband. He almost invariably shows great sensitivity to his wife's needs, and he willingly goes out of his way to meet them. He plainly feels great affection for her. When a friend remarks upon the extraordinary quality of John's concern for his wife, John responds without any self-indulgence or self-congratulation. "I've always thought that people should help each other when they're in a specially good position to do so. I know Anne better than anyone else does, so I know better what she wants and needs. Besides, I have such affection for her that it's no great burden – instead, I get a lot of satisfaction out of it. Just think how awful marriage would be, or life itself, if people didn't take special care of the ones they love." His friend accuses John of being unduly modest, but John's manner convinces him that he is telling the truth: this is really how he feels.

Lisa has gone through a series of disappointments over a short period, and has been profoundly depressed. In the end, however, with the help of others she has emerged from the long night of anxiety and melancholy. Only now is she able to talk openly with friends about her state of mind, and she turns to her oldest friend, Helen, who was a mainstay throughout. She'd like to find a way to thank Helen, since she's only too aware of how much of a burden she's been over these months, how much of a drag and a bore, as she puts it. "You don't have to thank me, Lisa," Helen replies, "you deserved it. It was the least I could do after all you've done for me. We're friends, remember? And we said a long time ago that we'd stick together no matter what. Some day I'll probably ask the same thing of you, and I know you'll come through. What else are friends for?" Lisa wonders whether Helen is saying this simply to avoid creating feelings of guilt, but Helen replies that she means every word – she couldn't bring herself to lie to Lisa if she tried.

## ii. WHAT'S MISSING?

What is troubling about the words of John and Helen? Both show stout character and moral awareness. John's remarks have a benevolent, consequentialist cast, while Helen reasons in a deontological language of duties, reciprocity, and respect. They are not self-centered or without feeling. Yet something seems wrong.

The place to look is not so much at what they say as what they don't say. Think, for example, of how John's remarks might sound to his wife. Anne might have hoped that it was, in some ultimate sense, in part for *her* sake and the sake of their love as such that John pays such special attention to her. That he devotes himself to her because of the characteristically good consequences of doing so seems to leave her, and their relationship as such, too far out of the picture – this despite the fact that these characteristically good consequences depend in important ways on his special relation to her. She is being taken into account by John, but it might seem she is justified in being hurt by the way she is being taken into account. It is as if John viewed her, their relationship, and even his own affection for her from a distant, objective point of view – a moral point of view where reasons must be reasons for any rational agent and so must have an impersonal character even when they deal with personal matters. His wife might think a more personal point of view would also be appropriate, a point of view from which "It's my wife" or "It's Anne" would have direct and special relevance, and play an unmediated role in his answer to the question "*Why* do you attend to her so?"

Something similar is missing from Helen's account of why she stood by Lisa. While we understand that the specific duties she feels toward Lisa depend upon particular features of their relationship, still we would not be surprised if Lisa finds Helen's response to her expression of gratitude quite distant, even chilling. We need not question whether she has strong feeling for Lisa, but we may wonder at how that feeling finds expression in Helen's thinking.[2]

John and Helen both show alienation: there would seem to be an estrangement between their affections and their rational, deliberative selves; an abstract and universalizing point of view mediates their responses to others and to their own sentiments. We should not assume that they have been caught in an uncharacteristic moment of moral reflection or after-the-fact rationalization; it is a settled part of their characters to think and act from a moral point of view. It is as if the world were for them a fabric of obligations and permissions in which personal considerations deserve recognition only to the extent that, and in the way that, such considerations find a place in this fabric.

To call John and Helen alienated from their affections or their intimates is not of itself to condemn them, nor is it to say that they are experiencing any sort of distress. One may be alienated from something without recognizing this as such or suffering in any conscious way from it, much as one may simply be uninterested in something without awareness or conscious suffering. But alienation is not mere lack of interest: John and Helen are not *uninterested* in their affections or in their intimates; rather, their interest takes a certain alienated form. While this alienation may not itself be a psychological affliction, it may be the basis of such afflictions – such as a sense of loneliness or emptiness – or of the loss of certain things of value – such as a sense of belonging or the pleasures of spontaneity. Moreover, their alienation may cause psychological distress in others, and make certain valuable sorts of relationships impossible.

However, we must be on guard lest oversimple categories distort our diagnosis. It seems to me wrong to picture the self as ordinarily divided into cognitive and affective halves, with deliberation and rationality belonging to the first, and sentiments belonging to the second. John's alienation is not a problem on the boundary of naturally given cognitive and affective selves, but a problem partially constituted by the bifurcation of his psyche into these separate spheres. *John's* deliberative self seems remarkably divorced from his affections, but not all psyches need be so divided. That there is a cognitive element in affection – that affection is not a mere "feeling" that is a given for the deliberative self but rather involves as well certain characteristic modes of thought and perception – is suggested by the difficulty some may have in believing that John really does love Anne if he persistently thinks about her in the way suggested by his remarks. Indeed, his affection for Anne does seem to have been demoted to a mere "feeling." For this reason among others, we should not think of John's alienation from his affections and his alienation from Anne as wholly independent phenomena, the one the cause of the other.[3] Of course, similar remarks apply to Helen.

### III. THE MORAL POINT OF VIEW

Perhaps the lives of John and Anne or Helen and Lisa would be happier or fuller if none of the alienation mentioned were present. But is this a problem for *morality*? If, as some have contended, to have a morality is to make normative judgments from a moral point of view and be guided by them, and if by its nature a moral point of view must exclude considerations that lack universality, then any genuinely moral way of going about life would seem liable to produce the sorts of alienation mentioned previously.[4] Thus it would be a conceptual confusion to ask that we never

154

be required by morality to go beyond a personal point of view, since to fail ever to look at things from an impersonal (or nonpersonal) point of view would be to fail ever to *be* distinctively moral – not immoralism, perhaps, but amoralism. This would not be to say that there are not other points of view on life worthy of our attention,[5] or that taking a moral point of view is always appropriate – one could say that John and Helen show no moral defect in thinking so impersonally, although they do moralize to excess. But the fact that a particular morality requires us to take an impersonal point of view could not sensibly be held against it, for that would be what makes it a morality at all.

This sort of position strikes me as entirely too complacent. First, we must somehow give an account of practical reasoning that does not merely multiply points of view and divide the self – a more unified account is needed. Second, we must recognize that loving relationships, friendships, group loyalties, and spontaneous actions are among the most important contributors to whatever it is that makes life worthwhile; any moral theory deserving serious consideration must itself give them serious considera-tion. As William K. Frankena has written, "Morality is made for man, not man for morality."[6] Moral considerations are often supposed to be overriding in practical reasoning. If we were to find that adopting a par-ticular morality led to irreconcilable conflict with central types of human well-being – as cases akin to John's and Helen's have led some to suspect – then this surely would give us good reason to doubt its claims.[7]

For example, in the closing sentences of *A Theory of Justice* John Rawls considers the "perspective of eternity," which is impartial across all indi-viduals and times, and writes that this is a "form of *thought and feeling* that rational persons can adopt in the world." "Purity of heart," he concludes, "would be to see clearly and act with grace and self-command from this point of view."[8] This may or may not be purity of heart, but it could not be the standpoint of actual life without radically detaching the individual from a range of personal concerns and commitments. Presumably we should not read Rawls as recommending that we adopt this point of view in the bulk of our actions in daily life, but the fact that so purely abstracted a perspective is portrayed as a kind of moral ideal should at least start us wondering.[9] If to be more perfectly moral is to ascend ever higher toward *sub specie aeternitatis* abstraction, perhaps we made a mistake in boarding the moral escalator in the first place. Some of the very "weaknesses" that prevent us from achieving this moral ideal – strong attachments to persons or projects – seem to be part of a considerably more compelling human ideal.

Should we say at this point that the lesson is that we should give a more prominent role to the value of nonalienation in our moral reasoning? That would be too little too late: the problem seems to be the way in which morality asks us to look at things, not just the things it asks us to look at.

## IV. THE "PARADOX OF HEDONISM"

Rather than enter directly into the question whether being moral is a matter of taking a moral point of view and whether there is thus some sort of necessary connection between being moral and being alienated in a way detrimental to human flourishing, I will consider a related problem the solution to which may suggest a way of steering around obstacles to a more direct approach.

One version of the so-called "paradox of hedonism" is that adopting as one's exclusive ultimate end in life the pursuit of maximum happiness may well prevent one from having certain experiences or engaging in certain sorts of relationships or commitments that are among the greatest sources of happiness.[10] The hedonist, looking around him, may discover that some of those who are less concerned with their own happiness than he is, and who view people and projects less instrumentally than he does, actually manage to live happier lives than he despite his dogged pursuit of happiness. The "paradox" is pragmatic, not logical, but it looks deep nonetheless: the hedonist, it would appear, ought not to be a hedonist. It seems, then, as if we have come across a second case in which mediating one's relations to people or projects by a particular point of view – in this case, a hedonistic point of view – may prevent one from attaining the fullest possible realization of sought-after values.

However, it is important to notice that even though adopting a hedonistic life project may tend to interfere with realizing that very project, there is no such natural exclusion between acting for the sake of another or a cause as such and recognizing how important this is to one's happiness. A spouse who acts for the sake of his mate may know full well that this is a source of deep satisfaction for him – in addition to providing him with reasons for acting internal to it, the relationship may also promote the external goal of achieving happiness. Moreover, while the pursuit of happiness may not be the reason he entered or sustains the relationship, he may also recognize that if it had not seemed likely to make him happy he would not have entered it, and that if it proved over time to be inconsistent with his happiness he would consider ending it.

156

It might be objected that one cannot really regard a person or a project as an end as such if one's commitment is in this way contingent or overridable. But were this so, we would be able to have very few commitments to ends as such. For example, one could not be committed to both one's spouse and one's child as ends as such, since at most one of these commitments could be overriding in cases of conflict. It is easy to confuse the notion of a commitment to an end *as such* (or *for its own sake*) with that of an *overriding* commitment, but strength is not the same as structure. To be committed to an end as such is a matter of (among other things) whether it furnishes one with reasons for acting that are not mediated by other concerns. It does not follow that these reasons must always outweigh whatever opposing reasons one may have, or that one may not at the same time have other, mediating reasons that also incline one to act on behalf of that end.

Actual commitments to ends as such, even when very strong, are subject to various qualifications and contingencies.[11] If a friend grows too predictable or moves off to a different part of the world, or if a planned life project proves less engaging or practical than one had imagined, commitments and affections naturally change. If a relationship were highly vulnerable to the least change, it would be strained to speak of genuine affection rather than, say, infatuation. But if members of a relationship came to believe that they would be better off without it, this ordinarily would be a nontrivial change, and it is not difficult to imagine that their commitment to the relationship might be contingent in this way but nonetheless real. Of course, a relationship involves a shared history and shared expectations as well as momentary experiences, and it is unusual that affection or concern can be changed overnight, or relationships begun or ended at will. Moreover, the sorts of affections and commitments that can play a decisive role in shaping one's life and in making possible the deeper sorts of satisfactions are not those that are easily overridden or subject to constant reassessment or second-guessing. Thus a sensible hedonist would not forever be subjecting his affections or commitments to egoistic calculation, nor would he attempt to break off a relationship or commitment merely because it might seem to him at a given moment that some other arrangement would make him happier. Commitments to others or to causes as such may be very closely linked to the self, and a hedonist who knows what he's about will not be one who turns on his self at the slightest provocation. Contingency is not expendability, and while some commitments are remarkably noncontingent – such as those of parent to child or patriot to country – it cannot be said that commitments of a more contingent sort are never genuine, or never conduce to the profounder sorts of happiness.[12]

Following these observations, we may reduce the force of the "paradox of hedonism" if we distinguish two forms of hedonism. *Subjective hedonism* is the view that one should adopt the hedonistic point of view in action, that is, that one should whenever possible attempt to determine which act seems most likely to contribute optimally to one's happiness, and behave accordingly. *Objective hedonism* is the view that one should follow that course of action that would in fact most contribute to one's happiness, even when this would involve *not* adopting the hedonistic point of view in action. An act will be called *subjectively hedonistic* if it is done from a hedonistic point of view; an act is *objectively hedonistic* if it is that act, of those available to the agent, that would most contribute to his happiness.[13] Let us call someone a *sophisticated hedonist* if he aims to lead an objectively hedonistic life (that is, the happiest life available to him in the circumstances) and yet is not committed to subjective hedonism. Thus, within the limits of what is psychologically possible, a sophisticated hedonist is prepared to eschew the hedonistic point of view whenever taking this point of view conflicts with following an objectively hedonistic course of action. The so-called paradox of hedonism shows that there will be such conflicts: certain acts or courses of action may be objectively hedonistic only if not subjectively hedonistic. When things are put this way, it seems that the sophisticated hedonist faces a problem rather than a paradox: how to act in order to achieve maximum possible happiness if this is at times – or even often – *not* a matter of carrying out hedonistic deliberations.

The answer in any particular case will be complex and contextual – it seems unlikely that any one method of decision making would always promote thought and action most conducive to one's happiness. A sophisticated hedonist might proceed precisely by looking at the complex and contextual: observing the actual modes of thought and action of those people who are in some ways like himself and who seem most happy. If our assumptions are right, he will find that few such individuals are subjective hedonists; instead, they act for the sake of a variety of ends as such. He may then set out to develop in himself the traits of character, ways of thought, types of commitment, and so on, that seem common in happy lives. For example, if he notes that the happiest people often have strong loyalties to friends, he must ask how he can become a more loyal friend – not merely how he can seem to be a loyal friend (since those he has observed are not happy because they merely seem loyal) – but how he can in fact be one.

Could one really make such changes if one had as a goal leading an optimally happy life? The answer seems to me a qualified *yes*, but let us first look at a simpler case. A highly competitive tennis player comes to realize that his obsession with winning is keeping him from playing his best. A pro tells him that if he wants to win he must devote himself more to the game and its play as such and think less about his performance. In the commitment and concentration made possible by this devotion, he is told, lies the secret of successful tennis. So he spends a good deal of time developing an enduring devotion to many aspects of the activity, and finds it peculiarly satisfying to become so absorbed in it. He plays better, and would have given up the program of change if he did not, but he now finds that he plays tennis more for its own sake, enjoying greater internal as well as external rewards from the sport. Such a person would not keep thinking – on or off the court – "No matter how I play, the only thing I really care about is whether I win!" He would recognize such thoughts as self-defeating, as evidence that his old, unhelpful way of looking at things was returning. Nor would such a person be self-deceiving. He need not hide from himself his goal of winning, for this goal is consistent with his increased devotion to the game. His commitment to the activity is not eclipsed by, but made more vivid by, his desire to succeed at it.

The same sort of story might be told about a sophisticated hedonist and friendship. An individual could realize that his instrumental attitude to-ward his friends prevents him from achieving the fullest happiness friend-ship affords. He could then attempt to focus more on his friends as such, doing this somewhat deliberately, perhaps, until it comes more naturally. He might then find his friendships improved and himself happier. If he found instead that his relationships were deteriorating or his happiness de-clining, he would reconsider the idea. None of this need be hidden from himself: the external goal of happiness reinforces the internal goals of his relationships. The sophisticated hedonist's motivational structure should therefore meet a *counterfactual condition:* he need not always act for the sake of happiness, since he may do various things for their own sake or for the sake of others, but he would not act as he does if it were not compatible with his leading an objectively hedonistic life. Of course, a sophisticated hedonist cannot guarantee that he will meet this counterfactual condition, but only attempt to meet it as fully as possible.

Success at tennis is a relatively circumscribed goal, leaving much else about one's life undefined. Maximizing one's happiness, by contrast, seems all consuming. Could commitments to other ends survive alongside it? Consider an analogy. Ned needs to make a living. More than that, he

159

needs to make as much money as he can – he has expensive tastes, a second marriage, and children reaching college age, and he does not have extensive means. He sets out to invest his money and his labor in ways he thinks will maximize return. Yet it does not follow that he acts as he does solely for the sake of earning as much as possible.[14] Although it is obviously true that he does what he does because he believes that it will maximize return, this does not preclude his doing it for other reasons as well, for example, for the sake of living well or taking care of his children. This may continue to be the case even if Ned comes to want money for its own sake, that is, if he comes to see the accumulation of wealth as intrinsically as well as extrinsically attractive.[15] Similarly, the stricture that one seek the objectively hedonistic life certainly provides one with considerable guidance, but it does not supply the whole of one's motives and goals in action.

My claim that the sophisticated hedonist can escape the paradox of hedonism was, however, qualified. It still seems possible that the happiest sorts of lives ordinarily attainable are those led by people who would reject even sophisticated hedonism, people whose character is such that if they were presented with a choice between two entire lives, one of which contains less total happiness but nonetheless realizes some other values more fully, they might well knowingly choose against maximal happiness. If this were so, it would show that a sophisticated hedonist might have reason for changing his beliefs so that he no longer accepts hedonism in any form. This still would not refute objective hedonism as an account of the (rational, prudential, or moral) *criterion* one's acts should meet, for it would be precisely in order to meet this criterion that the sophisticated hedonist would change his beliefs.[16]

## V. THE PLACE OF NON-ALIENATION AMONG HUMAN VALUES

Before discussing the applicability of what has been said about hedonism to morality, we should notice that alienation is not always a bad thing, that we may not want to overcome all forms of alienation, and that other values, which may conflict with non-alienation in particular cases, may at times have a greater claim on us. Let us look at a few such cases.

It has often been argued that a morality of duties and obligations may appropriately come into play in familial or friendly relationships when the relevant sentiments have given out, for instance, when one is exasperated with a friend, when love is tried, and so on.[17] 'Ought' implies 'can' (or, at least, 'could'), and while it may be better in human terms when we do what we ought to do at least in part out of feelings of love, friendship, or sympathy, there are times when we simply cannot muster these sentiments, and the right thing to do is to act as love or friendship or sympathy would have directed rather than refuse to perform any act done merely from a sense of duty.

But we should add a further role for unspontaneous, morally motivated action: even when love or concern is strong, it is often desirable that people achieve some distance from their sentiments or one another. A spouse may act toward his mate in a grossly overprotective way; a friend may indulge another's ultimately destructive tendencies; a parent may favor one child inordinately. Strong and immediate affection may overwhelm one's ability to see what another person actually needs or deserves. In such cases a certain distance between people or between an individual and his sentiments, and an intrusion of moral considerations into the gap thus created, may be a good thing, and part of genuine affection or commitment. The opposite view, that no such mediation is desirable as long as affection is strong, seems to me a piece of romanticism. Concern over alienation therefore ought not to take the form of a cult of "authenticity at any price."

Moreover, there will occur regular conflicts between avoiding alienation and achieving other important individual goals. One such goal is autonomy. Bernard Williams has emphasized that many of us have developed certain "ground projects" that give shape and meaning to our lives, and has drawn attention to the damage an individual may suffer if he is alienated from his ground projects by being forced to look at them as potentially overridable by moral considerations.[18] But against this it may be urged that it is crucial for autonomy that one hold one's commitments up for inspection – even one's ground projects. Our ground projects are often formed in our youth, in a particular family, class, or cultural background. It may be alienating and even disorienting to call these into question, but to fail to do so is to lose autonomy. Of course, autonomy could not sensibly require that we question all of our values and commitments at once, nor need it require us to be forever detached from what we are doing. It is quite possible to submit basic aspects of one's life to scrutiny and arrive at a set of autonomously chosen commitments that form the basis of an integrated life. Indeed, psychological conflicts and practical obstacles give us occasion for reexamining our basic commitments rather more often than we'd like.

At the same time, the tension between autonomy and non-alienation should not be exaggerated. Part of avoiding exaggeration is giving up the

Kantian notion that autonomy is a matter of escaping determination by any contingency whatsoever. Part, too, is refusing to conflate autonomy with sheer independence from others. Both Rousseau and Marx emphasized that achieving control over one's own life requires participation in certain sorts of social relations – in fact, relations in which various kinds of alienation have been minimized.

Autonomy is but one value that may enter into complex trade-offs with non-alienation. Alienation and inauthenticity do have their uses. The alienation of some individuals or groups from their milieu may at times be necessary for fundamental social criticism or cultural innovation. And without some degree of inauthenticity, it is doubtful whether civil relations among people could long be maintained. It would take little ingenuity, but too much of the reader's patience, to construct here examples involving troubling conflicts between non-alienation and virtually any other worthy goal.

## vi. REDUCING ALIENATION IN MORALITY

Let us now move to morality proper. To do this with any definiteness, we must have a particular morality in mind. For various reasons, I think that the most plausible sort of morality is consequentialist in form, assessing rightness in terms of contribution to the good. In attempting to sketch how we might reduce alienation in moral theory and practice, therefore, I will work within a consequentialist framework (although a number of the arguments I will make could be made, *mutatis mutandis*, by a deontologist).

Of course, one has adopted no morality in particular even in adopting consequentialism unless one says what the good is. Let us, then, dwell briefly on axiology. One mistake of dominant consequentialist theories, I believe, is their failure to see that things other than subjective states can have intrinsic value. Allied to this is a tendency to reduce all intrinsic values to one – happiness. Both of these features of classical utilitarianism reflect forms of alienation. First, in divorcing subjective states from their objective counterparts, and claiming that we seek the latter exclusively for the sake of the former, utilitarianism cuts us off from the world in a way made graphic by examples such as that of the experience machine, a hypothetical device that can be programmed to provide one with whatever subjective states he may desire. The experience machine affords us decisive subjective advantages over actual life: few, if any, in actual life think they have achieved all that they could want, but the machines makes possible for each an existence that he cannot distinguish from such a happy state of affairs.[19] Despite this striking advantage, most rebel at the notion of the experience machine. As Robert Nozick and others have pointed out, it seems to matter to us what we actually *do* and *are* as well as how life *appears* to us.[20] We see the point of our lives as bound up with the world and other people in ways not captured by subjectivism, and our sense of loss in contemplating a life tied to an experience machine, quite literally alienated from the surrounding world, suggests where subjectivism has gone astray. Second, the reduction of all goals to the purely abstract goal of happiness or pleasure, as in hedonistic utilitarianism, treats all other goals instrumentally. Knowledge or friendship may promote happiness, but is it a fair characterization of our commitment to these goals to say that this is the only sense in which they are ultimately valuable? Doesn't the insistence that there is an abstract and uniform goal lying behind all of our ends bespeak an alienation from these particular ends?

Rather than pursue these questions further here, let me suggest an approach to the good that seems to me less hopeless as a way of capturing human value: a pluralistic approach in which several goods are viewed as intrinsically, non-morally valuable – such as happiness, knowledge, purposeful activity, autonomy, solidarity, respect, and beauty.[21] These goods need not be ranked lexically, but may be attributed weights, and the criterion of rightness for an act would be that it must contribute to the weighted sum of these values in the long run. This creates the possibility of trade-offs among values of the kinds discussed in the previous section. However, I will not stop here to develop or defend such an account of the good and the right, since our task is to show how certain problems of alienation that arise in moral contexts might be dealt with if morality is assumed to have such a basis.

Consider, then, Juan, who, like John, has always seemed a model husband. When a friend remarks on the extraordinary concern he shows for his wife, Juan characteristically responds: "I love Linda. I even *like* her. So it means a lot to me to do things for her. After all we've been through, it's almost a part of me to do it." But his friend knows that Juan is a principled individual, and asks Juan how his marriage fits into that larger scheme. After all, he asks, it's fine for Juan and his wife to have such a close relationship, but what about all the other, needier people Juan could help if he broadened his horizon still further? Juan replies, "Look, it's a better world when people can have a relationship like ours – and nobody could if everyone were always asking themselves who's got the most need. It's not easy to make things work in this world, and one of the best things that happens to people is to have a close relationship like ours. You'd make things worse in a hurry if you broke up those close relationships for the sake of some higher goal. Anyhow, I know that you can't always put family first. The world isn't such a wonderful place that it's okay just to retreat into your own little circle. But still, you need that little circle. People get burned out, or lose touch, if they try to save the world by themselves. The ones who can stick with it and do a good job of making things better are usually the ones who can make that fit into a life that does not make them miserable. I haven't met any real saints lately, and I don't trust people who think they *are* saints."

If we contrast Juan with John, we do not find that the one allows moral considerations to enter his personal life while the other does not. Nor do we find that one is less serious in his moral concern. Rather, what Juan recognizes to be morally required is not by its nature incompatible with acting directly for the sake of another. It is important to Juan to subject his life to moral scrutiny – he is not merely stumped when asked for a defense of his acts above a personal level, he does not *just* say "Of course I take care of her, she's my wife!" or "It's Linda" and refuse to listen to the more impersonal considerations raised by his friend. It is consistent with what he says to imagine that his motivational structure has a form akin to that of the sophisticated hedonist, that is, his motivational structure meets a counterfactual condition: while he ordinarily does not do what he does simply for the sake of doing what's right, he would seek to lead a different sort of life if he did not think his were morally defensible. His love is not a romantic submersion in the other to the exclusion of worldly responsibilities, and to that extent it may be said to involve a degree of alienation from Linda. But this does not seem to drain human value from their relationship. Nor need one imagine that Linda would be saddened to hear Juan's words the way Anne might have been saddened to overhear the remarks of John.[22]

Moreover, because of his very willingness to question his life morally, Juan avoids a sort of alienation not sufficiently discussed – alienation from others, beyond one's intimate ties. Individuals who will not or cannot allow questions to arise about what they are doing from a broader per- spective are in an important way cut off from their society and the larger world. They may not be troubled by this in any very direct way, but even so they may fail to experience that powerful sense of purpose and mean- ing that comes from seeing oneself as part of something larger and more enduring than oneself or one's intimate circle. The search for such a sense of purpose and meaning seems to me ubiquitous – surely much of the impulse to religion, to ethnic or regional identification (most strikingly, in the "rediscovery" of such identities), or to institutional loyalty stems from this desire to see ourselves as part of a more general, lasting, and worthwhile scheme of things.[23] This presumably is part of what is meant by saying that secularization has led to a sense of meaninglessness, or that the decline of traditional communities and societies has meant an increase in anomie. (The sophisticated hedonist, too, should take note: one way to gain a firmer sense that one's life is worthwhile, a sense that may be important to realizing various values in one's own life, is to overcome alienation from others.)

Drawing upon our previous discussion of two kinds of hedonism, let us now distinguish two kinds of consequentialism. *Subjective consequentialism* is the view that whenever one faces a choice of actions, one should attempt to determine which act of those available would most promote the good, and should then try to act accordingly. One is behaving as subjective consequentialism requires – that is, leading a *subjectively consequentialist life* – to the extent that one uses and follows a distinctively consequentialist mode of decision making, consciously aiming at the overall good and conscientiously using the best available information with the greatest possible rigor. *Objective consequentialism* is the view that the criterion of the rightness of an act or course of action is whether it in fact would most promote the good of those acts available to the agent. Subjective consequentialism, like subjective hedonism, is a view that prescribes following a particular mode of deliberation in action; objective consequentialism, like objective hedonism, concerns the outcomes actually brought about, and thus deals with the question of deliberation only in terms of the tendencies of certain forms of decision making to promote appropriate outcomes. Let us reserve the expression *objectively consequentialist act* (*or life*) for those acts (or that life) of those available to the agent that would bring about the best outcomes.[24] To complete the parallel, let us say that a *sophisticated consequentialist* is someone who has a standing commitment to leading an objectively consequentialist life, but who need not set special stock in any particular form of decision making and therefore does not necessarily seek to lead a subjectively consequentialist life. Juan, it might be argued (if the details were filled in), is a sophisticated consequentialist, since he seems to believe he should act for the best but does not seem to feel it appropriate to bring a consequentialist calculus to bear on his every act.

Is it bizarre, or contradictory, that being a sophisticated consequentialist may involve rejecting subjective consequentialism? After all, doesn't an adherent of subjective consequentialism also seek to lead an objectively consequentialist life? He may, but then he is mistaken in thinking that this means he should always undertake a distinctively consequentialist deliberation when faced with a choice. To see his mistake, we need only consider some examples.

It is well known that in certain emergencies, the best outcome requires action so swift as to preclude consequentialist deliberation. Thus a sophisticated consequentialist has reason to inculcate in himself certain dispositions to act rapidly in obvious emergencies. The disposition is not a mere reflex, but a developed pattern of action deliberately acquired. A simple example, but it should dispel the air of paradox.

Many decisions are too insignificant to warrant consequentialist deliberation ("Which shoelace should I do up first?") or too predictable in outcome ("Should I meet my morning class today as scheduled or should I linger over the newspaper?"). A famous old conundrum for consequentialism falls into a similar category: before I deliberate about an act, it seems I must decide how much time would be optimal to allocate for this deliberation; but then I must first decide how much time would be optimal to allocate for this time-allocation decision; but before that I must decide how much time would be optimal to allocate for *that* decision; and so on. The sophisticated consequentialist can block this paralyzing regress by noting that often the best thing to do is not to ask questions about time allocation at all; instead, he may develop standing dispositions to give more or less time to decisions depending upon their perceived importance, the amount of information available, the predictability of his choice, and so on. I think we all have dispositions of this sort, which account for our patience with some prolonged deliberations but not others.

There are somewhat more intriguing examples that have more to do with psychological interference than mere time efficiency: the timid, put-upon employee who knows that if he deliberates about whether to ask for a raise he will succumb to his timidity and fail to demand what he actually deserves; the self-conscious man who knows that if, at social gatherings, he is forever wondering how he should act, his behavior will be awkward and unnatural, contrary to his goal of acting naturally and appropriately; the tightrope walker who knows he must not reflect on the value of keeping his concentration; and so on. People can learn to avoid certain characteristically self-defeating lines of thought – just as the tennis player in a previous example learned to avoid thinking constantly about winning – and the sophisticated consequentialist may learn that consequentialist deliberation is in a variety of cases self-defeating, so that other habits of thought should be cultivated.

The sophisticated consequentialist need not be deceiving himself or acting in bad faith when he avoids consequentialist reasoning. He can fully recognize that he is developing the dispositions he does because they are necessary for promoting the good. Of course, he cannot be preoccupied with this fact all the while, but then one cannot be *preoccupied* with anything without this interfering with normal or appropriate patterns of thought and action.

To the list of cases of interference we may add John, whose all-purpose willingness to look at things by subjective consequentialist lights prevents the realization in him and in his relationships with others of values that he would recognize to be crucially important.

Bernard Williams has said that it shows consequentialism to be in grave trouble that it may have to usher itself from the scene as a mode of decision making in a number of important areas of life.[25] Though I think he has exaggerated the extent to which we would have to exclude consequentialist considerations from our lives in order to avoid disastrous results, it is fair to ask: If maximizing the good were in fact to require that consequentialist reasoning be *wholly* excluded, would this refute consequentialism? Imagine an all-knowing demon who controls the fate of the world and who visits unspeakable punishment upon man to the extent that he does not employ a Kantian morality. (Obviously, the demon is not himself a Kantian.) If such a demon existed, sophisticated consequentialists would have reason to convert to Kantianism, perhaps even to make whatever provisions could be made to erase consequentialism from the human memory and prevent any resurgence of it.

Does this possibility show that objective consequentialism is self-defeating? On the contrary, it shows that objective consequentialism has the virtue of not blurring the distinction between the *truth-conditions* of an ethical theory and its *acceptance-conditions* in particular contexts, a distinction philosophers have generally recognized for theories concerning other subject matters. It might be objected that, unlike other theories, ethical theories must meet a condition of publicity, roughly to the effect that it must be possible under all circumstances for us to recognize a true ethical theory as such and to promulgate it publicly without thereby violating that theory itself.[26] Such a condition might be thought to follow from the social nature of morality. But any such condition would be question begging against consequentialist theories, since it would require that one class of actions – acts of adopting or promulgating an ethical theory – *not* be assessed in terms of their consequences. Moreover, I fail to see how such a condition could emanate from the social character of morality. To prescribe the adoption and promulgation of a mode of decision making regardless of its consequences seems to me radically detached from human concerns, social or otherwise. If it is argued that an ethical theory that fails to meet the publicity requirement could under certain conditions endorse a course of action leading to the abuse and manipulation of man by man, we need only reflect that no psychologically possible decision procedure can guarantee that its widespread adoption could never have such a result. A "consequentialist demon" might increase the amount of abuse and manipulation in the world in direct proportion to the extent that people act according to the categorical imperative. Objective consequentialism (unlike certain deontological theories) has valuable flexibility in permitting us to take consequences into account in assessing the appropriateness of certain modes of decision making, thereby avoiding any sort of self-defeating decision procedure worship.

A further objection is that the lack of any direct link between objective consequentialism and a particular mode of decision making leaves the view too vague to provide adequate guidance in practice. On the contrary, objective consequentialism sets a definite and distinctive criterion of right action, and it becomes an empirical question (though not an easy one) which modes of decision making should be employed and when. It would be a mistake for an objective consequentialist to attempt to tighten the connection between his criterion of rightness and any particular mode of decision making: someone who recommended a particular mode of decision making regardless of consequences would not be a hard-nosed, non-evasive objective consequentialist, but a self-contradicting one.

VII. CONTRASTING APPROACHES

The seeming "indirectness" of objective consequentialism may invite its confusion with familiar indirect consequentialist theories, such as rule-consequentialism. In fact, the subjective/objective distinction cuts across the rule/act distinction, and there are subjective and objective forms of both rule- and act-based theories. Thus far, we have dealt only with subjective and objective forms of act-consequentialism. By contrast, a *subjective rule*-consequentialist holds (roughly) that in deliberation we should always attempt to determine which act, of those available, conforms to that set of rules general acceptance of which would most promote the good; we then should attempt to perform this act. An *objective rule*-consequentialist sets actual conformity to the rules with the highest acceptance value as his criterion of right action, recognizing the possibility that the best set of rules might in some cases – or even always – recommend that one not perform rule-consequentialist deliberation.

Because I believe this last possibility must be taken seriously, I find the objective form of rule-consequentialism more plausible. Ultimately, however, I suspect that rule-consequentialism is untenable in either form, for it could recommend acts that (subjectively or objectively) accord with the best set of rules even when these rules are *not* in fact generally accepted, and when as a result these acts would have devastatingly bad consequences. "Let the rules with greatest acceptance utility be followed, though the heavens fall!" is no more plausible than *"Fiat justitia, ruat coelum!"* – and a good bit less ringing. Hence, the arguments in this article are based entirely upon act-consequentialism.

Indeed, once the subjective/objective distinction has been drawn, an act-consequentialist can capture some of the intuitions that have made rule- or trait-consequentialism appealing.[27] Surely part of the attraction of these indirect consequentialisms to the idea that one should have certain traits of character, or commitments to persons or principles, that are sturdy enough that one would at least sometimes refuse to forsake them even when this refusal is known to conflict with making some gain – perhaps small – in total utility. Unlike his subjective counterpart, the objective act-consequentialist is able to endorse characters and commitments that are sturdy in just this sense.

To see why, let us first return briefly to one of the simple examples of Section VI. A sophisticated act-consequentialist may recognize that if he were to develop a standing disposition to render prompt assistance in emergencies without going through elaborate act-consequentialist deliberation, there would almost certainly be cases in which he would perform acts worse than those he would have performed had he stopped to deliberate, for example, when his prompt action is misguided in a way he would have noticed had he thought the matter through. It may still be right for him to develop this disposition, for without it he would act rightly in emergencies still less often – a quick response is appropriate much more often than not, and it is not practically possible to develop a disposition that would lead one to respond promptly in exactly those cases where this would have the best results. While one can attempt to cultivate dispositions that are responsive to various factors that might indicate whether promptness is of greater importance than further thought, such refinements have their own costs and, given the limits of human resources, even the best cultivated dispositions will sometimes lead one astray. The objective act-consequentialist would thus recommend cultivating dispositions that will sometimes lead him to violate his own criterion of right action. Still, he will not, as a trait-consequentialist would, shift his criterion and say that an act is right if it stems from the traits it would be best overall to have (given the limits of what is humanly achievable, the balance of costs and benefits, and so on). Instead, he continues to believe that an act may stem from the dispositions it would be best to have, and yet be wrong (because it would produce worse consequences than other acts available to the agent in the circumstances).[28]

This line of argument can be extended to patterns of motivation, traits of character, and rules. A sophisticated act-consequentialist should realize that certain goods are reliably attainable – or attainable at all – only if people have well-developed characters; that the human psyche is capable of only so much self-regulation and refinement; and that human perception and reasoning are liable to a host of biases and errors. Therefore, individuals may be more likely to act rightly if they possess certain enduring motivational patterns, character traits, or *prima facie* commitments to rules in addition to whatever commitment they have to act for the best. Because such individuals would not consider consequences in all cases, they would miss a number of opportunities to maximize the good; but if they were instead always to attempt to assess outcomes, the overall result would be worse, for they would act correctly less often.[29]

We may now strengthen the argument to show that the objective act-consequentialist can approve of dispositions, characters, or commitments to rules that are sturdy in the sense previously mentioned, that is, that do not merely supplement a commitment to act for the best, but sometimes override it, so that one knowingly does what is contrary to maximizing the good. Consider again Juan and Linda, whom we imagine to have a commuting marriage. They normally get together only every other week, but one week she seems a bit depressed and harried, and so he decides to take an extra trip in order to be with her. If he did not travel, he would save a fairly large sum that he could send Oxfam to dig a well in a drought-stricken village. Even reckoning in Linda's uninterrupted malaise, Juan's guilt, and any ill effects on their relationship, it may be that for Juan to contribute the fare to Oxfam would produce better consequences overall than the unscheduled trip. Let us suppose that Juan knows this, and that he could stay home and write the check if he tried. Still, given Juan's character, he in fact will not try to perform this more beneficial act but will travel to see Linda instead. The objective act-consequentialist will say that Juan performed the wrong act on this occasion. Yet he may also say that if Juan had had a character that would have led him to perform the better

170

act (or made him more inclined to do so), he would have had to have been less devoted to Linda. Given the ways Juan can affect the world, it may be that if he were less devoted to Linda his overall contribution to human well-being would be less in the end, perhaps because he would become more cynical and self-centered. Thus it may be that Juan should have (should develop, encourage, and so on) a character such that he sometimes knowingly and deliberately acts contrary to his objective consequentialist duty. Any other character, of those actually available to him, would lead him to depart still further from an objectively consequentialist life. The issue is not whether staying home would *change* Juan's character – for we may suppose that it would not – but whether he would in fact decide to stay home if he had that character, of those available, that would lead him to perform the most beneficial overall sequence of acts. In some cases, then, there will exist an objective act-consequentialist argument for developing and sustaining characters of a kind Sidgwick and others have thought an act-consequentialist must condemn.[30]

### VIII. DEMANDS AND DISRUPTIONS

Before ending this discussion of consequentialism, let me mention one other large problem involving alienation that has seemed uniquely troubling for consequentialist theories and that shows how coming to terms with problems of alienation may be a social matter as well as a matter of individual psychology. Because consequentialist criteria of rightness are linked to maximal contribution to the good, whenever one does not perform the very best act one can, one is "negatively responsible" for any shortfall in total well-being that results. Bernard Williams has argued that to accept such a burden of responsibility would force most of us to abandon or be prepared to abandon many of our most basic individual commitments, alienating ourselves from the very things that mean the most to us.[31]

To be sure, objective act-consequentialism of the sort considered here is a demanding and potentially disruptive morality, even after allowances have been made for the psychological phenomena thus far discussed and for the difference between saying an act is wrong and saying that the agent ought to be blamed for it. But just *how* demanding or disruptive it would be for an individual is a function – as it arguably should be – of how bad the state of the world is, how others typically act, what institutions exist, and how much that individual is capable of doing. If wealth were more equitably distributed, if political systems were less repressive and more

171

responsive to the needs of their citizens, and if people were more generally prepared to accept certain responsibilities, then individuals' everyday lives would not have to be constantly disrupted for the sake of the good.

For example, in a society where there are no organized forms of disaster relief, it may be the case that if disaster were to strike a particular region, people all over the country would be obliged to make a special effort to provide aid. If, on the other hand, an adequate system of publicly financed disaster relief existed, then it probably would be a very poor idea for people to interrupt their normal lives and attempt to help – their efforts would probably be uncoordinated, ill-informed, an interference with skilled relief work, and economically disruptive (perhaps even damaging to the society's ability to pay for the relief effort).

By altering social and political arrangements we can lessen the disruptiveness of moral demands on our lives, and in the long run achieve better results than freelance good-doing. A consequentialist theory is therefore likely to recommend that accepting negative responsibility is more a matter of supporting certain social and political arrangements (or rearrangements) than of setting out individually to save the world. Moreover, it is clear that such social and political changes cannot be made unless the lives of individuals are psychologically supportable in the meanwhile, and this provides substantial reason for rejecting the notion that we should abandon all that matters to us as individuals and devote ourselves solely to net social welfare. Finally, in many cases what matters most is *perceived* rather than actual demandingness or disruptiveness, and this will be a relative matter, depending upon normal expectations. If certain social or political arrangements encourage higher contribution as a matter of course, individuals may not sense these moral demands as excessively intrusive.

To speak of social and political changes is, of course, to suggest eliminating the social and political preconditions for a number of existing projects and relationships, and such changes are likely to produce some degree of alienation in those whose lives have been disrupted. To an extent such people may be able to find new projects and relationships as well as maintain a number of old projects and relationships, and thereby avoid intolerable alienation. But not all will escape serious alienation. We thus have a case in which alienation will exist whichever course of action we follow – either the alienation of those who find the loss of the old order disorienting, or the continuing alienation of those who under the present order cannot lead lives expressive of their individuality or goals. It would seem that to follow the logic of Williams' position would have the unduly conservative result of favoring those less alienated in the present state of affairs over those who might lead more satisfactory lives if certain changes were to occur. Such conservativism could hardly be warranted by a concern about alienation if the changes in question would bring about social and political preconditions for a more widespread enjoyment of meaningful lives. For example, it is disruptive of the ground projects of many men that women have begun to demand and receive greater equality in social and personal spheres, but such disruption may be offset by the opening of more avenues of self-development to a greater number of people.

In responding to Williams' objection regarding negative responsibility, I have focused more on the problem of disruptiveness than the problem of demandingness, and more on the social than the personal level. More would need to be said than I am able to say here to come fully to terms with his objection, although some very general remarks may be in order. The consequentialist starts out from the relatively simple idea that certain things seem to matter to people above all else. His root conception of moral rightness is therefore that it should matter above all else whether people, insofar as possible, actually realize these ends.[32] Consequentialist moralities of the sort considered here undeniably set a demanding standard, calling upon us to do more for one another than is now the practice. But this standard plainly does not require that most people lead intolerable lives for the sake of some greater good: the greater good is empirically equivalent to the best possible lives for the largest possible number of people.[33] Objective consequentialism gives full expression to this root intuition by setting as the criterion of rightness actual contribution to the realization of human value, allowing practices and forms of reasoning to take whatever shape this requires. It is thus not equivalent to requiring a certain, alienated way of thinking about ourselves, our commitments, or how to act.

Samuel Scheffler has recently suggested that one response to the problems Williams raises about the impersonality and demandingness of consequentialism could be to depart from consequentialism at least far enough to recognize as a fundamental moral principle and agent-centered prerogative, roughly to the effect that one is not always obliged to maximize the good, although one is always permitted to do so if one wishes. This prerogative would make room for agents to give special attention to personal projects and commitments. However, the argument of this article, if successful, shows there to be a firm place in moral practice for prerogatives that afford such room even if one accepts a fully consequentialist fundamental moral theory.[34]

By way of conclusion, I would like to turn to alienation from morality itself, the experience (conscious or unconscious) of morality as an external set of demands not rooted in our lives or accommodating to our perspectives. Giving a convincing answer to the question "Why should I be moral?" must involve diminishing the extent that morality appears alien.

Part of constructing such an answer is a matter of showing that abiding by morality need not alienate us from the particular commitments that make life worthwhile, and in the previous sections we have begun to see how this might be possible within an objective act-consequentialist account of what morality requires. We saw how in general various sorts of projects or relationships can continue to be a source of intrinsic value even though one recognizes that they might have to undergo changes if they could not be defended in their present form on moral grounds. And again, knowing that a commitment is morally defensible may well deepen its value for us, and may also make it possible for us to feel part of a larger world in a way that is itself of great value. If our commitments are regarded by others as responsible and valuable (or if we have reason to think that others should so regard them), this may enhance the meaning or value they have for ourselves, while if they are regarded by others as irresponsible or worthless (especially if we suspect that others regard them so justly), this may make it more difficult for us to identify with them or find purpose or value in them. Our almost universal urge to rationalize our acts and lives attests to our wish to see what we do as defensible from a more general point of view. I do not deny that bringing a more general perspective to bear on one's life may be costly to the self – it may cause reevaluations that lower self-esteem and produce guilt, alienation, and even problems of identity. But I do want to challenge the simple story often told in which there is a personal point of view from which we glimpse meanings that then vanish into insignificance when we adopt a more general perspective. In thought and action we shuttle back and forth from more personal to less personal standpoints, and both play an important role in the process whereby purpose, meaning, and identity are generated and sustained.[35] Moreover, it may be part of mature commitments, even of the most intimate sort, that a measure of perspective beyond the personal be maintained.

These remarks about the role of general perspectives in individual lives lead us to what I think is an equally important part of answering the question "Why should I be moral?": reconceptualization of the terms of the discussion to avoid starting off in an alienated fashion and ending up with the result that morality still seems alien. Before pursuing this idea, let us quickly glance at two existing approaches to the question.

Morality may be conceived of as in essence selfless, impartial, impersonal. To act morally is to subordinate the self and all contingencies concerning the self's relations with others or the world to a set of imperatives binding on us solely as rational beings. We should be moral, in this view, because it is ideally rational. However, morality thus conceived seems bound to appear as alien in daily life. "Purity of heart" in Rawls' sense would be essential to acting morally, and the moral way of life would appear well removed from our actual existence, enmeshed as we are in a web of "particularistic" commitments – which happen to supply our *raisons d'être*.

A common alternative conception of morality is not as an elevated purity of heart but as a good strategy for the self. Hobbesian atomic individuals are posited and appeal is made to game theory to show that pay-offs to such individuals may be greater in certain conflict situations – such as reiterated prisoners' dilemmas – if they abide by certain constraints of a moral kind (at least, with regard to those who may reciprocate) rather than act merely prudentially. Behaving morally, then, may be an advantageous policy in certain social settings. However, it is not likely to be the *most* advantageous policy in general, when compared to a strategy that cunningly mixes some compliance with norms and some noncompliance; and presumably the Hobbesian individual is interested only in maximal self-advantage. Yet even if we leave aside worries about how far such arguments might be pushed, it needs to be said that morality as such would confront such an entrepreneurial self as an alien set of demands, for central to morality is the idea that others' interests must sometimes be given weight for reasons unrelated to one's own advantage.

Whatever their differences, these two apparently antithetical approaches to the question "Why should I be moral?" have remarkably similar underlying pictures of the problem. In these pictures, a presocial, rational, abstract individual is the starting point, and the task is to construct proper interpersonal relations out of such individuals. Of course, this conceit inverts reality: the rational individual of these approaches is a social and historical *product*. But that is old hat. We are not supposed to see this as any sort of history, we are told, but rather as a way of

175

conceptualizing the questions of morality. Yet why when conceptualizing are we drawn to such asocial and ahistorical images? My modest proposal is that we should keep our attention fixed on society and history at least long enough to try recasting the problem in more naturalistic terms.[36]

As a start, let us begin with individuals situated in society, complete with identities, commitments, and social relations. What are the ingredients of such identities, commitments, and relations? When one studies relationships of deep commitment – of parent to child, or wife to husband – at close range, it becomes artificial to impose a dichotomy between what is done for the self and what is done for the other. We cannot decompose such relationships into a vector of self-concern and a vector of other-concern, even though concern for the self and the other are both present. The other has come to figure in the self in a fundamental way – or, perhaps a better way of putting it, the other has become a reference point of the self. If it is part of one's identity to be the parent of Jill or the husband of Linda, then the self has reference points beyond the ego, and that which affects these reference points may affect the self in an unmediated way.[37] These reference points do not all fall within the circle of intimate relationships, either. Among the most important constituents of identities are social, cultural, or religious ties – one is a Jew, a Southerner, a farmer, or an alumnus of Old Ivy. Our identities exist in relational, not absolute, space, and except as they are fixed by reference points in others, in society, in culture, or in some larger constellation still, they are not fixed at all.[38]

There is a worthwhile analogy between meaning in lives and meaning in language. It has been a while since philosophers have thought it helpful to imagine that language is the arrangement resulting when we hook our private meanings up to a system of shared symbols. Meaning, we are told, resides to a crucial degree in use, in public contexts, in referential systems – it is possible for the self to use a language with meanings because the self is embedded in a set of social and historical practices. But ethical philosophers have continued to speak of the meaning of life in surprisingly private terms. Among recent attempts to give a foundation for morality, Nozick's perhaps places greatest weight on the idea of the meaning of life, which he sees as a matter of an individual's "ability to regulate and guide [his] life in accordance with some overall conception [he] chooses to accept," emphasizing the idea that an individual creates meaning through choice of a life plan; clearly, however, in order for choice to play a self-defining role, the options among which one chooses must already have some meaning independent of one's decisions.[39]

176

It is not only "the meaning of life" that carries such presuppositions. Consider, for example, another notion that has played a central role in moral discourse: respect. If the esteem of others is to matter to an individual those others must themselves have some significance to the individual; in order for their esteem to constitute the sought-after respect, the individual must himself have some degree of respect for them and their judgment.[40] If the self loses significance for others, this threatens its significance even for itself; if others lose significance for the self, this threatens to remove the basis for self-significance. It is a commonplace of psychology and sociology that bereaved or deracinated individuals suffer not only a sense of loss owing to broken connections with others, but also a loss in the solidity of the self, and may therefore come to lose interest in the self or even a clear sense of identity. Reconstructing the self and self-interest in such cases is as much a matter of constructing new relations to others and the world as it is a feat of self-supporting self-reconstruction. Distracted by the picture of a hypothetical, presocial individual, philosophers have found it very easy to assume, wrongly, that in the actual world concern for oneself and one's goals is quite automatic, needing no outside support, while a direct concern for others is inevitably problematic, needing some further rationale.

It does not follow that there is any sort of categorical imperative to care about others or the world beyond the self as such. It is quite possible to have few external reference points and go through life in an alienated way. Life need not have much meaning in order to go on, and one does not even have to care whether life goes on. We cannot show that moral skepticism is necessarily irrational by pointing to facts about meaning, but a naturalistic approach to morality need no more refute radical skepticism than does a naturalistic approach to epistemology. For actual people, there may be surprisingly little distance between asking in earnest "Why should I take any interest in anyone else?" and asking "Why should I take any interest in myself?"[41] The proper response to the former is not merely to point out the indirect benefits of caring about things beyond the self, although this surely should be done, but to show how denying the significance of anything beyond the self may undercut the basis of significance for the self. There is again a close, but not exact, parallel in language: people can get along without a language, although certainly not as well as they can with it; if someone were to ask "Why should I use my words the same way as others?" the proper response would not only be to point out the obvious benefits of using his words in this way, but also to point out that by refusing to use words the way others do he is undermining the basis of meaning in his own use of language.

These remarks need not lead us to a conservative traditionalism. We must share and preserve meanings in order to have a language at all, but we may use a common language to disagree and innovate. Contemporary philosophy of language makes us distrust any strict dichotomy between meaning, on the one hand, and belief and value, on the other; but there is obviously room within a system of meanings for divergence and change on empirical and normative matters. Language itself has undergone considerable change over the course of history, coevolving with beliefs and norms without in general violating the essential conditions of meaningfulness. Similarly, moral values and social practices may undergo change without obliterating the basis of meaningful lives, so long as certain essential conditions are fulfilled. (History does record some changes, such as the uprooting of tribal peoples, where these conditions were not met, with devastating results.)

A system of available, shared meanings would seem to be a precondition for sustaining the meaningfulness of individual lives in familiar sorts of social arrangements. Moreover, in such arrangements identity and self-significance seem to depend in part upon the significance of others to the self. If we are prepared to say that a sense of meaningfulness is a precondition for much else in life, then we may be on the way to answering the question "Why should I be moral?" for we have gone beyond pure egocentrism precisely by appealing to facts about the self.[42] Our preceding discussions have yielded two considerations that make the rest of the task of answering this question more tractable. First, we noted in discussing hedonism that individual lives seem most enjoyable when they involve commitments to causes beyond the self or to others as such. Further, we remarked that it is plausible that the happiest sorts of lives do not involve a commitment to hedonism even of a sophisticated sort. If a firm sense of meaningfulness is a precondition of the fullest happiness, this speculation becomes still more plausible. Second, we sketched a morality that began by taking seriously the various forms of human non-moral value, and then made room for morality in our lives by showing that we can raise moral questions without thereby destroying the possibility of realizing various intrinsic values from particular relationships and activities. That is, we saw how being moral might be compatible (at least in these respects) with living a desirable life. It would take another article, and a long one, to show how these various pieces of the answer to "Why should I be moral?" might be made less rough and fitted together into a more solid structure. But by adopting a nonalienated starting point – that of situated rather than presocial individuals – and by showing how some of the alienation associated with bringing morality to bear on our lives might be avoided, perhaps we have reduced the extent to which morality seems alien to us by its nature.

NOTES

*Philosophy and Public Affairs*, 13 (1984), 134–71.
* I am grateful to a number of people for criticisms of previous drafts of this paper and helpful suggestions for improving it. I would especially like to thank Marcia Baron, Stephen Darwall, William K. Frankena, Allan Gibbard, Samuel Scheffler, Rebecca Scott, Michael Stocker, Nicholas Sturgeon, Gregory Trianoski-Stillwell, and Susan Wolf.
1. The loss in question need not be a loss of something of value, and *a fortiori* need not be a bad thing overall: there are some people, institutions, or cultures alienation from which would be a boon. Alienation is a more or less troubling phenomenon depending upon what is lost; and in the cases to be considered, what is lost is for the most part of substantial value. It does not follow, as we will see in Section V, that in all such cases alienation is a bad thing on balance. Moreover, I do not assume that the loss in question represents an actual *decline* in some value as the result of a separation coming into being where once there was none. It seems reasonable to say that an individual can experience a loss in being alienated from nature, for example, without assuming that he was ever in communion with it, much as we say it is a loss for someone never to receive an education or never to appreciate music. Regrettably, various relevant kinds and sources of alienation cannot be discussed here. A general, historical discussion of alienation may be found in Richard Schacht, *Alienation* (Garden City, NY: Doubleday, 1971).
2. This is not to say that no questions arise about whether Helen's (or John's) feelings and attitudes constitute the fullest sort of affection, as will be seen shortly.
3. Moreover, there is a sense in which someone whose responses to his affections or feelings are characteristically mediated by a calculating point of view may fail to know himself fully, or may seem in a way unknowable to others, and this "cognitive distance" may itself be part of his alienation. I am indebted here to Allan Gibbard.
4. There is a wide range of views about the nature of the moral point of view and its proper role in moral life. Is it necessary that one actually act on universal principles, or merely that one be willing to universalize the principles upon which one acts? Does the moral point of view by its nature require us to consider everyone alike? Here I am using a rather strong reading of the moral point of view, according to which taking the moral point of view involves universalization and the equal consideration of all.
5. A moral point of view theorist might make use of the three points of view distinguished by Mill: the moral, the aesthetic, and the sympathetic. "The first addresses itself to our reason and conscience; the second to our imagination; the third to our human fellow-feeling," from "Bentham," reprinted in *John Stuart Mill: Utilitarianism and Other Writings*, Mary Warnock, ed. (New York: New American

179

Library, 1962) 121. What is morally right, in his view, may fail to be "loveable" (e.g., a parent strictly disciplining a child) or "beautiful" (e.g., an inauthentic gesture). Thus, the three points of view need not concur in their positive or negative assessments. Notice, however, that Mill has divided the self into three realms, of "reason and conscience," of "imagination," and of "human fellow-feeling"; notice, too, that he has chosen the word 'feeling' to characterize human affections.

6. William K. Frankena, *Ethics*, 2nd ed. (Englewood Cliffs, NJ: Prentice-Hall, 1973) 116. Moralities that do not accord with this dictum – or a modified version of it that includes all sentient beings – might be deemed alienated in a Feuerbachian sense.

7. Mill, for instance, calls the moral point of view "unquestionably the first and most important," and while he thinks it the error of the moralizer (such as Bentham) to elevate the moral point of view and "sink the [aesthetic and sympathetic] entirely," he does not explain how to avoid such a result if the moral point of view is to be, as he says it ought, "paramount." See his "Bentham," 121f.

Philosophers who have recently raised doubts about moralities for such reasons include Bernard Williams, in "A Critique of Utilitarianism," in J.J.C. Smart and B. Williams, *Utilitarianism: For and Against* (Cambridge: Cambridge University Press, 1973), and Michael Stocker, in "The Schizophrenia of Modern Ethical Theories," *Journal of Philosophy* 73 (1976), 453–66.

8. John Rawls, *A Theory of Justice* (Cambridge: Harvard University Press, 1971) 587, emphasis added.

9. I am not claiming that we should interpret all of Rawls' intricate moral theory in light of these few remarks. They are cited here merely to illustrate a certain tendency in moral thought, especially that of a Kantian inspiration.

10. This is a "paradox" for individual, egoistic hedonists. Other forms the "paradox of hedonism" may take are social in character: a society of egoistic hedonists might arguably achieve less total happiness than a society of more benevolent beings; or, taking happiness as the sole social goal might lead to a less happy society overall than could exist if a wider range of goals were pursued.

11. This is not to deny that there are indexical components to commitments.

12. It does seem likely to matter just what the commitment is contingent upon as well as just how contingent it is. I think it is an open question whether commitments contingent upon the satisfaction of egoistic hedonist criteria are of the sort that might figure in the happiest sorts of lives ordinarily available. We will return to this problem presently.

Those who have had close relationships often develop a sense of *duty* to one another that may outlast affection or emotional commitment, that is, they may have a sense of obligation to one another that is less contingent than affection or emotional commitment, and that should not simply be confused with them. If such a sense of obligation is in conflict with self-interest, and if it is a normal part of the most satisfying sorts of close relationships, then this may pose a problem for the egoistic hedonist.

13. A few remarks are needed. First, I will say that an act is available to an agent if he would succeed in performing it if he tried. Second, here and elsewhere in this article I mean to include quite "thick" descriptions of actions, so that it

180

may be part of an action that one perform it with a certain intention or goal. In the short run (but not so much the long run) intentions, goals, motives, and the like are usually less subject to our deliberate control than overt behavior – it is easier to say "I'm sorry" than to say it and mean it. This, however, is a fact about the relative availability of acts to the agent at a given time, and should not dictate what is to count as an act. Third, here and elsewhere I ignore for simplicity's sake the possibility that more than one course of action may be maximally valuable. And fourth, for reasons I will not enter into here, I have formulated objective hedonism in terms of actual outcomes rather than expected values (relative to the information available to the agent). One could make virtually the same argument using an expected value formulation.

14. Michael Stocker considers related cases in "Morally Good Intentions," *The Monist* 54 (1970), 124–41. I am much indebted to his discussion.

15. There may be a parallelism of sorts between Ned's coming to seek money for its own sake and a certain pattern of moral development: what is originally sought in order to live up to familial or social expectations may come to be an end in itself.

It might be objected that the goal of earning as much money as possible is quite unlike the goal of being as happy as possible, since money is plainly instrumentally valuable even when it is sought for its own sake. But happiness, too, is instrumentally valuable, for it may contribute to realizing such goals as being a likeable or successful person.

16. An important objection to the claim that objective hedonism may serve as the *moral* criterion one's acts should meet, even if this means not believing in hedonism, is that moral principles must meet a *publicity* condition. I will discuss this objection in Section VI.

17. See, for example, Stocker, "The Schizophrenia of Modern Ethical Theories."

18. Williams, "Critique."

19. At least one qualification is needed: the subjective states must be psychologically possible. Perhaps some of us desire what are, in effect, psychologically impossible states.

20. Robert Nozick, *Anarchy, State, and Utopia* (New York: Basic Books, 1974) 42ff.

21. To my knowledge, the best-developed method for justifying claims about intrinsic value involves thought-experiments of a familiar sort, in which, for example, we imagine two lives, or two worlds, alike in all but one respect, and then attempt to determine whether rational, well-informed, widely experienced individuals would (when vividly aware of both alternatives) be indifferent between the two or have a settled preference for one over the other. Since no one is ideally rational, fully informed, or infinitely experienced, the best we can do is to take more seriously the judgments of those who come nearer to approximating these conditions. Worse yet: the best we can do is to take more seriously the judgments of those we *think* better approximate these conditions. (I am not supposing that facts or experience somehow entail values, but that in rational agents, beliefs and values show a marked mutual influence and coherence.) We may overcome some narrowness if we look at behavior and preferences in other societies and other epochs, but even here we must rely upon interpretations colored by our own beliefs and values. Within the confines of this article I must leave unanswered a host

181

of deep and troubling questions about the nature of values and value judgments. Suffice it to say that there is no reason to think that we are in a position to give anything but a tentative list of intrinsic goods.

It becomes a complex matter to describe the psychology of intrinsic value. For example, should we say that one values a relationship of solidarity, say, a friendship, *because it is* a friendship? That makes it sound as if it were somehow instrumental to the realization of some abstract value, friendship. Surely this is a misdescription. We may be able to get a clearer idea of what is involved by considering the case of happiness. We certainly do not value a particular bit of experienced happiness because it is instrumental in the realization of the abstract goal, happiness – we value the experience for its own sake because it is a happy experience. Similarly, a friendship is itself the valued thing, the thing of a valued kind. Of course, one can say that one values friendship and therefore seeks friends, just as one can say one values happiness and therefore seeks happy experiences. But this locution must be contrasted with what is being said when, for example, one talks of seeking *things that make one happy*. Friends are not "things that make one achieve friendship" – they partially constitute friendships, just as particular happy experiences partially constitute happiness for an individual. Thus taking friendship as an intrinsic value does not entail viewing particular friendships instrumentally.

22. If one objects that Juan's commitment to Linda is lacking because it is contingent in some ways, the objector must show that the *kinds* of contingencies involved would destroy his relationship with Linda, especially since moral character often figures in commitments – the character of the other, or the compatibility of a commitment with one's having the sort of character one values – and the contingencies in Juan's case are due to his moral character.

23. I do not mean to suggest that such identities are always matters of choice for individuals. Quite the reverse, identities often arise through socialization, prejudice, and similar influences. The point rather is that there is a very general phenomenon of identification, badly in need of explanation, that to an important extent underlies such phenomena as socialization and prejudice, and that suggests the existence of certain needs in virtually all members of society – needs to which identification with entities beyond the self answers.

Many of us who resist raising questions about our lives from broader perspectives do so, I fear, not out of a sense that it would be difficult or impossible to lead a meaningful life if one entertained such perspectives, but rather out of a sense that our lives would not stand up to much scrutiny therefrom, so that leading a life that *would* seem meaningful from such perspectives would require us to change in some significant way.

24. Although the language here is causal – 'promoting' and 'bringing about' – it should be said that the relation of an act to the good need not always be causal. An act of learning may noncausally involve coming to have knowledge (an intrinsic good by my reckoning) as well as contributing causally to later realizations of intrinsic value. Causal consequences as such do not have a privileged status. As in the case of objective hedonism, I have formulated objective consequentialism in terms of actual outcomes (so-called "objective duty") rather than expected values relative to what is rational for the agent to believe ("subjective duty"). The main arguments of this article could be made using expected value, since the course

of action with highest expected value need not in general be the subjectively consequentialist one. See also notes 13 and 21.

Are there any subjective consequentialists? Well, various theorists have claimed that a consequentialist must be a subjective consequentialist in order to be genuine – see Williams, "Critique," 135, and Rawls, *Theory of Justice*, 182.

25. Williams, "Critique," 135.

26. For discussion of a publicity condition, see Rawls, *Theory of Justice*, 133, 177–82, 582. The question whether a publicity condition can be justified is a difficult one, deserving fuller discussion than I am able to give it here.

27. For an example of trait-consequentialism, see Robert M. Adams, "Motive Utilitarianism," *Journal of Philosophy* 73 (1976), 467-81.

28. By way of contrast, when Robert Adams considers application of a motive-utilitarian view to the ethics of actions, he suggests "conscience utilitarianism," the view that "we have a *moral duty* to do an act, if and only if it would be demanded of us by the most useful kind of conscience we could have," "Motive Utilitarianism," 479. Presumably, this means that it would be morally wrong to perform an act contrary to the demands of the most useful sort of conscience. I have resisted this sort of redefinition of rightness for actions, since I believe that the most useful sort of conscience may on occasion demand of us an act that does not have the best overall consequences of those available, and that performing this act would be wrong.

Of course, some difficulties attend the interpretation of this last sentence. I have assumed throughout that an act is available to an agent if he would succeed in performing it if he tried. I have also taken a rather simple view of the complex matter of attaching outcomes to specific acts. In those rare cases in which the performance of even one exceptional (purportedly optimizing) act would completely undermine the agent's standing (optimal) disposition, it might not be possible after all to say that the exceptional act would be the right one to perform in the circumstances. (This question will arise again shortly.)

29. One conclusion of this discussion is that we cannot realistically expect people's behavior to be in strict compliance with the counterfactual condition even if they are committed sophisticated consequentialists. At best, a sophisticated consequentialist tries to meet this condition. But it should be no surprise that in practice we are unlikely to be morally ideal. Imperfections in information alone are enough to make it very improbable that individuals will lead objectively consequentialist lives. Whether or when to *blame* people for real or apparent failures to behave ideally is, of course, another matter.

Note that we must take into account not just the frequency with which right acts are performed, but the actual balance of gains and losses to overall well-being that results. Relative frequency of right action will settle the matter only in the (unusual) case where the amount of good at stake in each act of a given kind – for example, each emergency one comes across – is the same.

30. In *The Methods of Ethics*, bk. IV, ch. v, sec. 4, Sidgwick discusses "the Ideal of character and conduct" that a utilitarian should recognize as "the sum of excellences or Perfections," and writes that "a Utilitarian must hold that it is always wrong for a man knowingly to do anything other than what he believes to be most conducive to Universal Happiness" (492). Here Sidgwick is uncharacteristically

confused – and in two ways. First, considering act-by-act evaluation, an objective utilitarian can hold that an agent may simply be wrong in believing that a given course of action is most conducive to universal happiness, and therefore it may be right for him knowingly to do something other than this. Second, following Sidgwick's concern in this passage and looking at enduring traits of character rather than isolated acts, and even assuming the agent's belief to be correct, an objective utilitarian can hold that the ideal character for an individual, or for people in general, may involve a willingness knowingly to act contrary to maximal happiness when this is done for the sake of certain deep personal commitments. See Henry Sidgwick, *The Methods of Ethics*, 7th ed. (New York: Dover, 1966) 492.

It might be thought counterintuitive to say, in the example given, that it is not right for Juan to travel to see Linda. But it must be kept in mind that for an act-consequentialist to say that an action is not right is not to say that it is without merit, only that it is not the very best act available to the agent. And an intuitive sense of the rightness of visiting Linda may be due less to an evaluation of the act itself than to a reaction to the sort of character a person would have to have in order to stay home and write a check to Oxfam under the circumstances. Perhaps he would have to be too distant or righteous to have much appeal to us – especially in view of the fact that it is his spouse's anguish that is at stake. We have already seen how an act-consequentialist may share this sort of character assessment.

31. Williams, "Critique," sec. 3.
32. I appealed to this "root conception" in rejecting rule-consequentialism in Section VII. Although consequentialism is often condemned for failing to provide an account of morality consistent with respect for persons, this root conception provides the basis for a highly plausible notion of such respect. I doubt, however, that any fundamental ethical dispute between consequentialists and deontologists can be resolved by appeal to the idea of respect for persons. The deontologist has his notion of respect – for example, that we not use people in certain ways – and the consequentialist has *his* – for example, that the good of every person has an equal claim upon us, a claim unmediated by any notion of right or contract, so that we should do the most possible to bring about outcomes that actually advance the good of persons. For every consequentially justified act of manipulation to which the deontologist can point with alarm there is a deontologically justified act that fails to promote the well-being of some person(s) as fully as possible to which the consequentialist can point, appalled. Which notion takes "respect for persons" more seriously? There may be no non-question-begging answer, especially once the consequentialist has recognized such things as autonomy or respect as intrinsically valuable.
33. The qualification 'empirically equivalent to' is needed because in certain empirically unrealistic cases, such as utility monsters, the injunction "Maximize overall realization of human value" cannot be met by improving the lives of as large a proportion of the population as possible. However, under plausible assumptions about this world (including diminishing marginal value) the equivalence holds.
34. For Scheffler's view, see *The Rejection of Consequentialism: A Philosophical Investigation of the Considerations Underlying Rival Moral Conceptions* (Oxford: Clarendon

Press, 1982). The consequentialist may also argue that at least some of the debate set in motion by Williams is more properly concerned with the question of the relation between moral imperatives and imperatives of rationality than with the content of moral imperatives as such. (See note 42.)

35. For example, posterity may figure in our thinking in ways we seldom articulate. Thus, nihilism has seemed to some an appropriate response to the idea that mankind will soon destroy itself. "Everything would lose its point" is a reaction quite distinct from "Then we should enjoy ourselves as much as possible in the meantime," and perhaps equally comprehensible.

36. I do not deny that considerations about payoffs of strategies in conflict situations may play a role in cultural or biological evolutionary explanations of certain moral sentiments or norms. Rather, I mean to suggest that there are characteristic sorts of abstractions and simplifications involved in game-theoretic analysis that may render it blind to certain phenomena crucial for understanding morality and its history, and for answering the question "Why should I be moral?" when posed by actual individuals.

37. Again we see the inadequacy of subjectivism about values. If, for example, part of one's identity is to be Jill's parent, then should Jill cease to exist, one's life could be said to have lost some of its purpose even if one were not aware of her death. As the example of the experience machine suggested previously, there is an objective side to talk about purpose.

38. Here I do not have in mind identity in the sense usually at stake in discussions of personal identity. The issue is not identity as principle of individuation, but as *experienced*, as a sense of self – the stuff actual identity crises are made of.

39. Nozick, *Anarchy*, 49. (I ignore here Nozick's more recent remarks about the meaning of life in his *Philosophical Explanations* [Cambridge: Harvard University Press, 1981].) The notion of a "rationally chosen life plan" has figured prominently in the literature recently, in part due to Rawls' use of it in characterizing the good (see Rawls, *Theory of Justice*, ch. VII, "Goodness as Rationality"). Rawls' theory of the good is a complex matter, and it is difficult to connect his claims in any direct way to a view about the meaning of life. However, see T. M. Scanlon, "Rawls' Theory of Justice," *University of Pennsylvania Law Review* 121 (1973), 1020–69, for an interpretation of Rawls in which the notion of an individual as above all a rational chooser – more committed to maintaining his status as a rational agent able to adopt and modify his goals than to any particular set of goals – functions as the ideal of a person implicit in Rawls' theory. On such a reading, we might interpolate into the original text the idea that meaning derives from autonomous individual choice, but this is highly speculative. In any event, recent discussions of rationally chosen life plans as the bearers of ultimate significance or value do not appear to me to do full justice to the ways in which lives actually come to be invested with meaning, especially since some meanings would have to be presupposed by any rational choice of a plan of life.

40. To be sure, this is but one of the forms of respect that are of importance to moral psychology. But as we see, self-respect has a number of interesting connections with respect for, and from, others.

41. This may be most evident in extreme cases. Survivors of Nazi death camps speak of the effort it sometimes took to sustain a will to survive, and of the importance

of others, and of the sense of others, to this. A survivor of Treblinka recalls, "In our group we shared everything; and at the moment one of the group ate something without sharing it, we knew it was the beginning of the end for him." (Quoted in Terrence Des Pres, *The Survivor: An Anatomy of Life in the Death Camps* [New York: Oxford University Press, 1976] 96.) Many survivors say that the idea of staying alive to "bear witness," in order that the deaths of so many would not escape the world's notice, was decisive in sustaining their own commitment to survival.

42. One need not be a skeptic about morality or alienated from it in any general sense in order for the question "Why should I be moral?" to arise with great urgency. If in a given instance doing what is right or having the best sort of character were to conflict head-on with acting on behalf of a person or a project that one simply could not go against without devastating the self, then it may fail to be reasonable from the agent's standpoint to do what is right. It is always *morally* wrong (though not always morally blameworthy) to fail to perform morally required acts, but in certain circumstances that may be the most reasonable thing to do – not because of some larger moral scheme, but because of what matters to particular individuals. Therefore, in seeking an answer to "Why should I be moral?" I do not assume that it must always be possible to show that the moral course of action is ideally rational or otherwise optimal from the standpoint of the agent. (I could be more specific here if I had a clearer idea of what rationality is.) It would seem ambitious enough to attempt to show that, in general, there are highly desirable lives available to individuals consistent with their being moral. While we might hope for something stronger, this could be enough – given what can also be said on behalf of morality from more general viewpoints – to make morality a worthy candidate for our allegiance as individuals.

It should perhaps be said that on an objective consequentialist account, being moral need not be a matter of consciously following distinctively moral imperatives, so that what is at stake in asking "Why should I be moral?" in connection with such a theory is whether one has good reason to lead one's life in such a way that an objective consequentialist criterion of rightness is met as nearly as possible. In a given instance, this criterion might be met by acting out of a deeply felt emotion or an entrenched trait of character, without consulting morality or even directly in the face of it. This, once more, is an indication of objective consequentialism's flexibility: the idea is to *be* and *do* good, not necessarily to *pursue* goodness.

# 7

# Locke, Stock, and Peril: Natural Property Rights, Pollution, and Risk*

### INTRODUCTION

Lockean natural rights theories have long been associated with *laissez-faire* policies on the part of the government, in large measure because of the sanctity they accord to individual rights, especially private property rights. However, I will argue that if one attempts to apply such theories to moral questions about pollution, they present a different face, one set so firmly against *laissez faire* – or *laissez polluer* – as to countenance serious restriction of what Lockeans have traditionally taken to be the proper sphere of individual freedom.

Curiously, Lockean theories also face a challenge from the opposite direction. They may be inadequately restrictive concerning the imposition upon others of unwanted risks that do not eventuate in actual property damage. As we will see, this challenge should be especially troubling for those who hold that Lockeanism gives expression to the Kantian idea of respect for persons.

I will consider various ways in which one might attempt to modify classical Lockeanism to avoid these difficulties, but it will emerge that these modifications generally raise more problems than they solve for the Lockean and result in views that lack much of the intuitive appeal of more orthodox Lockeanism.

In short, I will argue that Lockeanism, classical or revisionist, may be incapable of striking an appropriate balance between restrictiveness and permissiveness in matters involving pollution and risk. This failure raises doubts about the adequacy of a Lockean framework to our moral universe.

A simple, appealing picture of morality informs much contemporary thought and action. On this view, individuals have certain natural rights that give them freedom to act in certain ways and oblige others not to interfere. The archetype of such a right is the right of private property. If Harlan has exclusive ownership of a pumpkin, it is his to do with as he pleases, and no one may rightfully take it from him or hinder him in his enjoyment of it. His right entitles him to exclude others from making any use of his pumpkin to which he does not consent. Of course, Harlan's property right is limited by similar rights of others. He cannot, without permission, rightfully lob his pumpkin onto another's porch. He is free to transfer his pumpkin to another, or to give him use of it, and although such contracts or gifts, once made, bring with them new obligations to carry out promises rendered, these further limits are self-imposed.

In the classic, Lockean form of this view, individuals have some property rights wholly independent of civil law: property in one's own body and its capacities, and a right to appropriate common property for one's own use by mixing one's own labor with it, so long as one does not waste and "enough and as good" is left in common for others.[2] These initial, "natural" property rights form the basis for whatever further property rights individuals may acquire by harvesting the fruits of nature or exchanging goods or labor with others. In the fullness of time, some individuals may acquire more extensive property entitlements than others and may transfer this wealth to whomever they please, but all retain an equal, natural right not to be harmed in person or (other) property.[3]

From this Lockean view emerges an image of moral space akin to a map at a registrar of deeds. Individual entitlements or rights determine a patchwork of boundaries within which people are free to live as they choose so long as they respect the boundaries of others.[4] To learn one's moral obligations one need only consult the map. Would a given act involve crossing another's boundary?[5] If so, it is prohibited; if not, permitted.[6] This Lockean view is often called antipaternalistic because it holds that individuals are entitled to final say over what happens within their own boundaries. It is also often called libertarian, since it is so centrally concerned with preserving a field of individual freedom of choice. It is not, however, equivalent to the view that we should maximize individual freedom of choice: that is an aggregative, social goal, foreign to the Lockean picture. If the choices individuals make within their boundaries, and the mutual arrangements they make across their boundaries, do not result in a social scheme with maximum individual freedom, that is perfectly acceptable. Individual entitlements and decisions define the limits within which any social goal or policy may legitimately be pursued, including the policy of promoting freedom.

This Lockean view is opposed to balancing as well as aggregation. If I violate a boundary but in the process bring about some valuable result, this does not count as offsetting the original harm. For example, if the industrious Smith were to seize the laggard Jones's land, he might produce much more food, lowering food prices locally and making possible an improvement in local diet. But this improvement in efficiency would not undo the original violation of Jones's property right, even if Jones himself were ultimately made better off as a result. For it is up to Jones what becomes of Jones's land, and Smith would have acted without Jones's leave. Moreover, whether a given act violates one's property right is not a matter of whether one experiences unpleasant consequences from it. If I take an old pair of socks from your wardrobe without asking, I have violated your property right in them even if you had little use for them or fail ever to notice the theft. Of course, the fact that the object stolen is of little value may lead you to refrain from bringing the law down upon me, or may lead the law to be lenient about punishment. But I cannot plead that I have done nothing wrong if I have contrived to take another's property without ill effects. In this, as well as in its opposition to aggregation and balancing, Lockeanism is anticonsequentialist.

As I have said, this is an appealing picture. Some have argued that its opposition to aggregation and balancing of consequences gives expression to the moral separateness and uniqueness of individuals, while its opposition to paternalism expresses the moral autonomy of individuals. Indeed, this view may be seen as an attempt to capture the Kantian idea that individuals are the ultimate bearers of moral value, and that we should always treat individuals as ends, not as means alone.[7] If the view at first seems callous because it emphasizes obligations not to interfere with one another rather than obligations to assist one another, it must be remembered that the complement of my not being under an obligation to help another is that the other is not under an obligation to help me: we both enjoy a realm of free choice, within which we are at liberty to devote as much or as little of ourselves or our resources to others as we choose.

A strong historical connection exists between this Lockean view and the free market of classical capitalist theory. Individuals command property, which they may exchange by mutual agreement, and the standard of fair exchange is simply that the trade receives their free consent

189

(in the absence of fraud). What is produced and how, how the fruits of production are distributed, and similar matters are left up to individuals and to their particular decisions about work, consumption, and investment. Social principles of "just distribution," overall efficiency, or utility maximization are not to be imposed upon this process, although proponents of classical capitalism have argued that in a properly functioning market, the result of individual decisions will tend to be the efficient use of resources, the maximization of total wealth, a distribution of wealth that largely accords with marginal contribution to its production, and many other social goods besides.

This Lockean picture has, I think, impressed itself upon the consciousness of virtually all Americans, even those who would reject it. It is therefore important to ask what happens when a Lockean view confronts problems of pollution and risk.

POLLUTION AND BOUNDARY CROSSING

Lockean natural rights theories ought to be unequivocal about the moral impermissibility of many pollution-caused injuries. If I spray my lettuce with an insecticide that drifts onto your property, where you breathe it and develop a nervous disorder, I have crossed a boundary wrongfully.[8] I may not have intended this result, and it may not even have been something I could have foreseen (I did not know the stuff was dangerous to humans, perhaps), but these facts do not alter the fundamental one: I violated a boundary without permission or provocation. Unintended or unforeseeable violations may deserve different punishment from intentional, foreseeable ones, but on a Lockean view we have an objective obligation not to cross a boundary, intentionally or otherwise.[9] If I take your Buick thinking it mine, I am not a thief, but my possession of it is wrongful, and it must be given back intact. If I should damage it in the process, I would be obliged to repair it (as I would not be obliged to repair damage that happened to occur to my own car). Arguably, I may also owe you something to compensate you for any inconvenience my illegitimate taking caused you (as I would not be obliged to compensate you for inconveniences I cause you by the legitimate exercise of my rights). Violations of rights may not always warrant punishment, but we cannot "read backward" from the inappropriateness of punishment to the nonviolation of a right, any more than we can "read backward" from a judge's suspension of a criminal sentence to the nonviolation of a law. Precisely because Lockean views are so clear about the wrongfulness of crossing

190

boundaries unless permitted or provoked, they are (in theory at least) quite strict about pollution-caused injuries to persons or property, very much restricting the kinds of polluting activity that might legitimately go on.

For a polluting activity to be permissible, it would have to be shown to involve no wrongful boundary crossing, even of the slightest extent. There is no room in a Lockean view for regarding minor injuries inflicted across boundaries as morally permissible, since, as we saw, whether a boundary is crossed does not depend upon the magnitude of the effect, or the value of what was affected. Petty theft is still theft. Moreover, it is quite irrelevant that a pollution-caused injury may be temporary, for example, that one may recover from exposure to an airborne toxin and be good as new. Knife wounds, too, often mend nicely.

Nor should it matter whether the victim makes, or fails to make, a special effort to avoid a pollution-caused injury. The burden is plainly upon others not to act in such a way that one can escape harm from them while on one's own property or on common property only by making special efforts. If Gale throws a knife across my lawn, and it strikes me on the leg as I go about my business, it is no exculpation (on a Lockean view, at least) for him to claim that I could have escaped injury had I been wearing chain mail or had I earlier sold my property and moved out of his throwing range. A steel-mill owner cannot escape blame by saying that those who do not like his sulfur emissions are free to sell their homes and move elsewhere. His responsibility is to stay within his own boundaries; if his mill produces gases that corrode the lungs of those who own property in the vicinity, or who happen to be on nearby common property, he has done wrong. This is so even if the mill has been around longer than the current residents or passersby. Someone who voluntarily moves into a high-crime (or high-grime) neighborhood may have acted unwisely, but he has not laid down his rights, and those who invade his person or property violate these rights. We may have less sympathy for someone who does not take certain precautions to avoid wrongful harm at the hands of others and may feel less inclined to come to his assistance, but the duty to mind borders is in no way diminished by some people's incaution.

The question of when we can legitimately interpret an action (or inaction) as waiving a right is an entangling one, as is the related question of what it is we may interpret such an action as permitting. Does someone who knowingly and voluntarily accepts a risky job thereby give consent to whatever harm may befall him in the workplace? Presumably not; there is still the possibility that the employer acts negligently or maliciously. If I accept a position with someone well known for cheating his employees, it will still be wrong for him to do such a thing to me. On a Lockean view I *am* free to sign a contract laying down a number of my rights, that is, giving another permission to cross certain boundaries that would otherwise separate me from him. Moreover, some Lockean views permit my failure to object to the actions of another, or to quit his property when I am free to leave, to be interpreted as tacit consent to what is going on. Locke himself believed that by living in a country from which one is free to emigrate one gives tacit consent to its system of laws and governance – a claim Hume would later ridicule[10] – but he presumably would not say that living in a risky neighborhood gives tacit consent to the crimes that might befall one, or that crossing the street at a busy intersection rather than walking four blocks to a quieter one makes one fair game for motorists. Lockean tacit consent to the state does not make it legitimate for the state to violate my inalienable right to self-preservation or to appropriate my private property. These individual rights constrain what a state may legitimately do even when it is founded on the express consent of its people. (It is something else if the people also consent to give the state free access to their property.) Similarly, my rights in my person and property constrain what people may legitimately do to me even if I choose to live dangerously. (It is something else if I also declare my property to be anyone's for the taking.) Some Lockeans, including Locke, have argued that there are some natural rights that no apparent act of consent – tacit or express – could actually waive.[11]

Consent is a natural place to look for room within a Lockean scheme to provide greater freedom of action with regard to pollution, but I would like to postpone further consideration of this possibility in order to continue exploring the question of when, in cases where neither express nor tacit consent is present, a polluting activity constitutes a boundary crossing.

DISPOSITIONAL HARMS AND RISK

Among the effects of pollution are not only certain manifest injuries – property loss, illness, disability, death – but also increases in the probability individuals will suffer such injuries. How restrictive Lockean views are with regard to pollution will depend upon whether this latter sort of effect is also counted as a boundary crossing.

A Lockean may urge a fundamental distinction among ways of in-creasing the probability individuals will suffer harm: I may change the probability you will suffer a manifest injury by having an actual, causal effect on your person or property, or alternatively, by doing something potentially harmful that could causally impinge upon you. In the latter case, you and your property may emerge from the encounter with heightened risk wholly untouched, in the same condition you both would have been had the risky activity not taken place. In the former case, some actual physical change has been wrought by me in your person or property – for example, the sidestream smoke from my cigarette has clogged your alveoli, making you more likely to succumb to a respiratory infection. As it happens, you may in the end not contract any such infection, but you have suffered a physical change as the result of my actions that renders you less resilient, more vulnerable than before. This change may be difficult to detect and may make itself known in the population only by aggregate statistics. However, for many pollutants, such as tobacco smoke, statistics do not indicate the existence of a threshold of exposure below which there is no effect on the probability of infection. So we may suppose without being too unrealistic that each time I send some of my tobacco smoke your way you suffer some small physical change, not for the better. It seems to me that if exposure to a pollutant reduces your ability to resist infections, take vigorous exercise, perceive the environment (owing to impairment of the senses), and so on, then it has damaged your health, even if you do not in fact happen to contract an infection, seek vigorous exercise, or make fine perceptual discriminations. That is, health is a dispositional as well as manifest state, and if your capacities have been reduced by my polluting activities, then I have not merely raised the probability you will suffer harm, I have also harmed you. I have caused an actual, though perhaps not readily detectable, harm to you that has the additional (and sometimes more disturbing) effect of raising your probability of suffering further, more evident harm.

On the other hand, if your neighbor carries out an activity wholly on his own property, which raises the probability you will suffer harm – for example, operating an unsafe miniature fission reactor – and yet no actual harm results (the reactor does not malfunction) it would seem that no boundary has been crossed.[12] Let us call cases of this sort, where there is no actual physical change produced in a person or his property by an activity that nonetheless raises the probability he will suffer wrongful harm, the imposition of pure risk. In the purest cases of pure risk, the person whose probability of injury has been increased is wholly unaware of this circumstance, so that his life proceeds exactly as it would have had the risk-imposing activity never occurred. For example: you do not know

193

of your neighbor's reactor and suspect nothing unusual. Things get more complicated when we allow awareness (or other sorts of indirect effects) of the risk-imposing activity, but let's avoid complication for the moment.

Most of the cases of pollution that have awakened interest are cases in which some actual harms are caused within the exposed population in addition to any pure risk imposed.[13] If it is impermissible to cause actual harms, then these polluting activities are impermissible whether or not the imposition of pure risk is itself a harm. As a practical matter, then, what a Lockean should say about the permissibility of most polluting activities will not be much influenced by questions about pure risk. Moreover, his strictness about border crossings should suffice to rule out a much broader range of such activities than we currently prohibit. However, at least some polluting activities may result in nothing more than the imposition of pure risk, and some activities that are of concern with regard to air pollution are worrisome more because of their riskiness than because of the actual harm they are now causing, for example, the generation of power by nuclear fission. Further, pollution aside, many of the things we do impose upon others pure risk but only infrequently lead to actual harm, and it is of interest to ask what a Lockean might say about such activities in general.

COMMON PROPERTY

Again, we need a distinction. The fellow who operates an unsafe nuclear reactor entirely on his own property seems to cross no boundaries. What of the fellow who introduces some toxic substances into the atmosphere which, as it happens, no one ever inhales, although some are at risk of doing so? He has crossed no boundaries of private property, perhaps, but in the Lockean scheme the atmosphere is property, too: common property. By rendering a portion of the atmosphere toxic, he has in effect appropriated it from the commons, making it impossible for anyone else to use it without injury. For vividness, imagine that the toxins take the form of a cloud that floats intact around the earth's atmosphere. Locke permits such appropriation only under special conditions: one must mix one's labor with the property taken from the commons, one must not use it wastefully, and one must leave "enough and as good" in common for others. Let us suppose that the act involved mixing his labor and was not simply wasteful: the toxic substance is an unavoidable by-product of a process he was using to make a living.[14] Does he leave enough and as good in common for others?

The bare fact that no one happens to breathe that part of the atmosphere he has appropriated suggests that he left enough to go around. To be sure of this, we would have to be sure that no one had to make special efforts to avoid breathing the spoiled air. Assume that we do know this. Did he leave the air "as good" as before? We do not know exactly what Locke meant by this phrase, but let us suppose it to mean that the amount remaining in common after the appropriation is of the same quality as that which was originally appropriated. Here we may find that our polluter has transgressed even though no one breathed his toxins. If, for example, the bit of air he appropriated was cleaner than the atmospheric average at the time, he has violated the Lockean condition. Or suppose there is a general worsening of the air. He has (let us say) taken some air of 1982 quality and removed it from the commons. By 2050, there may not be enough air of 1982 quality to go around. That would not be entirely our friend's doing, of course, but Locke's condition could be interpreted in such a way that this should not matter; at least part of the scarcity of 1982-quality air is his doing.

The polluter could complain that it is unrealistic to imagine his toxins floating around as a cloud of quasi-private property; surely they would simply dissipate into the atmosphere, and surely it would be an exaggeration to say that he has privately appropriated all of the air into which these pollutants make their way. It is, in fact, unclear what a Lockean should say about this sort of case,[15] but let us grant that his original utilization of common property need not have the effect of appropriating for him all of the atmosphere subsequently tinged by this pollution. Thus, it would not be illegitimate for others to make use of this tinged air. It might, however, be harmful for them to do so, especially if the pollutants involved have no threshold of zero effect. By his initial use of common property in 1982, he will have had the effect that air regarded as common property in 2050 is less good. If there is not enough 1982-quality air available in 2050, then his original utilization seems impermissible on Lockean grounds.

Now our polluter may protest that eventually his toxins will, in effect, disappear, leaving the commons as good as before. If by this he means that they will settle out of the atmosphere, he does not strengthen his case, for then they may leave 2050 common land less good than 1982 common land. They might even fall on private property, an outright border crossing at any level of effect. If instead he means that they will become harmless with time, that of course depends upon the nature of the pollutants; some pollutants become *worse* health threats after undergoing chemical change or combination in the atmosphere. Moreover, even if a breakdown to harmless substances does occur, it will take time, so that there may be a period during which enough and as good has not been left in common. Most likely, what the polluter has in mind is the rather old-fashioned view that nature is so vast that his particular effect upon it is negligible, of trifling consequence.

This view is old-fashioned in at least two ways. First, no one today can fail to be impressed with the finitude of that part of nature we actually inhabit. Second, we now know that small causes needn't always have small effects. "There is evidence that cancers start from single cells and it is believed that a single molecule may be enough to start a cancer."[16] Even if one's polluting activities emit no more than one part per billion of a carcinogen, at this concentration there would be trillions of potentially cancer-causing molecules in a room-sized volume of air. Modern medicine aside, the polluter needs to be reminded that Lockean views do not say that whether a border is wrongfully crossed depends upon the magnitude of the effect. Taking from the commons, even ever so slightly, is taking the property of others.

Still, suppose that nature really were boundless. And suppose, too, as Locke did, that the provision against wastage drops out once an imperishable medium of exchange has been introduced. Would it even then be trivial that the requirement of leaving enough and as good be met? Nature may be infinite without all portions of it being equally accessible or equally worth having. It would hardly count as leaving "enough and as good" for future generations if they have to go to the ends of the universe or great effort to obtain it. If someone were to appropriate a bit of handily located and readily used common property, like the earth's atmosphere, leaving others plenty of good atmosphere frozen on the surface of a planet circling Alpha-Centauri, he would have violated the Lockean conditions.

There is, however, a more interesting point to be made. Suppose nature to exceed in extent what we could ever actually appropriate, and even to be equally valuable and equally accessible in its parts. Might we then take from the commons at will? If your *private* property exceeded in extent what you would ever actually use, I still would not be entitled to take a portion of it even though you were left enough and as good afterward. On the classical Lockean view, I would not be entitled to take part of your property even if I substituted for it something of equal value, unless I had your permission to do so. It emerges that Locke's justification of private appropriation from the commons rests upon an assumption that common property need not be accorded the same respect as private property, even that we need not accord others the same respect as (part) owners of common property that we owe them as owners (sometimes, part owners) of private property.[17]

What is the justification for this asymmetry? For Locke, the argument involves religious and practical considerations. He believes that God gave man the world in common in order that he might use it for his survival. He notes that as a practical matter, however, we cannot survive without appropriating from the commons: anything I take from nature and consume to sustain my own existence is for that reason no longer available to others. Further, as a practical matter, I cannot get the consent of all owners of common property – all mankind – before appropriating from it. So if we are to survive and flourish, which Locke believes to be both God's will and a law of reason, some nonconsensual way of legitimating private appropriation is needed.

Even if we leave God out of it, this is a plausible argument. But how can it be the basis for a Lockean property right that entitles an individual to exclude others from his private property even under those circumstances in which, by taking from it, they might enhance their chance of survival while still leaving him enough and as good? So long as there is enough and as good available to him either in common or in his remaining private holdings, or in the two together, the argument seems incapable of generating a right of exclusion. What of the fact that mixed in with his private holdings is his labor, something by nature belonging to him? Well, in his initial appropriation from the commons he, too, took something by nature belonging to other people.[18]

All along, Lockeans have taken common property – and our rights in it – less seriously than private property. If I besmirch part of your estate, this is a boundary crossing even if that besmirching never affects you materially. What I do reduces the capacities of your estate by effecting a physical change in it, and this, we say, is a wrongful harm even if you never attempt to use these capacities. For example, if I bespoil an out-of-the-way corner of your land and thereby lower its market value, I have wrongfully deprived you of property even if you never notice the spoilation or the loss in value. Why isn't a polluting act that reduces the capacities of common property (perhaps lowering its market value, too, were it to be sold), a violation of the property rights we all have in the commons, even if no one is ever materially affected by this act? Consistency would seem to demand that we put the two sorts of property on the same footing, at least in this regard.[19] But we have two choices of footing: we may promote common property to the status of private property, or we may demote private property to the status of common property.[20]

197

If we seize on the first alternative, then we must regard acts that introduce pollutants into common property without the permission of all mankind as boundary crossings, even if no individuals ever happen to have their own private holdings infringed. It would be irrelevant whether a polluter's effect were small, or whether enough and as good were left in common; just as it is irrelevant to whether I may rightfully take your private property that what I take is of little value, or that you have enough and as good private property left over. Most of the polluting acts we have heretofore called impositions of pure risk would become boundary crossings because they would involve violating property rights in the commons, and therefore would be morally impermissible harms. The result would be an extremely restrictive position on pollution. Indeed, there would not be much room for pollution left: one could befoul one's own, private nest, but only if nothing seeps over a border with common or private property. Even the idea of a private nest would become problematic, for appropriation of any property beyond one's mere self would require universal consent from mankind, including future generations. To make this first alternative workable, it would be necessary to develop a powerful doctrine of tacit or hypothetical consent. That may seem to be clutching at straws, given the difficulties of these notions, but they must be grasped at, for one cannot sensibly embrace the conclusion that there is no justified private appropriation from the commons. We must breathe, after all.

The second alternative, of demoting private property to the status of common property, fits better with the original Lockean argument and has less chokingly restrictive implications. (It should be kept in mind that we are talking here of natural property rights. There may be good pragmatic reasons for according different treatment to private and common property in civil law. On a Lockean view, however, civil law must respect natural rights. So unless citizens were to contract into some special arrangement, a civil code would have to accord property rights in the commons at least as much respect as they are due in a state of nature.) On this alternative, one may acquire private property from the commons by meeting the Lockean conditions – mixing one's labor, not wasting, leaving enough and as good for others – but this private property may in turn be appropriated by another if he mixes his labor with it, doesn't waste it, and leaves the original owner with enough and as good (in private or in readily accessible common property). Private property would no longer be inviolable, and this may make the second alternative unattractive to many. But if one believes in natural property rights, has doubts about tacit or hypothetical consent, and wants to be able to draw a breath without asking permission, this may be the best one can do.

Pollution of private or common property, so long as it leaves enough and as good remaining, may be permissible on this alternative, and so it is less restrictive about pollution than any version of Lockeanism thus far discussed. Even so, it would prohibit the imposition of pure risk in those cases where this involves lowering the quality of common property. That is a more restrictive policy on risk than many who think themselves Lockeans would accept, especially if we understand the criterion 'as good' broadly, to include not only the capacity of common property to support life, but also its aesthetic qualities: the clarity of the air, the naturalness of the landscape, and so on. Locke's view was that man was given the earth to enjoy, not merely to subsist on. Certainly, if someone physically changes another's private property in a way that reduces its aesthetic value, this is ordinarily regarded as a harm. If common property deserves equal respect, then ruining the aesthetic qualities of common property would be permissible only if the same were permitted of private property; since private property includes our bodies, I doubt many would accept the notion that aesthetic damage may be ignored as without moral significance. Similar remarks apply to, for example, the economic value of common property. Thus, if my factory's smokestack emits a noxious substance, which as it happens no one actually breathes, I may still have crossed boundaries impermissibly by reducing the value or capacity of common property as a sustainer of life, a source of aesthetic enjoyment, or an economic asset.

The phrase 'enough and as good' is sufficiently vague to leave it indeterminate just how much of a reduction in restrictiveness the second alternative would effect. The phrase may even be ambiguous: must what is left be as good in total as what was before, or (more weakly) must only that which is "enough" be as good as what was before? A very loose reading of the phrase – or of the other conditions of nonwastage and "mixing one's labor" – would leave private as well as public property quite open for use without the owner's consent.[21] However, one would be able to gain freedom in appropriating from common property only to the extent that one grants others similar liberties with one's own private property. This trade-off is only reasonable, for in both cases one is taking something owned by others.

Although advocates of Lockean natural rights theories have favored *laissez-faire* government and free-market solutions to a wide range of social problems, we have seen that such theories in fact furnish the basis for very tight governmental regulations on pollution. The reason is straightforward: the function of a Lockean state is to enforce property rights by prohibiting and policing unconsented-to boundary crossings, and pollution violates such rights. Since natural rights constrain civil rights, it would be impermissible for the state ever to permit crossings of natural boundaries for the sake of economic efficiency, social utility, or the like, unless all members of civil society consented to such an arrangement. On the classical view, it would be usurpation for the state to permit crossings of an individual's boundaries without his consent, even if this individual would be a net gainer in the end. Paternalism is simply an especially insidious form of usurpation.

We have seen that the restrictiveness of Lockean theories applies to dispositional as well as manifest harms, as long as the dispositional harm is due to actual physical effects of the polluting act. We have also seen that even when a polluting act merely increases the probability of manifest or dispositional harm, without having an actual physical effect on others, it may yet be impermissible on a Lockean view. Exactly which polluting acts are impermissible will depend upon how one resolves the asymmetry of private versus common property, or whether one finds a way of salvaging the classical, asymmetrical view. But on all plausible readings of these various forms of Lockeanism, the state should be much more vigorous in prohibiting and policing pollution than is now the case. A call for a return to Lockean property rights as the foundation of social justice is a call for greater, rather than lesser, governmental restriction on polluting activities. What else should we expect from a view that erects absolute boundaries around individuals and their possessions and makes individuals sovereign within these boundaries?

Yet in what remains of this chapter, I will try to argue that Lockean views, even in their most restrictive forms, may in some ways not be restrictive enough. A plausible moral theory, by my lights, would be less restrictive overall, but more restrictive in certain areas, in particular, with respect to the imposition of pure risk. Previously we considered a person who imposes risks but seems to cross no boundaries of either common or private property, the man who operates an unsafe nuclear reactor next door. As long as the reactor functions normally, he keeps within the boundaries separating his private domain from all others. On Lockean views, his should be a morally neutral act.[22]

The Lockean accepts the deontological notion that some acts – for example, the violation of a natural right – are intrinsically wrong, even when they happen to have good consequences.[23] Let us accept this idea for now. If any act is intrinsically wrong, it would seem intrinsically wrong intentionally to raise the probability innocents will suffer harm. This is just a probabilistic form of the familiar principle that it is intrinsically wrong to bring deliberate harm to innocents. Is intent essential? If we hold the description of an act, $A$, constant, then it would be odd to say both (1) it is intrinsically wrong to do $A$ with intent to do $A$, and (2) $A$ itself is morally neutral. It seems more reasonable to say that there must be something wrong with $A$ in the first place, which explains why intending to do $A$ is intrinsically wrong. In the case where $A$ is "acting so as to harm innocents," this is readily granted by most deontologists. Should it not also be granted when $A$ is "acting so as to raise the probability of harm to innocents"? If this is so, then operating (what one does not realize is) an unsafe reactor in one's basement is not morally indifferent after all, for we would certainly want to say that doing so with intent to imperil others by operating an unsafe reactor is wrong. The contrary urge we have, to say that there is nothing wrong with operating an unsafe reactor so long as one is intending only to operate a safe reactor, is the urge to displace attention from the evaluation of acts to the evaluation of agents. If the agent has reason to believe the reactor is no threat, he is doing nothing contrary to his subjective duty: his duty relative to what he believes (or has reason to believe) is the case. But there is also the question whether what he is doing is something he would be obliged not to do if he had full knowledge of the facts, that is, whether he is failing to do his objective duty. In practice, we often take subjective duty as the best approximation of objective duty, but recognize that the two may fail to coincide when we are mistaken about the facts. Is the man operating an unsafe reactor doing his objective duty? Of course not. One is objectively obliged not to maintain an unsafe condition that threatens innocents (other things equal), even if this is being done without evil intent.

Can we explain what is morally wrong with such an act in terms of the crossing of boundaries or the violation of property rights? What territorial right is violated if someone acts within his private domain in such a way as to increase the probability another will suffer wrongful harm, yet no such harm actually results?

It seems that the Lockean must recognize there to be something wrong with acts that raise the probability others will suffer wrongful harm. One motivation for the Lockean scheme draws upon the idea of respecting others and their rights. It certainly would raise a question about the extent to which I respect your rights if I thought it permissible to expose them to arbitrarily high increases in the probability they would be violated, so long as these probabilities did not chance to be realized. (In many cases, even if I deliberately set out to harm you I could do no more than to raise the probability you will be injured: I may take a shot at you, but my aim is imperfect.) To avoid entanglement in questions about intent, let us say in a hypothetical mode that if I were to know that an act of mine would increase the probability another would suffer wrongful harm, then, other things equal, respect for that person would be a reason for not performing it. Respect for others is not simply a matter of not happening to violate their rights, but of taking some care that my actions not happen to do so. If I treat your belongings carelessly when they are on loan to me, you may legitimately feel that I showed inadequate respect for your property even if no actual damage happened to occur. Moreover, it seems incompatible with the Kantian dictum of treating others as ends, not as means alone, to think there is nothing wrong in pursuing one's own interests even when this involves exposing others to arbitrarily high levels of risk, so long as no boundaries actually are crossed. "A miss is as good as a mile" seems too expedient an attitude to be consistent with respecting others as ends in themselves.

However, acceptance of this argument would precipitate an important change in the simplest version of the Lockean picture, for it would mean that the rights of others are not simply side constraints determining an arena within which I am free to go about my business as I please.[24] Rather, I am under other-regarding obligations even on my own turf. My freedom to swing my arm does not stop at your nose, but at some point where I begin to show inadequate respect for you by putting your nose at too much risk. Lockeans face something of a dilemma here. On the one hand, if they do not take risk into account except when it involves the crossing of a boundary of common or private property, then although they preserve the simple, territorial picture of morality that attracts many to Lockeanism, they will fail to take into account all that we mean when we talk of respect for others or their rights. On the other hand, if they take risk into account, then they will face some large difficulties: either they must redefine the moral boundaries to make them more restrictive, or they must admit that there is more to morality than staying within one's boundaries. This last admission would open the way for a more thorough rethinking of the Lockean picture.

Let us call an act that raises the probability another will suffer wrongful harm as a causal outcome of one's own behavior, where we leave it open whether this harmful outcome actually obtains, an *endangering* act. We may ask whether risk presents Lockeans with a genuine dilemma by considering several ways in which a Lockean might attempt to treat endangerment within the original spirit of his view.

## REVISIONIST LOCKEANISM

### *Self-defense*

For a certain range of cases, Locke himself has developed a doctrine for dealing with risk prior to actual border crossing, for he wrote that an individual who

> declare[s] by word or action, not a passionate and hasty but a sedate, settled design upon another's life, puts him[self] in a state of war with him against whom he has declared such an intention, and so has exposed his life to the other's power... it being reasonable and just I should have a right to destroy that which threatens me with destruction.[25]

Someone who deliberately puts me at risk has, then, violated the side constraints even before any actual injury is inflicted, and I would be entitled to use force or otherwise violate his territory if this were necessary to stop him. The motivation for such a principle is clear enough: were I to have to wait until actual injury has occurred, I would be defenseless against many serious harms. The classical Lockean, then, may claim to have a doctrine to deal with the imposition of risk, even when the risk remains pure.

However, we have already seen that it is plausible to say that endangerment morally ought not to happen, other things equal, even when it is not intended as such, and so does not involve any sort of settled design or declaration of war. One may endanger innocently if one's acts pose a threat to the rights of others but one is not at fault for failing to realize this; one may endanger negligently if one's failure to realize the threat one's acts pose is culpable in some way (e.g., is the result of a history of carelessness or inattention); and one may endanger deliberately if one actually intends that one's acts imperil others. (There are other categories as well.) Locke's doctrine applies only to the last case and so gives us no basis for constraining the innocent or negligent endangerer. Of course, we ordinarily judge the character of the deliberate endangerer more severely than that of the negligent endangerer, and we may have nothing bad to say about the character of the innocent endangerer. But in all cases we may judge the endangering act as one that, other things equal, ought not to be done (assuming that a nonendangering alternative is available to the agent). What is needed, then, is a development of Locke's theory to cover all sorts of endangerment.

This development must perform two tasks. First, it must answer such questions as when endangerment is wrong, what counteractions are justified against it, and so on. Second, it must tell us what it is about (say) innocent endangerment that makes it wrong, since such endangerment may not involve any actual boundary crossings and does not involve evil intent. We will consider two proposals, focusing initially on how they would accomplish the second task.

(1) If we cannot locate the wrongness of innocent endangerment in the psychology of the endangerer, we may yet look to the psychology of those endangered. If it is a harm to step on someone's toes, should it not be a harm to cause the often more severe and lasting discomfort that fear of harm may cause? Fear may be as debilitating as physical injury and may even bring about a number of physical disorders. Why draw boundary lines so as to include trivial physical damage and exclude grave mental damage? Is this any more than a fetishism of the tangible?

These strike me as important questions for the Lockean to ask himself, but Lockeans may be suspicious of the notion of psychological harm.[26] One may, after all, be concerned to distinguish "real harms," such as damage to property, from "imagined harms," such as the offense others might take at one's ideas or habits. If it were morally required that we avoid innocently causing certain psychological responses in others, it would be difficult to imagine what a Lockean system of boundaries might look like. Psychological effects flow across existing boundaries in a marvelous variety of ways, some of which depend much more heavily upon how others regard us than upon what we actually do. A natural right that no one else act in such a way as to cause one psychological distress would radically change the character of a Lockean scheme of things.

This is not of itself a conclusive argument against such a right. Moreover, one certainly cannot argue that damage to property is in general more troubling to individuals, or more a sign of disrespect for them, or more likely to involve treating them as a mere means, than the psychological distress they may suffer at the hands of others. If anything, the opposite seems true. It is therefore something of a mystery why psychological effects play so small a role in Lockean views. After all, such views usually do incorporate a prohibition against fraud, which essentially involves a psychological effect.

I suspect that a number of long-standing convictions are at work: ideas and feelings may be viewed as simply unreal in a way that land or limbs are not; individuals are thought to have more control over their mental states and how these are affected by the acts of others than they do over their physical states, so it is more likely that they could contrive to manufacture mental harms;[27] physical harm is more publicly observable than psychological harm, so its authenticity, origin, and extent are more reliably assessable. In some cases, however, psychological damage is real, nonmanufactured, and observable enough.

It seems implausible to claim that my natural rights are violated by an otherwise innocent act of another that causes me fear if the fear is an irrational reaction to the act or if the fear, while rational, has as its object no piece of potential wrongdoing on the part of the other – for example, if you inform me by word or deed that my neighbor is coming after me with a hayfork, thereby exciting in me considerable rational fear of wrongdoing, but not on your part. (Is there anything intrinsically wrong with causing the anxiety that fear involves if the fear would be rational in the circumstances? Does it matter whether the object of fear is human wrongdoing or some natural calamity? Of course, it seems wrong to torment people with fear – rational or irrational – but the wrongness here could be laid to one's intention to disturb or to one's negligence in attending to how one's behavior affects others.)

Let us consider only the simplest case: Should a Lockean admit a natural right that others not act so as to cause one rational fear that one will suffer wrongful harm from them? Someone might argue that this right would do more to restrict our behavior than it would to enhance the quality of our lives or our freedom of action. But this is not a Lockean argument, for it uses aggregative, balancing considerations about consequences to test whether a right exists. A Lockean might try a different sort of argument, seemingly popular today: we cannot live in a no-risk society, so we must learn to live with a degree of rational fear rather than obsessively try to eliminate it from our lives. However, a Lockean presumably would reject the comparable argument that since we cannot live in a crime-free society, we must accept some criminal activity as permissible. Natural rights should not lose their hold upon us merely because we cannot eliminate all violations of them; nor is the impossibility of eliminating all violations a reason not to seek to minimize violation.

I know of no convincing argument that a Lockean, concerned that individuals be respected as ends, could use to refute the claim that we have a natural right that others not act in such a way as to cause us rational fear of suffering wrongful harm at their hands.[28] Yet even admitting such a right would not wholly solve the Lockean's problem of capturing the wrongness of endangerment. For endangerment seems wrong even when it arouses no fear in those at risk, for example, when they simply are unaware of their peril. We might reformulate the right as a right that no one act in a way that *would* awaken rational fear of wrongful harm from him were his actions to be known and their possible consequences grasped. But is that all that is wrong with endangerment? Would it make any difference to the wrongness of my playing Russian roulette on my sleeping roommate that he is someone who constitutionally feels no fear? In such a case, is the wrongness attributable to the fact that someone else, less fearless, would feel fear if he knew *he* were being exposed to such endangerment? Kantians, at least, would presumably deny this. They have held that the wrong done to an individual by (for example) fraud or coercion is not just a matter of the discomfort such an act, if known, would cause him (or an average person). Rather, Kantians have argued that such acts fail to show adequate respect for the individual as an autonomous being, discomfort apart. Therefore Lockeans who would employ a Kantian interpretation of the notion of respect for persons and rights must affirm that what makes endangering acts wrong is not merely the uncomfortable psychological states they may cause in others. This would also fit with the Lockean treatment of actual – as opposed to potential – property crimes, for there it was not essential that the property loss was accompanied by any psychological distress.

(2) Let us, then, consider a second proposal, one that makes no essential reference to psychological states, either on the part of the endangerer or the endangered. Intent and fear alike are displaced from the center of the ethical analysis of endangerment, and a new natural right is recognized: as long as one remains within the bounds of one's own property or common property, one has a right against being exposed by the actions of others – even when they, too, remain on their own or common property – to an increase in the probability one will suffer wrongful harm.[29] This seems a natural extension of the Lockean natural right not to suffer wrongful harm to

the case where violation is merely probable. If you like, it recognizes one's safety, or freedom from risk of wrongful harm, as part of one's property.

However, such a natural right would impose heavy restrictions upon the free action of others. Do you have a natural right that I not read *Crime and Punishment* if this would cause a smallish increase in the probability that I might one day rob and bludgeon you? Even inaction on my part may add something to the probability you will suffer wrongful harm, for example, if I fail to speak sternly to a surly youth, perhaps encouraging him down the road to delinquency. Holders of a Lockean view would no doubt object strongly to such a right, pointing out that it would intrude grossly into an individual's proper sphere of action. Yet on Lockean views an individual's proper sphere of action is not an independent concept. It is defined as the area left open by the exercise of natural rights (one's own and others'), and so cannot be used to determine those rights.[30] Now, I am perfectly sympathetic with the claim that to recognize a right against endangerment would be to restrict individual freedom excessively, but Lockeans should be wary of such arguments: they suggest the possibility of trading off individual territorial rights for some other good, namely, freedom. If natural rights are not set as prior constraints upon the pursuit of any good, even freedom, then all rights in the Lockean canon should be subject to reevaluation. The cautious Lockean will retain the priority of natural rights and look for some nonconsequentialist reason for rejecting or qualifying an extremely restrictive right against endangerment. Several possibilities suggest themselves: one might exclude reciprocal risk, or set a threshold of acceptable risk, or introduce a notion of proximate causation; one might make use of quasi-contractual notions such as tacit or hypothetical consent; or one might pursue a strategy using elements of both these suggestions. In what follows, I will review some of these possibilities.

### Reciprocal Risk

Special principles regarding endangerment might not be needed within a Lockean scheme if there were a mutual imposition of risk throughout civil society and states of nature. If this were the case, then all wrongdoing involved in endangerment would in effect cancel out, and it might be possible to avoid the problem of redefining boundaries altogether. This would not be a satisfactory resolution from a theoretical standpoint (are we to limit application of Lockean theory to those societies and those times when the imposition of risk is nearly reciprocal?), but it would as a practical matter eliminate the risk-based problem of finding a middle course between extremes of permissiveness and restrictiveness.

Unfortunately, however, the imposition of risk is manifestly not reciprocal. Not only do some face risks owing to the actions of others upon whom they themselves impose no risks, but imbalance in the magnitude of risks imposed is at least as common as balance. This is especially clear in the three cases with which this chapter is concerned: ambient air pollution, pollution in the workplace, and side-stream tobacco smoke.

The Lockean might admit that the imposition of risk is not in fact reciprocal, but then say that it should obey a principle of reciprocity. This would allow individuals substantial freedom of action as long as they do not impose risks upon others greater than those imposed upon them. Such a principle would offer an explanation of what is wrong with smoking in public places or the emission of high levels of pollutants by certain industries: the risk imposed upon others is out of balance with the risk experienced at the hands of others. A normative appeal to reciprocity, however, gives rise to problems absent from its descriptive use. It is barely conceivable that one could keep track of all the risk one experiences and regulate the risk one creates so as to apportion it accordingly, matching both agents and magnitudes. Moreover, the principle has the consequence that it would be impermissible to impose any risks upon future generations, powerless as they are to impose risks upon us. Since virtually any course of action we are likely to pursue will impose risks upon future generations, this principle would hardly enable us to avoid excesses of restrictiveness.

### Acceptable Risk and Tacit Consent

Complexities of reciprocal apportionment of risk and quandaries about future generations could be avoided if a threshold level of acceptable risk could be established. Let us suppose that we can identify a level of risk that people in general find tolerable. We might then posit a natural right not to be exposed by the actions of others to increases above this threshold in one's risk of wrongful harm. This approach would return some of the neatness of the original Lockean view: so long as one stays below the threshold, one is free to act as one pleases without regard to possible effects on others. Moreover, there is a plausible associated notion of respect for persons: to respect a person involves (among other things) refraining from exposing him to unusual ("unacceptable") levels of risk. Since reciprocity is not presupposed, such a principle could apply across generations.

208

How might a threshold of acceptable risk be fixed? One could simply observe what levels of risk people do in fact accept in their daily lives without taking special precautions or demanding special compensation, and then infer that this level must not be intolerable. In effect, one is assuming something like tacit consent to this risk level.

It might be objected that people notoriously vary in their willingness to accept risks and that we have no business assuming tacit consent to average levels of risk on the part of those who are atypically risk averse. But let us not quarrel about this, for the whole proposal is deeply confused.

The fact that I daily tolerate a level of risk $r$ in no way shows that I am indifferent about whether an additional risk of magnitude $r$ is imposed upon me, yet the right at issue concerns increments of risk. Moreover, if rational individuals accept a level of risk $r$, we may be sure that is because they feel they gain something in return, if only convenience. Whether such individuals would find objectionable the imposition upon them of some further risk, even if very much less than $r$, will depend upon whether they receive something worth the risk in return. It makes no more sense to ask for a level of "acceptable risk" in general than for an "acceptable price" in general. Is five dollars an acceptable price? Well, what is it the price of? Something I want? Is the same thing or a good substitute available to me elsewhere at lesser cost? What are the total resources available to me at the time, and what other spending options exist? It would not be rational for me to accept a one-in-a-million chance of harm if it brought with it no possible benefits, or if other alternatives offered lower risk or greater benefits without greater cost. By looking at the choice behavior of rational individuals, then, we do not discern anything like a threshold of significance with regard to risk; risks are accepted relative to a particular range of options, with an eye to possible benefits.[31]

Suppose, however, that sense could be made of the idea of taking a certain degree of endangerment as a threshold of significance. Would the Lockean's problems be solved? Let us call risk or increments of risk below this threshold level trivial. For simplicity, let us ignore questions about benefits, and imagine that the Lockean arrives at the following principle: one has a natural right that others not cause a nontrivial increase in the probability that one will suffer wrongful harm as a consequence of their actions.[32] Like other Lockean rights, this one would be quite restrictive regarding polluting activity; just how restrictive depends upon what counts as a trivial degree of risk.

Yet it is not clear how such a right would be deployed within a Lockean scheme, for Lockean rights characteristically apply between individuals.

209

Consider the following sort of case. A polluting act by one individual spreads a toxic substance over a large area. Each of the individuals in that area suffers only a trivial increase in the probability of suffering a wrongful harm as a result, so no individual rights against endangerment are violated. But the probability that *someone* in the area will be wrongfully harmed may be nontrivial – indeed, it may be arbitrarily close to one – suggesting that the act should be impermissible even though it violates no individual's Lockean rights. In another sort of case, a number of people act separately in ways that each causes a trivial increase in the probability I will suffer wrongful harm. But the result is a nontrivial increase in the probability I will suffer wrongful harm from someone (though not from any one person in particular). Again, no individual violates another individual's rights, but nontrivial risk – indeed, arbitrarily great risk – has been imposed. In an extreme case of this kind, two independent acts, each imposing trivial risk on its own, together produce almost certain harm, as when two pollutants, individually not very toxic but in combination lethal, are independently released in my neighborhood.

Other things equal, a rational person would be just as disturbed at the prospect of suffering wrongful harm at the hands of two independent agents as two acting in conspiracy, or at the hands of someone (he knows not whom) as at the hands of a particular individual. When we apply the Lockean framework to questions of social policy as well as individual conduct, it becomes still more obscure why it should matter whether a nontrivial increase in risk is due to the act of one individual or two, or whether an effect will be borne by individuals as a group rather than singly. The image of individuals holding rights against individuals, and of individual trespass as the paradigm of impermissible action, ceases to be illuminating. It would seem appropriate to depart from classical Lockeanism enough to take into account aggregative effects of endangering behavior, but there is no obvious extension of individualist natural rights theory to cover such cases. (We encountered similar difficulties handling aggregative effects in discussing Lockean views about appropriation from the commons.)

The very use of a notion of acceptable risk has already called for a significant departure from classical Lockeanism, for the notion of a threshold of "significant effect" has no answer in traditional Lockean property rights. The consistent Lockean must explain why it is morally impermissible for me to commit trivial theft, but permissible for me to endanger others to a small degree. Of course, he may say that deliberate or negligent endangerment is always wrong, regardless of degree – the threshold applies only to innocent endangerment. However, in the case of private property, Lockeans have held that it is (objectively) wrong for me to take something belonging to another even if I do so innocently. This disparity in the treatment of innocent endangerment versus innocent misappropriation could not be justified by a Lockean on the grounds that it is socially efficient to enforce laws against theft rigorously while permitting some latitude when it comes to endangerment. This may indeed be an efficient arrangement, but we are here concerned not with civil codes but with natural rights, which cannot be overridden or abridged – on a Lockean view – for the sake of efficiency. Nor can a Lockean justify the disparity by pointing to our general social tolerance of low levels of risk; we also tolerate low levels of theft.

The notion of an acceptable level of risk thus proves both dubious in itself and difficult to render consistent with a Lockean natural rights theory. There may be some hope for a natural right based upon a threshold of risk, but only if some imposing problems can be solved in a Lockean spirit, and I see no such solutions in the offing.

### Causal Proximity and Complexity

I burn some coal to heat my house; sulfur compounds released in combustion enter the atmosphere; in time, these compounds are picked up by water droplets in the clouds, forming dilute sulfuric acid; these acid droplets then rain down on the surface of the earth, slightly blighting your health and home. A Lockean might note that tort law embodies criteria of proximate causation that lessen or remove liability for certain highly mediated outcomes of one's acts. By emphasizing the indirect character of many pollution-caused harms or risks, a Lockean might be able to find elbow room within his scheme. One would be obliged only to refrain from those acts that would proximately cause (or threaten to proximately cause) wrongful harm.

Intuitively, there is great appeal to such a suggestion, but I suspect that much of the appeal comes from what has by now become a familiar confusion: mistaking the question "How much responsibility should we assign to an individual for a given harm?" for the question "Other things equal, is it right or wrong in an objective sense to initiate a chain of events resulting in harm to an innocent?" In the former case, but not the latter, length and complexity of causal chains seem potentially relevant; yet it is the latter that concerns us. Suppose that, to scare a crow away from the soup pot at our campsite, I pitch a rock at him, which ricochets off the pot, strikes a tree branch, rolls down the side of a tent, and drops squarely into the mouth of a sleeping fellow camper, chipping his expensive bridgework. Clearly, if I could have foreseen the whole sequence, I would have been obliged not to toss the stone, that is, I objectively ought not to have performed the act. Would this judgment be altered in the least if a few more steps had occurred between my act and his harm? One may of course think I deserve less punishment than someone who deliberately took aim at his dozing friend, but even here intent matters more than directness: if I *had* been aiming at my friend, but my arm was unreliable, the stone might have ricocheted off the pot, struck a branch, . . . and I would be as culpable as if I had had a more accurate arm. Length and complexity of causal chain have much to do with foreseeability, and therefore with assessments of intent or negligence, but long and involved causal chains that terminate in wrongful harm are not more objectively permissible than short, straightforward ones, other things equal.[33]

### Consent, Hypothetical Consent, and Compensation

Perhaps it is time to stop casting about for an appropriate way of avoiding or weakening a Lockean natural right against endangerment. After all, the Lockean has at his disposal a device for achieving great flexibility in restriction and permission even if the right is absolute: consent. Individuals are entitled to exchange, sell, or give away their rights against endangerment. Through the arrangements made among individuals, the Lockean scheme makes a place for trade-offs of rights against benefits. To carry justificatory force, such consent would have to be free and undeceived (at least, the deception could not have come from the other parties to the agreement). Must the consent also be informed? (*How* informed?) Rather than take up these issues, let us suppose that the Lockean has devised an acceptable account of the criteria of legitimate consent.

Arguably, there are cases in which free and informed consent has been given, yet one ought not to perform the consented-to act. For example, if the agreed-upon terms of a contract prove quite onerous, it may be that I should release the other party (perhaps in return for some compensation) even though I have much to gain by holding him to it. Agreements have a way of becoming onerous even when entered into with what was at the time good information and reasonable care; one can simply be exceptionally unlucky with what was a rational, calculated risk. When this occurs, it may be unconscionable to hold someone to a conscionable contract. In another kind of case, a smoker may find it rare for anyone to refuse his request for permission to light, yet it may still be wrong in some such cases for the smoker to exploit this reticence. It is hardly a new idea that there may be obligations to others not based upon rights. I may, for example, be morally obliged to help you if you are in need and the necessary aid would not be burdensome to me, but not because you have a right to my assistance. Mightn't there also be humanitarian obligations not to cross voluntarily opened borders in some circumstances? Such speculations may not be very libertarian in spirit, but a reasonable notion of respect for persons as ends would seem to involve some humanitarian obligations of this kind. Thus, a Lockean scheme seeking to express such a notion may be unable to treat consent – even when free and informed – as an unproblematic source of justification for the imposition of harm or risk.

Let us ignore such problems, and accept for now the view that individual sovereignty includes the sovereignty of consent. Certainly, it is part of the attractive antipaternalism of Lockeanism that individuals are treated as the ultimate judges and guardians of their own interests.

Even so, it may not be feasible to make widespread use of explicit consent to gain flexibility regarding endangerment. Someone contemplating an activity that involves releasing harmful substances into the air seldom is able to confine the risk thereby imposed to those individuals he has been able to consult fully in advance. And a single individual, even though only marginally affected, would be entitled to veto any such activity, however much it may benefit others, by exercising his right against endangerment. Moreover, some of those put at risk may yet be unborn, and no existing individual can bargain for the claims of future individuals.

If it is in practice often impossible to obtain explicit consent to endangerment, a Lockean may propose as an alternative a scheme of after-the-fact compensation to those exposed to harm or risk.[34] If a polluting activity harms an individual, the compensation required would be such that the victim would have been indifferent before the fact between not suffering the harm at all and suffering the harm but receiving the compensation given. If a local factory blackens my house, and the factory pays to have it repainted and provides me with a small sum to cover inconvenience, I may end up as pleased with this outcome as I would have been had the blackening not occurred. If an individual is simply put at risk, the appropriate level of compensation would be the premium one would have had to pay prior to the exposure to make him indifferent between being exposed to the risk (and receiving the premium) and not. The premium need not be a sure thing; individuals may prefer a state of affairs in which they face increased risk of some harm but at the same time enjoy a higher probability of receiving some benefit. When this standard of compensation for harm or risk is used, one is in a sense obtaining hypothetical consent to a package of harm or risk plus compensation: the package would have been acceptable if offered. Such a scheme has some practical advantages over requiring explicit consent before the fact. First, future generations cannot be consulted, but they can be compensated (if, e.g., this generation leaves behind substantial benefits to offset the risks we bequeath to others). Second, one gains flexibility, for in some circumstances it may be more manageable to provide compensation after the fact than to seek to obtain consent beforehand. Whenever compensation would cost less than the amount to be gained by the endangering act, this flexibility would permit a gain in overall efficiency, for once compensation has been made, no one will be worse off, and at least some will be better off, than otherwise would have been the case.

There are, to be sure, limits upon compensability. If an individual dies or loses something irreplaceable, no after-the-fact benefit could compensate him for the harm done. Since many of the injuries we must consider in discussing pollution – whether as actual harms or as things at risk – are of this sort, the scope for avoiding restrictive prohibitions through a system of compensation is much reduced.

Moreover, it may in many cases be no more practical to determine and distribute required levels of compensation to a diverse – and often future – population than to seek their consent. It might be possible to fix on some sort of average level of compensation for broad classes of polluting activities and broad categories of affected populations. But where in the Lockean scheme is there room for the idea that undercompensation to an individual, or obliging an individual to overcompensate, is permissible if it would be inefficient to determine the actual level of compensation needed? Yet polluters, even small-scale polluters such as smokers, generally cannot keep track of everyone they have harmed or put at risk, of the magnitude of harm or risk in each case, and so on. Is one to imagine a smoker passing out nickels to those who ride with him five floors in an elevator, dimes to those riding ten floors, and so forth, with double pay for those with weak hearts? Would it really be a lessening of restrictiveness if individuals were required to bear such a burden of monitoring effects, determining compensations, securing compensation from those who resist paying, and so on? More sensible would be (for example) a scheme of taxation on tobacco, with benefits paid out to nonsmokers. Such a scheme would lead to much over- and undercompensation, but probably not more than individual efforts.

214

A more fundamental difficulty with any scheme for compensation is that it runs afoul of a fundamental motivation of Lockean views: their antipaternalism. Even if reimburse you after the fact for damages I cause to your person or property, I have failed to respect your right to have the last say over what becomes of both. Nor is this problem removed if I compensate you as well for any damage to your self-esteem. Any attempt to use a notion akin to hypothetical consent within a Lockean framework must confront the fact that even though someone might have consented to an arrangement $C$ were he rational, well informed, and so on, we are not letting *him* decide if we do not actually ask his leave and simply impose $C$ upon him. How can it be said that $C$ is "imposed" upon the individual if he is able to say what would count as compensation? In any practicable scheme of compensation, the injured individual could not be allowed final say in determining the appropriate level of compensation, for this would permit exorbitant after-the-fact demands. Instead, some interpersonal means must be found to determine appropriate levels, one consequence of which would be that individuals – if they are to be compensated at all – may have to accept levels of compensation they would not agree to.

It would seem to be a clear case of using someone – not necessarily misusing him, but using him – if I were to harm or endanger him in order to pursue my own interests, but then made sure to provide after-the-fact compensation at a level he would have to take or leave. Why is this something less than treating him as a Kantian end-in-himself? Several elements seem to be involved. First, there is a preemption of his actual will and of his sovereignty, his entitlement to decide certain matters himself. Second, such preemption reflects an attitude according to which what matters is that people receive certain outcomes, even if they did not participate in bringing the outcomes about through an exercise of autonomous choice. Third, in the simplest sorts of cases, compensation really is nothing but a price attached to the pursuit of one's own ends, a toll one must pay in order to get on with it, a fee that frees one from the obligation of consulting others. Nothing in the compensation mechanism itself prevents one from taking this instrumental view of others, and much encourages it. Finally, ability to compensate will vary with ability to pay, so that those with greater resources will gain greater release from restriction than those with less. If in a Kantian "kingdom of ends" we are all equal and the ends of others are equally our ends, then we seem a long way from such a kingdom in a world in which the better-off are able to preempt the wills of the less well-off through the mechanism of compensation, but not conversely. A rich man may be able to ride his hounds over a peasant's land and then make this up to the peasant monetarily, but in so doing does he show respect for the peasant's property rights, or for the peasant as an equal in the kingdom of ends?

We must make a distinction. Once an unconsented-to harm of endangerment has occurred, is it a respectful thing to compensate? Probably so. But is it a respectful thing to harm or endanger without consent, perhaps even deliberately, so long as one later compensates? Probably not. From a social standpoint, it is, we have seen, efficient to permit boundary violations whenever the violater can compensate his victims and still come out ahead. But one of the central themes of the Lockean tradition has been that individual rights take precedence over efficiency.

Now, it seems to me quite important that it be at times morally permissible to pursue activities that give rise to unconsented-to harms or endangerment when these activities in the end yield a substantial balance of benefits over burdens. Without this possibility, society could not achieve much by way of development. Yet moral theories of a Lockean structure and Kantian inspiration tend to exclude such quasi-utilitarian balancing as disrespectful of persons. Now, the balancing involved in a scheme of violation-and-compensation is not strictly utilitarian, for it is person-specific, requiring that a surplus of benefits over burdens accrue to the particular individuals bearing the burdens of harm or endangerment, and not merely to society as a whole. Yet Kant tells us not to use others solely as means, even as means to their own ends, and libertarians tell us that we cannot force things upon people even when they themselves are the beneficiaries. A scheme permitting trade-offs of benefits against rights, even when person-specific, is thus in important ways conceptually closer to utilitarianism than to either Kant or classical natural rights theory.

It is instructive that Lockeans typically have not advocated a scheme of violation-and-compensation as a way of loosening the restrictiveness of private property in general. For example, one might avoid the need for "excessive governmental regulation and enforcement" of prohibitions against theft or assault by permitting the thief or assailant to compensate afterward, or, if compensation is not forthcoming, allowing the victims to have recourse to the tort system.[35] Instead, most Lockeans have advocated direct state enforcement through criminal law of rights against theft and assault, and for good reasons: a system of violation-and-compensation would place the burden on the victim; it would allow preventable crimes to occur; it would fail whenever compensation is not possible owing to the nature of the harm or the resources of the harmer; it would be unreliable (many would fail ever to receive compensation because they are unable to pursue their cases, or because small losses would not be worth pursuing); it would not be an adequate deterrent to crime and so would increase insecurity; it would give rise to "free-rider" problems; and so on.[36]

These reasons apply with equal force to the environmental case. In fact, it may in general be harder for individuals to detect and assess pollution-caused injury or risk than is the case in ordinary crimes against person or property. The information-gathering burden on victims would be enormous, substantially diminishing the probability that polluters would voluntarily compensate (since they could often hope to escape detection) or be brought successfully to trial for failure to compensate. Once one makes a serious assessment of what it would involve for individuals to keep up with current knowledge of the effects of pollutants and to trace the origin of the pollutants to which they are exposed, it becomes obvious that a system of regular public regulation, monitoring, and policing would secure substantial gains in efficiency over individual enforcement through threat of suit. Moreover, such governmental activity need not violate any Lockean rights, for no one is entitled to harm or endanger, with or without permission.[37]

Both schemes – direct enforcement by the state and individual enforcement through violation-and-compensation – would require that it be permissible under some circumstances to enter private property to monitor potential hazards. How else could one determine whether another is putting one at risk by acts carried out entirely on his own property? The entitlement to inspect would require that property rights be retailored, just as they are tailored in civil law by the notion of a reasonable search. Government enforcement would have the advantage of limiting the total amount of inspecting activity needed by reducing duplication: government inspectors, but not private individuals, could be required to make public record of their findings. Moreover, public inspectors could be required to carry identification and to follow certain procedures.

Note that if the Lockean picture were modified to demote private property to the status of common property, compensation without consent might be fit in more consistently. Under this modification one could appropriate another's property without consent so long as one left enough and as good either in his remaining private holdings or in readily accessible common property. If a given appropriation would not leave enough and as good in this sense, it might still be permissible if one were to substitute something of value equal to whatever is taken. (Would one also have to compensate for distress?) Compensation, then, would emerge as a special case of meeting the conditions necessary for appropriation.

A Lockean may use compensation to gain lessened restrictiveness either by making special provision for a scheme of compensation without consent, or by treating private property on a par with common property. Both are major changes and would result in moral theories with different, and almost certainly less, intuitive appeal than the orthodox view. They appear to fall between two stools, being defective both with regard to social efficiency – and so not attractive to utilitarians – and with regard to respect for persons – and so not attractive to Kantians.

Lockeans, then, do seem to face a genuine dilemma. The orthodox view turns out to be vastly restrictive of individual freedom when it comes to pollution-caused harm, but insufficiently restrictive when it comes to pollution-caused risk. Revisions of the orthodox view may permit a more sensible balance, but involve significant departures from Lockeanism and bring with them a host of new problems.

SUMMARY AND CONCLUSION

The injuries and endangerment we may experience from pollution have excited among Lockeans an ingenious interest in incorporating greater flexibility into their view, an interest much less commonly directed at the restrictiveness of the system of private property in general. After all, the system of private property calls for centralized, direct governmental regulation, yet it is viewed by Lockeans as the very bulwark of freedom. What structure of governmental permissions and prohibitions should be in place regarding pollution is a subject beyond the scope of this chapter. My point is the modest one that it seems hardly defensible to treat airborne harms differently from handborne harms. I cannot here canvass all the ways a Lockean might attempt to come to terms with risk and injury from pollution, but we may draw some tentative conclusions.

First, if we treat injuries due to polluting activities comparably with injuries that happen to be caused by other means, we find that the Lockean view in its classical form is highly restrictive about pollution, very much the opposite of the *laissez-faire* doctrines associated with it. It should be viewed as no more probable that problems posed by pollution could be handled by a self-regulating market than problems of property crime in general. Much of the appeal of Lockean views is that they seem to afford a way of securing considerable freedom of action for individuals, but this is so only if we disregard the injuries individuals may cause each other through the medium of the environment. We cannot argue that Lockeanism is internally inconsistent if it turns out that this doctrine would, if put into practice, be very restrictive of freedom of action, for Lockeanism does not require that freedom should be maximized. But Lockeanism will lose much of its attractiveness unless there is good reason to think that a society founded upon Lockean principles would permit very substantial freedom of action. Owing to environmental effects, Lockeanism would, if put into practice, impose much more severe restraints upon individual action than, for example, the most elaborate existing environmental laws and regulations.

Second, if we look at the specific issue of risk, as opposed to actual injury, we find that classical Lockeanism may fail to be restrictive enough, especially if it is to be thought of as giving expression to the Kantian notion of respect for persons.

Third, there are some systematic – but unmotivated – asymmetries in the classical Lockean view, most notably with regard to the treatment of ownership rights in common property versus private property.

Fourth, the search for a Lockean scheme that strikes a more appropriate balance between restrictiveness and permissiveness suggests a number of modifications of the classical theory: one may need to question the absoluteness of certain rights; to introduce considerations of balancing benefits and burdens; to contemplate collective or aggregative entitlements or obligations as well as individual rights; to challenge the idea that so long as one operates within one's own boundaries and intends no harm, one need acknowledge no other-oriented constraints or obligations; to recognize limitations on the justifying role of consent – tacit, explicit, or hypothetical; to rethink the Lockean notion of privacy; and to give a fuller account of the notion of showing respect for persons.

All this is a rather roundabout way of arguing what perhaps cannot be argued more directly: if we take seriously the fact that we find ourselves situated in, and connected through, an environment, we are soon impressed with the inaptness of a conception of morality that pictures individuals as set apart by propertylike boundaries, having their effect upon one another largely through intentional action, limiting their intercourse by choice, and free to act as they please within their boundaries, although absolutely constrained by them. The result of this conception is gross restrictiveness here, gross latitude there, and, in general, an inadequate vocabulary for debating, or even expressing, a number of pressing moral issues concerning the environment.

It does not follow that one ought to give up the notion of individual natural rights as the basis of morality and adopt utilitarianism. But the arguments made here at least suggest that a plausible morality will involve at base more than a scheme of presocial, territorial individual rights and will make room for a number of notions – balancing, aggregation, and the like – more commonly associated with utilitarian than natural-rights theories.[38]

NOTES

*To Breathe Freely*, Mary Gibson, ed. (Totowa, NJ: Rowman and Littlefield, 1985).

* I am grateful to members of the Working Group on Risk, Consent, and Air for their comments on an earlier version of this chapter. I should mention especially Judith Jarvis Thomson, Samuel Scheffler, Mary Gibson, and Douglas MacLean. I would also like to thank Rebecca Scott for much helpful discussion.

1. I do not attempt here a full characterization of the doctrines of John Locke. Rather, I seek to draw out certain main features of an influential view that takes a number of central Lockean doctrines as its foundation. For example, although contemporary libertarians often draw heavily from Locke, it would be misleading to call Locke himself a libertarian.

2. See John Locke, *The Second Treatise of Government* (Indianapolis: Bobbs-Merrill, 1952) ch. 5. All references to Locke are to this work.

3. At this point in the argument, Locke has assumed the existence of an imperishable medium of exchange; otherwise, any wealth amassed beyond what one could use would perish and be wasted. Locke, sec. 51.

4. Perhaps the most explicit use of this boundary-based image of moral space is in Robert Nozick, *Anarchy, State, and Utopia* (New York: Basic Books, 1974) ch. 3. All references to Nozick are to this work.

   A right in such a scheme is a moral liberty or entitlement to do or refrain as one pleases, and it entails the existence of an obligation on the part of others not to interfere. In effect, then, it establishes a border. One possible exercise of such a right is to grant to another part or all of one's entitlement, that is, to issue a pass (the border stays put, but the other is free to cross – perhaps subject to certain conditions), to transfer a deed (the border stays put, but the rightful occupant changes), or to establish joint ownership (no property line separates joint owners, but there may be some agreed-upon limits governing use; in effect, if we think of the uses of properties as quasi-spatial dimensions of it, such limitations are internal boundaries).

5. Or, would it involve crossing an internal boundary of jointly owned property? (See note 4.)

6. A complication arises where another has a "settled design" upon one's life or possessions; then self-defense permits interfering with him even before he crosses one's boundaries. He has, according to Locke, declared an unjust war upon one and thereby forfeited his rights against interference. See Locke, sec. 16.

   A futher complication is that in a state of nature Locke gives to all the right to enforce the laws of nature. One may, presumably, cross a boundary for this purpose without asking permission, for example, to retrieve stolen property and secure as well any of the thief's property needed for "reparation and restraint" (sec. 8). This boundary crossing, too, comes under the head of states of war (ch. 2).

7. For example, this view is taken by Nozick, 30ff.

8. Hereinafter, when I speak of crossing a boundary wrongfully, I will mean that the crossing was not freely consented to, is not a legitimate act of self-defense, and is not a legitimate effort to enforce the laws of nature.

9. An objective obligation is an obligation one would recognize if one knew all the principles of morality and all the relevant facts about one's situation and drew the appropriate moral conclusion. (It does not follow that one necessarily would be moved by this conclusion.) Subjective obligations are relative to what one believes, perhaps wrongly, to be the case. For discussion of the distinction, see Richard B. Brandt, *Ethical Theory* (Englewood Cliffs, NJ: Prentice-Hall, 1959) 362ff.

10. Hume wrote that "a poor peasant or artisan . . . [who] knows no foreign language or manners and lives from day to day by the small wages which he acquires" cannot seriously be said to give consent to his government simply by remaining in his place. "We may as well assert that a man, by remaining in a vessel, freely consents to the dominion of the master, though he was carried on board while asleep and must leap into the ocean and perish the moment he leaves her." David Hume, "Of the Original Contract," in *David Hume's Political Essays*, C. W. Hendel, ed. (Indianapolis: Bobbs-Merrill, 1953) 51.

11. Locke himself held that we could not trade away our right to life or sell ourselves into slavery, this being contrary both to reason and to the will of our ultimate owner, God (secs. 6 and 25). Nozick, on the other hand, imposes no such restriction (331).

12. I assume that your neighbor is not operating the reactor in a Kamikazelike effort to put your life at risk, that is, has no "settled design" to harm you, and so his behavior does not fall under Locke's special provision for self-defense. The question of intent will be discussed further.

13. I am availing myself here of the notion of a probabilistic cause. Roughly, a factor $C$ is a (partial) probabilistic cause of event $E$ at time $t$ if, were $C$ not present at $t$, but conditions up to it were otherwise exactly the same, the objective probability of $E$ at $t$ would have been lower than in fact it was. Thus characterized, this notion is neutral on the question of whether there is an underlying determinism.

14. Interestingly, Locke thought that in a state of nature no one would bother to appropriate in a wasteful fashion, since it would simply be a net loss to expend one's labor and then not put the product to good use (sec. 51). This would be so only if it were true that the simplest way of obtaining something for one's own use did not commonly involve despoiling other parts of common property not put to good use. Historically, the opposite has often been true and special care and effort would have been necessary to avoid wasteful despoilation.

15. Regarding this unclarity, see Nozick, 174–5, where he rather surprisingly leaves the unclarity unresolved.

One common form of pollution, dumping toxic wastes into the soil, can be quite a bit like creating a cloud of pollutants in the atmosphere, although this sort of pollution is usually accompanied by some leaching into ground water, streams, etc.

16. Talbot Page, "A Generic View of Toxic Chemicals and Similar Risks," *Ecology Law Quarterly* 7 (1978), 207–44, 222n. Page cites K. S. Crump, D. G. Hoel, C. H. Langley, and R. Peto, "Fundamental Carcinogenic Processes and Their Implications for Low Dose Risk Assessment," *Cancer Research* 36 (1976), 2973–9, and Jerome Cornfield, "Carcinogenic Risk Assessment," *Science* 198 (1977), 693–9.

17. It should be noted that the requirement of consent before taking private property applies among joint owners. Thus, if two of us were to inherit an estate jointly, I could not simply take whatever I wished from the estate so long as you were left "enough and as good"; some sort of agreement would be needed before the estate could be rightfully partitioned. Express consent may not be needed when tradition or custom establishes rules governing joint property or where the joint owners are in some other, special legal relationship (such as marriage). Locke notices the need for consent when he considers "the joint property of this country or this parish," which he distinguishes from common property in a state of nature by noting that it is "common in respect of some men, [but] it is not so to all mankind." He treats this as, in effect, jointly owned private property, saying that "no one can enclose or appropriate any part without the consent of all his fellow commoners." (Locke adds, as a quite separate consideration, that in practice if one were to appropriate part of such property one would not ordinarily leave "enough and as good" behind in common.) An asymmetry therefore exists between jointly held common property and jointly held private property, even though it would seem as if the difference in the end could be no more than a matter of the size of the joint-holding group: a parish, a country, or mankind. See Locke, sec. 35.

18. There are other problems with Locke's argument. For example, it at best justifies private consumption, but not private ownership of land or of other productive resources that might be put to common use in creating the requisites of private consumption.

19. Perhaps some of the special status often attributed to private property derives from considerations of privacy and from the especially intimate relationship we may have with our own possessions. This is a mire of issues – not the least of which concern the private and intimate relationship we may have with common property – which I will simply refrain from wading into. This is consistent with our purposes, for what is at issue is not a bare right to hold some property privately, but a right of exclusion that can be extended over property in no way intimate to us or necessary for us.

20. There is a third option: to drop the notion of *natural* property rights altogether. This leaves the possibility of arguing for a system of civil property rights (see following text) and is compatible with recognizing other natural rights in terms of which such a system might be justified.

21. At least at one point, Locke himself suggests a very loose reading. He considers the "rule of property, viz., that every man should have as much as he could make use of" and says it "would hold still in the world without straitening anybody, since there is land enough in the world to suffice double the inhabitants," had not money been introduced (sec. 36). The criterion that others not be "straitened" is clearly weaker than that they be left enough and as good. Elsewhere, Locke says that 'enough and as good' means "there was never the less left for others" and that

"he that leaves as much as another can make use of does as good as take nothing at all" (sec. 33). These latter remarks suggest a stricter and perhaps more appropriate standard: that no one's prospects be reduced by another's appropriation.

22. Again, we assume that it is not part of his motive to put you at risk by operating an unsafe reactor.

23. Depending upon details of particular Lockean theories, it may be that extreme gains or losses in social utility or in consequent rights observance would offset violations of individual rights. Nozick, for one, says the question of absoluteness "is one I hope largely to avoid," 30n.

24. The expression 'side constraint' and the image associated with it are found in Nozick, 28ff.

25. Locke, *The Second Treatise of Government*, sec. 16.

26. Nozick, in ch. 4 of *Anarchy, State, and Utopia*, does use the concept of fear in discussing risk, although he does not give a general theory of how the concept of fear would be integrated into his treatment of natural rights. One may also ask whether it is a harm to cause fear even when no actual risk is involved (and when causing such fear involves no deliberate acts of deception, etc.).

27. Someone might say: "But some people are just more sensitive than others, and it would not be fair that they should therefore have more extensive claims upon the rest of us not to be harmed psychologically. They do not *deserve* such sensitivity – they may merely be born with it or have inculcated it in themselves." This would be a peculiar objection in the mouth of a Lockean, for some are born with greater property than others, and some acquire greater property through their own efforts, thereby gaining – justifiably, in the Lockean's eyes – more extensive claims against others than the rest of us enjoy.

In comparison with the acquisition of property, is it simply too easy, and of too little benefit to others, to develop a thin skin? Of course, it sometimes is quite easy to acquire property (e.g., by inheritance) and quite unhelpful to others, but that aside, it might be thought that permitting individuals to enlarge their sphere of moral claims through the acquisition of property provides an incentive to industriousness, which often benefits others as well as the agent. By contrast, it is hard to see what beneficial incentives would arise from allowing individuals to enlarge their sphere of moral claims through the cultivation of exquisite sensitivity or the manufacture of psychological harms. This is plausible enough, but unfortunately for the Lockean it is a straightforwardly utilitarian argument.

28. Could it be said that someone is *helping* you by tipping you off, that is, giving you grounds for rational fear of wrongdoing on his part if his plan is in fact to harm you? In those cases where you are able to put this information to good use, there is some benefit along with the (perhaps protracted) anxiety. However, it is a general feature of harm-causing acts that they may in certain circumstances also confer benefits, so we cannot use this point to settle the question whether causing rational fear of wrongdoing on one's own part is a harm.

29. Does the reference to probability reintroduce psychological states, in the form of degrees of belief? Not necessarily. First, the probability in question could be an objective probability, such as a propensity or a relative frequency, and thus be fully independent of what the agents in question believe. Second, for those

who do not admit of irreducible objective probability, it could be interpreted as an idealized subjective probability – a rational degree of belief conditioned upon all relevant evidence. This is manifestly not a psychological state of any sort as such – such probabilities exist at a time whether or not anyone thinks of them.

An important question hinges upon the interpretation of probability given here. Is it objectively wrong, for example, to introduce a drug that in fact is harmless but for which there is not adequate evidence to warrant the conclusion that it is harmless? That is, is it objectively wrong to act in a way that could be said to increase the subjective probability another will suffer harm even if no increase in objective probability actually occurs? My inclination is to say that what is wrong in such cases is that one is acting contrary to one's subjective duty, although, fortuitously, this turns out not to be contrary to one's objective duty.

30. On this point, see the otherwise quite baffling definition of 'voluntary action' given by Nozick:

Whether a person's actions are voluntary depends upon what it is that limits his alternatives. . . . Other people's actions place limits on one's available opportunities. Whether this makes one's resulting action non-voluntary depends upon whether these others had the right to act as they did (262).

On this account, I leave your home voluntarily if you tell me (which is within your right) that if I do not do so you will call the police.

While this clearly is inadequate as an account of voluntariness, one can see the Lockean forces that drove Nozick to this position: whether an act is within one's proper sphere of free action depends upon whether the constraints others impose upon it are within their right to impose. However, not all acts within one's proper sphere of free action need be voluntary; whether they are depends as well upon the psychology of the agent. Moreover, acts outside one's proper sphere of free action may be quite voluntary, albeit wrong.

31. Further, if it is rational for individuals to assess costs versus benefits in evaluating the acceptability of risks, this seems equally rational at the social level. Yet the Lockean view precludes social aggregation and balancing.

It does not follow that so-called "cost-benefit analysis" is a uniquely rational way of making social policy. Indeed, it does not follow that cost-benefit analysis is even minimally rational, for it suffers the following defects (among others): it fails to take into account the declining marginal utility of money (and of other ways in which distribution may affect utility at a given cost/benefit ratio); it ignores the disparities between utilities and prices (including the fact that prices, but not utilities, reflect ability to pay, and that future utilities cannot be discounted the way future prices can); and it often substitutes the demonstration of a net surplus of benefit over cost for a demonstration that a given course of action is optimal. For further discussion, see my "Costs and Benefits of Cost-Benefit Analysis: A Response to Bantz and MacLean," in *PSA 1982,* vol. 2 (East Lansing, MI: Philosophy of Science Association, 1983) and "Cost–Benefit Analysis as a Source of Information about Welfare," in P. B. Hammond and R. Coppock, eds., *Valuing Health Risks, Costs, and Benefits for Environmental Decision Making* (Washington, DC: National Academy Press, 1990).

32. A similiar principle is suggested by Judith Jarvis Thomson in "Imposing Risks," in Mary Gibson, ed., *To Breathe Freely* (Totowa, NJ: Rowman and Littlefield, 1985).
33. I am grateful to Judith Jarvis Thomson and David Lewis for discussion of the possible importance of a causal proximity condition.
34. One such scheme is Nozick's. I follow his account in most details. See Nozick, *Anarchy, State, and Utopia*, ch. 4.
35. This is fact parallels proposals one hears from libertarian quarters for dealing with pollution. The parallel is rather close in the case of Nozick. Just how close is hard to say, owing to loose ends in Nozick's account and to my imperfect understanding of the whole of his view.
36. Would anyone be interested in perpetrating aboveboard theft-and-compensation? One might dearly love to gain use or possession of a particular piece of property one does not happen to own and be prepared to compensate the owner adequately after the fact, but for one reason or another be unwilling or unable to obtain express consent to such an arrangement. Indeed, if one could simply make more efficient use of certain property than its present holder, one might be able to take it without permission, use it, pay full compensation (i.e., give the owner the equivalent of what he would have had if he had kept possession of the property), and still come out ahead. (See the following discussion of demoting private property.) Aboveboard *assault*-and-compensation may have substantial appeal to various individuals for reasons we need not go into here.
37. Some Lockeans would insist that individuals remain free to sell or waive their rights against harm or endangerment, just as they should be free to sell or waive rights against assault or theft.
38. My sense of fairness forces me to note that a previously mentioned difficulty poses a problem for those utilitarian theories that assess the objective rightness or wrongness of acts in terms of the value of the *actual* consequences they produce. (Those utilitarian theories based upon the *expected value* of acts will not have this problem.) The existence of an unactualized possibility of harm will not show up among manifest consequences, but this means such theories will not reflect pure risk as such. Two acts with the same manifest consequences, but differing in that one imposes a substantial (but unactualized) risk while the other does not, would be judged morally equivalent, other things equal. This is somewhat counterintuitive. Consider a closely related problem. Suppose that an act of mine substantially augments the market value of your house, that is, increases the price that would be paid for it were it to be sold. But suppose further that this increase in value is only temporary, that you do not sell during this period, and, indeed, that you never learn of this change in value. Have you benefited from my action? (Does one benefit by receiving a lottery ticket, hopefulness aside, only if it wins?) If this is a benefit, then we should count possibilities, not just actualities, among the valuable consequences of actions – even possibilities that are never actualized. That would allow a consequentialist to capture the intuitive judgment that, other things equal, it is objectively worse to impose more rather than less risk, even if the risk remains pure. Of course, we would need to explain why mere possibilities are benefits (or harms) and to ask whether, for example, any amount of merely possible benefit (or harm) could outweigh even the smallest actual benefit (or harm). I leave these puzzles for another occasion.

# 8

## How Thinking about Character and Utilitarianism Might Lead to Rethinking the Character of Utilitarianism

### I

"One cannot properly judge actions by their outcomes alone. The motive from which an act is performed is independently important, and makes a distinctive contribution to moral assessment not only of the actor, but of the action. Moreover, if morality is to achieve a secure place in individual lives and social practices, it is necessary that agents develop firm characters to guide their choices and to provide others with a stable basis of expectation and trust. Any sensible moral theory therefore must give a central role to the encouragement and possession of virtuous character."

When such thoughts are heard, can it be more than a moment before a condemnation of act utilitarianism follows? Still, many critics of *act* utilitarianism remain drawn to what I will call the guiding utilitarian idea, namely, that the final ground of moral assessment – including assessment of character – must lie in effects on people's well-being.[1] For such critics, a favored strategy has been to turn to indirect forms of utilitarianism, such as rule utilitarianism. And indeed, moral philosophers in general appear increasingly to be convinced that *if* utilitarianism is to be defensible, it will be in an indirect form.

Perhaps, then, with these remarks about the importance of character fresh in our minds and with some sympathy for the guiding utilitarian idea alive in our hearts, we should consider the possibility of formulating an indirect utilitarianism worthy of the name *character utilitarianism*. And that is indeed what I propose to do, by considering two forms character utilitarianism might take. In the end, however, it will seem doubtful whether either form can satisfactorily accommodate our concerns about character, and this will in a roundabout way tell us something about how utilitarianism has been conceived and about how a reconception of it might better serve the guiding utilitarian idea. Sometimes in philosophy, getting there is half the fun. In the case of character utilitarianism, not getting there will have to be all of it.

II

One form character utilitarianism might take would follow the model of rule utilitarianism and hold that an act is right just in case it would be done by someone having a character,[2] the general possession of which would bring about at least as much utility as any alternative.

To assess this possibility, let us look directly to the model. Rule utilitarianism sometimes is defended along lines that echo the remarks about character voiced at the outset: "We need rules in moral life because it is a poor idea to send moral agents into the world without the guidance they afford. Moral decisions often involve complex problems that call for large amounts of information and stable, coordinated responses. Further, individuals inevitably slant deliberation in their own favor. If moral agents were left to their own devices it would be worse overall than if they were to follow shared rules of the kind that would be chosen on broadly utilitarian grounds."

For present purposes, let us define rule utilitarianism as the moral theory that deems an act right just in case the act conforms to a set of rules the general acceptance of which would bring about at least as much utility as any alternative.[3] Do the preceding reflections about the need for rules lend support to rule utilitarianism?

Nothing in rule utilitarianism as here defined inherently mitigates against case-by-case deliberation by individual moral agents. Since it is highly unlikely that the rules prevalent in any given agent's society are optimal, it is as much the task of a rule-utilitarian deliberator to figure out which sets of rules would be optimal as it is the task of an act-utilitarian deliberator to figure out which acts would be.[4] In answering such questions the rule-utilitarian deliberator would face essentially similar problems arising from changing or incomplete information, tendencies toward personal bias, and the like. And a society of rule-utilitarian deliberators would have problems of coordination akin to those afflicting act-utilitarian deliberators. Indeed, since multiple sets of rules may be optimal, even well-informed, unbiased, continent rule-utilitarian deliberators could fail to coordinate.[5] Finally, although rule utilitarianism places the question whether an act *would conform to* certain rules at the center

227

of moral evaluation, it characteristically attaches no direct significance to the question whether an act *is in fact done from respect for* a rule.

Rule utilitarianism is a theory of the moral rightness of individual acts, not a moral endorsement of rules or rule-following deliberation or rule-governed action. To be sure, it is an indirect theory, for it applies the test of utility to rules rather than individual acts. But its appeal to rules in giving a criterion of the rightness of acts must not be confused with its according actual, shared rules – and their many benefits – a prominent place in moral life. It might of course turn out that acts promoting the widespread adoption and following of useful rules would be approved by rule utilitarianism; but then equally it might turn out that such acts would be approved by act utilitarianism. The case of rule utilitarianism should make us wary of the idea that if one is concerned about $X$'s, one should be an $X$-utilitarian.

Similarly, character utilitarianism, if defined as previously mentioned, is a theory of the rightness of individual acts, and although it appeals to character in giving a criterion of rightness, it no more than act utilitarianism assigns a special place to the cultivation or exercise of character in practice, and it no more than act utilitarianism makes the moral evaluation of an act depend upon the motive from which the act was actually performed.

III

Perhaps, then, character utilitarianism should be built on a different model. We might take its lines from motive utilitarianism, as discussed by Robert M. Adams,[6] and adopt as its ultimate concern the moral value of actual possession of character. Suppose we were to define character utilitarianism as the moral theory according to which a character is morally better the higher the utility of general possession of that character. Would this give us what we want?

Not obviously. Once again, let us examine the model before the copy. The characterization of motive utilitarianism that Adams seems to prefer is the following: A motive, among those humanly possible, is morally better the higher the average utility of anyone's having it on any occasion.[7]

Motive utilitarianism begins with the moral evaluation of actual possession of motives – but it also ends there. It does not, for example, tell us whether right action depends upon motive. Indeed, it has no implications, even indirect, for the assessment of actions. The having of a motive is not an action; and though the cultivation of morally good motives normally would involve various sorts of actions, motive utilitarianism is silent on whether we should act in such a way as to encourage good motives in ourselves or others (as Adams notes, 481). Moreover, in the assessment of motives it ignores a range of questions that would be central to any discussion of the appropriate role of motives in our moral life, for example, questions about the cost or likelihood of bringing people to have certain motives, and so on.

Motive utilitarianism is what William K. Frankena has called an *aretaic* theory – a normative theory of moral *value* – and thus stands in contrast with *deontic* theories – normative theories of moral *obligation*.[8] Deontic theories take as fundamental the question what it would be morally right or wrong to do, whereas aretaic theories take as fundamental the question what would be morally good or bad. Among deontic theories are divine command ethics, natural law ethics, Kantian ethics, and act and rule utilitarianism; among aretaic theories, ethics of virtue and motive utilitarianism. Adams draws this distinction in his own way by distinguishing the (deontic) question "What should I do?" from the (aretaic) question "Have I lived well?" and he remarks that motive utilitarianism is concerned with questions of the latter sort (474). He in effect observes that an aretaic theory need not be bound by a constraint comparable to the "*ought* implies *can*" restriction on deontic theories, for he notes that one may be liable to the judgment that one has not lived well even though one's life has been among the best of those "causally possible" for one to lead (475). It is, for example, legitimate within an aretaic theory to ask, "Is Jack morally perfect?" where this question is only minimally bounded by the bare constraints of what it takes to be a person.[9] It is legitimate to ask this, and not to worry about whether Jack is actually capable of moral perfection, because an aretaic judgment of perfection does not imply that he *ought* to be perfect, or is *obligated* to be perfect, or is *wrong* for being imperfect.[10]

It comes as something of a surprise, then, when Adams speaks of motives as "right" (471), says that "from a motive-utilitarian point of view Jack ought ... to have been as weakly interested in maximizing utility as he was" (471–2), and worries therefore about "incompatibility" between "right action, by act-utilitarian standards" and "right motivation, by motive-utilitarian standards" (475). However, since rightness in action concerns choice among causally possible options, whereas having the best motives (at least, according to motive utilitarianism) does not, it is not obvious that there is a common dimension of assessment along which this incompatibility could arise.

To adapt an example of Adams's: Wretch that I am, I cannot have the best motives humanly possible, and so I could not bring myself to "love righteousness and my neighbors"; instead, "I did my duty out of fear of hellfire for the most part" (475). Act utilitarianism says that if indeed I did not do my duty, then I acted rightly, for doing my duty amounted to acting in ways, of those available to me, most conducive to net utility. Motive utilitarianism does not contradict this by telling me I did anything wrong. Rather, it simply says that, whatever I did, I failed to possess the best sort of motives humanly possible. Is there any incompatibility here? (Is there any incompatibility in saying, "Lefty pitches the baseball as fast as he can, as fast as any coach could ask him to, but he still is not the best fastball pitcher humanly possible"?)

Perhaps incompatibility is more likely to arise when we shift from general to specific standards of excellence, and confine ourselves to that which is causally possible for given individuals. We might for example ask not whether Jack has perfect motives, but whether he has the best motives among those possible for him. Here 'best possible' presumably means "bringing about – directly by their possession or indirectly by their effects – at least as much net utility as any others he might actually have had." However, this last phrase is ambiguous. One way Jack might have had better motives is that he might have been brought up differently, had better luck in his youth, and so on. (Lefty pitches as fast as he can, but still is not the best fastball pitcher he could have been, since he might have had better coaching in Little League.) Such possibilities raise no issues about the rightness of Jack's actions, for they are not acts on his part.

Alternatively, Jack might have had better motives as a result of having made different choices or tried harder. Would this show that he did not act rightly? Whenever a choice is made that affects what motives one will have, the utility or disutility of the consequences of this choice will in part be the direct or indirect result of one's possession of these motives. Suppose Jack has made motive-affecting choices in ways that did not bring him to have the best possible motives of those available to him. Still, he may have acted rightly, since the costs that would have been involved in acquiring motives that would subsequently have made the greatest possible contribution to utility – as opposed to more easily acquired motives whose subsequent contribution was less – might have been sufficiently high to offset the gains. Thus an act-utilitarian standard of right action need not recommend choosing in such a way as to have the best possible motives among those causally accessible to the agent.[11] This might be thought to be a kind of incompatibility between act and motive utilitarianism.

Consider now the other direction of comparison. Could it be the case that if Jack had the best possible motives (of those causally accessible to him) he would in some circumstances act wrongly by act-utilitarian standards? It may bring about the greatest utility on the whole if Jack is strongly motivated to be honest, so strongly that he does not even try to deceive – though he would succeed were he to try – in some cases in which this would be optimal. This could come about if the psychological changes necessary for Jack to become more likely to deceive in such cases would inevitably increase Jack's tendency to deceive in many nonoptimal cases as well. Thus there is no necessary coincidence between having the best motives by motive-utilitarian standards and acting rightly by act-utilitarian standards. This, too, might seem an incompatibility.

In can be replied that there is no strict incompatibility in either case, since judgments of the rightness of acts and judgments of the goodness of (possession of) motives lack a common subject matter. (Lefty has the best strikeout record in the league, but a mediocre earned-run average.) Motive utilitarianism, even in its individualistic form (480), does not imply that one ought to have the best motives among those available. And act utilitarianism, because it does not until supplemented – for example, by motive utilitarianism – contain a theory of moral value, does not imply that the moral value of motives is determined exclusively by their contribution to right action.

IV

Yet one who aspires to be a character utilitarian may find this rather beside the point. For, to him, the issue is not one of incompatibility in a logical sense. Rather, he has the concerns about the place of character in morality expressed in the opening paragraph of this paper, and he thinks, "If I accept both character utilitarianism and act utilitarianism, then an evaluative dualism may arise in which what I deem right in action lacks an appropriate connection with what I deem good in character. In a number of cases, the two aspects of evaluation will simply go their separate ways, whereas my hope was to integrate them."[12]

Suppose, for example, that part of the best character available to Mel is a powerful sense of parental responsibility. This is so, we may suppose, because with this sense he will receive great satisfaction from helping his child – a highly useful thing that he is more likely to do, and do well, if he finds enjoyment in it – and because without it he would become more self-absorbed and less motivated to take into account the interests of others in general. Consider now a choice he faces between conferring a smallish benefit upon his young son and conferring a considerably larger benefit upon people unknown to him. Mel could spend an afternoon taking his son and a friend on an outing he knows they would especially like, or he could find a sitter to mind his son at home while he goes out to spend the afternoon canvassing for grass-roots economic development in Central America.

We need not imagine that the sort of parental concern that would be part of the best character available to Mel is one that would dispose him in such cases *always* to elect to spend time with his child – surely there would be room for activities of both sorts. But suppose that on this particular Saturday Mel has just returned home from an extended, utility-maximizing trip. An act-utilitarian computation reveals that it nonetheless would bring about more intrinsic good were he to go door-to-door for agricultural self-help projects. All things considered – including, for example, long-term effects on his character and his relation with his son – it would be wrong according to act utilitarianism for Mel to take his son on the outing, and he accordingly is morally obliged not to do so. Yet it may also be the case that if Mel had the best sort of character available to him he would on this Saturday deliberately sidestep his all-things-considered obligation and go on the outing. And here there is a rub. The normative force of claims about "the best sort of character" available to one is unclear and perhaps unimpressive or unpointed in comparison to claims about one's "all-things-considered moral obligation." It is not unusual in ethics to come across conflicts among duties each of which is weighty, but this case is of a different nature. An all-things-considered duty stands on one side, while on the other there is no duty at all, for motive utilitarianism does not enjoin us to act as someone with good character would. So if, contrary to duty, Mel does go on the outing – either because he has a good character or because he is trying to act as someone with good character would – how is Mel to regard the moral status of what he is doing? And how can Mel really embrace his character in a moral sense? Yet it may be crucial to achieving the good effects of this character that he so embrace it.

An act utilitarian can respond that the impression that judgments of character are inconsequential in guiding action is something like an illusion of perspective. When we broaden our gaze to take in decisions that will affect the sort of character we have – and many of our decisions have such effects – we will find within act utilitarianism all the injunctive force we need to give weight to character. Act utilitarianism does not tell us to maximize episodes of right action; its concern is only and always with maximizing utility.[13] Thus when Mel contemplates his past, and considers choices that would have altered his commitment to his child in such a way as to have made it likely that he would have decided to go door-to-door that Saturday, he will see that, on our hypothesis,[14] he was at the time under an all-things-considered act-utilitarian injunction to act to promote instead a parental commitment that would lead him to favor going on the outing. Here, the act utilitarian argues, is the sought-after normative affirmation of character: the best way to achieve good results almost always involves taking seriously the development of firm character, where "taking seriously" includes embracing a character even though it will sometimes lead to wrong action.

If our would-be character utilitarian complains that what he wanted was an affirmation of the intrinsic rather than strategic value of character, the act utilitarian has two lines of reply. First, to the extent that the character utilitarian has in mind whatever intrinsic *non*-moral value character may have, the act utilitarian of course affirms this and allows it to enter directly into his calculations of utility. Second, to the extent that the character utilitarian has in mind whatever intrinsic *moral* value character may have, then he is in effect supposing the falsity of his own view, since the point of character utilitarianism is to give an account of moral value without appealing to any notion of *intrinsic* moral goodness.

Of course, the sorts of character that act utilitarianism would recommend that we develop will not in general be exactly the ones that an aretaic character utilitarian would identify as "best (among those available) to have." For, as we have already noted in connection with motives, act utilitarianism takes into account not only how much utility arises from the having of a character, but also how much is lost or gained in the acquiring, teaching, or encouraging of a character, and how much utility arises from act-affected sources other than character and the consequences of character. However, the value of having a character will certainly figure prominently in act-utilitarian assessment, and so character-utilitarian evaluations will certainly have a place in the scheme. Moreover, one can accept an act-utilitarian account of rightness in action without being (what might be called) a *hegemonic* act utilitarian, that is, without believing that all moral evaluation is based at bottom upon evaluations of the rightness of acts. One could, for example, hold that whenever there is direct concern with moral evaluation of character, character utilitarianism can stand entirely on its own alongside act utilitarianism, fielding whatever questions come its way.

233

Still, the aspiring character utilitarian may have the uncomfortable sense that his concerns have somehow been shoved to the periphery. Perhaps act utilitarianism can issue an endorsement of cultivating firm traits of character, but some of the issues raised by the remarks about character and action with which this paper began remain unresolved.

First, what of the idea that motives make a distinctive contribution to the moral assessment of an act, a contribution in some ways independent of the consequences of the act?

Suppose that Frank has a character that is among the best available to him, and that indeed is among the best humanly possible. But he is human, and in order that he be sufficiently sensitive to, and critical of, unjustified inequality he must also harbor a trace of resentment of just about any inequality. As a result, he finds a certain satisfaction in seeing those of high status taken down a peg or two. An opportunity presents itself for him to facilitate this in the large firm for which he works. He is asked his candid opinion of Richard, a superior in the firm who is being considered for an employee award. Now Frank is honest and cooperative. And his honest opinion is that Richard is worthy, though overrated. Ordinarily, Frank's reluctance to damage a candidate's chances for something as peripheral as an employee award would outweigh his cooperative desire to supply an honest answer to a legitimate question, and he would find some polite way – undamaging to the candidate – to beg off. In this case, however, he reflects for a moment, and then quite deliberately says, "I think he's overrated, though, of course, there is no question of such a choice actually embarrassing you." Frank is giving a candid opinion, and one that he has reason to believe will have good effects, since it seems likely to advance the candidacy of some less senior employees whom Frank believes to be at least as deserving of the award as Richard and also to be more likely to benefit significantly from it. But deep down Frank is also hoping that his carefully chosen remark will tilt the decision against Richard, and what lies behind his hope is largely the idea that this would be something good *not* happening to Richard, to whom so many good things have already happened. However, without realizing it, Frank has said exactly what his questioner wanted to hear – the only thing holding up giving the award to Richard was precisely this person's idiosyncratic fear that the choice would somehow prove embarrassing.

Suppose now that for the award to go to Richard would for complicated reasons do considerably more good than Frank had imagined – so much more that Frank's response turns out to have been utility maximizing. Yet don't we feel a bit queasy about the moral status of Frank's action? Are we content to call it right, as an act–utilitarian standard would indicate?[15] And if the function of a character–utilitarian standard is simply to answer questions about the moral value of character within the realm of what is causally possible for humans, then it too will find nothing to criticize about Frank – he is as good as a human can be. What would seem to be needed is a way of reaching a motivation-related evaluation that applies to individual actions and that is not a function solely of consequences.

Second, we have not fully quieted the earlier worry about chafing between acting from good character and the act–utilitarian insistence that it is always all-things-considered obligatory to maximize the good. The possibility of chafing does not exist because, as it is sometimes said, act utilitarianism requires that agents actually consult the test of utility in deliberating about their choices.[16] Insofar as deliberation is an action, or can be influenced by action, act utilitarianism requires optimality, whether or not this involves distinctively utilitarian deliberation or a resolve to act in an optimal way, and it may on occasion (or even always) involve neither, but rather a tendency to act, say, from character.[17]

Instead, chafing threatens largely because it seems to us so plausible that acting optimally will not infrequently require action that in one way or another goes against good character. The conflict suggested in the case of Mel, between optimal action and the natural action-tendencies of parental concern, arises not only on the odd Saturday afternoon, but daily, whenever he faces a decision about how to make use of his time or money or energy. And it arises not only for parental concern, but for any special relation he might have with other individuals or groups, or with his work or avocations. The ubiquity of such potential for conflict in Mel's life – and in our lives – is the joint product of human psychology and the world in which we and Mel now find ourselves. On the one side, there are many in severe need who could benefit dramatically from reallocation even of small resources. On the other, there are few among those with ample resources who could be unstintingly responsive to this need except at great personal cost. Not all of this cost would be due to selfishness in any narrow or pejorative sense. For some will arise from possible impairment of an individual's ability to have in any deep way the more particular attachments and engagements of family, friendship, and work that anchor the self and supply much of the structure and interest of life.

To be sure, act utilitarianism does not tell us to set out to destroy these attachments in order to clear the way for doing impersonal good. It can recognize that people will be able to act reliably to promote the general good only if they can sustain the integrity and interest of their own lives. Act utilitarianism, therefore, may school us in the importance of acting so as to develop and maintain practices and characters that merge a tendency to promote general well-being with other psychological characteristics that lend integrity and interest to lives. So far so good. But it tells us one thing further: Someone with as good a character as possible in this sense nonetheless does what is morally *impermissible* whenever, owing to such character, he fails to the slightest degree to optimize when given the chance.

There will be cases in which it is uncontroversial that the best character available to an agent can lead to wrong action. Consider the example involving Frank, but remove the supposition that Frank could have had reasonable confidence that his remark would have positive effects overall. Assume, perhaps, that he knows Richard to be aware of being in the running for the award and to be prone to respond in an exaggerated way to anything that hints of failure. Assume that Frank can (correctly) see that these considerations would be just enough to make it optimal in the circumstances to keep his opinion of Richard to himself. And assume that, when voiced, Frank's opinion will – as he hopes – steer the award away from Richard. Thus redescribed, Frank's action would count as wrong by an act-utilitarian standard. And it would probably strike most of us as morally wrong, even though it would stem from the best character available to him.

But there are many cases on the other side. It is rather unintuitive, for example, to judge it morally wrong for Mel to go on the Saturday afternoon outing. In a more general example, the most generous people I know give something like 15 percent of their income to charities and other worthwhile causes. Assume that this approaches the "maximum sustainable yield" for most people. Perhaps anyone who committed himself on a regular basis to giving substantially more, say, 30 percent, would after several years feel so cramped that he would lose interest in the whole thing. Or perhaps he would have so hardened his heart against providing for his own or his family's "less needy" desires as to become a crank whose example leads his children to swear off all but minimal charitable contributions for the remainder of their natural lives. Yet, on any given occasion of making a gift, any of my generous friends could give more than 15 percent without noticeable harm and to considerable good effect. Thus, on each occasion when they give 15 percent they act wrongly, contrary to their moral duty. That is, with regard to charitable giving, they act wrongly almost all the time. In that respect, they act like me, even though I give only a few percent. Wrong is wrong, after all.

But most of us would be inclined to say that they do not really act like me – they act much better. Indeed, it would accord with ordinary usage to say that when they give 15 percent they not only act better, they act rightly, even beyond the call of duty. This would sit comfortably alongside the idea that they have something close to the best character available to them. But it contradicts act utilitarianism.

Now act utilitarians will rush to tell us that they have the wherewithall to explain the moral distinction between my acts and those of my more generous friends. For example, act utilitarians can distinguish the question whether an act is wrong from the question whether it would be right to blame the agent for it. Yet I may be morally countersuggestive while my generous friends, bless them, respond constructively to moral criticism. If criticized, they would nudge their annual charitable contributions still closer to the sustainable limit and add some further, exceptional gifts from time to time. Thus it could be right in act–utilitarian terms to blame them for giving "only" 15 percent, but not to blame me for giving a paltry few percent. Similarly, to heap praise upon the charitable acts of such people might simply embarrass them and fill the rest of us with envy and self-loathing, making us less charitable out of a mixture of spite and increased consumption as we apply to our wounded self-esteem the balm of luxury.

If indirect act–utilitarian approaches seem not to yield the judgments wanted, an act utilitarian might attempt to generate the judgments directly by introducing a vocabulary of degrees of wrongness in which to say that, for example, while both my giving 2 percent and their giving 15 percent are wrong, mine is wronger. Yet wrongness may not be the concept for the job.

For a start, 'right' and 'wrong' mark a binary distinction – hence the oddness of 'wronger' – and it may be useful in moral theorizing to keep them that way, especially since we already have a serviceable vocabulary of degree in moral assessment: 'better' and 'worse,' 'more valuable' and 'less valuable,' and so on.

More importantly, the binary character of 'right' and 'wrong' reflects deeper facts about their use. Right and wrong are quasi-juridical notions, linked to requirement and impermissibility, and it is clear why this is usually seen as a dualism – perhaps with a vague boundary – rather than as a matter of degree.

Now it seems inconsistent with anything like our ordinary under-standing of 'morally right' to say that the boundary separating the right from the wrong is to be sharply drawn infinitesimally below the very best action possible. 'Wrong' does mark a kind of discontinuity in moral evaluation, but one associated with real unacceptability. For this reason 'right,' though not itself a matter of degree, covers actions that are entirely acceptable given reasonable expectations as well as those that are optimal. 'Wrong' comes into clear application only when we reach actions far enough below normal expectations to warrant real criticism or censure.

As quasi-juridical notions, rightness and wrongness are to be found ready-made in some conceptions of the basis of morality, such as those of divine command and natural law. Not so in the case of the underlying conception of utilitarianism, which consists not in laws or commands directed at individuals, but in overall states of affairs that realize varying amounts of value. Individual acts are parts of these states of affairs, and are both bearers and causes of value. But they are not the only parts, the only bearers, or the only causes. Intrinsic good is realizable in human lives through being and doing alike – through experience, acts, characters, institutions, and practices. All of these phenomena interact, and the utilitarian perspective upon them – and the value they realize – is global rather than local, symmetrical rather than agent-centered. (Perhaps for these reasons, a direct utilitarian standard has always had greater plausibility as a criterion of choice in public policy than in personal ethics.[18]) Obviously a complex treatment will be needed to accommodate within a scheme of global, symmetrical evaluations of continuously valued states of affairs an account of one multiply entangled, discontinuous, asymmetrical, local component of moral evaluation, such as rightness in action.

The utilitarian can – and typically does – pull out one contributor to value and one component of moral evaluation and link them in a fairly simple, direct or indirect way. The act utilitarian does this in giving his account of moral rightness. 'Right' becomes as a result a term of art, and incongruities arise partly because most of us will continue to understand the term as carrying many of its traditional connections – for example, with reasonable expectations, praising and blaming, etc. – and partly, too, because the utilitarian himself continues to draw upon some traditional connections – for example, with all-things-considered obligation. A dilemma may present itself. Either the act utilitarian is also making, say, 'all-things-considered obligation' a term of art – with a change in its role that removes obligation so far from reasonable expectation that we no longer expect most people in our society to come close to carrying out their obligations – or the act utilitarian is retaining our familiar sense of, and role for, 'all-things-considered obligation,' in which case most

238

people will be amazed at what is expected of them and at what they are liable to criticism for failing to do.[19]

The source of this dilemma is familiar in contemporary philosophy. Once one accepts a reasonable degree of holism about discourse and practice, one accepts that any attempt to introduce new meanings or roles into this network will involve two complementary processes. First, it will bring about alterations in the meanings and roles of other elements of discourse and practice, and thus run the risk of changing the subject. Second, it will itself be vulnerable to alteration beyond original specification as a result of "backward linkages" from the rest of the network, and thus run the risk of saying something unintended. The utilitarian who is attempting a quite systematic account of ethics must be very careful which part of the network of moral discourse and practice he seizes upon when he begins his reconstruction. It may be inadvisable to proceed as the act utilitarian does, by initially taking up the threads that converge on the notion of moral rightness. Although reconstruction must eventually come to this notion, if a utilitarian ties a tight knot between the goodness of states of affairs and the rightness of individual actions he may find that he is unable to get back the slack he needs for successful reconstruction except by unraveling the strands connecting right action to obligation, reasonable expectation, blameworthiness, and so on – increasingly changing the subject. The importance of where the utilitarian takes – or makes – his slack becomes especially evident when, out of a concern with character, we look up from the traditional focus upon right action and glimpse the multiple dimensions and questions of moral assessment that need to be tied together without creating excessive strain.

VI

What is the alternative to commencing utilitarian reconstruction deontically, with a theory of right action? Some distinctly nonutilitarian philosophers appear to favor outright abandonment of the categories of right and wrong in ethics, but it seems to me that in morality as in law, there is a highly useful function to be served by the particular sort of guidance such notions provide to agents. We thus do have a reason for attempting to give some account of deontic judgments within moral theory, but it is a further question whether moral theory should start with such judgments.

Aretaic theories afford an example of how one might start elsewhere, namely, with assessments of moral value. But as the name suggests, such theories have largely been concerned with virtue, and what is needed is a broader category than *arete*. For want of anything better, I will forgo the felicity of Greek roots and introduce the harsh latinate term *valoric* to cover direct assessments of what is better or worse from a moral point of view, whether these assessments be made of acts, agents, characters, institutions, or whatever. When the moral point of view in question bases its assessments ultimately upon an impartial reckoning of the non-moral good realized, we have what may be called *valoric utilitarianism*.

Valoric utilitarianism starts out from the guiding utilitarian idea that no sort of act or motive or institution has intrinsic moral value and that whatever value it has from a moral point of view depends in the final reckoning upon how it affects human well-being. There are, of course, multiple valoric utilitarian positions, depending upon how well-being is understood and upon whether effects on well-being are evaluated in terms of total amount of utility realized, average amount, distributed amount,[20] or whatever. In what follows I will be concerned only with a maximizing valoric utilitarianism. Although I will not defend this choice here, it must be admitted to be a choice – nothing in the theory of non-moral value tells us that for purposes of moral evaluation greater total non-moral value is always superior to lesser, a claim that belongs to the realm of moral theory proper.

Is it therefore a claim about moral value? In a sense, yes, for it is a matter of what is "better rather than worse from a moral point of view." It would however be confusing to appropriate the familiar term 'moral value' for such claims. A maximizing[21] valoric utilitarian assessment of an action or a character would consist in asking directly how much net non-moral value would be realized by, and as a result of, its occurrence or existence. But notoriously, an act or character can strike us as morally bad even though it happens to bring about very good results. Like 'right' and 'wrong,' 'morally good' and 'morally bad' owe their content in part to judgments about *kinds* of actions or characters and about what *characteristically* goes along with them, and in part as well to judgments about the *normal range* of human variation. Moreover, 'morally good' tends in ordinary use to be applied only to the limited range of human thought and action that involves *moral conscientiousness*, and so would not be applied to actions of, say, spontaneous affection that, although highly beneficial, lack distinctively moral motivation.

Valoric utilitarians thus should not assume that their notion of "better or worse from a moral point of view" coincides with our notion of moral value. They will almost certainly have to use complex and indirect means to give an account of judgments of moral value (in the ordinary sense) and thus should insist that they are using 'better or worse from a moral point of view' as a technical term. To emphasize this while at the same time avoiding a cumbersome phrase, let us remint an expression coined by Bertrand Russell, and speak of acts or character traits that are better rather than worse from a moral point of view as more or less *morally fortunate*.[22] Thus one could speak of Frank's unenthusiastic remark (under the original assumptions) as morally most fortunate relative to available alternatives, even if not morally right or morally good as we ordinarily understand these terms. Frank's overall character, too, would be morally most fortunate relative to available alternatives, and here ordinary usage might deem this character morally good. Moreover, valoric utilitarianism would say that it is unfortunate, relative to a perhaps unattainable ideal of character, that Frank's moral outrage at unjustified inequalities must be allied to his rather spiteful resentment of all inequalities, just as ordinary usage would say that owing to this spiteful streak Frank, though good, is not perfect. Put another way, among the motives underlying Frank's act are some that, even though they are part of a character both fortunate and good, are not themselves either fortunate or good.

As this example suggests, valoric utilitarianism has direct application not only to acts, but also to any object of moral assessment. In this way it differs not only from familiar indirect utilitarianisms, but also from direct act utilitarianism. One can ask how morally fortunate an individual act is, or how morally fortunate actions of that kind usually are, or how morally fortunate it would be if everyone regularly took such actions, and so on. And one may ask how morally fortunate it is that on a given occasion an individual possesses or acts from a given character, or how morally fortunate a character of that kind usually is, or how morally fortunate it would be if most people had such characters, and so on. And thus far, we have spoken only of valoric utilitarian judgments based upon the *absolute* amount of non-moral value that is or would be brought about.

In moral practice we have a special interest in judgments based upon the *relative* amount of non-moral value that acts, characters, etc. would bring about, especially those within the range of alternatives causally accessible to us. For example, we often want to know which acts, among those the agent would succeed in performing if he tried, would bring about at least as much non-moral value as any others.[23] I suppose one could call the view that such acts are morally most fortunate "act-token valoric utilitarianism," but this view would not as such be a theory of moral rightness, nor would it be in competition with "act-type valoric utilitarianism" or "rule valoric utilitarianism" or "character valoric utilitarianism." "Rule valoric utilitarianism" and "character valoric utilitarianism," for example, are direct views about the fortunateness of rules or characters, not indirect views about the fortunateness of acts.

Consider again my generous friends. According to valoric utilitarianism, (1) it is very fortunate relative to available alternatives that they give 15 percent of their income to worthy causes – since this does a large amount of good compared to most other uses of these funds – but (2) it would be still more fortunate if on occasion or regularly they were to give 30 percent. Yet (3) it is most fortunate relative to available alternatives that they have the characters they do, even though these characters lead them not to give more than 15 percent. For although it would be more fortunate for them to have characters that would lead them always to give 30 percent, such characters are not causally accessible to them, and we have supposed that it would in fact be less fortunate were they to have characters that would lead them to be strongly inclined to try to give 30 percent. Moreover, (4) their acts of donation are more substantially more fortunate than mine, despite the fact that (5) chastising them for not giving more would, owing to their more measured and appropriate response, be more fortunate than chastising me.

Consider, too, Mel's Saturday afternoon. The valoric utilitarian would say that (1) it would be more fortunate were Mel to go off canvassing, but (2) less fortunate were he to have the sort of character that would make it highly likely for him to do so. Valoric utilitarianism would also say that, (3) given the resources available to Mel and the world as it is, it would be more fortunate were his psychology such that he would reliably do more for Central American peasants and others in great need, even if this meant doing less for his kith and kin. Yet valoric utilitarianism would also say that (4) it would be more fortunate were the world and Mel's psychology such that he could live a life in which contribution to his own good and the good of kith and kin were more consonant with maximizing the general good, at least, so long as this were achieved by raising the resources available to others rather than simply lowering the resources available to Mel.

So far the valoric utilitarian's judgments do not strike me as either morally complacent or grossly at odds with our moral concepts. For example, although the value of doing more non-moral good has been recognized, no claim has been made to the effect that it is always wrong to fail to optimize.

However, the rejoinder will be made: perhaps nothing jarring has been said about right or wrong, but that may only be because nothing has been said about them. And it must be admitted that, as described thus far, valoric utilitarianism is indeed an incomplete, and to that extent unspecific, moral theory. Note, however, that it is also in its own way quite a bit more comprehensive theory than familiar deontic utilitarianisms, for it furnishes assessments of what is better or worse from a moral point of view not only with regard to acts, but also motives, characters, distributions of resources, and so on. Moreover, in its hegemonic form – the form with which we are concerned here[24] – valoric utilitarianism is quite specific in at least one respect about how it is to be completed. For it tells us that all moral evaluation – evaluations of moral rightness, moral goodness, and the like – are to be traced back to assessments of the total amount of non-moral good realized in the world, that is, to what is more rather than less fortunate. Upon this base would be built accounts of these other species of moral evaluation, and once the valoric utilitarian moves beyond judgments of what is more or less morally fortunate, about which he is relentlessly direct, he is free to become indirect. Indirect and intricate. For in view of what has been said about the holism of moral discourse, any plausible account of, say, moral rightness can be expected to be quite elaborate, involving not only questions about rules or principles, but also about motivations, dispositions to feel guilt or attribute blame, and so on. Thus a valoric utilitarian account of rightness might deem an action right if it would conform to normative practices – comprising rules, motivations, dispositions, etc. – that would be fortunate.[25] But if it is to overcome some of the difficulties facing existing indirect utilitarianisms, the valoric account may have to avoid certain idealizations and abstractions. For example, it may have to attach primary significance not to the question "Which practices would be most fortunate if generally observed?" but rather "Which practices are most fortunate given circumstances as they are and will be?" And it may also have to attach importance not simply to whether an action *would* be performed if the agent had fortunate motives, dispositions, etc., but also to whether it actually was the result of such causes.

Given the characteristic structure of valoric utilitarianism, it may be able to escape the charge of "rule worship" that has been laid against various forms of deontic indirect utilitarianism. For in an instance in which an act in conformity with fortunate normative practices would lead to bad outcomes, the valoric utilitarian is able to say that it would be morally more fortunate – that is, better from a moral point of view – if the practice were violated and a more beneficial act performed. This application of direct utilitarian assessment is not, it must be noted, a judgment of

243

rightness. The act in violation of fortunate normative practices remains wrong, and this accommodates the commonsense thought that certain sorts of action – torture, deception, the sacrifice of innocents – are wrong even when, owing to unusual circumstances, they are beneficial.

This may seem puzzling. "What am I to do," an agent seeking moral advice in such circumstances may ask, "that which is most fortunate or that which is right?" Shouldn't there be a definite answer as to which evaluation to follow? There are definite answers, but there is no one question. If the agent wants to know which acts, of those available to him, are most highly valued from a moral point of view, he receives one answer. If he wants to know which acts would be right or wrong, he receives another. It is a familiar feature of ordinary moral life that in doing something right, one is not always doing the best – there is, after all, supererogation. Moreover, in doing something right, for example, in rejecting certain sorts of deception, one may be doing a good bit of harm. Insofar as the moral point of view is concerned, it is preferable if the most fortunate act is performed. But the most fortunate act may be blameworthy by the sorts of standards that ground judgments of right and wrong. This is a bit like the fact that the morally fortunate thing to do may be illegal and appropriately punished. It is a bit more like the fact that the best thing to do from the standpoint of promoting the law itself may be illegal.

Perhaps, however, the agent is asking a different question still. He may want to know whether he has more reason to do what is morally fortunate or what is morally right. This, however, is not a question to refer to moral standards or even to the moral point of view. For it is the office of practical reason to answer questions about the place of morally fortunate – or morally right – action in a rational life.

It would be a very large task to develop a valoric utilitarian reconstruction of the discourse and practice of assessments of moral rightness, or, for that matter, of moral goodness or social justice. Such a reconstruction would have to withstand stresses from several directions at once – from the need to retain continuity with existing language and practice as well as the need to avoid complacency and make appropriate improvements. Whether such a reconstruction could give character and rules a significance in morality closer to roles suggested by the imagined defenses of character and rules quoted in the initial sections of this paper cannot be judged until we have before us a more definite idea of what such a reconstruction might look like.

Still, those drawn to the guiding idea of utilitarianism may wish to consider the possibility that valoric utilitarianism gives the most direct expression of what they find attractive in that idea. And it is possible to say something about what valoric accounts of rightness or goodness might look like. For act and rule utilitarianism could be seen as more or less simple prototypes of how one might develop an account of moral rightness in action within a valoric framework; and motive and character utilitarianism (in the second form discussed) could be seen as prototypes of how one might develop an account of moral goodness of motive or character within such a framework. The difficulties these prototypes have faced in meeting the simultaneous stresses of necessary continuity with existing practices and appropriate reform are instructive, for they show where the valorist needs to work outward from the guiding utilitarian idea with greater sophistication. Of course, if, even after considerable time, more successful prototypes were not forthcoming, then this failure might provide a different sort of instruction, to the effect that the fault lies with the guiding idea itself. Those who are already impatient with utilitarianism may feel they have seen more than enough to reach such a judgment – Is utilitarianism asking for our patience for another century or two? To them I can only say that, by this standard, the grace period of deontology would also have expired.

## VII

We have taken a curious route from our starting point. Consideration of how judgments of character might figure in a utilitarian moral theory have led us not to new advancements in utilitarianism, but rather to a new starting point, one further back than where we began. That could be fortunate for utilitarianism. Progress sometimes comes from taking a fresh start. But at the same time, the view from the valoric starting point is not entirely cheering to the utilitarian, since from this vantage utilitarianism as it stands seems to lack a satisfactory account not only of goodness of character, but even of the category of moral assessment with which it has most preoccupied itself, right action. And it will be cold comfort to the valoric utilitarian to learn that, in the eyes of many moral philosophers, that much of valoric utilitarianism is obviously true.[26]

NOTES

*Midwest Studies in Philosophy*, xiii (1988).
1. One might expand this guiding idea to include all sentient beings. In this paper it is restricted to people, though not on principled grounds.

2. Throughout I speak of having a character rather than having specific traits of character. The view could be formulated in either way, but there may be something to be said for the more holistic notion, just as in contemporary rule utilitarianism reference is usually made not to individual rules, but to sets of rules or "moral codes."

3. Many formulations of the notion of 'general acceptance' exist. Some, for example, ignore questions of teaching or socialization and simply assume widespread – or even ideal – compliance. Others more plausibly incorporate costs of teaching, difficulty of internalization, and so on, in assessing optimality and do not assume anything like ideal compliance. Similarly, rule utilitarians may differ over whether they are recommending *action in accord with optimal rules* or *active consultation of optimal rules in deliberation*. Since there can be no guarantee that the former always requires – or even always permits – the latter, and since in cases of conflict it seems at odds with a broadly consequentialist spirit to treat a form of deliberation as intrinsically required, I have taken for our definition a version of rule utilitarianism that adopts the former line.

4. I mean by 'rule-utilitarian deliberator' to designate, not someone who – in deliberation or action – actually lives up to the requirements of rule utilitarianism, but someone who *tries* to do so in the following sense: he accepts the rule-utilitarian account of rightness and he conscientiously endeavors to determine which acts, of those available to him, would satisfy it. Similarly for 'act-utilitarian deliberator.' It is important to see that neither theory need set forward such conscious, conscientious striving as a moral ideal. We will return to this point in the following text, in connection with act utilitarianism.

5. It is perhaps a defect of rule utilitarianism that it could turn out that agents would escape rule-utilitarian criticism despite their failure to coordinate if each could correctly claim to be conforming to one of the optimal sets of rules. (I suppose any optimal set of rules would somewhere contain an injunction to coordinate, but our example supposes that the injunctions of the equi-optimal sets of rules have already been taken into account.) Actual-outcome act utilitarianism, by contrast, would condemn an agent's failure to coordinate optimally whenever it was in his power to do so. This, of course, would leave untouched the interesting problems of how agents might actually go about achieving coordination.

6. See R. M. Adams, "Motive Utilitarianism," *The Journal of Philosophy* 73 (1976), 467–81, esp. 480. Otherwise unattributed page citations in the text refer to this work.

7. For the sake of consistency with the rest of this paper, I have put his definition (480) in terms of actual rather than expected utility.

8. See William K. Frankena, *Ethics*, 2nd ed. (Englewood Cliffs, NJ, 1973) 121, 122.

9. Adams restricts the question of what motives "the morally perfect person" would have to "patterns of motivation that are causally possible for human beings" (470), but we may also wish to consider persons more broadly. A Kantian might, for example, want to say that a morally perfect *person* would have a holy will, while a morally perfect *human* would have at best a good will.

10. But doesn't calling something good entail a claim that it "ought to exist"? Philosophers have indeed often spoken as if this were so, but to whom or what would this

'ought' be addressed in those cases where we speak of the goodness of impossible perfection?

11. Because the difference in the question arises from the fact that the act utilitarian casts his evaluative net wider, this situation could arise even if the acquisition of motives were assumed to be effortless. For example, it may be that, of the sets of motives available to me, $M$ would bring about more utility than any other, and *a fortiori* more than $N$. However, perhaps in order to have motives $M$, I must also as a matter of psychological necessity have beliefs $B$, which themselves directly bring me a certain amount of utility; on the other hand, in order to have motives $N$ I must have beliefs $C$, which, we will suppose, directly bring me more utility than $B$. The beliefs are not caused or otherwise brought about by having the motives, and so their direct utility does not figure in the evaluation of the motives or the effects of these motives. It therefore could turn out that although motives $M$ would bring about more utility than motives $N$, the motive-belief package $M + B$ would bring about less utility than $N + C$. If we consider a choice among acts that would determine which of these packages I would (effortlessly, we suppose) come to have, an act-utilitarian standard would favor promoting $N + C$.

12. Adams may be expressing a similar concern when he speaks of "the way that the motives, and especially the kind of conscience, regarded as right must be related to the acts regarded as right in anything that is to count as a morality" (479), and it may be this concern that lies behind his talk of incompatibility.

13. Contrast here the claim of Bernard Williams that act utilitarianism "contains something which a utilitarian would see as a certain weakness, a traditional idea which it unreflectively harbors. This is, that the best world must be one in which right action is maximized." B. Williams, "A Critique of Utilitarianism," in *Utilitarianism: For and Against*, J. J. C. Smart and B. Williams, eds. (Cambridge, 1975) 129.

14. That is, on the assumption that, were Mel's parental attachment to weaken, the result would be that he would bring about less utility in the long run. Note that this assumption is in a relevant sense more inclusive than the assumption that strong parental attachment is among the motives it would be best for him to have. See the following text.

15. I have tried to formulate the example so that the act would be right on either a prospective or an actualist account of act-utilitarian duty.

16. Williams disagrees, arguing that "There is no distinctive place for *direct* utilitarianism unless it is, within fairly narrow limits, a doctrine about how one should decide what to do" ("A Critique of Utilitarianism," 128).

17. For discussion, see P. Railton, "Alienation, Consequentialism, and the Demands of Morality," *Philosophy and Public Affairs* 13 (Spring 1984), 134–71, esp. 148–56. Reprinted here as Chapter 6.

18. Presumably the global, symmetrical character of the underlying conception of utilitarianism – which yields "no comprehensible difference which consists just in my bringing about a certain outcome rather than someone else's producing it" – helps account for Williams' criticism that utilitarianism cannot give a plausible account of agency and moreover leaves individuals forever at the mercy of a "universal satisfaction system" ("A Critique of Utilitarianism," 96, 118). Although

I would emphasize that these are features of the *underlying* utilitarian conception, and not necessarily of all accounts of right action justified by appeal to that conception, it must be said that Williams' criticism has made vivid an important part of what would be involved in giving a satisfactory utilitarian account of right action.

19. I was guilty of failure to take the full measure of this dilemma when, in a footnote to "Alienation, Consequentialism, and the Demands of Morality," I attempted without saying as much to pick and choose among the connections the expression 'right' – as used by an act utilitarian – would retain with existing usage (160n).

20. The role of distribution here would be distinct both from the role distribution would play if it had intrinsic *non*-moral value – which could then be figured directly into a maximizing or averaging scheme without loss – and from the role distribution would play if it had intrinsic *moral* value in the narrow sense. I suppose that a defense of allowing distribution the role in question would have to take the form of showing distributive constraints to be partly *constitutive* of the moral point of view.

21. Hereinafter, this qualification will be dropped.

22. See B. Russell, "The Elements of Ethics," reprinted in *Readings in Ethical Theory*, 2nd ed., Wilfrid Sellars and John Hospers, eds. (Englewood Cliffs, NJ, 1970) 12. Russell uses the term for a somewhat different purpose, to pick out those acts that actually (as opposed to prospectively) have good consequences.

23. This is what we would like to know, although of course we seldom do, and so settle instead for some prospective estimation of the value that would be realized. It seems to me that valoric utilitarianism is most plausibly formulated in terms of *actual* non-moral value realized, although the valorist's account of such notions as moral rightness, goodness, and so on, may well appeal to *prospective* value. It is, I think, because of utilitarians' undue focus upon the question of right action that it has seemed so natural to formulate their view, at base, in terms of prospective value. For how can one say that agents are *obliged* to act as full information would indicate, given that they never will have full information? Once, however, we see the problem of constructing an account of moral obligation from the standpoint of what I have called the guiding idea of utilitarianism, it becomes more plausible that it is actual well-being that matters at bottom, and that prospective value matters because it is predictive of actual value.

24. Just as act utilitarianism could be held in a nonhegemonic way (e.g., in tandem with motive utilitarianism), so can valoric utilitarianism (e.g., in tandem with act utilitarianism). However, since our aim here is to get some idea of what a nondeontic utilitarianism might look like, and in particular to see how an integrated valoric utilitarian approach to the various species of moral evaluation might be made, it will best suit our purposes to focus upon hegemonic valoric utilitarianism, which denies deontic judgments any independent foundation.

25. Compare here Richard B. Brandt's notion of a "moral code," as presented in *A Theory of the Good and the Right* (Oxford, 1979) ch. 9.

26. I would like to thank William K. Frankena for very helpful comments on an earlier draft of this paper.

# 9

## Pluralism, Dilemma, and the
## Expression of Moral Conflict

### INTRODUCTION

Talk of pluralism and of dilemma are everywhere in the air in contemporary ethics. And everywhere something called "moral theory" is coming in for a thumping. There is, it seems to me, ample reason for taking this talk of pluralism and dilemma seriously, and for trying to be as clear as we can about how it might bear on the enterprise of moral theorizing.

Pluralism and dilemma come onto the scene as purported facts of moral experience – and who can wonder? The fabric of our moral life is a patchwork, not a system. It has been long in making, and in it we find remnants of sacred as well as secular ways of thought, past social conflicts and compromises, changing conceptions of man and the world, codes of loyalty and honor, ideals of impartiality and mercy, cultural intersections, and legal systems. Nor is it finished. And the very stuff of this fabric – human wants and interests, passions and ideas – promises to resist ironing out.

Of course, it is typical in philosophy to confront a patchwork realm of human thought and practice, whether it is philosophy of mind, philosophy of language, metaphysics, or epistemology. Philosophers characteristically find themselves torn between plausible general principles and more satisfactory "intuitive fit," or between fidelity to what lies within the realm and coherence with the present state of knowledge at large. But morality may be exceptional. Philosophical accounts of morality that achieve generality at the expense of intuitive fit, or borrow heavily from outside ethics, may seem not only counterintuitive, but wrong-headed, crass, disqualified. Surely there is something to this reaction. Morality plays an exceptional role in guiding our lives, and in how we see ourselves.

249

Yet "moral exceptionalism" is too pat. Other concepts that have preoccupied philosophical theorizing – *knowledge, mind, personal identity, action,* even *meaning* itself – also have a central role in how we live and how we see ourselves. One need not be obsessed with tidiness and system to worry whether we can take these concepts at face value. As yet we understand ourselves and our practices only imperfectly, and seeking a widely informed, critical perspective may be the best antidote to claims of obviousness, naturalness, and irreducibility. Why seek an antidote? We see in hindsight how many conceptual schemes and human practices have wrapped themselves in claims of obviousness and naturalness, only to come to be seen as misleading or worse.

Indeed, the very character of moral thought cuts *against* a philosophical approach that aims to leave everything as it was. Knowing what we know about the real world, I expect we would be *morally* suspicious of an approach that could find nothing to question in existing moral thought and practice. The reforming ambitions of a Bentham in applying an all-purpose "test of utility" to the most diverse aspects of society and culture may strike us as ham-handed, but the Philosophical Radicals did have a point. Much of English common law and common sense was deeply laced with prejudice and privilege, and utilitarianism gave these philosophers a critical purchase of real moral force on entrenched practices. This would have been impossible in an approach to morality that insisted on remaining closer to the intuitive, "obvious" ground. Moreover, this critical purchase could be applied even to some of the less savory aspects of the "utilitarian tradition" itself. Utilitarianism affords a standpoint from which to reject proposals advanced in the name of "the general welfare" that rest on dubious political, psychological, or economic assumptions. If technocratic elites or one-party states are unreliable guardians of the common good, utilitarianism enables us to say why they should not be put in charge.

As I score things, the generalizing philosophical reformers of the nineteenth and twentieth centuries are still ahead of the quietistic particularists on moral points: in the great social movements for abolition, the extension of suffrage, social welfare legislation, and civil rights and gender equality, the universalizing reformers were right on the largest questions of principle in opposing "natural hierarchy" and "commonsense intuition"; they were wrong mainly in the area of governance – trusting too much to centralized institutions. If we now focus so sharply on the defects of universalizing reformers in this last respect, that is in large measure because their innovations in the domain of principle have become the moral status quo.

At the same time, other historical trends pushed the generalization of moral thought. Expanding political units and increasing economic inter-dependency have brought very heterogeneous populations into what are, in name or in effect, single polities. After the European wars of religion, the emerging national societies had to contend with considerable diversity in their population's background beliefs, values, and norms. If a stable, mutually beneficial *modus vivendi* was to be secured, it would have to be founded on interests and identities of a more abstract and general kind.[1] Religious tolerance requires that we see the views of others *as religions*, rather than mere heresies. This calls for adopting some critical distance not only on their convictions, but on our own as well.[2] Unsurprisingly, the public conceptions of morality that emerged in these polities were abstract, secular, general, individualistic, and voluntaristic, and did not rest justification on "thick" moral concepts or particularistic common sense. Generalizing moral theory is thus a characteristic part of contemporary moral practice – however things were (or might by philosophers be imagined to have been) in the Greek city-states or on feudal manors.[3]

This hopelessly stylized history, if it contains any truth, suggests why we may be past the point at which the move toward generality and abstraction in moral theorizing can simply be reversed. However, caution is called for. The modern period has witnessed a sustained effort to develop relatively unified normative theories, Kantian and utilitarian, in particular. Yet hard-to-ignore intuitive anomalies and other recalcitrant phenomena of commonsense moral thought and practice persist. Card-carrying moral theorists, among whose number I count myself, should ask what might be learned from this rather than wishing it away.

Generally speaking, theories confronted with recalcitrant experience can respond in four ways: (1) *accommodation* by enriching the core theory, or providing for a more sophisticated application of its principles to practice; (2) *explaining away* apparent moral conflicts or anomalies, for example, by showing the conflict to be no more than apparent, or by showing how the moral anomalies arise from assumptions questionable on other grounds; (3) *riding roughshod* over offending intuitions in the name of theoretical power and simplicity; or (4) *losing credibility*. The rising chorus of criticisms of moral theory suggests that the glory days of riding roughshod are over for now – moral theory must either find more compelling ways of accommodating or explaining away, or lose its credibility. Borrowing some terminology very loosely from Imre Lakatos' work in the philosophy of science,[4] we might say that we have reached a point at which the great generalizing moral theories – progressive as they

were in relation to more conservative approaches to ethics in the past –
are now "degenerating." Their accommodations and explanations look
increasingly ad hoc, and alternative approaches to moral philosophy, less
systematic in ambition and "closer to the ground" of actual practice, are
now the chief sources of advances in moral understanding.

Such an assessment might be premature. The capacities of well-known
generalizing moral theories to contend with such phenomena of moral
experience as pluralism and dilemma have yet to be fully explored. Of
course, many philosophers have understandably become impatient with
these generalizing theories and their seemingly incorrigible defenders. In
this paper, I will try to work "from the ground up" – from examples *to*
theory – to suggest that there might be some life in the old theories yet.

## I. KANTIAN PLURALISM?

Morality, it seems, should not be thought of as a specialized body of
doctrine wheeled out on special occasions. Instead, it should be deeply
kneaded into our thoughts and lives. But consider Harold:

*Harold* is a conscientious individual. Though warm-hearted and sensitive
by nature, he refuses to be led around by feeling and "intuition," and
seldom fails to bring a principled moral perspective to bear on his decisions. He articulates definite moral principles, subjects them to a high
degree of scrutiny, and consults them regularly rather than yielding to
his more spontaneous impulses. He is prepared to subordinate even his
strongest natural inclinations to their deliverances.

Now we might find Harold in various ways uncongenial or rigid, but let
us try to focus on our *moral* response. There is much to admire in Harold,
yet I doubt we see him as a *highly skilled* moral agent. It would be one
thing if we thought he simply lacked the ability to be a skilled moral agent –
perhaps because he failed to possess the requisite feelings or intelligence –
and therefore is compensating as best he can. But Harold seems not to
be making the best possible use of the faculties he does have to act in a
morally reliable way.

Compare Harold's conduct as a moral agent to other forms of skilled,
practical activity: the conduct of skilled builders, doctors, politicians,
teachers, detectives, or experimental scientists. None of these are areas
of life in which "mere feeling" or "blind inclination" could reliably lead
to successful performance. These skills involve experience, knowledge,

close observation, practiced judgment, an ability to rethink and improvise, and so on. Often they involve as well a significant period of education and apprenticeship. Effective practitioners may know, more or less explicitly, various rules or abstract principles; and they'll tend to be alert to clues that a given circumstance calls for consulting a rule or guideline. But many will look at you with skepticism if you ask them to articulate a simple, definite, and perfectly general scheme of principles for their craft. They may draw on quite complex and systematic theoretical knowledge, but exercise of their practical activity is largely guided by a diverse bundle of "ground level" ways of thinking, noticing, and feeling.

For the orthodox Kantian, the accommodation of deliberative or motivational pluralism within the domain of moral agency seems problematic – the good will, and the test of the categorical imperative, appear to exclude other determinants from shaping morally worthy practical thought. Moreover, Kant apparently deemed them entirely sufficient:

Inexperienced in the course of the world, incapable of being prepared for whatever might come to pass in it, I ask myself only: can you also will that your maxim become a universal law? . . . Here it would be easy to show how common human reason, with this compass in hand, knows very well how to distinguish in every case that comes up what is good and what is evil, what is in conformity with duty or contrary to duty. . . .[5]

There is something attractively democratic in the idea that moral knowledge is not a specialized body of theory and moral agency not a rarified excellence, accessible only to the best and brightest. But there is also something puzzling in the thought that the complex moral questions with which we are confronted could be handled straightforwardly and reliably by a relatively simple, perfectly definite and general, rule. Could a naive and inexperienced individual who constantly consults and dutifully follows the moral "compass" – testing his maxims for universalizability– really be as skillful at finding the way through the tangled moral woods of life as a skilled woodsman at finding his way in an actual forest?

Of course, no Kantian need deny that experience, sensitized feelings, and the like are useful "heuristically" in identifying what morality requires. However, when we think of such motives to moral action as benevolence, loyalty, or affection, it seems that these are not only useful, but in themselves morally estimable. Kant, however, takes a dim view of any "inclination," even when it leads to morally appropriate action. "All so-called moral interest consists solely in respect for the law," he writes in the *Groundwork*. Action done from benevolent inclination "if fortunately directed to what in fact accords with duty ... deserve[s] praise and encouragement but no esteem."[6] Kant appears to be hostile even to the idea that benevolence might be a morally worthy motive and guide to action so long as we are prepared to check it regularly against the moral law:

The moral disposition is necessarily connected with consciousness of the determination of the will *directly by the law*. ... Inclination is blind and servile, whether it is kindly or not, and when morality is in question, reason must not play the part of mere guardian to inclination but, disregarding it altogether, must attend solely to its own interest as pure practical reason.[7]

Thus, "an act from duty wholly excludes the influence of inclination," so that if the act is to command respect it must involve a will that "overpowers ... or at least excludes" inclination.[8]

Is there any room here to accommodate the intuitively compelling pluralistic idea that spontaneous action guided by motives of benevolence, loyalty, or affection, can be an estimable form of moral agency? Answering this question is a task perhaps better left in the hands of those who know Kant better than I, but it does strike me that a promising Kantian response is available. To give it, we will need to set aside or modify certain of Kant's less central (to my untutored mind!) views. And Kant interpretation apart, if we no longer find these particular views credible, it seems worthwhile to ask what insight Kant's moral philosophy might afford in their absence.

First, suppose we gave up Kant's hedonistic understanding of "empirical" motivation. Sympathy, as seen by Kant, is an "inclination" that is, like all inclinations, essentially self-regarding and pleasure-oriented. Sympathetic joy, for example, is simply a pleasure stimulated by the presence of another's pleasure; sympathetic pain is simply a pain of one's own, a resonance with the pain of another.[9] These are feelings that require no conceptualization of the other as any sort of *end*, feelings an infant might have in response to a pet's evident pleasure or distress. Because Kant sees all inclination as in this way "solipsistic," even when they happen to be stimulated by an external state,[10] nothing in inclination could possibly count as viewing another as an end-in-himself. I suspect that if we thought of a benevolent person as someone led around by the feeling of sympathy, we'd share Kant's view that this is – though often endearing – not a form of moral agency or character at all, even when it leads to morally fortunate behavior.

If one agent is ever to take another seriously as an end-in-himself, then mere inclination cannot be the guiding motive. Someone we commonsensically deem benevolent, and especially someone who seems skilled at this, *does* treat others as ends-in-themselves – it hardly suffices simply to vibrate sympathetically to the feelings of others, and indeed this can be an obstacle to skilled benevolence. For example, a benevolent person cannot simply be deeply depressed when learning of another's deep depression – "Now you've made *me* feel bad, too!" Depression is a state of reduced motivation and inability to pursue alternatives, and a benevolent response is, however empathetic with the sufferer, also a matter of being positively, perhaps even urgently motivated to think of and pursue ways to aid that person. A skilled benevolent person coming upon the scene of a recent accident does not respond by sharing the victims' overwhelming shock and stunned pain, but by finding in herself a focused energy she did not have before, an active desire to do something to help. A benevolent feeling in response to the trauma of others involves some sympathetic pain, but additionally involves a recognition the other is like oneself, with concerns and a well-being that give oneself urgent reasons for action. A skilled benevolent person is attuned in her responses to the feelings of others, but also to their ends and needs, and to the needs of the situation. That is, benevolently motivated action is a form of end-based practical agency, where the end is not self-regarding. Addressing the needs of someone whose feelings and circumstances one does not share can involve considerable personal discomfort, even internal conflict. Moreover, it may require checking various more "natural" impulses. Some people love the idea of being a hero, riding gloriously to the rescue – the distress of others is, perhaps perversely, in part a means to this end. Benevolence as we ordinarily understand it isn't like that. It involves a certain satisfaction at being able to help, and a definite frustration if one cannot help, but it need not be self-promoting or grandiose. True benevolence may call for checking *that* natural motivation as well. As one skillfully benevolent friend once put it to me, shrewdly: "I've discovered that there's almost no limit to the amount of good you can do at this University, so long as you don't want credit for it." By her actions, she showed that this was true of her.

Kant's psychology does have a place that might accommodate practical attunement to others as ends-in-themselves, but not among inclinations.[11] He distinguishes a "faculty of desire," which moves us to bring about objects or states that correspond to concepts or representations.[12] Desire is related to happiness – to satisfy a desire yields happiness, to fail yields frustration – but what *stimulates* and *guides* one's conduct when acting on desire is a direct attraction to the concept or representation as such, not happiness as such.[13] Indeed, the concept or representation that serves as a guide in desire can be entirely without reference to my personal condition, so that desire can be a *"sense-free inclination (propensio intellectualis)."*[14]

For Kant, desire does not by its nature oppose dutiful action; rather, it makes dutiful action possible. In the faculty of desire we find not only the will, but also *moral feeling* – a direct liking of the moral law, permitting it to stimulate and guide action.[15] Without this feeling, he argues, we would be incapable of recognizing dutifulness, and would be "morally dead," however agreeable or fortunate our inclinations might be.[16] Given the moral feeling, we will admire the dutifulness we see in others – even when it comes at our expense – and will take genuine satisfaction in our own moral actions – even when they involve overcoming our inclinations. But this pleasure is the result of, rather than the cause of, our prior motivational interest in the moral law.[17]

Now, if Kant could accept the idea that the good of another or of others in general, considered as ends-in-themselves, could be an object of *direct* liking, then benevolence could be located in the faculty of desire. Because the idea under which one is motivated, and by which one is guided, is that of the good of another as an end-in-himself, without reference to one's own personal condition, benevolent feeling would be a "sense-free inclination." Skillful benevolence – good competence in being guided by this concept – would involve as well experience, perceptiveness, imagination, and self-discipline. It involves an ability to ask oneself "What does this person really need? What would be best for him in the circumstances?" But it need not involve invocation of the moral *law* as such.

Skilled benevolence will tend to conform to what the moral law would demand, and non-accidentally so. An inexperienced person attempting to add a porch to his house may happen to build well spontaneously, yet could not rationally expect to do so without consulting and following more experienced individuals, instructions, or manuals. A skilled builder can rationally expect to build well – the proper end of his craft – without consulting rules, though advice, manuals, and rules are sometimes most helpful. Such a builder anticipates difficulties, appreciates priorities, seizes upon opportunities, is alert to pitfalls, and learns from her inevitable mistakes as she goes along. A skillfully benevolent agent does likewise. Common sense recognizes the practical difference between skilled versus unskilled craft, and the moral between benevolence versus mere sentimentality, friendship versus blind loyalty, probity versus guilelessness, and courage versus rashness or vainglory. And it grants esteem accordingly.[18]

Now it might be objected that a Kantian morality, as a morality of duty, cannot accord a place to moral motivation by benevolence, however skilled, since benevolence still involves a benevolent feeling for others, which is beyond the scope of the voluntary. *Ought* implies *can*, and though a conscientious individual lacking in benevolent feeling can dutifully will herself to act as benevolence might require, she cannot will the feeling or will benevolent motivation. Yet Kant already recognizes that morally worthy motivation may presuppose a feeling we cannot voluntarily acquire, and that cannot itself be an object of duty. This, in fact, is precisely how he views the indispensable subjective condition for dutiful action, the "moral feeling":

Since any consciousness of obligation depends upon moral feeling ... there can be no duty to have moral feeling or acquire it....[19]

This feeling is not voluntary; rather, Kant claims, "every human being (as a moral being) has it in him originally," and "[o]bligation with regard to moral feeling can be only to *cultivate* it and to strengthen it...."[20] Similarly, we might say that every human being *as a benevolent being* has the benevolent feeling (or some capacity to develop it) within him, and that our duty can only be to cultivate it. Perhaps some members of our species lack any capacity to develop the moral feeling, or benevolence. But then they could be neither benevolent nor dutiful. It would be wrong to assume that the same "capacity for feeling" underlies dutifulness and benevolence – we can at least imagine someone who could have direct feeling for the moral law but lack benevolent feeling for others as such. This is perhaps what Kant calls "practical love":

beneficence from duty, when no inclination impels it ... [which] resides in the will and not in the propensities of feeling.[21]

But I suppose we could equally imagine someone capable of direct feeling for others as ends-in-themselves but not for the moral law as such. In a *pluralistic Kantianism*, such a person would not be "morally dead" – he would be capable of morally appropriate action in virtue of a morally appropriate motivation, rather than because of some morally irrelevant incentive. He would be "dead" to dutifulness as such – direct appeal to the moral law might leave him cold. But we could appeal to his benevolence to attend to others as ends-in-themselves, and to motivate acts in accord with duty's demands. Perhaps this would deserve the neo-Kantian name "practical dutifulness"?[22]

But what of the idea that Kantian morality is a matter of *rational requirement*? Kant does not assume that the "moral feeling" will be present in all rational beings, since perfectly rational beings would have no sense of dutifulness, and feel no *ought*. But he does appear to assume that all imperfectly rational beings, like ourselves, will have the moral feeling "originally." Whether or not this strikes us as plausible, we surely may not want to assume the same of benevolence. Therefore the place of benevolence in a Kantian pluralism would likely be different from the place of conscientiousness. A pluralistic Kantian could insist – not without plausibility – that we should not think of "conscientiousness" as simply slotting into a list of morally worthy motives, somewhere after affection and benevolence, and before courage. Conscientiousness, the Kantian pluralist can claim, comes with any capacity to recognize a moral *ought*, and thus Harold-like dutifulness would be the ultimate "fall back" for morality even for someone lacking benevolent feeling or personal courage. Someone capable of benevolence but not conscientiousness, on the other hand, might be a good companion and in many ways estimable, but lacking a distinctively moral perspective.

Does this mean that in those of us capable of benevolent feeling or personal courage as well as dutifulness, these other motives cannot themselves be any part of the ground of rational requirement? No. There can, for example, be rational theoretical requirements grounded in part in sense perception, even though some rational beings are blind. And Kant recognizes that aesthetic judgments of beauty constitute rational requirements for humans, even though rationality alone is not sufficient ground for such judgments.[23]

Finally, have we simply given up on the "attractive, democratic idea of moral agency" previously mentioned? Someone unequipped with the feelings essential for benevolence, courage, or affection simply could not *be* benevolent, courageous, or a loving person, much less a skillful one. Is that an unacceptable thing for a moral theory to say? Precisely because *ought* implies *can*, a Kantian pluralism would not view this as a *defect* for which the person can be held responsible or merit blame. Such a person could, moreover, win our high admiration by his conscientiousness. Still, we need not regard him as the most reliable or authoritative of moral guides for our own conduct – any more than we must regard the judgments of someone tone deaf as aesthetically authoritative concerning beauty in music despite her most conscientious book learning.

The emotional equipment needed to attain a reasonable degree of skilled benevolence does seem widespread, and the skills involved in its effective attunement seem widely accessible in daily life. It certainly is not like a rare athletic or musical talent. Moreover, many of these same abilities are, I suspect, equally necessary for skilled conscientiousness. Why "skilled" – isn't conscientiousness sufficient unto itself? Standing behind Kant's moral theory – as, he believes, a necessary postulate – is a natural order created by a divine intelligence. In this order, if we mortals will but do our part, by striving conscientiously to act with goodwill, we need not worry about the long-term results – for ourselves, or for the world at large.[24] If we no longer feel confident assuming such an order, it falls to us to take greater responsibility for outcomes – if we don't look after them, who will? But this requires us to ask how one might gain, or lose, credibility as a moral actor or judge. That is, it requires us to temper a democratic respect for all opinions with a sober assessment of what it would take to know what we're doing.

It would be unreasonable to expect the same level of skill in everyone on all matters, or to credit oneself automatically as among the most highly skilled in every department. I am a child and a parent, a student and a teacher, a male and a spouse, living in middle-class America. There are many realms of human activity I have entered into to some degree, many that are virtually unknown to me. I don't really think I can demand on democratic (or any other) grounds, even that you take *my* opinions and actions in parenting, pedagogy, marriage, or morality as having as much authority for yourself as the opinions and actions of those with greater experience, knowledge, sensitivity, or demonstrated practical success in these various areas. I can, however, democratically ask you to respect my efforts as well as your own for what they are, and to give each of us credit rather than blame if we are doing the best we can with what we have to work with. This does not strike at the heart of our moral personalities or self-respect, neither does it undermine the basis for a democratic moral community. There's no one among us whose voice is always right, no one whose voice is never worth listening to.

A genuinely Kantian pluralism would have at least two distinctive features, both of interest and merit, to my mind. First, as noted, it would emphasize the special place of conscientiousness among worthy motives to morality, and its special relationship to duty and blame. This would *not* be a matter of insisting that conscientiousness is always the higher or more re-liable motive to moral action, or that all dimensions of moral insight must be accessible to the conscientious. After all, a distinctively Kantian aesthet-ics does not insist that conscientious scholarly judgment is always a higher and more reliable aesthetic authority than the exercise of discriminating sensation, or that it can yield every aesthetic insight sensation would afford.

Second, a distinctively Kantian pluralism would insist that no motive to moral conduct – not even conscientiousness – should be thought of as an independent "moral sense" or special source of intuitive knowledge of moral requirement. The moral feeling itself is, for the Kantian, a subjective condition of duty, not a standard of it – "one cannot validly judge for others by means of his own feeling."[25] The *objective criterion* of what is morally required with respect to others (or with respect to "duties to self") is quite independent of any such "feeling" or "sentiment" on my part, and can be stated without reference to it. Indeed, all such feelings presuppose such a criterion, which underwrites the objective concepts to which the moral feeling and benevolence orient us and through which they move us.[26]

II. KANTIAN DILEMMA?

Kant may have been mistaken on the psychological question whether conscientiousness alone could be the basis for acting toward others as ends-in-themselves, and commonsense moral experience may convince us that the morally worthy motives are plural. A credible Kantian pluralism can accommodate this, I have tried to suggest, without selling its Kantian soul. But it would be a further, more questionable, and much more threatening claim to say that Kant is mistaken about the existence of a unified objective criterion of moral requirement and permission underlying the diverse range of commonsense moral judgments.

We should expect, therefore, that Kantianism might have a more difficult time making its peace with moral dilemma. Why cannot a unified standard of duty produce dilemmas? The short argument here returns us to the principle that *ought* implies *can*. If act *a* is a duty, and act *b* is a duty, and one cannot perform both *a* and *b*, then a collision with "*ought* implies *can*" looms.

Could an orthodox Kantianism get into this difficulty? Suppose that one has a duty to keep one's promises. Now consider:

*Bemis and Benchley*

I have borrowed money from Bemis with a promise to repay him on the spot should he find himself in urgent need of money. And I have made a similar promise to Benchley. The amounts of money are not large,

260

and I have every reason to believe that I could meet both demands at once – perhaps simply by borrowing against my credit line. However, an unforeseeable medical emergency has arisen for me, depleting my available funds. Coincidentally, the bank holding my credit line has just had a fire and lost its records. Still more coincidentally, both Bemis and Benchley find they have urgent need of money at this very juncture and turn to me, desperate. Fortunately, I do have on hand the funds to pay back one; unfortunately, not enough for both. I seem to face two competing moral duties, neither of which is cancelled or overridden by the other. By at least one familiar definition, this is a moral dilemma.[27]

A Kantian should, I think, object. Is there this alleged "duty to keep one's promises"? That seems like a Kantian idea, but for the Kantian the objective test of action is whether the *subjective maxim* of a contemplated act can be universalized. Thus, making a promise with the intent to break it should this prove convenient fails the test.[28] But that is not what I am contemplating in this case. I sincerely promised to pay both back on notice of urgency, and now I am equally sincerely addressing the question "What to do?" given a non-negligent inability to follow through to the full. There is no perfectly general "duty to repay one's debts" that can be divorced from the will of the agent in a given set of circumstances. Any such talk is moral shorthand.

What might my subjective maxim be? How about: "Make proportionate payments to each of the lenders, while undertaking with them a new commitment to pay the balance as soon as possible, augmented by offering interest to compensate for the added time and inconvenience." This maxim could, as far as I can see, stand the test of universalization. Morever, it would show me a way out of my seeming dilemma – what appeared to be an inescapable collision of duties has been "explained away" – but not in a fashion that objectionably "gets Railton off the hook" or "fails to give the conflicting commitments their due" or that "treats Bemis and Benchley as mere means to my ends."

Next step. An offer has been made by me. Should Bemis and Benchley accept? Each must form his own subjective maxim. Each tries: "Hold a borrower to the strict letter of his original agreement, if his funds permit [in this case, they do – I could repay either in full]; if any other claims are made upon these funds, demand to be first in line." This maxim could not be universalized. If each individual who has a claim upon a scarce resource insists on being first in line, then there is no line, and "being first" would have no application. Next each tries: "Accept a good-faith offer from a borrower to pay off his creditors over time on equal terms, even if this means not getting repaid in full immediately and that proves inconvenient." This could pass the test, so Bemis and Benchley do not refuse and do not attempt to elbow each other aside. Once again, it seems to me, the Kantian answer seems aptly "responsive" to the conflicting commonsense obligations at stake, and shows respect for all persons involved as ends rather than means alone.

But what of poor Bemis and Benchley? Now they are each stuck short of funds, with their creditors bearing down. Repeat the cycle. They make a good-faith offer to their creditors. Assuming no negligence anywhere along the line, their creditors cannot give them in return only unthinking refusals to renegotiate. At least, they cannot do this under any sort of pious moral cover story of an alleged "absolute duty to repay your debts."

The Kantian's maxim-oriented approach is not a dodge, not ad hoc. Rather, it is a direct expression of the Kantian way of viewing morality. Morality is not a list of duties based on autonomous "moral facts"; it is an exercise of *practical reason*. We use practical reason to help us think through how to act in good faith in the circumstances that face us, however regrettable these may be. Had my inability to pay been the result of deceit or negligence on my part, I still could not be obliged to hand over money I did not have, but I could be blamed, judged, and punished. If my inability to pay is non-culpable, then morality should not rush to find me in an impossible moral bind and lash me mercilessly for having been so unreasonable as to have been colossally unlucky. Instead, it should encourage the fullest use of practical intelligence in actively looking for a good-faith way for each to proceed.

Whether practical intelligence can help us find a tolerable way out will, of course, depend upon just how regrettable the circumstances are. We might all run out of luck, and morality cannot prevent this. But there is one large domain, however, where we can make our fortune good or ill, yet it is unclear whether orthodox Kantianism would enable us to do so. The test of subjective maxims is applied individually, with regard to *hypothetical* universalizability but without regard to what others *actually* do. As a result, we may face serious coordination problems. Two of us are attacked by an assailant. Failing upon him together, we could subdue him. Running in criss-crossing directions, we could confuse him and both escape. Each subjective maxim could be universalized − if everyone did as it said, we could consistently think and will the outcome − so each course of action is permitted. But then you might jump him while I run zigzagging off. You'd be assaulted, and I wouldn't even be making a beeline for help. To be sure, we would each of us act in good faith, but is this really practical reason at work?

The example is silly, but the point serious. To coordinate effectively we need to monitor "in real time" what others of us are actually doing or setting about to do, as well as what would be permitted by a scheme of universal legislation. Now nothing seems to stop Kantian agents from such monitoring, but what rationally obliges them to do it? We should be able to take advantage here precisely of the way in which Kantian morality *is* a theory of practical reason in action. When Donald Regan attempted to formulate a general rule for coordination, the best he could come up with was not a fixed rule, but a procedure for agents to follow, involving attentiveness to what others were doing and thinking:

> The basic idea is that each agent should proceed in two steps: First he should identify the other agents who are willing and able to co-operate. . . . Then he should do his part in the best plan of behaviour for the group consisting of himself and the others so identified, in view of the behaviour of non-members of that group.[29]

This sort of procedure could be universalized, and its best results arise when it is in fact universalized. But it can help us be more responsive to problems of coordination even if not, and it certainly would seem to be part of rationality to internalize it somehow.

A Kantian might be able to construct an argument to the effect that there is an "imperfect" duty – arising from our separate wills to see our ends realized – to cultivate such a coordinative disposition. How, though, would this interact with the act-by-act individual test of subjective maxims? For surely having the disposition is not enough. We need to attune ourselves to cases where coordination is in the offing, and develop ways of helping bring it into play. As we noted at the end of the previous section, if there is no natural order to look after things once we individually do our parts, we'll have to do better collectively at looking out for ourselves. But in the case of the assault, for example, can we identify any Kantian misstep in the procedure we separately followed in applying the test of universalization to our subjective maxims? We did lose a perfectly good chance to coordinate, perhaps with disastrous results. The question is not whether a theory of practical reason can guarantee coordination. That is hardly possible. The question is whether it makes us appropriately attentive to, and primed for, the real possibilities we encounter, and to laying the social basis for more such possibilities in the future.

Often accused of excessive rigidity, Kantian moral theory can show – in its approach to commonsense "conflicts of duties" – an impressive suppleness. We'll need to see more clearly how this suppleness can be made to work when practical intelligence calls for coordination.[30]

## III. UTILITARIAN PLURALISM AND DILEMMA?

By its nature, utilitarianism need not be a theory of moral deliberation or motivation.[31] But it might be thought that there is something in utilitarianism inhospitable to the idea of genuine moral dilemma. Any utilitarian worth her salt, it will be said, must agree that if moral requirements seem to conflict, this can be no more than apparent – the overarching obligation is to maximize expected utility. Any seeming plurality of duties, or dilemma among duties, should dissolve upon utilitarian reflection.

To be sure, it will quickly be conceded, there can be utilitarian "ties." That is, two or more courses of action might promise equal expected utility overall, so that the utilitarian standard would not yield an univocal answer. Yet this may not be a deep sense of moral dilemma or moral pluralism, since each course of action will be morally permitted according to the utilitarian, and she will be morally indifferent which is taken. True dilemmas, it will be argued, must involve choosing between courses of action when doing so seems genuinely *contrary to a non-overridden moral obligation,* perhaps thereby doing something *morally impermissible,* and leaving a serious *moral residue.*

*Coventry*

It is wartime, and your intelligence service has just broken the secret code of your enemy. You learn that a major city has been targeted for saturation bombing. By alerting the city, it could be evacuated in time to save the lives of thousands, but the evacuation would very likely tip off the enemy that his code has been broken. He would change the code, and you'd lose a potentially very significant weapon – perhaps costing you victory, and surely resulting in a longer war with greater casualties on both sides. But can you really fail to warn the thousands of civilians in the city, standing by silently while they suffer this horror? And what if you happen to have family members in the city? Could you invite *them* to leave immediately on some pretext – but then leave everyone else to their fate?

There are so many imponderables – what right have you to make any "calculation" rather than send the alert? Perhaps the "broken code" is actually a trick to get you to reveal your sources of secret information by your behavior, while encouraging you to abstain from offering a "suspicious" amount of resistance to the wings of bombers that soon will descend upon one of your major cities? Or perhaps enemy agents have already learned that the code has been broken, so that it will be changed no matter what you do, while your citizens are killed and mutilated by the bombing? Even trying the gruesome calculation seems only to yield expected utilities that may be impossible to distinguish. Given the clear and present danger, and your sworn civic responsibilities, would it even be permissible not to evacuate?

Here is a classic moral dilemma, yet the utilitarian response seems so lame: the expected utilities are pretty equal, so either course is permissible; no moral residue either way; "flip a coin and get a good night's sleep"; "no point in crying over split milk." Can't a utilitarian do better than this?

She can. True, so-called "act-utilitarianism" is typically formulated as a monistic theory of obligation and permission: an act $a$ is morally permitted iff $a$ possesses, of those acts available to the agent, expected utility at least as great as any other available act; an act $a^*$ is morally required iff $a^*$ is the uniquely permitted act in the circumstances. A serious difficulty for this theory is that common sense surrounds the notions of moral requirement and permission with various truisms, notably, that there is a distinction between what is morally required and what is supererogatory or morally best, and that sanctions of criticism, punishment, and guilt are typically merited only by failures to do what is morally required – not by failures to do what is morally optimal. Partly out of respect for this point, utilitarians have been drawn over the years to a more Millian account of moral requirement. According to Mill, an act of type $A$ is morally required iff prevalence of a code of conduct sanctioning acts of type $A$ – by attaching negative opinion, punishment, or guilt to nonperformance in suitable circumstances – would tend to maximize overall utility in comparison with other codes that might be taught and adopted.[32]

Such *indirect-utilitarian theories of moral requirement* face various challenges and difficulties in formulation, but let us not try here to put such a theory into better shape. Rather, we will simply note that an indirect-utilitarian theory of moral requirement could have the effect of introducing irreducible pluralism in the domain of moral requirement. Why "irreducible" – isn't it plain as the nose on a man's face that all the requirements really boil down to one overriding requirement, to maximize expected utility?

This objection simply misunderstands the indirect theory. For such a theory might not even support a requirement that individual acts maximize expected utility – such a requirement is unlikely to figure among those included in an optimal moral code. For example, it is unlikely that social moral censure should be attached to anyone who acts in a way that fails to promote maximal expected utility. To be sure, the theory offers a univocal utilitarian standard for evaluating codes, but that is not itself a standard of moral obligation or requirement. Nor is this evaluation itself a direct source of obligation. An optimal code is unlikely to contain a requirement that agents always choose acts of a kind that would most promote adoption of an optimal code, or face moral censure. Censure can be overused, and serious coordination problems would beset any attempt to articulate an act-by-act requirement of this kind.[33] So far are we from having a "fixed, reductive, monistic" theory of moral requirement to pin on indirect utilitarians, that basic questions about how to formulate a utilitarian theory of moral requirement are very much alive among them.

We can say at least this much, perhaps. Given what we know of how humans learn and think, how emotions tend to attach to certain *classes* of actions and reactions, and how our emotional repertoire has likely been shaped through evolutionary history, it seems probable that a fairly diverse set of independently characterized moral requirements would figure in a viable indirect-utilitarian account of moral requirement.[34] We might expect, for example, requirements not to steal or aggress, requirements of kinship and fidelity, requirements of reciprocity and charitable aid, and so on. These would of course be *prima facie* requirements in Ross' sense – they could conflict without fixed hierarchy, and override without canceling. And Rossian *prima facie* duties are a paradigm of pluralism about moral requirement.[35] The indirect utilitarian is likely to emphasize the important contributions to our shared moral life made by a tendency to feel guilt, or feel a need for apology or compensation, in the event of overriding a *prima facie* duty. Such feelings would tend to deepen not only one's awareness of the requirement, but heighten one's sensitivity to other people's needs and expectations, and to those values that the requirement protects or promotes in the first place.

Return now to the example, Coventry. An optimal moral code is almost certain to contain a *prima facie* duty to warn innocent people of immediate threats to their lives, where this is feasible. Moreover, it is almost certain to contain a *prima facie* duty both to fight against aggressors and a *prima facie* duty of humanitarianism, which would favor trying to minimize casualties from warfare. These *prima facie* duties conflict without clearly overriding in the case of Coventry, so that no matter what one does some degree of "moral residue" will be left, in the form of remorse and guilt, and the need to make amends. For example, a decision to sacrifice the city would also call for a subsequent special commitment to aid the citizens in the wake of the attack or rebuild its shattered structures and economy after the war. Anyone who had genuinely taken to heart these *prima facie* duties, and was aware of the powerful considerations of human well-being that stand behind them, would find it difficult to avoid a powerful sense of guilt from either decision about warning the city.

A utilitarian need not regard any moral residue as "crying over spilt milk," or dismiss moral pluralism as superficial or conventional. What drives utilitarianism, at base, is a concern above all for human well-being. Any course of action involving considerable human suffering can hardly be viewed with indifference, even if it must be embraced as the lesser of two evils. And although Benthamite utilitarianism is famously monistic about intrinsic good, most utilitarians today accept the idea that intrinsic value itself is irreducibly plural. Part of the poignancy of many dilemmatic moral situations, it seems to me, arises not from the sense that *obligations* are in conflict, but that *values* are (we will return to this in Section IV). For a utilitarian who is pluralistic about intrinsic good, these conflicts can go to the very bottom of morality and human concern.

Still, mustn't any utilitarian who permits calculation be in some sense a monist about intrinsic good? For how, without a common metric, could value comparisons be possible at all? But mathematicians have known since the time of Pythagoras that values can be *comparable* without being strictly *commensurable*. More prosaically, we can say that I am confident that one cloud or one mountain is larger than another even though I cannot specify a precise quantitative measure for "size of cloud" or "size of mountain." In individual choice we often decide between values we know we cannot quantify or co-measure univocally, but which we can compare. I cannot say just how much aesthetics and authenticity matter relative to economic cost, but I do feel confident that a more authentic wood selection for restoring my bannister is worth paying a bit for, but not half my annual income.

One might protest that a utilitarian "irreducible pluralism" about moral obligation remains in some sense ersatz, since it does not reflect diverse fundamental sources of moral requirement. All requirements arise directly or indirectly from considerations of well-being. But it is a substantive issue what the normative moral *sources* of plural *prima facie* moral requirements might be. It would simply beg the question against utilitarianism (as it would against Kantianism) to insist that the plurality of moral requirements reflect a plurality of *independent obligations* "all the way down." Moreover, as previously mentioned, the utilitarian can defend the idea that there is pluralism all the way down – not multiple obligations, but multiple intrinsic values, sometimes in conflict, and typically realized in different ways.

## IV. MORAL EXPRESSION

Once we recognize that conflicting moral requirements may be just one kind of moral dilemma, our minds should be open to more systematic rethinking of the subject. Let me introduce a few more examples.

### The Forum

You've been asked to participate in a television forum on an important subject, about which you feel you have something worthwhile, but infrequently heard, to say. The forum, which appears regularly, is something of a media phenomenon and is run by a telegenic fellow academic bent on propelling himself into public life. The wider public pays surprisingly much attention to this forum, in part because of its reputation for handling tough issues and for representing "both sides." You and your associates, on the other hand, have long viewed it as tendentious at best in its framing of issues and its choice of participants. Indeed, you're a bit surprised to be invited, since your sort of viewpoint is seldom allowed to express itself there. You're pretty sure that if you participate you would reach people who would not otherwise be exposed to views like yours, and equally sure that if you don't agree to participate the next person to be asked would be unlikely to represent your viewpoint. Moreover, if you refuse you would give your self-aggrandizing colleague the opportunity to say in public that some of those vocal in criticizing the forum for lack of openness have actually turned down invitations to appear. At the same time, you're very reluctant to lend your name to this enterprise, and to lend to it whatever appearance of legitimacy and fair-mindedness this would yield. It also is well-known that the forum pays a handsome honorarium, and that being in the good graces of its very influential host can boost a career. Even your associates – especially your associates? – are likely to be somewhat suspicious of your motives in participating. In truth, you know enough about yourself to recognize that these blandishments are not without appeal

268

and would almost certainly have some effect on how you would conduct yourself. You would feel much less compromised never to be involved.

In such a case you certainly might feel faced with a moral dilemma, but I doubt that you would feel yourself to be under two conflicting moral obligations – to participate and to decline. Indeed, I doubt that you are morally *obliged* either to participate or decline, although you might well feel a generalized obligation of public responsibility that itself dictates neither choice definitively. As the case has been described, either course strikes me as morally *permissible*. The man running the forum is an opinionated opportunist, but not a moral monster; the expression of your point of view on the subject of the forum would have various benefits, but it would not save a major urban center from bombardment. Though either choice seems morally permissible all things considered, you feel strongly conflicted over what to do. Perhaps we should describe your quandary not in terms of obligation at all, but as being torn over what it would be best to do, or over what a decent person with political savvy would do in the circumstances.

*Violin Lessons*

Let us suppose that developing true virtuosity at the violin requires sustained, intensive instruction at an early age. Absent this, we'll imagine, there is almost no chance of developing the highest order of talent. Your four-year-old child shows real interest in the violin, and truly startling promise. After some inquiries, you learn that Kelso is the premier teacher in town. Kelso auditions your child and, with visible excitement, proposes an intense regimen of private lessons. Your child takes to Kelso, loves playing the violin, and badly wants to take the lessons. Kelso strikes you as marvelously skilled and devoted, but also perhaps a bit too eager to enlarge his own reputation. On the other hand, a less ambitious instructor might not be willing to invest the extraordinary personal effort that developing a prodigy requires. And you know your child: she loves the violin and her lessons, and has real determination, but the required level of participation in lessons, practicing, and recitals week-in and week-out would try you both in a host of ways, and would powerfully shape the character of a large portion of the time you are able to spend together. Moreover, it would significantly affect her relations with her peers and, especially, her two older siblings. You would of course make every effort to keep in balance the time and attention received by all three of your

269

children. But you know that this would not be entirely possible, given the constraints upon your own time and the special sort of recognition your youngest would doubtless receive from outside the family. Further, you see only too clearly that the intensive course of instruction and performance would throw *you* together with a different group of adults than you otherwise would have sought out, would preempt a number of activities normally part of your life, and so on.

In this case, too, you might feel that you are facing something of a moral dilemma as well as a personal dilemma – you are making a decision with potentially profound implications for your daughter's life and the lives of others. The dilemmatic character of your situation arises not because you see yourself as having clear, conflicting moral obligations to undertake and not undertake the intensive instruction. Your chief obligation here is to the well-being of your children, and it would be implausible to claim that either choice is mandated by that parental duty. I think we may suppose that either choice is, all things considered, morally permissible. But what is the best or wisest thing to do?

Some of the difficulty in deciding might be attributable to lack of information: talent of the highest order is rare, and many prodigies do not flourish and develop into successful adult virtuosi. But one can imagine that your quandary would not be resolved even if you had much less uncertainty. Suppose yourself to have strong, convincing evidence that your child would, after prolonged and intense training, develop into a successful first or second violin in a major orchestra, with a chance to do something few of us ever can – namely, to participate at the highest level in giving life to some of the greatest accomplishments of art and aesthetic delight to thousands – but also the ordinary mix of happiness and unhappiness in life, and with a persistent sense of a lost childhood, an unresolved hostility to an overbearing parent, and rather nonexistent relations with siblings who never fully overcame their jealousy. Suppose, too, that you have strong evidence that the alternative life for her would involve good success and roughly comparable happiness in some other, more prosaic and less intensely engaging and rewarding area of endeavor, and better family relations overall, though not without occasional pangs of longing on her part at the thought of the violin career that might have been, accompanied by accusatory thoughts directed at the parent who let the talent go underdeveloped and the overly conventional family that held her back. In such a case, it is indeed no straightforward matter to ask "Which life seems to suit my child best?", since the choices one now makes will shape in important ways the sort of person one's child becomes.

In this case, your sense of dilemma (if I have succeeded in confronting you with such a sense) might stem less from a sense of conflicting, nonoverridden obligations than from a sense of conflicting, difficult to compare – perhaps even incommensurable – *values, loyalties,* and *ideals.* At stake are aesthetic values, values of parent-child or child-peer relationships, values of accomplishment and autonomy, relationships with specific individuals, and so on. You are deciding for others as well as yourself, and you know only too well that, whichever way you decide, something very significant will irretrievably be lost – a "normal" childhood, say, or an unusual talent and the access to aesthetic accomplishment this talent affords. This sense of inevitable loss seems characteristic of much of our thinking about moral dilemmas, even when the loss or failing in question is not – or is not entirely – a matter of failure to meet moral obligations.

The Forum and Violin Lessons have as well at least two other features characteristic of much commonsense thinking about dilemmas. First, the agent is called upon *to choose rather than compromise or postpone* – not because of some specifically moral requirement, but by the sheer force of circumstance. That is, you are presented with alternatives that do not appear to admit readily of degree, and that cannot be postponed without *de facto* deciding the matter.[36] Had your child not been so talented and enthusiastic, or had the invitation to the forum not come, you would not face these hard choices. But you now do face these choices, and unfortunately some of the usual ways of "balancing" or "hedging" to reconcile conflicting pulls in decision making are not open to you. A half-hearted regimen of instruction would simply fail to promote the kind of development essential for virtuosity. And there is no intermediate level of involvement in a televised forum. Moreover, you are in no position to reshape the forum – it will take place on the scheduled date, with or without you, and postponement of the decision would only cause the invitation to go to someone else, who would almost certainly not be someone you would have chosen. If you attempt to make a public spectacle of refusing to participate, it will only make you look somewhat ridiculous and attract negative publicity to your point of view.

Second, both examples illustrate, in somewhat different ways, the *expressive* aspect of moral dilemmas. To participate in the forum would appear to be making a statement you do not in fact endorse, but could not expect fully to cancel, a statement to the effect that the forum is quite open after all, and that you respect this activity on the part of your colleague.

271

To fail to participate would appear to manifest an unwillingness to take a public stand and defend one's principles in an open setting, or a snobbish refusal to risk entering a popular forum. In the second example, to commit yourself and your child to intensive violin instruction, a commitment that includes sticking with it even when it becomes a source of family conflict, also seems to be making a statement you cannot expect fully to cancel: that you attach greater importance to developing a prodigy than to fostering a "normal" childhood; and that this one child, because of her talent, deserves more of your time and attention than the other children.

We often find dilemmatic situations uncomfortable because they seem to lead us to act in ways we ordinarily would have quite sufficient grounds to criticize and avoid. They therefore "taint" or "compromise" us in ways we find destructive of the messages we ordinarily hope to convey with our actions. There is more to this than feeling regret or remorse at certain consequences in the aftermath of decision – though that, too, is important here. For one also feels as if circumstances prevent one from fully being, or from communicating to others by one's actions that one is, the sort of person one hopes to be.

Let me now add several more examples, some of them central cases in the literature. The first is perhaps the most famous.

*Sartre's Student*

During the Second World War, one of Sartre's students came to him with a dilemma:

His father was quarreling with his mother and was also inclined to be a 'collaborator'; his elder brother had been killed in the German offensive of 1940 and this young man, with a sentiment somewhat primitive but generous, burned to avenge him. His mother was living alone with him, deeply afflicted by the semi-treason of his father and by the death of her eldest son, and her one consolation was in this young man. But he, at this moment, had the choice between going to England to join the Free French forces or of staying near his mother and helping her to live. He fully realized that this woman lived only for him and that his disappearance – or perhaps his death – would plunge her into despair. He also realized that, concretely and in fact, every action he performed on his mother's behalf would be sure of effect in the sense of aiding her to live, whereas anything he did in order to go and fight would be an ambiguous action which might vanish like water into sand and serve no purpose. For instance, to set out for England he would have to wait indefinitely in a Spanish camp on the way through Spain; or, arriving in England or in Algiers he might be put into an office to fill up forms. Consequently, he found himself confronted by two very different modes of action; the one concrete, immediate, but directed towards only one individual; the other an action addressed to an end infinitely greater, a national collectivity, but for that reason ambiguous – and it might be frustrated on the way. At the same time, he was hesitating between two kinds of morality; on the one side, the morality of sympathy, of personal devotion and, on the other side a morality of wider scope of more debatable validity. He had to choose between the two.[37]

Now I suppose one might interpret this as a case of clearly conflicting obligations – an obligation to his mother colliding with an obligation to democracy or his countrymen – but that does not seem to me the most compelling diagnosis.

First, the cause of Free France really seems to be a *moral ideal* for the student, not a duty. Perhaps everyone in occupied France had some moral obligation to avoid or resist various sorts of collaboration so long as the personal cost were not too great. But it would be a singularly demanding moral conception that claimed that every young male in France was under a moral *requirement* to undertake the perilous course of joining the Free French.

Second, as a parent I rebel at the suggestion that an adult child, such as this student, has a clear moral *duty* to remain with a parent in such circumstances. It would seem to me a supererogatory, not mandatory, act of filial devotion to remain with a parent in such a case. Here, too, there is a *moral ideal* at work, in this case, of "personal devotion," to use Sartre's phrase.

Now, it might be said that, whether or not *we* view this case as one of conflicting obligations, the student himself does. Both courses of action strike him as something that morally *must* be done, and that is what accounts for the poignancy of his case. I am not sure this is right, or that every moral 'must' is the 'must' of obligation.[38] Nonetheless, what seems most important here is that even if one imagines oneself in such a situation without seeing the alternatives as requirements – seeing them rather as reflecting ideals to which one's life has been or could become strongly devoted – the sense of being in a moral dilemma does not seem to go away. One can, for example, imagine oneself saying, of each alternative, "Could I really do *that* – abandon my mother/leave the dangers of freeing ourselves from the Nazis to others – and still be the sort of person I want to be?"

It certainly seems as if Sartre favors understanding the student's dilemma in terms of competing ideals rather than conflicting obligations. He describes it as "hesitat[ion] between two kinds of morality," directed at (or devoted to) different ends. Indeed, we know from Sartre's philosophy in general that he is more likely to see choice as inexorably staking out one's identity rather than as a response to objectively given duty. Sartre's philosophy draws our attention especially to the expressive and self-defining characteristics of choice and commitment, and this certainly seems to capture something important to our commonsense experience of moral dilemmas.

Sartre's Student shares with The Forum and Violin Lessons several crucial features, already mentioned. First, all three involve circumstances in which, whatever we do – even if we remain "inactive" – a choice concerning what common sense would regard as the nub of the matter will *de facto* have been made. Second, all three make it clear that a sense of uncancellable moral cost can accompany not only violation of duty, but also decisions (or failures to decide) that have the effect of foreclosing the realization of certain values. And third, all three draw our attention to the expressive aspect of choice. Making certain choices involves making a statement the meaning of which (like the meaning of the sentences we utter) belongs in part to a public arena and cannot be stipulated at will. Indeed, we can no more stipulate the meaning of our actions than we can stipulate their consequences.

Consider the following thought. Perhaps Sartre's student does not face quite the dilemma it seems. After all, there are many clandestine ways of helping the Free French while remaining in France and attending to most of his mother's needs. To be sure, she might not approve of his running this risk, so that a pure ideal of filial devotion might point to avoiding all entanglement with anti-Vichy forces. But it is not too improbable to assume that he could keep her in the dark about this sort of activity, while still doing virtually all that a devoted child would to provide her comfort, companionship, and so on. Yet we can readily imagine that Sartre's student would not want to hear of this Solomonic solution. His state of mind finds him torn between two poles of pure commitment, and it is a choice of that sort – rather than a compromise – that he might feel he must make. I would suggest that the felt 'must' here, if indeed there is one, has much to do with the expressive dimension of choice – with what an action says or seems to be saying about the agent – and little to do with the notion of duty. Some confirmation for this is to be found in the student's worry that, if he leaves the country to join the Free French, he might be "put into an office to fill up forms." Any war effort requires form-fillers as well as combatants. Fulfillment of his duties, reassertion of the "national collectivity," and even revenge for his brother's death could all be advanced materially by hard work in a London office. What office work – or, for that matter, somewhat less dramatic clandestine work for the Resistance while remaining at home with his mother – might lack is not so much efficacy in achieving certain moral or quasi-moral ends as the vivid expressive power that the student needs in order for his actions to speak with the voice he seeks.

That the plight of Sartre's student, described as Sartre describes it, has been seen as paradigmatically dilemmatic is some reason for broadening our understanding of dilemma to include conflicting ideals and to recognize that we can be as torn by meanings as by duties.

The expressive dimension of choice seems especially prominent in the following example, which is called a moral dilemma by no less an authority on conventional norms than *The New York Times*.

### The Governor

According to the *Times*,[39] Governor Cuomo of New York faces a "moral dilemma." A federal court has ruled that an inmate currently on death row in Texas must be returned to New York to finish a 20-years-to-life sentence for murder. The inmate, Thomas Grasso, prefers death over imprisonment, and wishes to stay in Texas, where he would soon be executed. Cuomo as Governor is legally permitted to waive the return to New York, which would spare Grasso many years in prison – though it would cost him his life. Alternatively, Cuomo can insist that Grasso spend two decades imprisoned in New York anticipating a return to Texas, where he would subsequently be executed. Waiving the return might seem at first to be the humane thing to do, but it would involve sending a man directly to his death. Moreover, Cuomo is a well-known opponent of the death penalty, and very likely would publicly be seen to be – and perhaps would feel himself to be – acquiescent to, even complicitous in, a system of administering the death penalty were he to waive Grasso's return. Of course, there is some chance that Texas (of all places) will eliminate the death penalty during the next 20 years, or that through some entirely unforeseen development the condemned man will be shown to have been coerced into a false confession, or that Grasso will die in prison in New York of natural causes before his return to Texas (imagine seeing *this* as a possible silver lining!). Most important, there is the chance that Grasso is mistaken, and that living the next 20 years – albeit in a prison in upstate New York, and always awaiting execution – would be a substantial benefit to him.

It does not seem that Cuomo faces obvious, competing, symmetric moral requirements or obligations. One might say that he has both an obligation to the prisoner to be humane and an obligation to the citizenry to be just. But sheer justice would appear to permit either course. And although there are humanitarian considerations on both sides of this question, the (imperfect) duty to be humane does not appear to be sufficiently symmetrically disposed to explain the sense of dilemma. One feature this case shares with those that have gone before is that it is not hard to imagine feeling guilt or remorse in the aftermath of making either decision. Has one assisted in the execution of a fellow human? Or, is one subjecting a fellow human to years of suffering in order simply to keep one's own hands clear of any taint of involvement in an execution?

To understand this dilemma, I suspect we must pay attention not only to effects on the prisoner's well-being, but also to the special role of a public figure in declaring, by his or her actions, allegiance to principle. What would Cuomo be saying were he to take either choice? Perhaps he opposes the death penalty partly on humanitarian grounds. Would it be an advertisement for humane treatment of prisoners to require a man to live some 20 years of a life he does not want, only to be put to death, as opposed to granting his wish to have done with it? Perhaps the *Times* is right in calling this a moral dilemma, rather than a mere political quandary, in part because expression is so intimately tied to evaluation. As we noted previously, part of what is unsettling about moral dilemmas is that we find ourselves facing a situation in which the case for either action, though perhaps somewhat imponderable, is one that normally would be morally sufficient. To act in a dilemma is therefore to act contrary to what one is accustomed to regard as sufficient grounds, grounds that anyone alive to the values or obligations at stake would ordinarily take to be determinative. How, then, to manifest in action one's respect for these values or obligations?

The cases of moral dilemma we have considered all involve the thought that, whichever path is taken, there will be a "moral residue" – morally intelligible grounds for guilt or remorse over what one has done, given what one has forsaken. But mere conflict in obligation, or the presence of conflicting, normally sufficient reasons need not leave a residue. To the extent that we are inclined to think of residue as a central feature of dilemma, the presence of conflicting duties thus is neither necessary nor sufficient. Consider next a case similar to one discussed by Philippa Foot.[40]

*Overbooking*

You have made an appointment to meet Winkle in a park on the West Side at noon on the 16th and to meet Squires in a park on the East Side at noon next Monday. You have, however, made an honest mistake: misreading the calendar you failed to notice that next Monday *is* the 16th. But now you have made two promises that cannot both be kept. Unfortunately, you learn of the mistake only at the last minute – there is no time to notify either Winkle or Squires to rearrange schedules, and one of them must be left hanging (or both!). You flip a coin and head for the West Side. There you meet Winkle, explain the difficulty, and apologize for having to reschedule. Winkle is, surprisingly, pleased – an old friend turned up unannounced that morning and talked his ear off, and he'd love to have his noon hour free to finish some work needed by that afternoon. You rush to take a cab to the East Side, and seek out Squires, thirty minutes late. Unforeseeably, Squires, too, was late for the appointment, and feels some measure of relief when you come charging up to him in the park in an apologetic state. At least, he thinks, he didn't miss you and offend you by being late himself. The two of you quickly sort out what has happened, each laughingly dismisses any apologies from the other, and you head off for a somewhat abbreviated lunch.

You were under conflicting obligations in this case, and did not really live up to both fully. Yet in the circumstances your conduct seems to have left no moral residue. So it would to that extent be odd to think that you genuinely faced a moral dilemma rather than a practical problem.

The idea of a genuine dilemma cannot be captured, however, by the idea of being led by circumstances into acting in a way that inevitably produces regrettable harm. For this is a feature in many cases in which there is no dilemma, real or perceived. Thus, when a stronger obligation overrides a much weaker one, for example, when someone stops to aid a fallen bicyclist even though this makes her late for dinner, the agent faces no real dilemma, and it would be morally inappropriate for someone else to blame her morally or for her to spend time in self-blame. And should it happen that the agent feels only regret at the inconvenience she knowingly has caused, rather than guilt or remorse, there would be nothing to say against this morally.

But not all cases of this structure can be "domesticated" morally in quite this way. The case of the two loans, discussed in Section II, might be modified. What if I have promised both Bemis and Benchley something indivisible, for which compensation seems out of the question – for example, the saving of their lives, or the life of one of their children? I am, let us say, a surgeon who has promised to each, and to the families of each, that if I am at the hospital I will be available on a moment's notice in Emergency to perform a lengthy, life-saving operation should the need arise. Each family has derived substantial comfort from the assurance on my part. Unexpectedly, both Bemis and Benchley fall into immediate danger of death at the same time while I am on duty – and no other surgeons are available. Or suppose that one of the two falls into such danger at the same moment as someone else, whom hospital triage procedures would normally favor, but to whom I have made no personal promise? Should the promise matter?

Or suppose that no "professional norm" is relevant. I have taken their children to the beach, promising reassuringly to serve as lifeguard, yet Bemis, Jr. and Benchley, Jr. have simultaneously come into immediate danger of drowning.

No line of reasoning concerning partial soultions and renegotiated "making good" on the promises or duties here seems applicable. Moreover, unlike the first, indebtedness case, these cases seem to call for deep remorse, whatever I do. Of course, it is imperative that in none of the three cases I simply fail to act, lacking sufficient reason to keep one duty rather than another. And it would seem in all three cases that there would be something inappropriate if Beemis or Benchley or the anonymous patient, or their families, were to think I acted in a morally unacceptable or despicable way if I elected to save one when I couldn't save all, though it would be morally unacceptable and despicable were *I* to feel no grief or remorse, or to take no steps to apologize to, and comfort or assist in some way, the families of those who die. We should all try to be as understanding and sensitive as possible, and also ultimately forgiving of others and of oneself, consistent with the normal range of human emotion. The real challenge here for moral theory appears to be less of the shape "How to decide whether I should save just one?" or even "How to decide which?", than "How to express through my acts and feelings my awareness of what has been lost?" We would be left hanging by a moral theory that gets us through dilemmas using principles of choice, but leaves open the question of why, having gotten through, this still is not "right" or "enough." And to the extent that the real issues about moral dilemma concern *how to feel*, we are left hanging by a practical theory that sticks to the categories of moral action.

Following out somewhat the Millian line of thought discussed previously, in cases of this kind, or even in the original case of the two loans, it might be that anyone with sufficiently strong moral motivation would tend to feel not only regret, but guilt, in view of the pain and loss caused. This is in part an empirical question, and it is not impossible to imagine someone of strong moral motivation who would feel nothing other than acute regret. Were I, or even one of the bereaved families, to see matters more in terms of regret than guilt and blame, this would not itself seem morally repugnant. It is easy in cases of dilemma to fall too quickly into the assumption that moral sensitivity would have to translate into blackest guilt, or that such guilt might not also be in some measure to be *struggled with* morally. Two final examples.

### Sophie's Choice

This example, like Sartre's discussion of his student's quandary, has taken on a life of its own in the literature on moral dilemma, somewhat independent of the original work that inspired it.[41] So I will describe it only briefly, in what I take to be its canonical form.

Sophie is imprisoned in a Nazi concentration camp, and a guard forces upon her the following choice. If she will select one of her children to be killed, the other will be allowed to live. If she refuses to select one, both will be killed. We will assume – contrary to the original – that the children are as nearly alike as possible in any dimension one might take to be relevant.

Sophie is obliged to protect the well-being of each child, and in this case it would appear that her obligation to each is equally strong, neither overriding the other. Her situation thus appears to fulfill the standard characterization of a moral dilemma. Moreover, any choice she makes would appear to leave a dreadful residue: it would be, for Sophie, grounds not only for regret, but for lasting and deeply justified remorse. But compare:

### Ruth's Choice

Ruth is a single parent who has given birth to Siamese twins. The hospital doctors tell her that both will die unless a complex and uncertain surgical operation is performed at once that will disconnect the two, after which only one will have the requisites for survival. Ruth is asked whether she consents to this procedure, which will involve selecting one of the two twins to emerge (if the operation is successful) capable of sustained life. Assuming that the surgeon discovers nothing new on the operating table, this could be done by lot if Ruth so wishes. Her obligations to each child again seem equally compelling, and neither overrides the other. Thus she faces a dilemma in the standard sense.[42]

But what of residue? Would it be a sign of morally defective character were she not to experience lasting guilt at having made a choice, for example, to consent to the operation and use of the lot? Suppose that Ruth resolves not to dwell upon her choice in the future, but to prevent it from casting a cloud over her life with her new child by seeing it as nothing more than a regrettable way of having done what was necessary to save his life. She resolves to fight back any tendency to feel guilt, difficult as this might be. Suppose that this resolve proves highly successful. Would anyone think that she *ought* to feel greater regret or remorse, with the inevitable effects this would have upon her psyche and her child's?

Several differences between the two cases stand out for our attention. First, in Ruth's case, quite unlike Sophie's, entry into the process of choice does not itself involve an act expressive of complicity with grave moral wrong. Second, in Ruth's case, again unlike Sophie's, the children have not lived long enough to develop established relationships with their mother or distinctive individual identities. Third, for various reasons, the most psychologically salient aspect of Ruth's Choice is the saving of a life, while the most psychologically salient aspect of Sophie's Choice is the taking of a life. These three considerations do not have to do with whether Sophie and Ruth face conflicting, nonoverridden obligations to promote the life and well-being of each of their children. Presumably, both have such obligations if either does. That Sophie's Choice would have greater moral remainder is therefore not a consequence solely of its involving conflicting obligations – Ruth's Choice is not different in that regard. Nor is the difference really one in the magnitude of value directly at stake – the loss of an innocent life. Indeed, given the cases as described here, it might even be obvious that both Ruth and Sophie should follow the same course: to accept the need to choose and to choose by lot. If commonsense is much more likely to regard Sophie's Choice as an archetype of moral dilemma, I suspect that is due instead to the different expressive significance of choice in her circumstances and, perhaps above all, to the greater depth of her relationship to her individual children.

But there is also a symmetry to be found in both Sophie's and Ruth's Choice, at least as we have described them here. And if the remarks made about symmetry are correct, then this symmetry should have a mitigating effect, and we should be able to modify the cases to create situations in which symmetry is not present and in which it therefore is even less obvious that there is a morally acceptable choice. Thus consider a modification of the case in which she must choose, not between two of her children, but between a single child of her own and the children of five others, or between the death of a single child and the destruction of a document that is the only source of information on whereabouts of thousands of children who have been separated from their families. In these modified cases, a decision to use the lot no longer seems appropriate – an exercise of direct personal choice seems expressively appropriate, even if we recognize that any personal decision in such circumstances is going to be little more than desperately arbitrary.

Return now briefly to our two paradigm moral theories, Kantian and utilitarian. Neither sort of theory seems, in its original formulations, to give us a clear way of incorporating talk of the expressive dimension into our moral assessment of acts or states of affairs. For the expressive character of an act is not clearly within the scope of duty, nor need it be a "welfare outcome" in the ordinary sense. The meaning of an act, like the meanings of a word, goes well beyond what our individual will can control, as we saw in the preceding examples. And meaning can be "backward-looking" rather than consequential – an act can show respect for persons, and give greater meaning to lives, now gone. This may have future effects on welfare, but the meaning will not *be* that effect – just as two statements with different meaning, literally or poetically, can have the same truth value.[43]

Meaning is, of course, in itself morally neutral. Acts can express vengeance, contempt, indifference, benevolence, or love. Since meaning is substantially independent of will, an orthodox Kantian might insist that even though an act of dutiful apology, say, will not have the same meaning as an act of spontaneous contrition – "You *say* you're sorry, but you don't really *feel* sorry!" is the beginning of many a familial spat - moral obligation can extend only to the former. And since meaning is substantially independent of well-being, an orthodox utilitarian might insist that "respect for the meaning of past lives," for example, is an attractive concept only until we notice that many past lives have been lost fighting on behalf of intolerant or vengeful goals. Should we wish that their sacrifice was not in vain, still, do we really want it to have the meaning *they* tried to give it? Human life is infused with meaning, and would be unintelligible without an appreciation of meanings. But however much meaning contributes to the value of life – or even to the possibility of many of our most cherished values – in itself it is a dimension distinct from value. The utilitarian can argue that individual meanings are not *values*-in-themselves that intrinsically merit our devotion, and that respect for meanings makes *moral* sense only insofar as it is part of what, over time, makes human existence better.

It does seem to me that some of the dilemmas and conflicts faced in morally troubling cases will not be thoroughly understood until moral theory has confronted questions of meaning more deeply. As yet I see no conclusive reason why this confrontation could not occur or be productive. Still, I would be whistling in the dark if I claimed that we have a ready understanding of how questions of meaning are to be integrated into the venerable value- or duty-based moral traditions. But then, I don't know of an alternative moral tradition better equipped to grapple with meaning.

## v. CONCLUSION: THE STATUS OF MORALITY

Consider what one might call the *Straightforward Argument*. According to this argument, phenomena such as moral dilemma and irreducible moral pluralism pose a fundamental difficulty for moral realism, that is, for the view that moral judgments sometimes express literally true claims.[44] Truth is held to be *bivalent* – that is, for any well-formed, definite proposition $p$, either $p$ or not-$p$ is true. But if dilemma arises, then it looks as if "He ought to stay home with his mother and not run off to join the Free French" and "He ought to run off to join the Free French and not stay home with his mother" are either both true, or neither. And if irreducible pluralism yields an incommensurability, for example, then "His duty to his mother is weightier" could fail to be either true or false.

But the Straightforward Argument falsely assumes that "He ought to $A$" and "He ought not to $A$" describe logically incompatible states of affairs. We saw in the case of Mill in Section III that a conflict of moral requirement can arise within a consistently described state of affairs. Similarly, as we noticed, magnitudes can be incommensurable within a consistently describable state of affairs. Is there, then, any less "straightforward" argument from moral dilemma or moral pluralism to moral anti-realism?

On the contrary, perhaps. One could make a case that pluralism and dilemma reveal, often quite starkly and wrenchingly, how real value and obligation seem to be, and how reluctant we are to treat them as somehow conventional or "constructed."

But one might have a worry about "moral reality" from a different direction. To speak of 'moral reality' suggests a "moral order" – a coherent way that things might be and we might be. Of course the orderliness could be *practical* rather than *metaphysical* – the coherence a matter of reasons for action. Still, dilemma and incommensurability threaten even practical coherence. Historically, philosophers as different as Aristotle and Kant have been said to suppose that morality would lose any rational foundation if no such moral order could be assumed.

One can detect at least two distinct elements in the long-standing idea that some degree of moral order must be presupposed if morality is to be well-founded. To the first we are inclined to attach less philosophical significance nowadays: there must be a definite path of right action by which one can accord with divine will, and which therefore will unite duty with happiness – if not in this life, then in an afterlife. Here the idea of "rational foundation" is closely allied with "intelligent Creator" and "enlightened self-interest." It now seems clear any incentive or coherence supplied to morality in this way is external to it.

A second idea of "rational foundation" depends upon no theistic or teleological assumptions. Moreover, if it involves "self-interest" at all, this is in a very broad sense of the term – the sense in which the unity of the self is, for an agent, always an interest. "Leading a moral life" cannot be an organizing principle in the development of individual character and in the conduct of personal choice, it is held, if following this principle does not afford some coherence to one's life. It must, for example, generate self-sustaining motivations, and provide some degree of intelligibility in thought and feeling. If fundamental moral conflict were the heart of daily life, and no moral perspective could give enduring guidance concerning which way to turn, but only deepen our sense of conflict and guilt, then there would be little prospect for "leading a moral life" to be a way of making sense of oneself and one's place in the world. Horrid circumstances have sometimes thrust morally aware individuals into just such torment, and we cannot ask morality to guarantee that there will be no horrors, or that life will make much sense within them. But neither could we ask that morality retain its place in life if we saw no hope for the horror to end.

We might, for example, be led to an "error theory" of morality if insufficient unity or practical coherence could be found among the elements central to everyday moral thought. Morality is rich with truisms – that morality contributes to the conditions for social harmony and the promotion of individual well-being, that it affords guidance in choice, and that the various virtues it recognizes are substantially compatible and self-reinforcing. If sufficiently many of these fail to obtain, we might think that it is a mistake to use moral categories as organizing principles.[45] It is perhaps in this way that we can understand the existentialist insistence upon the devastation of conventional morality by honest recognition of the absurdity of choice and the hopelessness of the life to which humans have been abandoned, now that "God is dead."[46]

So what might have looked like a "merely practical" problem for morality could become a theoretical problem as well. It is a question not only of what to do, but of what to think. Pervasive dilemma and conflict might lead us to think that there is no unified set of phenomena fit to play the role of moral properties, properly so called.

Notice the role of the word 'pervasive.' The problem does not arise from the bare possibility or existence of moral dilemma or irreducible pluralism. Rather – somewhat surprisingly? – it depends upon *how much* or *what kinds of* dilemma or incommensurability we face. Neither of these is exactly a given. For what we do as agents to shape our acts, institutions, and circumstances will also shape how frequently we confront dilemmatic circumstances or intolerable conflicts in value or requirement. Some of the seemingly unmanageable conflicts we now face – between personal life and social good, say – are the result of morally questionable, but also morally alterable, institutions, practices, and inequalities. It might be an unalterable fact of life that the world does not support the sort of coherence that morality presupposes. But this cannot be shown by finding a handful of examples of striking moral dilemmas and conflicts, especially if we fail to ask how many of their sources might be in some measure within our control – if not as individuals at a moment, then collectively over time.

Moreover, we should not take the notion of *coherent perspective* too strictly. Some degree of coherence certainly is needed in life. But a life can remain full of meanings, and sources of intelligibility and value, even though it lacks a high degree of univalence. In matters of language, prudence, culture, and belief we can face – even embrace – enormous amounts of dissonance and complexity without letting go altogether of the idea that there are things to be said, and better or worse ways of proceeding. We should not be quick to write off morality because our world is complex and conflicting, though perhaps we should write off moralities that would represent it as otherwise or make no sense if it were.

Even our everyday notion of truth brings with it the semantic paradoxes, yet they do not seem to destabilize truth and meaning in ordinary language, and we are able to use ordinary language to help us state and explore these very paradoxes. Coming to terms with paradox may mean understanding it, not dissolving it. Discussions of moral dilemma often serve to illuminate just how much our developed moral theories can help

284

us, after all, to understand and appreciate the sorts of conflict and loss that are in question, and where these should and should not unsettle moral practice.

I therefore would modestly propose that the debate over moral dilemma and pluralism spend more time with the questions "How much?" and "What kinds?" than it has in the past. How much irreconcilable conflict is there? How much could this be affected by changing human institutions and practices? How much is due to our failure to integrate expressive dimensions into moral theory? How much unity or coherence really is presupposed by the idea of a moral life or a moral point of view? My own sense is that we tend to overestimate this last, and this leads us to downplay the quite substantial amount we might do to eliminate various conflicts in fact, rather than obsess about them in theory or be crushed by them in practice.

We want our actions and institutions to say something about ourselves, typically something positive or at least not manifestly negative. We build monuments, hold celebrations and solemn rituals, and cover our conduct and history with explanations. Dilemma and unresolved conflict threaten to interrupt this impressive spectacle, however, since they make it inevitable that our actions also say something negative, no matter what we try. Yet this reveals an unexpected affinity between realism, on the one hand, and dilemma and pluralism, on the other. For each contains the idea of the robustness of moral phenomena. Recalcitrant phenomena in general force theorists to try to discern what is central and what is not. In the moral case, coming to terms with recalcitrant pluralism and dilemma may, curiously, strengthen rather than weaken our understanding of even the most abstract conceptions in ethical theory, and remind us why the need for such theories also refuses, recalcitrantly, to go away.[47]

### NOTES

This paper combines material from two previously published papers, "Pluralism, Determinacy, and Dilemma," *Ethics* 102 (1992), 720–42 and "Some Types of Moral Dilemma," in G. Mason, ed., *Moral Dilemma* (Oxford: Oxford University Press, 1996), along with some revisions and additional material.

1. When such an abstract conception of shared citizenship fails to achieve or hold a prominent position among other loyalties, as in Eastern Europe, polities can be maintained only by constant threat of repression. Once the threat of repression becomes less credible, polities crumble and mutual benefits of cooperation are lost.
2. Hobbes, for example, can be seen as urging that even the religious enthusiast attend to his interests as a human being, rather than simply seeing himself as a soldier in the Army of Christ. For relevant discussion, see Albert O. Hirschman, *The Passions*

and the Interests: Political Arguments for Capitalism before Its Triumph (Princeton, NJ: Princeton University Press, 1977).

3. For some discussion, see P. Railton, "Moral Theory as a Moral Practice," Noûs 25 (1991), 185–90.

4. See Imre Lakatos, "Falsification and the Methodology of Scientific Research Programmes," in I. Lakatos and A. Musgrave, eds., Criticism and the Growth of Knowledge (Cambridge: Cambridge University Press, 1970).

5. Immanuel Kant, Groundwork of the Metaphysics of Morals, M. J. Gregor, trans, in M. J. Gregor, ed., Immanuel Kant: Practical Philosophy (Cambridge: Cambridge University Press, 1996) A403–4.

6. Immanel Kant, Foundations of the Metaphysics of Morals, L. W. Beck, trans. (Indianapolis: Bobbs-Merrill, 1959) 14 (A398).

7. Immanuel Kant, Critique of Practical Reason, M. J. Gregor, trans., in Gregor, ed., Kant: Practical Philosophy, A116, A118.

8. Kant, Foundations, 17 (A401).

9. "Sympathetic joy and sadness (sympathia moralis) are sensible feelings of pleasure or displeasure (which are therefore to be called "aesthetic") at another's state of joy or pain (shared feeling, sympathetic feeling). Nature has already implanted in human beings receptivity to this feeling." Immanuel Kant, The Metaphysics of Morals, M. J. Gregor, trans., in Gregor, ed., Kant: Practical Philosophy, A456.

10. "All the inclinations together (which can be brought into a tolerable system and the satisfaction of which is then called one's own happiness) constitute regard for oneself (solipsismus)." Immanuel Kant, Critique of Practical Reason, M. J. Gregor, trans., in Gregor, ed., Kant: Practical Philosophy, A73.

11. Kant's famous formula is, of course, to treat humanity in others as an end-in-itself, rather than to treat them directly as ends-in-themselves. If one wishes to insist upon this aspect of the formula, then transpose the present discussion of benevolence into the register of humaneness or, what we sometimes praise as an individual's profound humanity.

12. "The faculty of desire is the faculty to be, by means of one's representations, the cause of the objects of those representations." Immanuel Kant, The Metaphysics of Morals, M. J. Gregor, trans., in Gregor, ed., Kant: Practical Philosophy, A211.

13. "So if a pleasure necessarily precedes a desire, the practical pleasure must be called an interest of inclination. But if a pleasure can only follow upon an antecedent determination of the faculty of desire it is an intellectual pleasure, and the interest in the object must be called an interest of reason. . . ." Kant, Metaphysics of Morals, A212.

14. Kant, Metaphysics of Morals, A212–13.

15. Respect for the moral law – "reverence" – is a kind of direct love, and ". . . only the love that is delight [Liebe des Wohlgefallens] (amor complacentiae) is direct." Kant, Metaphysics of Morals, A402. Moreover, "the good is the object of the will (a power of desire that is determined by reason). But to will something and to have a liking for its existence, i.e., to take an interest in it, are identical." Immanuel Kant, Critique of Judgment, W. S. Pluhar, trans. (Indianapolis: Hackett, 1987) A209.

16. "Moral feeling. This is the susceptibility to feel pleasure or displeasure merely from being aware that our actions are consistent with or contrary to the law of duty." Kant, Metaphysics of Morals, A399.

17. "*Moral feeling*. This is the susceptibility to feel pleasure or displeasure merely from being aware that our actions are consistent with or contrary to the law of duty. Every determination of choice proceeds *from the representation of a possible action to the deed*, through the feeling of pleasure or displeasure, taking an interest in the action or its effect. The state of *feeling* here (the way in which inner sense is affected) is either *pathological* or *moral*. The former is that feeling which precedes the representation of the law; the latter, that which can only follow upon it." Kant, *Metaphysics of Morals*, A399.

18. It is, of course, a further question whether there *are* "character traits" in the ordinary sense. For some reasons to think that commonsense characterology might misrepresent actual psychology, see P. Railton, "Made in the Shade: Moral Compatibilism and the Aims of Moral Theory," *Canadian Journal of Philosophy*, suppl. vol. 21 (1999), 79–106; Gilbert Harman, "Moral Philosophy Meets Social Psychology: Virtue Ethics and the Fundamental Attribution Error," *Proceedings of the Aristotelian Society* 99 (1999), 315–31; and John Doris, "Persons, Situations, and Virtue Ethics," *Noûs* 32 (1998), 504–30.

19. Kant, *Metaphysics of Morals*, A399–400. See also: "Respect (*reverentia*) is, again, something merely subjective, a feeling of a special kind, not a judgment about an object that it would be a duty to bring about or promote. For, such a duty, regarded as a duty, could be represented to us only through the *respect* we have for it. A duty to have respect would thus amount to being put under obligation to duties." *Metaphysics of Morals*, A402.

20. *Metaphysics of Morals*, A399–400.

21. *Foundations*, 16 (A399).

22. As we ordinarily understand them, benevolence, affections, and so on are capacities that involve a degree of "empirical determination" (and, in some cases, a "particularity") of the will. This could conflict deeply with the orthodox Kantian idea of autonomous, noumenal agency. It would take a firm grasp of the nature and centrality of the idea of *noumenal* agency in Kant – and of the possibility of developing a Kantian but nonnoumenal account of free will – to say whether a genuinely Kantian motivational pluralism along the lines suggested here is possible. Various neo-Kantians have shown a willingness to dispense with or reinterpret the doctrine of the noumenal self, offering a different sort of account of the normatively central Kantian notions of *autonomy* and *universality* in agency (see, e.g., John Rawls' contractarian reinterpretation of these notions in *A Theory of Justice* [Cambridge: Harvard University Press, 1971] 251–7). Such neo-Kantians could, I think, avail themselves of the form of deliberative and motivational pluralism about moral agency sketched here. Since the orthodox Kantian doctrines of noumenal agency and acausal freedom of the will are "limit points" of the critical philosophy, a great deal of Kant's analysis of moral agency might be preseved without including them.

23. ". . . beauty [holds] only for human beings, i.e., beings who are animal and yet rational, though it is not enough that they be rational (e.g., spirits) but they must be animal as well. . . ." Kant, *Critique of Judgment*, A210.

24. ". . . the existence of a cause of all nature, distinct from nature, which contains the ground of this connection, namely of the exact correspondence of happiness with morality, is also *postulated*. . . . [T]he supreme cause of nature, insofar as it

must be postulated for the highest good, is a being that is the cause of nature by *understanding* and *will* (hence its author), that is, **God**." Kant, *Critique of Practical Reason*, A125.

25. Kant, *Foundations*, 17 (A401).
26. "The concept of duty, therefore, requires of the action *objective* accord with the law but requires of the maxim of the action *subjective* respect for the law, as the sole way of determining the will by the law." Kant, *Critique of Practical Reason*, A81. Moreover, ". . . the concept of a duty, observance or transgression of which is indeed connected with a pleasure or displeasure of a distinctive kind (moral *feeling*), although in practical laws of reason we take no account of these feelings (since they have nothing to do with the [objective] *basis* of practical laws but only with subjective *effect* in the mind when our choice is determined by them, which can differ from one subject to another . . .)." Kant, *Metaphysics of Morals*, A221.
27. In an influential book, Walter Sinnott-Armstrong characterizes a moral dilemma as a situation in which one faces two or more competing but undefeated moral requirements. See W. Sinnott-Armstrong, *Moral Dilemmas* (Oxford: Blackwell, 1988).
28. Kant, *Groundwork*, A422.
29. Regan's final version of the procedure is considerably more complex. See Donald H. Regan, *Utilitarianism and Cooperation* (Oxford: Clarendon, 1980) x, chs. 9–10.
30. Interestingly, contemporary "social contract" forms of Kantian thought – such as Rawls, *A Theory of Justice* – do not avoid the problems of coordination mentioned. For they arrive at a fixed list of rights or duties *on the assumption* of nearly full compliance with these rights and duties, and lack a theory of how to proceed in conditions far from full compliance.
31. For related discussion, see R. E. Bales, "Act Utilitarianism: Account of Right-Making Characteristics or Decision-Making Procedure?", *American Philosophical Quarterly* 8 (1971), 257–65; R. M. Adams, "Motive Utilitarianism," *Journal of Philosophy* 73 (1976), 467–81; P. Railton, "Alienation, Consequentialism, and the Demands of Morality," *Philosophy and Public Affairs* 13 (1984), 134–71, reprinted here as Chapter 6; Derek Parfit, *Reasons and Persons* (Oxford: Oxford University Press, 1984); and P. Railton, "How Thinking about Character and Utilitarianism Might Lead Us to Rethink the Character of Utilitarianism," *Midwest Studies in Philosophy* 13 (1988), 398–416, reprinted here as Chapter 8.
32. See J. S. Mill, *Utilitarianism*, 303, ch. 5, as reprinted in Warnock.
33. Serious coordination problems beset virtually every aspect of "optimal code" indirect utilitarianism – depending upon what others actually do, adherence to or promotion of an ideal code may have disastrous consequences. (This is the utilitarian version of the contractarian problem mentioned in note 25.) As far as I know, there is no "fixed formula" of indirect utilitarianism that will give us an adequate account of real-world coordination problems. Once again, see Regan, *Utilitarianism and Cooperation*.
34. Mention of evolution and moral emotion is liable to rouse suspicion. Critics and defenders of "evolutionary approaches to ethics" alike have often claimed that evolutionarily shaped emotions or motivations could never be redeployed on behalf of morality, for morality is impartial or "altruistic" and evolutionary selection is not – the vaunted objectivity of morality would be a sham. Such

288

claims overlook the fact that the same argument could be made for the idea that human *cognition* and *belief* could never be redeployed on behalf of *science*, for science purports to be impartial and universal, while evolutionary selection is not – the vaunted objectivity of science (including, of course, evolutionary science) would also have to be dismissed as a sham. For discussion, see P. Railton, "Darwinian Building Blocks," *Journal of Consciousness Studies* 7 (2000), 55–60.

35. See W. D. Ross, *The Right and the Good* (Oxford: Clarendon, 1930).

36. Of course, it is true in general that whenever one makes or postpones a decision one forgoes *some* opportunities irrevocably. What presses us in the direction of a sense of urgency or dilemma has more to do with the *kinds* of opportunities that will be forgone – for example, they have very important benefits, or others like them will not recur, or they are of a kind one would never otherwise pass up – and the *difficulty of offsetting or compensating* for the lost opportunities.

37. The case appears in Jean-Paul Sartre, *Existentialism Is a Humanism*, Walter Kaufmann, trans., in W. Kaufmann, *Existentialism from Dostoyevsky to Sartre* (New York: Vintage, 1984) 203–4.

38. Perhaps there is a French cultural norm at work here as well, assigning to adult children greater responsibility for their parents.

39. October 9, 1993.

40. See Philippa Foot, *Virtues and Vices* (Oxford: Oxford University Press, 1983) 387.

41. William Styron, *Sophie's Choice* (New York: Random House, 1979), with apologies to the author.

42. The case is not silly. A similar circumstance arose a few years after this was originally written.

43. Even in all possible worlds. '2 + 2 = 4' does not have the same meaning as '1 + 3 = 4,' yet they are both true in all possible worlds.

44. This is a simplification. For further discussion, see P. Railton, "Moral Realism," *Philosophical Review* 95 (1986), 163–207. Reprinted here as Chapter 1.

45. Richard Boyd suggests a similar kind of concern in his discussion of "homeostatic clusters." See his "How to be a Moral Realist," in G. Sayre-McCord, ed., *Essays on Moral Realism* (Ithaca: Cornell University Press, 1988).

46. Sartre writes:

> The existentialist is strongly opposed to a certain type of secular morality which seeks to suppress God at the least possible expense . . . [and which introduces the idea that] it must be considered obligatory *a priori* to be honest, not to lie, not to beat one's wife, to bring up children, and so forth; . . . the existentialist, in the contrary, finds it extremely embarrassing that God does not exist. . . . Everything is indeed permitted if God does not exist.
>
> (Sartre, *Existentialism Is a Humanism*, 201–2)

47. Of course, however congenial this idea might be to the realist – however little it might point us away from realism – it is not the unique possession of realists.

An earlier version of part of this paper was presented at a conference on moral dilemma, held at the University of Minnesota. I am grateful to my coparticipants at that conference, and especially to Walter Sinnott-Armstrong for comments and to Gene Mason for suggesting many editorial improvements. I am also indebted to the participants in the *Ethics* Symposium on "Pluralism and Ethical Theory" held at Rollins College, and in particular to John Deigh (who presented a reply). Some of this material was presented to a seminar at New York University School of Law led by Thomas Nagel and Ronald Dworkin, and I thank them and others present for much stimulating conversation about dilemma, determinacy, and realism. I owe a particular debt to Peter Vranas, for drawing my attention to Kant's account of respect in the *Metaphysics of Morals*.

# Part III

*The Authority of Ethics and
Value – The Problem of Normativity*

# 10

## *On the Hypothetical and Non-Hypothetical in Reasoning about Belief and Action**

> I am sure that I do not understand the idea of a reason for acting, and I wonder whether anyone else does either.
>
> Philippa Foot

Perhaps it shouldn't be surprising when a central notion of common sense proves elusive on reflection – that's what makes the philosophical world go round. And some aspects of practical rationality seem obvious enough: rational agents form intentions, adjust means and ends, and so on. Yet even very elementary questions can excite not only controversy between conflicting, entrenched positions, but also expert bafflement.

An indirect approach suggests itself: it might help us to understand reasons for action if we started with reasons for belief. First, action involves belief. Second, one of the most crucial and problematic notions in practical reason – the notion of *non-hypothetical* reasons or requirements (reasons or requirements not dependent upon contingent ends of the agent) – appears to be well domesticated within the literature on theoretical reasons.[1] On the usual view of things, two agents in the same epistemic situation (same evidence, same background beliefs) would have the same reasons for believing any given proposition, regardless of possible differences in their personal goals.[2]

Can the "usual view of things" in the theoretical realm be given a principled basis? If so, can a similarly non-hypothetical basis be found in the practical realm? In what follows, we will be developing a sequence of arguments that purport to show just this. These arguments turn on considerations concerning belief and action of a kind David Velleman has called *constitutive*.[3] By way of conclusion, we will ask what the limitations of such arguments might be.

## I. REASONING ABOUT BELIEF

Let us begin with Gary, a student in our introductory course on the Theory of Knowledge one autumn term. He's confronting epistemology as a discipline for the first time, and he's been staring with silent but disarming intentness from the back of the room for several weeks. Now he's ready to speak: "These philosophers we've been reading seem to agree that there are certain standards of belief, standards we should follow even when they lead us to conclusions we don't like. They spend all their time disagreeing about exactly what these standards are, but they just seem to assume that we'll want to follow them. Suppose I don't? What can they say to me?"

One can imagine our initial response: "Well, you understand why you should eat your vegetables? You may not care about these epistemic standards as such, but you do care a lot about other things. And you're more likely to get what you want if you have warranted beliefs. Following epistemic norms won't guarantee reliability, but there isn't any better alternative short of magic or luck."

Notice, though, that this line of response is *non-epistemic* and *hypothetical*. It advertises the existence of benefits accruing to an agent who follows epistemic norms, but the values or goals in question are not distinctively epistemic, nor do we assume that they carry distinctive epistemic presuppositions. To be sure, this hypothetical justification is, or purports to be, quite *robust*. Virtually any goal Gary might have would be well served by his following epistemic norms. Indeed, we might at this point refer Gary to the Dutch Book argument, to show that he is at risk of being a sure loser if he does not conform his degrees of belief to certain probabilistic principles.

Gary has obviously been preparing his case. He counters by asking the class to imagine an individual dying of an incurable disease, to whom little or nothing matters besides peace of mind. Belief in the Hereafter would comfort him mightily and would come to him spontaneously if he could just relax his epistemic scruples. What makes us think that the balance of non-epistemic considerations will always favor keeping those scruples? Gary pushes his question: he wants to know whether there are any considerations that require or favor following epistemic standards that don't depend at all on our personal goals.

We can, of course, point out that although someone might find the thought of an afterlife reassuring, reassurance is not evidence and so does not yield *epistemic reasons for belief* in the Hereafter, only *practical reasons for being a believer in* the Hereafter. Epistemic evaluation, then, appears to be quite untouched by Gary's deathbed example.

Gary, however, finds this serene lack of regard for whether agents are comforted or tormented by their beliefs off-putting. Moreover, he cannot see how appealing to "epistemic reasons" could provide any sort of answer to his initial question. Isn't it circular to invoke epistemic reasons on behalf of epistemology? The fact that these epistemic reasons are themselves non-hypothetical is beside the point. After all, there are lots of norms that lay down standards that pay no attention to the agent's particular goals.

Gary asks us to consider "anti-epistemology," which tells us to reduce our belief in proportion as evidence increases. This norm is just as non-hypothetical as orthodox epistemology, since it prescribes degrees of belief without making any allowance for the agent's personal goals. Why should we submit ourselves to the old-fashioned rigors of epistemology rather than take on the exciting new challenges of anti-epistemology?

It plainly will not do for us to say to him that epistemic norms recommend non-hypothetically against this, since anti-epistemic norms speak non-hypothetically for it. Of course, it is unlikely that Gary or anyone else would really be prepared to abide by anti-epistemic norms. Only a very singular set of personal goals and circumstances could make anti-epistemic thinking much of a boon. But we can see that this again affords no more than a very robust hypothetical and practical justification.

After all, we reflect, Gary might find himself in some pretty unusual circumstances. Perhaps it is he who lies on the deathbed, yearning for peace of mind. Or perhaps a powerful, mind-reading anti-epistemic demon is prepared to torment him mercilessly unless his beliefs fly in the face of evidence. We consider responding, "Look. Belief isn't voluntary. You can't just decide what to believe." But this threatens to show too much. There won't be much left of normative epistemology unless we recognize some forms of control over what we come to believe. However, there is something that might help explain the oft-repeated phrase that belief isn't voluntary, and that might also help with Gary.

Consider a form of "Moore's paradox" – the extreme oddness of:

(1) $h$ is true, but I don't believe it.

According to anti-epistemology, the more one takes the evidence to favor $h$, the weaker should be one's belief that $h$. In the limit, then, we find the anti-epistemologist saying:

(2) I recognize that the evidence for $h$ has become conclusive, so I don't believe that $h$ in the least.

But (2) seems (almost?) as odd as (1). Maybe anti-epistemology isn't a real alternative after all.

What makes (1) – and perhaps by extension (2) as well – so odd? Various explanations have been proposed. One might start by noting that belief is a propositional attitude partly characterized by its representation of its object as true. "Belief is believing true," the saying goes.

But this is too quick. For even the propositional attitude of "pretending that $h$" amounts to "pretending that $h$ is true" – such is the 'believe' in 'make-believe.' And there is nothing paradoxical about:

(3) $h$ is true (or: I recognize that the evidence that $h$ is true has become conclusive) but I'm pretending otherwise.

So we must go further. We might say this: a belief that $h$ "aims at" the truth of $h$.[4] A belief that $h$ necessarily "misses its target" when $h$ is false, whereas a pretence that $h$ does not. Beliefs are evaluable as true or false, and are false whenever their propositional objects are. To have mastered the distinction between belief and pretense is in part to understand this. That suggests:

(4) A believer that $h$ holds that, necessarily, her belief that $h$ is false if $h$ itself is false.

This, however, is overloaded conceptually. Most of us think that school-age children have genuine beliefs and can distinguish belief from pretense quite well, even though we suspect that they do not explicitly hold the modal attitude expressed in (4). Rather, they manifest their awareness of the special tie between belief and truth implicitly, by showing sensitivity to the distinction between what is the case (as far as they can tell) and what they would like to be the case, and through their responses to evidence for or against $h$. Believers in effect hold their beliefs to be *accountable* to truth.[5]

To be sure, it is not false belief as such that is paradoxical. There is nothing odd about:

(5) $h$ is true, but I wrongly disbelieved it at the time.

Paradox emerges in (1) – or in (2) – not because the belief in question is false or incongruous with the world, but because the belief is incongruous with something else the agent already thinks.

What is the nature of this incongruity, and what sort of problem is it for the believer? There is, I am sure, often incongruity among my beliefs. To the extent that I remain unaware of incongruity, no Moore-like paradox arises. I can, for example, unthinkingly pick up the telephone to call the repair office to report that my phone is dead. This is a state manifesting incongruous beliefs, but not one that seems unattainable. By contrast, the state of mind that would be accurately expressed by (1) – or by (2) – seems not foolish but opaque. What *could* someone who confidently uttered (1) – or (2) – have in mind?[6]

The distinctive propositional attitude of belief is therefore one that not only represents its propositional contents as true, but also one that cannot represent itself as unresponsive to – unaccountable to – their truth. This is still an unacceptably crude formulation.[7] But fortunately for present purposes we need only a rough idea, since even the rough idea enables us to explain why anti-epistemology is untenable. In order for a propositional attitude to be an attitude of *belief*, it cannot represent itself as wholly unaccountable to truth or evidence.

We've been lost in thought for a bit, but now are in a position to respond to Gary with what looks like a non-hypothetical argument. For we can say why he must, at least in the limit, accord some deference to what he takes to be truth and evidence thereof in his belief-formation. It is part of the *price of admission* to belief as a propositional attitude that one not represent one's attitude as unaccountable to truth. Someone unwilling to pay this price – who, for example, insists that he will represent himself as accepting propositions just as it suits his fancy and without any commitment to their truth – would not succeed in *believing* these propositions at all. The special relation between belief and truth thus comes with the territory of belief, and is not hypothetical upon any contingent aim of the believer.

None of this argues against the possibility of belief that is in fact – even as the outcome of prior design – unresponsive to evidence or truth. One could, it seems, have some success in coming to believe certain convenient falsehoods through a suitable program of self-imposed indoctrination. What this argument purports to show is not the impossibility of such a program but a *design constraint* upon it: if one is to succeed, one must somehow contrive to veil the program's true nature from oneself. Transparent anti-epistemology, for example, is not an option.

Gary might, however, think that we have overstated what has been shown. He can say, "Your answer to my challenge is still hypothetical, as far as I can see. It presupposes that I am in, or plan to enter, the belief business. But what if I opt out? Why can't I just do without belief, and manage my affairs instead with other propositional attitudes lacking its particular relation to truth?"

Here we might be tempted to reply, "Well, why not do without automobiles and manage instead with boats? Beliefs, after all, play many roles in one's mental economy – in inference, deliberation, action, even emotion. They are evolutionarily 'made for' these roles, and it is by no means obvious how many of these roles could be played by propositional attitudes other than belief.[8] Just ask whether a strong desire for self-defense, plus a *pretense* that a mortal enemy lurks behind the next hedge, would do the job in producing an action-guiding intention to engage in all-out self-defense."

Gary is tenacious. "Still hypothetical. You're telling me that people typically have goals that are better served by having some attitudes that play all the roles of belief – just as people typically have goals that are better served if they have vehicles that can play all the roles of cars, and don't have only bicycles and boats." In atypical circumstances, he observes, things might be otherwise. He can remember one incident involving a broken guardrail on the coastal highway south of Monterey when he quite suddenly found himself thinking just how much there is to be said for boats as opposed to cars.

"Very well," we reply, "you want a non-hypothetical argument and you will have it. But remember: To show that a norm or reason is non-hypothetical is not to show that it is utterly without condition. It is only to show that it would necessarily apply to any agent as such, regardless of her contingent personal ends.

"So. Consider how deeply implicated belief is in our notion of agency. An agent acts on intentions and plans, which constitutively involve beliefs and are formed deliberatively in part on the basis of beliefs. To replace *all* belief with (say) wishing would be to form no intentions at all. Moreover, our notion of ourselves as agents extended over time constitutively involves *memories* and *expectations*. These, too, involve beliefs. There is all the difference in the world between believing that one is the father of John, or believing that one will experience the pains of an unattended-to toothache, and pretending or merely supposing these things. To delete all forms of belief from your mental repertoire would leave you with no recognizable notion of identity.

"Being 'in the belief business' therefore isn't as optional as you imagine. It is a precondition of agency. So the argument is non-hypothetical in a familiar sense: as an agent you must possess beliefs; as a believe you must represent certain of your propositional attitudes as accountable to truth and as disciplined by truth-orientated norms (at least, in the limit); therefore, as an agent you must so represent at least some of your attitudes, irrespective of what other goals this might or might not serve."

The argument is not dispositive. But it does place a certain burden on Gary. It seems that he would have to exhibit the compatibility of our notions of practical deliberation, agency, personal identity, etc. with a mental economy that contains no beliefs. The magnitude of this burden affords a *prima facie* case for the following claim: paying the price of admission to belief is necessary to gain entry to agency. A self-representation of certain of one's attitudes as "aiming at" truth is *partially constitutive* of belief, which in turn is *partially constitutive* of agency. Let us, then, call this sort of argument a *constitutive argument*.

Unlike our first, hypothetical, eat-your-vegetables defense of conforming to norms of theoretical reason, this constitutive argument concerns not an agent's actual conformity (or attempt to conform) to epistemic norms but her self-representation as such. Moreover, it concerns only a limiting case, the case of deeming certain evidence to be conclusive. Not very much normative epistemology can be wrung from that. Finally, Gary might surprise us and successfully discharge his burden of proof by showing that a genuinely alternative propositional attitude – or constellation of such attitudes – could play as many of the roles of belief as one would need to attain agency.

Rather than explore these issues further at this point, let us simply note that despite its limitations, the constitutive argument provides a *prima facie* case for the non-hypothetical status of certain broad epistemic requirements.

## II. REASONING ABOUT ACTION

It is now the spring term. We find Gary, undaunted as ever, in our Introduction to the Theory of Action. This time he sits in the front row; and has his question ready earlier in the term. "These philosophers," he begins, "each has his own view about what practical reasoning requires. But what makes any of these views something I have to pay attention to? How could any of them insist that I pay attention to their favorite norms if I didn't care to? They might not be *my* favorite norms." In particular, he concludes, he'd like to know how the practical case compares with the discussion of theoretical reasoning last term.

Let us see how much parallelism we can find. In the autumn we began with a non-epistemic but robust hypothetical defense of familiar standards of theoretical reason: Gary could expect to do better relative to almost any of the goals he might have if he formed warranted beliefs. In effect, this constituted a *practical* defense of theoretical reason. Would a parallel in the present case be a practical defense of paying heed to norms of practical reason? This time that would seem circular at the outset.

There is, however, at least one way of construing the question that would avoid circularity – though this might not satisfy Gary. We can distinguish two ways in which an agent's deliberations, decisions, and actions might be said to follow a norm: objectively versus subjectively.

We will say that an agent's deliberations, decisions, and actions are *in objective conformity with* a norm to the extent that he is actually succeeding in complying with whatever the norm prescribes. Consider a norm that directs one to act so as to maximize one's self-interest. An agent would be in (full) objective conformity with this norm just in case his acts were those, relative to available alternatives, that would maximally benefit him.

It would not follow, however, that this agent is acting exclusively for his own sake, or even with his own benefit in mind. That is, it would not follow that this agent's deliberation and actions are *subjectively patterned on* a norm of maximizing self-interest.[9]

Using this distinction, we can interpret the question whether there might be a practical defense for paying heed to norms of practical reasoning in the following, non-circular way. Given any particular norm of practical reason, one can ask whether in a particular instance – or in general – subjectively patterning one's deliberation on this norm would constitute behavior in objective conformity with it. For many norms much of the time, the most promising way of achieving objective conformity will indeed be subjectively to pattern one's deliberation on the norm. But not always. It seems plausible, for example, that if one were to regulate one's conduct by self-consciously and exclusively consulting one's self-interest one would be incapable of the sorts of commitment to other individuals or to groups or causes that are the source of some of life's deeper satisfactions.

If Gary wants to know whether, in his circumstances – or in general – one would have good (objective) practical reason to be (subjectively) practically rational, then he will be asking a genuine question to which the answer is not preordained. For many theories of practical reason, it is a contingent matter.

But Gary is growing restless. He meant his question to be less internal to the domain of theories of practical reason. "Objective or subjective," he says, "it matters little to me how you put it. I want to know whether you can give a good, non-circular defense of having anything to do with norms of practical reason. Why should I be bothered?"

This is starting to look like an impossible request. For either the defense presupposes a set of norms of practical reason, which would appear to be question begging, or the defense makes no such presupposition, and there is nowhere to start.

However, something more might be said within the domain of practical reasoning. Philosophers often engage in a process that looks like a non-circular practical defense of practical norms – a process that sometimes leads them well away from their starting points.

The process begins with our many intuitive notions about which actions or principles of action make – or do not make – sense. These notions are much less coherent or articulate than a "theory of practical reason." Here, for example, is an appeal to intuition meant to raise doubts about whether maximizing one's expected utility really makes sense even as a basis for self-interested choice:

You are forced to play Russian roulette – but you can buy your way out. One bullet is placed in a six-cylinder revolver ... What is the most you would pay to have the bullet removed?

Next ... You are forced to play Russian roulette with four bullets in the revolver. Answer a new question: What is the most you would pay ... to have *one* of the four bullets removed, leaving three? More? Or less?[10]

Most say "less." Maximizing expected utility seems to say "more." This has the form of the "Allais Paradox," though one might say that it is no paradox at all, but merely a counterintuitive result. For our purposes what is most important is that the example does not appear to depend for its force upon people's acceptance of some alternative theory of practical rationality. Indeed, popular intuitions have proved exceedingly difficult to describe in any general, coherent way.

In consequence, one can also have the opposite response to the case: after being told that the choice "more" would maximize expected utility, one might come to think that one *should* accept this answer as rational and simply ignore its intuitive oddness. Indeed, a considerable literature in cognitive psychology suggests that commonsense reasoning is prone to various errors and fallacies in assessing probabilities and risks.[11]

Such dialogue – an interplay of examples, intuitive responses, empirical theory, and proposed norms – is a form of *wide reflective equilibrium*. The critique and acceptance of norms of deliberation through such dialogue is surely a form of reasoning that deserves the name 'practical.' Yet reflective equilibrium arguments need not take a particular set of practical norms for granted. Inarticulate commonsense notions of practical rationality will figure in such a process and partially shape it, but they need not serve as a *constraint* on the process, or leave it intact.

A wide reflective equilibrium argument thus might answer to the demand for a non-circular practical justification, but would it be convincing to Gary? Convincing or not, he'd point out, the argument would nonetheless be *hypothetical*: which adjustments we are prepared to make in response to various intuitive tensions is sure to depend upon our particular goals and priorities.

Therefore Gary still wants to know whether there exists a non-hypothetical argument concerning fidelity to norms of practical reasoning, akin to the constitutive argument made in the case of theoretical reasoning. One established way of approaching this question is to ask whether there is anything in the realm of action that plays the role that truth plays in the realm of belief. We can think of ourselves as looking for a feature $F$ such that one must represent oneself as "aiming at" $F$ in action in approximately the same sense in which one must represent oneself as "aiming at" truth in belief.

Among philosophical accounts of the nature of intentional action that might be seen as offering a candidate for $F$, two have perhaps attracted the greatest interest historically. For each, I will argue, it is possible to construct a constitutive argument. Let us call the two philosophical accounts of agency we will be considering *High Brow* and *Low Brow*.

High Brow is a view with excellent pedigree, tracing its ancestry back to ancient Greece. According to High Brow, just as belief necessarily "aims at" the True, action necessarily "aims at" the Good. Deliberation seeks to identify the good, and action is guided by it. In choosing an action we place it (or find it to be) in a positive evaluative light, and deem it choiceworthy.

Note that the High Brow's claims concern action as such, not merely *rational* action. The constitutive argument for belief held that a self-presentation as "aiming at" the truth is part of what makes a propositional attitude be one of belief, rational or irrational alike. Similarly, the High Brow claims that action that is irrational – as distinct from arational or non-rational behavior such as reflexes or kicking in one's sleep – is also in some sense "aimed at" the good. Weakness of the will, as it is ordinarily understood, is a paradigm of practical irrationality that clearly manifests this. The akratic agent is said to be "aiming at" the good but falling short due (say) to insufficient motivation or "willpower."

Of course, our description of High Brow is quite vague. Action requires representing one's choice in a positive evaluative light, but which? There are many varieties of goodness: good for oneself, good for one's kith and kin, morally good, aesthetically good, and so on. One might formulate High Brow by identifying one of these goods, or perhaps a *summum bonum*, as the true end of all action. This would, however, be needlessly ambitious for our purposes. We seek a constitutive feature of action as uncontroversial upon reflection as the connection between belief and truth, and a generic value claim is much less controversial. Action, our High Brow will say, involves representing the act chosen or the ends for which it is done as good *in some self-acknowledged sense*.

Despite its generic character, this claim is non-trivial. It implies, among other things, that individuals incapable of representing an end or a course of conduct as good – nonhuman animals, or (perhaps) human infants – would also be incapable of agency, properly so-called. Moreover, those among our fellow adults who have a latent capacity to represent a course of conduct as good, but who fail to develop or exercise it – that is, who fail or refuse to *acknowledge* any good – would also lack agency, properly so-called. Their lot might be a kind of motivation-driven behavior that nonetheless remained in some profound sense aimless. Alternatively – and perhaps far more likely – individuals claiming not to acknowledge any good are actually kidding themselves. Their deliberation and action reveal their nihilism to be no more than a posture.

This suggests a High Brow response to Gary. Suppose that a visiting High Brow philosopher has just given a guest lecture in our class on practical reason. Gary's eager hand is up. Why, he asks, must he pay any attention to the good when deciding what to do? What magical force would stop him from simply ignoring questions of good and bad, or flying in their face, and acting as he pleases?

The High Brow philosopher can reply: "I have claimed that deliberation and choice constitutively involve representing what you choose as in some sense good. You can no more decide to ignore questions of good and bad – of choiceworthiness – in your deliberation and action than you can decide to introspect someone else's thoughts rather than your own. No 'magical force' is needed to police this constraint. Of course, you might lack the nerve, or will, or energy to follow through on your judgments of choice-worthiness. But to the extent that you are aware of this, you yourself will be sensible of it *as a lack*, a gap between what you value and what you do. You will be in no position to say 'Well, that's nothing *to me.*' If it weren't *something* to you, it wouldn't have been a choice in the first place."[12]

Gary is being attributed paradoxical claims, which might be thought to echo – though in a practical setting – Moore:

(6) I believe I have reason to choose act *A*, but I can't see anything good about it.
(7) Act *A* would be good, but that's no reason for *me* to choose it.

One way of explaining the oddness of (6) and (7), according to the view under consideration, is that they seem to suggest the existence of a gap within practical deliberation that makes room for a purely *hypothetical* dependence of an agent's deliberation on judgments about the good. This gap presumably would need to be filled by the agent's possession of some independent, intermediating goal, such as that of "doing what is good." But such a view would be deeply confused, according to the High Brow. The deliberative role of judgments of goodness is indispensable and needs no mediation – it simply comes with the territory of acting. To use our previous phrase, it is *partially constitutive* of agency that one perceive the landscape in an evaluative light, and steer toward the good as one sees it. Gary proposed to act in the face of, or indifferent to, questions of goodness. But anyone who managed to become a complete stranger to goodness would simply have dismantled his capacity for deliberate action and begun a life of merely behaving, of roaming at the behest of his appetites.

We thus have arrived at an argument in the practical realm that affords an interesting parallel to the argument made in the theoretical realm: both appeal to a constitutive condition to identify a non-hypothetical element in reasoning.

High Brow is, however, highbrow. Many philosophers, in my experience, are not. Gary, it seems, isn't either. He points to a long line of Low Brow thinkers, beginning perhaps with Hume, who have denied that an agent engaged in deliberate action necessarily "aims at" the good.

If not the good, then what does action "aim at"? To Hume is often ascribed the view that agency aims at no more than the satisfaction of current desires. But this might be wrong about Hume, and it in any event is not necessary for a Low Brow. Just as High Brow comes in both generic and brand-name forms – the latter identify a particular sort of good as "the aim" of action – so does Low Brow. We can see Hume as endorsing in the first instance a generic Low Brow position: agents necessarily possess and act on *ends*, and this involves both a *representational* and a *motivational* component, though neither component need involve a judgment of, or an "aiming at," what is good. The belief/desire view often attributed to Hume is an example of this type. According to it, motivationally inert beliefs will suffice for representation, and non-evaluative, intrinsic attractions and aversions will suffice for motivation. Hume famously wrote:

> Ask a man *why he uses exercise*; he will answer *because he desires to keep his health*. If you then enquire *why he desires to keep his health*, he will readily reply *because sickness is painful*. If you push your enquiries further and desire a reason *why he hates pain*, it is impossible he can ever give any. This is an ultimate end, and is never referred to any other object.[13]

Humean individuals engage in both theoretical and practical reasoning. They inquire into causes and effects; form beliefs about the conduciveness of means to ends; take into account the relative strength and independence of desires; acquire habits; form intentions to act; and formulate and respond to rules and sanctions. Their conduct therefore can, it is claimed, be given fully fledged intentional, rational-agent explanations. Why-questions about their conduct can often be answered correctly by citing *their reasons* for behaving as they do, and these will include: how they represented the situation, what their goals were, how they weighed their various ends, how they adjusted means and ends, and so on.

Our interest in Humean individuals lies precisely with the claim that they exemplify agency even though they do not by their nature "aim at" the good. We need not evaluate the stronger claim that reason giving always terminates in current intrinsic desires (or that belief must be motivationally inert).

The tenability of any Low Brow position therefore depends upon the possibility of distinguishing *the possession of ends* from *the making of judgments that certain ends are good*. Desire appears at first to afford a clear case: we often speak of acting on desire (so desire seems capable of playing the necessary role in choice) and also of desiring something that we do not take to be good (so desiring seems suitably distinct from evaluating).

But such claims might be challenged. To desire, it can be argued, is to represent as desirable, and desirability is itself a species of good. When we speak of desiring that which we take to be bad, this can be understood as (say) reflecting the difference between a *prima facie* and a conclusionary judgment of value. This is, however, a very demanding position. It would force us to deny that young children, who (it seems) lack the evaluative concept of desirability, have desires. To reject the evaluative notion of desire need not be to treat desire as a mere animal appetite (whatever that might be). There is a great deal of psychic distance between a fish that swims to the surface "because it is hungry" and a child who responds to our question "Why did you come downstairs?" with the answer "I'm hungry." We can begin to account for this difference by pointing out that the child "acted on a desire" in a way that the fish did not, and this despite our reluctance to suppose that the child has judged there to be something further that is good about having breakfast.[14]

Perhaps a more promising challenge to the Low Brow's distinction would be to argue that even if desires (say) are non-evaluative, they cannot function as *ends* until some suitable evaluative judgment has at least tacitly been made. This view is less severe. A young child can be spoken of as having desires in the familiar sense, but even when these "mere desires" cause her behavior, a child cannot be seen as *acting on reasons* or as *possessing an end that furnishes her rationale in acting* until she is capable of exercising a certain amount of judgment as to the appropriateness or worthwhileness of acting on her desires.

Perhaps the best Low Brow defense is to give illustrative examples. First, consider a case of a kind brought to our attention by Jean Hampton.[15] Our two children have been begging all week to go to the shore. Both, however, dislike long summer car rides. When the weekend comes one child absolutely refuses to get into the car. "But we're going to the beach, which you love!" "I don't care. I don't want to ride in this stuffy old car. I hate it! I won't do it." He has to be carried bodily to the car and buckled in, thrashing. Once in the car, he still refuses to be jollied along. "It's *your* fault I'm in this stuffy old car! I told you I hate it." The second child confines her thrashing to loud complaints. "Not another car ride! Last time I felt sick the whole time!" But when the time comes to leave she climbs into her seat of her own accord, waiting sulkily to be buckled in. On her face is a look that says "Okay, I'll ride in the car, but don't expect me to like it."

The second child possesses a capacity for self-control (relative to her weightier desires) that the first child lacks, though, according to the Low Brow, we need not also impute to the second child a judgment that being at the beach is a good thing – beyond her strong desire for it. There is a sense in which the second child's thinking and conduct, but not the first's, accord the strong desire to be at the beach the force of a *rationale* for the despised beach trip. The desire speaks on behalf of means toward its fulfillment, even unwanted means. By contrast, for the first child the desire to be at the beach does not yet function as end-setting, and his conduct is not rationalized even by his own desires.

Second, consider an example inspired by a case due to Michael Smith.[16] Two "unwilling addicts" – individuals who strongly desire heroin but who also very much wish they did not[17] – are both beginning their day. Each has overslept – it is now too late even to consider going to work. "I've got to quit this stuff. It's ruining my life. I won't even have a job by the end of the week – if I haven't been fired already." This is no new resolve. Each has already judged his taking of heroin to be a bad thing on the whole. Though neither reconsiders this judgment, as the day grows longer the desire for heroin becomes fierce. By noon, each has set out to get a fix. One locates a needle and, trembling, injects himself. The other, who is just as aware as the first of how to use heroin, locates a needle and hungrily tries to eat it. He chokes to death.

We now ask why each has used the needle as he did. For the first, we are able to cite a reason, *his* reason: he strongly wanted to dose himself with heroin, and he knew that this is how to do it. For the second, we are at a loss. Without further information we must see his needle-eating conduct as inexplicable by any "rational agent" explanation. Perhaps sheer craving somehow overcame him. The difference in intelligibility between the two cases is not attributable to the addicts' differing capacities to form and be guided by judgments of the good – they formed the same judgment on this score, and equally failed to be guided by it – but to their differing ability to adjust means to ends. Thus although we almost certainly regard the conduct of neither as truly *rational*, we do see the one's conduct as having a *rationale* in terms of what he believes and desires that the other's does not.

These two examples give us at least a *prima facie* case for the Low Brow's distinguishing of the notion of an agent having and acting on ends from the High Brow notion of an agent aiming at the good.[18] We now must ask whether Low Brow conceptions of agency – which ordinarily are seen as allergic to anything non-hypothetical – can support a constitutive argument of their own. Perhaps so. Consider the Moore-like statement:

(8) *E* is an end of mine, but that's nothing to me in my deliberation.[19]

Our original Moore-ism

(I) *h* is true, but I don't believe it

is a statement that could easily be true (there are many truths I do not believe) but that seemed deeply problematic for any agent to assert.

Something similar holds for (8). It is hardly odd for someone to fail in a given case to take one of his ends into account. He might not even notice its relevance. But asserting (8) would be peculiar indeed, according to the Low Brow, since we have no clear idea what it could amount to for $E$ to be acknowledged by me as an end of mine if it counted for nothing in my deliberation whether or not $E$ is realized. Of course, we must make room for inattention, distraction, and depression. The connection suggested in (8) is non-hypothetical not in the sense that it has no conditions, but in the sense that it does not presuppose a further, contingent desire on my part "that I realize my ends" or "that I realize end $E$."

It should be emphasized that (8)'s oddness manifests a *structural* connection, which, though non-hypothetical, is not a device for generating univalent, non-hypothetical imperatives. Thus, if an end $E$ of mine would be advanced by act $A$, this can be taken as either counting in favor of performing $A$ or counting against retaining $E$. If success in the army requires unquestioning obedience, for example, I might consider giving up my military ambitions.[20] The oddness of (8) points to the unavailability of a third option: genuinely retaining the end while in effect setting oneself to accord it no deliberative relevance. To see one's deliberation as guided (at least in part, in the limit, other things equal, in normal circumstances, etc.) by one's own ends thus comes along with the mere possession of ends.

Suppose, then, that a Low Brow philosopher visits our class. At the lecture's end, Gary raises his characteristic challenge. "Maybe I can't have an end unless I take that to count in some way in thinking about how to act. Fair enough. But that's still hypothetical. You yourself admit that very young children might have desires or appetites but no ends as such. Maybe they know something you don't."

The Low Brow philosopher can respond. "You, like most of us, have ends, desires, appetites. Nothing prevents you from becoming a being with appetites and desires but no ends. There are lots of such beings around: infants, maybe animals. You could join their ranks. But then you would cease *acting* on desire – you'd merely be behaving. If you are to remain an agent, you must have ends. And once you acknowledge ends – as you've conceded – you must (in the limit, under ordinary conditions, etc.) be to some degree engaged in the business of weighing courses of conduct in light of their tendency to contribute to the realization of your ends." So, we reach a "principled basis" for a Low Brow non-hypothetical response to Gary. An agent as such must in effect see herself as deliberating in a way that gives weight (in the limit, etc.) to the realization of what she takes to be her ends, independently of what these particular ends might be.[21] This is so even for agents who are acting *irrationally* relative to their ends.

## III. STOCKTAKING

The High road and the Low road thus both lead to non-hypothetical requirements for practical reasoning. The path in each case proceeds using a constitutive argument that has much in common with the constitutive argument made for theoretical reasoning. In all three cases a linkage is made to the (alleged) nature of agency, thereby avoiding dependence upon contingent personal goals.

But have we found convincing answers to Gary's questions? Or convincing grounds for rejecting them? To simplify exposition, I will begin by narrowing the argumentative field, focusing largely on the case of theoretical reasoning and the Low Brow version of the practical case.[22]

Constitutive arguments have the strength that comes from purportedly necessary connections. And necessity is hard to argue with, even for Gary. But this strength can also be a weakness. If the necessity turns out to be linguistic, the argument may lack the power to sustain substantive conclusions. And if the necessity is of a more substantive kind, then the argument may have the unintended effect of pulling the claws of the very criticisms one wishes to make.[23] We now face both of these dangers. Let us look at them in turn.

First, the linguistic danger. Consider the Low Brow constitutive argument that connects taking oneself to have an end $E$ with taking oneself to be responsive in deliberation to whether $E$ is realized. Someone might see this as an analytic truth: "That's just what it *means* for $E$ to be an end of yours – an end is something you see yourself as giving weight to in deliberation." Gary, however, sought answers to seemingly substantive practical and epistemic questions: "Why do things that way?", he wanted to know. It would be surprising if we could give an answer with nothing more than a few definitions. To be genuinely responsive to the concerns expressed, constitutive arguments must capture a substantive – not merely linguistic – necessity.

This brings us to the second danger, the danger of pulling the claws of criticism.[24] Assume, for example, that the connection between taking oneself to have an end and according that end deliberative weight is a substantively necessary, non-analytic connection of the same modality as the connection between being gold and having atomic number 79. What would we then be able to say by way of *criticism* of an agent who refused to give deliberative weight to his own acknowledged end $E$? Would he be "necessarily deliberatively defective" or perhaps "self-defeatingly irrational"?

If the constitutive argument is right, we cannot even raise the question! To fail to take oneself as according $E$ deliberative weight is to fail to acknowledge $E$ as an end. But then the agent cannot merit the label 'self-defeating' or 'irrational' with respect to $E$. An analogy: to discover that the metal in the sample tray on one's laboratory bench has atomic number 82 is not to discover that it is "defective gold," but rather that it is not gold at all.

A similar problem confronts all constitutive arguments. Suppose, for example, that someone has a propositional attitude toward $p$ that involves, among other things, her representing $p$ as true. Thus far, this attitude is a candidate for belief. But suppose further that she sees no relevance to this attitude of admitted evidence against $p$, even evidence she recognizes to be conclusive. When challenged, she is not defensive and produces no elaborate rationale, but simply points out that she is quite indifferent as to whether her attitude toward $p$ is responsive to the truth of $p$.

According to the constitutive argument, she does not have an irrational or epistemically defective belief that $p$; she simply fails to *believe* that $p$ at all. Perhaps she instead is *supposing* that $p$. What if she nonetheless claims that her attitude toward $p$ is one of belief? It would seem that, on the strength of the constitutive argument, our only criticism could be that she has *mislabeled* her propositional attitude (like our mislabeling of the metal sample). Labeling errors are not, however, defects of rationality. Once she has found the right word for her propositional attitude, the criticism would vanish.

To be sure, we could at this point invoke a more general, higher-order constitutive argument. If we were to come across someone who failed quite generally to deliberate in a way that he takes to be responsive to his ends, or who failed quite generally to form propositional attitudes that he takes to be responsive to evidence, we could argue that such an individual thereby would fail to possess ends or beliefs at all, and thus would fail to be an agent.

Indeed, we might raise the stakes still higher. Perhaps *speaking a natural language* itself presupposes the formation of beliefs and intentions, so that an individual without beliefs or intentions could not even offer an *argument* on behalf of his way of life – his vocalizations would not constitute speech. This is beginning to sound serious! Or is it? Now when he emits the sounds $bĭ\text{-}l\bar{e}f'$ or $ăk'\text{-}shən$ we cannot even charge him with a linguistic mistake.

It seems that we are turning up the volume of criticism while simultaneously ensuring that the purported target of our criticism is ever more profoundly deaf. If we rely on these ascending constitutive arguments, we quickly reach a point in which the only thing left to say of someone is to dismiss him as not one of us. This is xenophobia, not criticism.

Eager for a secure justification, a knock-down answer to the likes of Gary, we sought a requirement – a "must" – that applies non-hypothetically, arising from the very conditions of agency. That now looks unwise. For then there could be no such thing as failure to conform *on the part of an agent*. Perhaps we have asked too much, or the wrong thing, of our constitutive claims.

We may begin to regroup by recognizing that we have formulated the constitutive arguments too rigidly. Having beliefs and having ends are, even in the limit, complex phenomena to which we have not done justice. Beliefs, for example, come in degrees, and are not all or nothing. Moreover, having a belief involves possessing a large bundle of dispositions – not only to represent one's thinking in certain ways, but also to infer, to notice, to act, to avow, to assert, to claim a measure of authority, and so on. Psychological realism alone compels us to recognize that many of the attitudes in ourselves and others that we unhesitatingly call beliefs may from time to time lack one or another of the complex bundle of attitudes and dispositions paradigmatically associated with belief as an ideal type. Interpretative charity often demands that we be latitudinarian with respect to departures from the ideal type.

Now consider a person who has a propositional attitude toward $p$ that he deems to be belief, but that he does not – or does not with any consistency – hold accountable to admitted evidence concerning the truth of $p$. If that person nonetheless allows this attitude to play all the other roles of belief – in assertion, in intention-formation, in expectation, etc. – then he will almost certainly find himself in a variety of difficulties, difficulties more serious than mislabeling, difficulties that mere relabeling could not remove. Given his attitude's extensive overlap with characteristic roles of belief, we would have some interpretative justification for calling it a 'belief'; but given its unresponsiveness to admitted evidence, we would also have some interpretative ground for calling it a 'belief *manqué*,' or even a "rationally defective" or "irrational" belief.

311

Why "rationally defective"? Consider an example. Suppose that I am a nervous flyer. I recognize there to be compelling statistical evidence that commercial airplane travel is very safe. Moreover, my frequency of electing to travel by air fits with what one would expect of an individual who deems it safe; for example, a small difference in travel time or cost will tip me toward air rather than rail or car. Yet I find that nontheless, in the sense in which belief is connected with expectation and perception, I do not seem really to *believe* that air travel is relatively safe. This is not because my attitude is a mere supposition or pretense or of the like – it has less in common with these attitudes than it does with belief, as my travel choices show. One might with some justice interpret me as partly believing that taking wing in a commercial airliner is safe, and partly disbelieving this.

But the division between belief and disbelief here is not a simple probability distribution, the way that I "distribute" my belief over 'Clinton will win in November' and 'Clinton will not.' For in a suitably abstract context, I will sincerely and confidently assert the view or place a bet that flying on a commercial airliner is much safer than driving to work. In a different context, when I'm aboard a jet taxiing for takeoff, I may find myself irresistibly believing that I am in a very precarious situation, wishing I were anywhere else, jumping to conclusions about the meaning of small sounds or little bumps and jiggles, and so on. By way of contrast, despite what I know of statistics, I have no such belief when speeding through traffic in my rattletrap of a car, clutching a cup of coffee between my knees, late for work (again!). How would I myself describe things? I would probably say that my beliefs on such subjects as the relative safety of air versus car travel, the safety of the particular flights or car trips on which I find myself, and so forth are simply not wholly rational.[25]

We need to effect a similar relaxation of the Low Brow constitutive argument in the case of practical reasoning. When deliberating about what to do, a rational person takes her ends into account. But to have an end paradigmatically involves possession of a complex bundle of attitudes and dispositions, involving action, perception, sentiment, belief, and so on. As in the case of belief, interpretative charity will often license attributing an end to a person even though some of these elements are missing, or inconsistently present. An agent who arranges a considerable part of her life in order to promote a long-term goal will from time to time find herself in contexts in which she is attracted to other things, feels alternative pressures exclusively, or even lacks interest in her life. In such cases, even though she may see the bearing of her long-term goal, and even though she may remain disposed to avow it, she may nonetheless find herself giving it no weight in certain deliberations.[26] Do we say she no longer has the end? Or that she has the end but isn't at the moment being fully rational with respect to it? The agent herself – at least, if she is like me – will sometimes opt for the latter description.

Failures of rationality come in many shapes and sizes, and do not form a unified type. But it may be useful to think of some forms of theoretical or practical irrationality as instances of incomplete-yet-nearly-complete approximation of believing or having an end. How many of the elements in the bundle must one possess to be "nearly complete"? There are limits, but vague limits, no doubt. And dynamic, holistic limits – they concern chunks of one's thought and stretches of time. Particular elements may come and go, but may do so in mutually compensating ways or so that, at any given time, enough hold.

We thus remove from the constitutive arguments an artificial rigidity. But are we any closer to an answer to Gary? We may have made matters worse. If having a belief or possessing an end is a complex phenomenon, with vague and holistic limits, then we have left behind the Manichaean world of the original argument. In that world there seemed to be only stark choices: to be an agent or . . . infantile, or a beast. Now it seems one could pass almost imperceptibly from belief to near belief, and thus from agency to something else. And that something else therefore might not be so terribly alien.[27]

Gary asked why he should pay attention to epistemic norms. If we reply that this is necessary in order to be a believer and thus to be an agent, he can respond: "But just how severe a cost does this threaten me with? Somewhere on the continuum between the ideal type of belief, on the one end, and clear non-belief on the other, there is a region that forms the borderland of genuine belief. I want to know why my attitudes should be on one side rather than the other of that borderland. The claim that I would cease to be an agent on one side of the region sounds dramatic. But if life on the believer side of the borderland has certain pluses and minuses, how do we know in advance that the balance must be worse on the other side? Mightn't it even be better, on the whole?"

Consider two possibilities. First, suppose that there is more that Gary would find enjoyable or valuable on the believer side of the borderland. Then we have a reply to Gary, but it once more looks hypothetical – whether Gary finds life sweet or sour seems unlikely to be independent of what he happens to desire. Second, suppose the opposite: there is more that Gary would find enjoyable or valuable on the other side. Then our reply to Gary can only be, "The enjoyment, however great, would not be that of an agent. The value would not be the value of the life of an agent."[28] This reply is indeed non-hypothetical, but Gary could be excused if he finds it unconvincing.

We might at this point be inclined to be dismissive. Surely once one has demonstrated that a condition is essential to agency one has justification enough. After all, we *are* agents and that seems to be a very deep fact about us. Justification has to start somewhere, and if it is to be justification *for us* it had better start where we are. Indeed, the mere fact of Gary's asking such a question, posed as matter for choice, seems to presuppose that he, too, is an agent. Yet all the same can be said for two much more difficult-to-dismiss questions.

Consider first a patient with a painful, incurable disease who wonders whether to elect to end his life by euthanasia rather than live out the disease's wretched course, destroying his family's finances and becoming every day less the sort of person he has aspired to be. He is an agent, and moreover his very posing of the matter as a question of choice presupposes his agency. To choose euthanasia would, however, be to put an end to his agency. Does this suffice to show that there can be no question of justified voluntary euthanasia? Can we say that, since life is a necessary condition of agency, "choice of euthanasia" is ruled out as a practical contradiction? Most of us, I suspect, do not think so. The considerations on the side of ending his life, and thereby resigning agency, might be more compelling than the considerations on the side of continuing it. But then we can understand the idea of a rationally justified transition from agency to non-agency.

Second, imagine a Schellingesque case of a kind discussed by Derek Parfit.[29] You have been captured by mobsters. They seek revenge on members of your family who have testified against them and who now have new identities and locations thanks to the Federal Witness Protection Program. The mobsters will torture you to reveal your family members' whereabouts. You know that you will not be able to resist this torture. If you could abolish your agency by knocking yourself senseless – perhaps irrevocably – your captors could not extract from you the information they need. Does the fact that you would be crossing the borderland into non-agency show that such a choice could not be a genuine or appropriate option for you as an agent?

Dramas aside, non-agency need not be the end of life as we know it. We all pass from non-agency to agency sometime during the first years of life, and, arguably, we all commute daily back and forth to a state in which agency is at least temporarily disengaged when we sleep and awaken.

314

Suppose we were to say to Gary: "The pleasures (or other advantages) on the other side of the borderland couldn't possibly count *for you*. They wouldn't be *yours*. You're an agent – that's one of the deepest facts about you – and they'd be the pleasures of a non-agent." This way of speaking is belied by our comfort with speaking of a life that stretches from birth to death as the life of a single person, despite its various transitions to and from non-agency, active versus suspended agency, and the like. We cannot simply refuse questions of partial or even complete border crossing.

Previously we spoke of the "price of admission" to belief, action, or agency. Now we are discussing the "exit price," temporary or permanent. Often that price will be high. Now is the time to remind ourselves, and Gary, that most of us most of the time will be in a much better position to figure out and accomplish what matters to us if we are agents. But a high-priced option is very different from an impossibility. High prices are sometimes worth paying, and circumstances (such as facing the end of one's life) can drive down the price. We arrive, then, at a somewhat unanticipated sense in which one might intelligibly ask for "reasons for action" – reasons for agency versus non-agency as a way of being.

This very observation does show, however, that there is a sense in which Gary has not succeeded – even slightly – in suggesting anything like the possibility of an alternative to familiar forms of practical reasoning. When he asks, in effect, whether the exit price is worth paying, he is asking whether *being an agent* is the best or only way of getting what he most wants from life. This is itself a means/ends form of reasoning of the familiar, Low Brow sort. It therefore betrays Gary's deference to (at least) Low Brow notions of agency after all. When Gary contemplates a border crossing and asks whether life on the other side might be an improvement, he is giving deliberative weight to the tendency of a means to promote an end.

Perhaps the grass really is greener on the other side. But then not only would Gary have good reason in the familiar sense for crossing over, he would also have good reason *to be* and *to stay* on the other side even after he ceased himself to be a fully fledged agent. Indeed, unless Gary takes for granted means/ends reasoning, it is unclear what bearing the (possibly) high quality of life on the other side of the borderland would have upon what he should do.

We might be able to put this point more clearly by invoking another turn-of-the-century Englishman's paradox, not G. E. Moore's this time, but Lewis Carroll's.[30] Achilles entertains an argument:

(9) If $p$ then $q$

(10) $p$

(C) So: $q$.

Carroll's Tortoise asks Achilles whether there isn't a gap in this argument, a missing premiss. Couldn't one grant both premisses but fail to be driven to the conclusion unless one also granted:

(11) If [(if $p$ then $q$) & $p$] then $q$

to effect the connection between (9) and (10) and (C)?

This seems reasonable to Achilles, on whom it only slowly dawns that he has just launched a regress. For suppose our premisses now enlarged to be (9)–(11). Tortoise will cheerfully argue that we would need a new premiss to effect *their* relevance to the conclusion, namely:

(12) If { ([(if $p$ then $q$) & $p$] then $q$) & (if $p$ then $q$) & $p$ } then $q$.

Were (12) added, Tortoise would notice the need for yet another premiss to link (9)–(12) with the conclusion (C). And so on.

The moral: one cannot treat rules of inference (such as *modus ponens*) as premisses, on pain of regress. Put another way (and using Carroll's own terminology): We cannot see rules of inference in logical argument as *hypotheticals*. This is not to say that we should see them as *necessary* or *non-hypothetical premisses*. Far from it. Taking premiss (12) to be a necessary truth – or as "constitutive of logical inference" – would no more enable it to stop the regress than taking it to be simply true. Rules of inference differ essentially in *role* from premisses, not in modality.

Somewhat similarly, we should not be led by questions such as Gary's to think of the mutual bearing of ends upon means as itself hypothetical, or as something like a premiss in our deliberation about action, on pain of regress. For suppose we started with the practical argument:

(13) $E$ is an end of mine

(14) Means $M$ would secure $E$

(C*) So: There is that much to be said deliberatively in favor of my doing $M$, or against my having $E$.

And suppose Gary asked, "Isn't this argument missing something? – Doesn't it suppose not only that I have end $E$, but that I also have the further aim, call it $F$, of choosing so as to bring about the realization of my ends? If I didn't have that further end, couldn't I reject any relevance of (13) and (14) to my deliberation?" It would seem that we need to add this premiss:

(15) $F$ [ = choosing so as to bring about the realization of my ends] is an end of mine.

But if one did not already recognize that having an end makes deliberatively relevant questions about the means that would advance it – if, that is, (13)–(14) were insufficient to support the conclusion ($C^*$) – then adding the further premiss (15) could hardly help. And notice that the situation would not be improved by claiming that the end $F$ is somehow necessary for agents as such. For if one cannot see the bearing of having an end upon the choice of actions, then knowing an end to be necessary would not enlighten one on that score.

So we arrive again at what we want to say to Gary. Not: "Giving deliberative weight to one's ends is constitutive of agency, and you are, after all, an agent." He might sensibly wonder whether *that* state of affairs should continue. Rather, we want to say: "You already defer, in posing this question, to the very thing you seek to challenge. You must already see – and feel – the 'practical logic' of what you claim to find arbitrary or problematic: the bearing of ends upon means. If you reply, 'Well, so that's just another end of mine – I can change it' then we can answer 'No, on pain of regress, it cannot be just another end of yours.' "

Does this show that Gary cannot be raising a genuine issue about whether or not to be rational? Return to our previous distinction between subjective and objective notions of conformity to norms.

Gary was dismissive of this distinction, since his ambition was to ask a question less "internal" to the theory of practical reason in its orthodox form. "Subjective or objective," he said in effect, "I want to know whether rationality's worth it." It now appears that he succeeded instead in asking a more "internal" question. Roughly: "I want to know whether subjectively patterning my thinking along means/ends lines would really be in objective conformity with realizing my ends – especially, the end of living well." This question, more internal than he imagined, is also more real than others have imagined. Constitutive arguments of the kind considered here can neither answer it nor set it aside. The Low Brow argument, if successful, would show that subjective patterning to means/ends reasoning – that is, representing oneself as deliberatively adjusting means and ends – is partially constitutive of agency. But whether a life of subjective patterning would be in objective accord with realizing one's most important ends is another question. Arguably, it is Gary's real question.

317

Gary is asking, not "Do ends bear on means?", but "Why be the sort of creature who asks about ends and means?"

Lewis Carroll's paradox is sometimes used to argue that there cannot really be an "alternative logic" – we cannot drop or pick up rules of inference like premisses. But this paradox cannot really establish that orthodox logic will be adequate to – or necessary for – the fullest possible development of our thought and experience. The paradox shows instead that a certain way of thinking about how an alternative logic might be introduced or argued for is absurd. We cannot say, for example, "Just compare the implications of existing logical rules with those of my new rules. . . ." The very notion of *implication* presupposes that logical rules are already in place. Similarly, the present discussion cannot demonstrate that Low Brow means/ends reasoning will be adequate to – or necessary for – the fullest possible development of our thought and experience. We can at most show the absurdity of attempting to give a Low Brow rationale (in terms of objective conformity) for questioning whether Low Brow reasons (again, in the objective sense) are relevant for what to do or how to live. Gary seemed to be pursuing such a rationale, so his line of questioning can come to look a bit silly. One can't lift oneself by one's own bootstraps, but he seems to have managed to pull himself down thereby.

Yet Gary isn't without a "less internal" response. He can, without absurdity, be seen as trying to find a way of keeping us aware that no one really knows where reflective equilibrium and our evolving experience might take us. Each step in a reflective equilibrium process is linked by intelligible forms of reasoning to the step before, but this does not mean that we could not take steps that would, in sum, yield the result that our conception of reasoning itself has changed. Experience has held some interesting surprises for those who thought certain principles – such as the Principle of Sufficient Reason – were constitutive of the entire possible domain of thought and action. Perhaps Gary just wants to remind us of this. Moreover, he could insist, it seems inevitable that wherever reflective equilibrium takes us, its route will depend upon facts about us and our contingent nature. As Gary never tires of pointing out, this shows our reasoning is never on a wholly non-hypothetical footing.

Where, then, are we left? We began with the question whether a non-hypothetical account could be given of why we must conform to certain forms of theoretical or practical reasoning. In that context, we developed several constitutive arguments that showed some prospect of returning an intelligible, positive answer. We now have also seen the limitations of such arguments. Especially, they cannot supply a self-sufficient non-hypothetical response.[31]

But we should not imagine that this means we are left with wholly hypothetical considerations. Another conclusion to be drawn from the Low Brow constitutive argument is that each element – hypothetical and non-hypothetical, end-setting and ends/means-adjusting – has its own distinctive role to play in reasoning about action. Neither can do the other's job. To ask, of a given act of Low Brow reasoning, whether it owes its conclusion to hypothetical or non-hypothetical considerations is a bit like asking, of an act of deductive theoretical reasoning, whether it owes the belief-guiding force of its conclusion to the reasoner's hypothetical deference to the premises or her non-hypothetical deference to the rules of logic.[32] The answer, of course, is always both.[33]

NOTES

*Ethics and Practical Reason*, Garrett Cullity and Berys Gaut, eds. (Oxford: Clarendon Press, 1997).

\* I would like to dedicate this essay to the memory of Jean Hampton, who taught us much about practical rationality.

1. This will function herein as something like a stipulation about the meaning of 'non-hypothetical.' Thus, reasons that depend upon ends *necessary* for agents as such would count as non-hypothetical for present purposes. One might distinguish *personal-goal* non-hypotheticalness (absence of dependence upon contingently held *ends* of the agent) from *personal-belief* non-hypotheticalness (absence of dependence upon contingently held *beliefs* of the agent). What I refer to in the text as 'well domesticated within the literature on theoretical reasons' is the idea that epistemic reasons are *personal-goal* non-hypothetical.

2. I write 'personal goals' because there is a school within contemporary epistemology according to which theoretical reason is *end-orientated*. But the ends in question typically are assumed to belong to a special class of *epistemic* ends that are subject to at most limited variation across rational individuals.

3. See David Velleman, "The Guise of the Good," *Noûs* 26 (1992), 3–26 and "The Possibility of Practical Reason," *Ethics* 106 (1996), 694–726. I am much indebted to Velleman's discussions and to his comments on earlier papers, though I do not mean to suggest that he would agree with my use of the notion. See also his "Deciding How to Decide," in G. Cullity and B. Gaut, eds., *Ethics and Practical Reason* (Oxford: Clarendon, 1997).

4. Bernard Williams gives a seminal discussion of belief as "aiming at" truth in "Deciding to Believe," in his *Problems of the Self* (Cambridge: Cambridge University Press, 1973) 136–51.

5. More precisely, a believer-that-$h$ holds *this* attitude accountable to the truth of $h$. It cannot be essential to belief (in beings with finite minds, such as us) to hold that, for all $p$, if $p$ is true then one should believe it.

6. See Section III for some further discussion.

7. For some further discussion, see P. Railton, "Truth, Reason, and the Regulation of Belief," *Philosophical Issues* 5 (1994), 71–94.

8. Those who think of *being a belief* as a purely functional property will presumably hold that any attitude playing all the roles of belief would simply *be* a belief. Here, however, we are supposing that the attitude would lack at least some of the central roles of belief, namely those involved in the "internal relation" between what one believes and what one takes to be true or evidential.

9. Subjective patterning on a norm $N$ need not involve a second-order thought to the effect that "I do this in order to satisfy norm $N$."

10. The example itself is used by Daniel Kahneman and Amos Tversky, "Prospect Theory: An Analysis of Decision under Risk," *Econometrica* 47 (1979), 263–91, at 283, and attributed to Richard Zeckhauser. The version given here is quoted from Allan Gibbard, *Wise Choices, Apt Feelings* (Cambridge: Harvard University Press, 1990) 15.

11. See for example Daniel Kahneman, Paul Slovic, and Amos Tversky, eds., *Judgment Under Uncertainty: Heuristics and Biases* (New York: Cambridge University Press, 1982).

12. Sometimes, of course, we just *pick* rather than choose. This can be seen, however, as a species of action in which it is decided simply to select an option rather than deliberate further.

13. David Hume, *An Enquiry Concerning the Principles of Morals*, app. 1, "Concerning Moral Sentiment."

14. We have been working throughout with generic High Brow views because of their greater plausibility. That complicates the present discussion, however, since open-endedness about the notion of the good can make it difficult to distinguish such views from Humean Low Brow views. Unless a certain amount of substance is built into the idea of goodness, it will be rather too easy (and uninformative) to think of any sort of desiring as "deeming to be good."

15. I am grateful to Shelly Kagan for bringing this sort of example to my attention.

16. Personal communication. He is obviously not to be held responsible either for the claims made about the example or for the interpretation offered of it.

17. Psychologists would, I think, challenge the suggestion that the cravings of an addict can be understood as a subspecies of our familiar notion of desire. Let us, however, follow philosophical convention and set that concern aside.

18. The Low Brow need not rule out the possibility of an agent also inquiring into or aiming at the good. His point is simply that this is at most an *option* for agents, and perhaps also that it presupposes the means/ends relationships that are the stuff of Low Brow agency.

19. In this formula, $E$ must be understood as occurrently taken by me as an end of mine. As with belief, there is nothing odd about the diachronic case:

(8′) I once deemed $E$ to be an end of mine, but that now counts for nothing in my deliberation.

20. This is like the relevance of *modus ponens* to inference. If I already believe that (if $p$ then $q$) and come to believe that $p$, should I conclude $q$? Perhaps, in light of $q$'s implausibility, I should question one or both of the premises.

21. It should perhaps be emphasized again that an agent's ends need not be self-oriented. They could include the well-being of others, moral or aesthetic causes, and so on.

22. This might not be wholly unfair to High Brow theories. After all, High Brows can agree that means/ends reasoning is a central part of agency (even, of course, irrational agency).

23. For a discussion of related concerns about the critical limitations of constitutive or linguistically necessary principles, though in connection with a conception of instrumental *rationality* rather than agency, see Christine Korsgaard, "The Normativity of Instrumental Reason," in Cullity and Gaut, eds., *Ethics and Practical Reason*.

24. I am indebted here to Shelly Kagan.

25. In cases like this, we might seem to be flirting with Moore's paradox. That is, I might be tempted to say: "Yes, I grant that it is unquestionably true that commercial air travel is safer than car travel, but I don't really believe it." Once we realize all that "coming to believe" actually involves, this looks more like a needlessly paradoxical way of expressing a fairly familiar sort of imperfection in rational belief.

26. This sort of case differs from classic cases of weakness of the will, in which the agent feels the positive deliberative force of an end, but is swayed to act otherwise. The case I am imagining is less psychologically conflictual.

27. Bas van Fraassen recommends that the community of scientists take an attitude of *acceptance* rather than belief toward the truth of their theories, but should *also* behave as scientists in every other respect – inferential, experimental, etc. – as if they believed the theories to be true. If sustainable, this attitude would be a form of near belief. Could it, perhaps, even spread beyond scientific theories? See *The Scientific Image* (Oxford: Clarendon, 1980). For critical discussion, see P. Railton, "Truth, Reason, and the Regulation of Belief."

28. Note that we cannot uncontroversially say "The value would not be *true* value." We will see shortly some examples where ends of (what we agents deem) true value can be attained only at some cost to one's own agency.

29. Derek Parfit, *Reasons and Persons* (Oxford: Clarendon, 1984) 12–13.

30. See Lewis Carroll, "What the Tortoise said to Achilles," *Mind* 4 (1895), 278–80. I have altered Carroll's example slightly.

31. We have not, however, tried to demonstrate the impossibility of other types of argument that could provide the grounds for "purely" non-hypothetical justifications.

32. I am grateful to John Searle for suggesting an error in the original version of this remark. Searle's concern, however, appears to be with the *logical validity* of a deduction, rather than the phenomenon of *theoretical reasoning* as such. See John R. Searle, *Rationality in Action* (Cambridge: MIT Press, 2001) 19–20.

33. I am grateful to a number of people for helpful comments and conversation. In particular, I should mention Garrett Cullity, Stephen Darwall, Berys Gaut, Allan Gibbard, Shelly Kagan, Michael Smith, David Velleman, and an anonymous referee.

# 11

# Normative Force and Normative Freedom: Hume and Kant, but Not Hume Versus Kant

Our notion of normativity appears to combine, in a way difficult to understand but seemingly familiar from experience, elements of force and freedom. On the one hand, a normative claim is thought to have a kind of compelling authority; on the other hand, if our respecting it is to be an appropriate species of respect, it must not be coerced, automatic, or trivially guaranteed by definition. Both Hume and Kant, I argue, looked to aesthetic experience as a convincing example exhibiting this marriage of force and freedom, as well as showing how our judgment can come to be properly attuned to the features that constitute value. This image of attunement carries over into their respective accounts of moral judgment. The seemingly radical difference between their moral theories may be traceable not to a different conception of normativity, but to a difference in their empirical psychological theories – a difference we can readily spot in their accounts of aesthetics.

## INTRODUCTION

'Normativity' is, for better or worse, the chief term we philosophers seem to have settled upon for discussing some central but deeply puzzling phenomena of human life. We use it to mark a distinction, not between the good and the bad (or between the right and the wrong, the correct and the incorrect), but rather between the good or bad (or between right or wrong, . . .), on the one hand, and the actual, possible, or usual, on the other. Ethics, aesthetics, epistemology, rationality, semantics – all these areas of philosophical inquiry draw us into a discussion of normativity. And they do so not because we philosophers import this notion into our inquiries, but because – sometimes rather belatedly – we discover it there whether we went looking for it or not.

I said 'for better or worse' because, while it is useful to bring these various normative phenomena together, the term 'normativity' itself bears the stamp of but one aspect of such phenomena: *norms* – rules or standards. The etymology of the English term *norm* traces it back to the Latin *norma*, a builder's square. The term *rule* also seems to come to us from the building trade – it descends from the Latin *regulus*, a straightedge or ruler. Now anyone who has sawn a board or chiseled a stone recognizes what it is to take a square or a ruler as a guide in cutting, and thus to treat gaps between the actual cut and the square or ruler to show there is something to be "corrected" in the cut rather than the tool. So we have here a seemingly concrete example of "action-guidingness" and an associated "standard of correctness," different from the merely actual, at work.[1]

Because the *norma* (or *regulus*) is a tool whose application is so transparent to us, it can prove a useful example. But there is a danger as well as an aptness in using such a model when we attempt to construct a philosophical account of normativity. A builder can consult his *norma* to guide himself in making cuts and to judge whether his work "measures up," but does this tool, or any tool, tell him why or when his cuts should measure up to the *norma*? In most cases it is of course evident why they should, and there certainly is no mystery why the builder's square is ubiquitous in the building trade. But what if an arch is needed, or a compound curve – is it still the case that cuts are always to be made following the square-angled *norma*?

Understanding how a *norma* or a norm could possess legitimate regulative standing thus also requires us to ask: What is it in general for a rule or standard to *apply*? There is no special difficulty about saying what it is for a rule to apply in (what we might call) a "formal" sense. A *norma* can be applied to a cut and we can find the cut to fit or not. But in this sense the *norma* applies even when we needed to cut a curve. So when do we say a rule *applies* or is *in force* in the sense that it is *to be followed*? Clearly, we have simply re-encountered the question of action-guidingness, now in the form of a distinction between "formal" and (what we might call) "normative" applicability. If at this point we ask for another rule, a "rule of application," the threat of regress emerges at once – for how to distinguish those cases in which the rule of application itself normatively applies among those in which it merely formally applies?

We could block the regress if there were a super-rule (rationality) that always normatively applies and that directs us regarding the applicability of all other rules. Unfortunately, however, the useful transparency of anything like the *norma* – or of such familiar examples as rules of a game – is lost once we speak of super-rules. For we can intelligibly ask when to use the *norma* – or when to play a game – and why. But somehow, a super-rule is supposed to prevent such questions about itself from arising.

Even as strong a proponent of rules and rationality as Kant seemed able to see the sense of asking what might be "the purpose of nature in attaching reason to our will as its governor" (G 305).[2] This is a question about the *normative* applicability of "rules of reason," that is, a question about the source of reason's normative authority.

Authority is an impressive thing. At least, it is when it works. We speak of rules *binding* us, or being *in force*, even when we would rather not comply. This suggests a certain image of what it would be to explain or ground normative authority. Sheer force is sometimes called upon to enforce norms, but it is not much of a model of the "coercive power" of norms as such. Rousseau noted that "If force compels obedience, there is no need to invoke a duty to obey."[3] A sufficiently great actual force simply *is* irresistible. Familiar rules and *oughts*, even stringent ones, are not like that – we can and do resist them, as Kant noted:

The moral law is holy (inviolable). Man is certainly unholy enough, but humanity in his person must be holy to him (CPrR 87).

Clearly the *must* here is not the *must* of something irresistible – the moral law is normatively, not actually, "inviolable." Since an *ought* is to apply to us even when we fall short, its force (and recognition thereof) must leave that option open. If "guidance by norms" is to play a nontrivial role in explaining an individual's or a group's behavior, then the normative domain must be a domain of freedom as well as "bindingness."

This need for a "possibility of incorrectness" is often remarked upon in philosophical discussions of normativity, usually in connection with physical or causal possibility. But it is no less important to make room for the *logical* or *conceptual* possibility of error. It is sometimes said, for example, that a *free agent* is by definition guided by rationality or a good will. There is no objection to this kind of definition as such, but it does not capture the sense of "freedom" we need here.

Consider a more mundane example. Suppose that I have written you a letter and have spelled 'correspondence' correctly, rather than as the often-seen 'correspondance.' You, the reader, aware that my spelling is at best uncertain, remark upon my unexpected success to a colleague and wonder aloud whether it was accident or competence. You are, in effect, assessing two explanations, according to one of which I spelled it with an 'e' by chance, while according to the other I did it on purpose (though perhaps without explicit deliberation) – as a manifestation of my internalization of, and deference to, this particular norm of English spelling. Suppose your friend replies, "No, there simply is no question of why Railton spelled 'correspondence' with an 'e'. *Spelling* is a normative concept – acts of spelling constitutively involve satisfying the norms of spelling. So he *couldn't* have spelled the word with an 'a' – to have written 'correspondance' wouldn't have counted as a spelling of 'correspondence' at all."

Now there certainly is a "normative sense" of spelling, according to which 'correspondance' cannot count as a spelling of 'correspondence.' In this sense, it is analytic that spelling is correct, and even losers in spelling bees never spell incorrectly. That's why, thought it may sound odd to say so, when we ask why or how someone spelled correctly we typically are *not* using the term in this "normative sense." As you intended your question to your colleague, my spelling 'correspondence' with an 'e' was either a happy accident or a pleasant surprise, not an analytic truth.

If a normative *must* is to have a distinctive place in the world, then, it cannot be the *must* either of natural law or of conceptual necessity. Natural law and conceptual necessities are "always at work," even when we're tired, weak-willed, lazy, disobedient, evil, or ignorant. No worry about anyone violating *them*. But normative guidance requires some contribution on our part, in a domain where freedom in the "non-normative" sense makes some vigilance or effort necessary.

However, having escaped the danger of missing the phenomenon of normative guidance altogether by assimilating it to a kind of unfreedom, we had better be careful not to think of it as simply a matter of free willing. First, many of the *attitudes* (and associated motives and emotions) basic to normative conduct – attitudes of belief, desire, admiration, regret, approval, anger, and so on – appear not to be wholly within the scope of direct willing.[4] Kant, for example, distinguishes attitudes of love and reverence (*reverentia*), which are not directly subject to the will and cannot strictly be objects of duty (MM 401–3), from attitudes that accord to others a respectful observance (*observantia*) of their rights or goals, which can be required of us as a duty (MM 449, 467–8; compare G 399).[5] Kant does not conclude that attitudes of the first sort are therefore irrelevant to the domain of normative governance – on the contrary, according to the interpretation to be discussed in the following text, they are to be found at the very bottom of his view, as a source or "basis" of duties (cf. MM 402–3).

Second, even if we restrict attention to those areas of normative governance in which the will seemingly can be effective – in selecting among acts, in regulating the more voluntary attitudes (such as acceptance or acknowledgment), and in shaping indirectly over time the less voluntary attitudes and motives (such as esteem, reverence, or liking) – it seems we cannot capture all of normative guidance with the notion of freely willing. For though the will may guide us, what guides the will? If we say, simply, "*We* do – we exercise our normative freedom and choose," this appears to get at only half the truth. For what makes an exercise of will a *choice*, rather than a mere *fiat*? And what would make a choice a moral one – or a rational, aesthetic, prudential, or epistemic one? Could the bare fact that a will is *my* will make it (say) a *good* will?

## REASON AND NORMATIVITY

Kant tells us that reason's "highest practical function" is to enable us to discover and "establish" the good will (G 396), but speaking of reason and rationality can be ambiguous, at least in ordinary discourse. Let us distinguish, roughly, two senses of 'rational choice.'

In the first sense, a rational choice is a *well-reasoned* choice, one that is (or, perhaps, could in principle be) supported by a chain of deliberation in accord with norms of good reasoning. In the second sense, a rational choice is a choice *appropriately responsive to reasons*, whether or not it is (or, perhaps, even could in principle be) supported by such deliberation.

A simple example might help here. Consider a circumstance in which it would be best to pick an option from among those saliently available, rather than to deliberate – perhaps time is short, or perhaps the question is of little significance. To be "appropriately responsive to reasons" would involve prompt and decisive selection of one option and moving on. If we were even to stop and deliberate about *whether* to deliberate, we might miss our chance, or waste valuable time. In such cases, the two senses of 'rational choice' come apart in practice.

Yet we might hold that this represents no deep ambiguity in our basic thinking about practical rationality. For it seems we could, in principle, in a restrospective "context of justification," give a well-reasoned argument in favor of selecting without deliberation in certain circumstances. Indeed, it is not uncommon to find philosophers supposing that the two senses of 'rational choice' always come to the same thing, at least once we understand "well-reasoned" in terms of an in-principle constructable argument in the context of justification rather than a piece of actual cogitation in heat of the moment. And in this coming together of "well-reasoned" and "responsive to reasons" we might hope to find the secret to explaining how the free and forceful elements of normativity can be combined. Perhaps we can understand normative force on the model of appreciating *the force of argument*.

The force of argument has many features that make it an appealing general model for normative guidance. Unlike an irresistible coercive or natural force, the force of argument is one we can fail to follow. We have all departed from laws of logic by reasoning fallaciously, and we have all had the experience of finding our actual belief tendencies somewhat recalcitrant in the face of an argument whose validity and premises we cannot fault. The connection between the force of argument and belief is a normative one, rather than a matter of nomic or conceptual necessity.

At the same time, our response to the force of argument seems appropriately free without being arbitrarily willful. When we feel "trapped" by an argument or "caught" in a contradiction, we want out, but we are not inclined to think that we can, with sufficient power of will or strength of desire, bend the logical relations and escape. Moreover, even though logical relations thus stand independent of our will and wishes, recognition of them does not seem to be at odds with our capacity for autonomy in thought and belief. Since we take our beliefs to aim at truth and to be responsive to logic and evidence – one might even say this sort of commitment is *constitutive* of belief as an attitude[6] – we do not need to be subject to some further coercion or external sanction in order for self-acknowledged logical implications to be felt as putting normative pressure on us. We think we can see responsiveness to argument as a form of *epistemic attunement* of just the sort that belief might be said to present itself as having – attunement to content, to relations of implication and evidence, and so on.

"The force of argument" is indeed a central example of the peculiar mixture of force and freedom that we take normative guidance to involve. If it were possible to understand all normative guidance on this model, then we might hope that the two senses of 'rational choice' would never lead to genuinely divided loyalty and that we had gotten to the bottom of things normative. No doubt the lasting appeal of rationalism in philosophy is partly explained by this.

But I will spend most of the balance of this paper discussing – in a very preliminary way – some ways in which the force of argument seems unable to afford a general model of normative guidance, or to take us to the bottom of all things normative. I will look first at what might seem the most hospitable territory for the force of argument: epistemology, or reasons for belief. Second, I will look at another domain of judgment, which might at first strike us as peripheral but instead emerges as central: aesthetics. Third, I will consider the classic turf for normativity: morality.

## NORMATIVE AUTHORITY FOR BELIEF

We face a problem at the very outset attempting to understand normative authority in the domains of theoretical or practical reason in terms of the force of argument. For arguments and the logical relations they involve operate on, and conclude in, *propositions*. But according to a long tradition that seems worth maintaining, the conclusion of a piece of practical reasoning is an action and the conclusion of a piece of theoretical reasoning is a belief, and neither a belief nor an action is a proposition. If we are somehow to connect the propositional conclusion of an argument to a phenomenon like belief or action, it seems as if some nonargumentative but nonetheless *justifying* or *"rationalizing"* relationship must be found. Can we do this without already introducing a species of normative authorization not encompassed by the power of argument?

This is a contested matter. For example, we are inclined to speak of sensory experience as paradigmatically justifying perceptual belief, yet it is far from obvious that the content of experience itself is propositional, or that the justificatory relationship of this content to perceptual belief can fully be captured in deductive or inductive relations among propositions. To explore these questions would take us into deep waters. But perhaps we can give a less controversial example of justified belief to illustrate how difficult it would be to reconstruct all epistemic justification propositionally.

So as not to prejudice matters against "propositionalism," let us make some favorable assumptions. Suppose that we were able to give an uncontroversial account of "the force of argument" in the inductive case, that is, of what it is for a hypothesis to be inductively supported to a certain degree by a given body of evidence. And suppose as well that we can state the "rationalizing" relationship linking justified belief to inductive argument by a simple formula: a *belief that h* of strength *r* is justified in epistemic context *C* if *h* is inductively supported in *C* to degree *r*.

Focus now on beliefs that ascribe self-identity. Some such beliefs, I trust, are in fact epistemically justified. Can we give an account of this justification in propositional terms, even under our favorable assumptions? Perhaps, one might suppose, they are justified on the basis of an inductive inference from certain coherences and continuities among one's experiences. Consider an argument of the form:

(SI)   I have experience e1 at t-3
       I have experience e2 at t-2.
       I have experience e3 at t-1.
       I have experience e4 at t.
       Experiences e1 – e4 exhibit coherence and continuity.
       I therefore conclude (with strength *r*) that I am self-identically me through-
       out the time interval (t-3) to *t*.

Yet it is clear that this argument simply *presupposes* self-identity, since it is formulated in terms of (a presumably unequivocating) first-personal '*I*'. Now propositions are essentially third-personal, so we would have to reformulate the argument replacing 'I' and 'me' with 'Peter Railton.' Suppose this is done, and suppose there is no doubt about the truth of the premises or the argument's inductive legitimacy. We now have a conclusion about Peter Railton, but it tells me nothing yet about *my* identity. That is, it does not yet sustain a conclusion licensing a *de se* self-identity ascription on my part.[7] It does not tell me that 'Peter Railton' refers to me.

If experiential induction, propositionally construed, will not suffice, where does my sense of self-identity and my entitlement (if any) to the first-personal 'I' come from? Presumably I arrive at a *sense* of being me (and here, and now) in part from something like what has been called *proprioceptive* aspects of my experience (both conscious and nonconscious) – a kind of feeling or expectation that pervades my mental life and that, so far as I can see, cannot in principle be rendered as a third-personal propositional content.[8] Now, if we dismiss this as no more than my "sense" of self-identity, and insist that we would need *evidence* reconstructable in argumentative form in order to *warrant* such a conclusion, we will find ourselves cut off from any possible avenue of justification. This could leave us stranded as theoretical reasoners, since without any entitlement to the '*I*,' how am I ever to be responsive in my belief to the evidence *I* have? – A lot of people have a lot of evidence, much of it conflicting, but whose should weigh with me? To justify my beliefs I need to identify myself in the space of epistemic reasons.

Hume himself seems to have become sensible of such a defect in any purely continuity-and-coherence–based approach to personal identity, such as the one he experimented with in the *Treatise*. He reflected in an Appendix:

> If perceptions are distinct existences, they form a whole only by being connected
> together. But no connexions among distinct existences are ever discoverable

by human understanding. We only *feel* a connexion or determination of the thought . . . the ideas are felt to be connected together, and naturally introduce each other (T 635).[9]

He is at a loss to describe this feeling, or to explain it as based upon principles. "[T]his difficulty," he concedes, "is too hard for my understanding" (T 636).

Just what a fix we could end up in is seen at the end of Part I of the *Treatise*, where Hume gives a perhaps inadvertent intimation of the problem his later reflection brought clearly into focus. Hume is describing the depths of the mental distress he reaches as a result of an "*intense*" commitment to following the rationalistic maxim to restrict belief to those matters where we can give a reasoned justification. He finds that, as a result, he loses any entitlement to confidence in induction, memory, external body, or even deduction. Eventually he "can look upon no opinion even as more probable or likely than another," and calls out in desperation, "Where am I, or what?" (T 269). Rigorous adherence to the self-imposed rationalist maxim prevents him from attributing any epistemic authority to his "natural introduction" to the self through an unreasoned "feeling" of it – and he thus loses his grip on self-location and self-identity.

Having seen what it would be to reach this point, Hume cannot convince himself that epistemology would be well served by unqualified obedience to the rationalistic maxim. Why is it, he wonders, that

. . . I must torture my brain . . . at the very time I cannot satisfy myself concerning the reasonableness of so painful an application, nor have any tolerable prospect of arriving by its means at truth or certainty? Under what obligation do I lie . . . ? (T 270).

Hume remains concerned with reasonableness, truth, and probability. He is, however, "sceptical" that trusting *only* the force of argument will enable us to be fully responsive to these concerns.

. . . understanding, when it acts alone, and according to its most general principles, entirely subverts itself, and leaves not the lowest degree of evidence in any proposition, either in philosophy or in common life. . . . I am ready to reject all belief and reasoning. . . . Whose favor shall I court, and whose anger must I dread? What beings surround me? and on whom have I any influence, or who have any influence on me? I am confounded . . . and begin to fancy myself . . . utterly depriv'd of the use of every member and faculty (T 268–9).

Far from consolidating belief around a core of rational certainty like the Cartesian *cogito*, Hume finds himself in a complete collapse of normative epistemic guidance – there remains no discernment concerning evidence or probability, no sense of anyone's authority, even one's own. His "distribution of credence" has become entirely undiscriminating, even with respect to logical relations and "the force of argument." How, for example, are we to *reason* in the "context of justification" about the relationship between our beliefs and their grounds if we accord immediate experience no *prima facie* authority to support belief even concerning the content of our own thoughts?

If belief and reasoning are to be resurrected, we will need to authorize ourselves to draw directly upon a wider base of epistemic resources, without asking for reconstructability as argument, even in the context of justification. But what to add? Belief, we've noticed, is not a bare proposition, but an *attitude* toward propositions. Hume puts it starkly: "*Belief is nothing but a peculiar feeling, different from the simple conception* [of its object]" (T 624). If we consider *de se* belief, Hume's suggestion would seem to be that this attitude is a feeling that is *to be regulated* (at least in part) by "self-introducing" (we might say "self-intimating") feelings. A feeling regulating a feeling? Hume writes that "*Belief is more properly an act of the sensitive, than of the cogitative part of our natures*" (T 181). Hume appears to apply this idea well beyond self-identifying belief, stressing the role of feelings in shaping belief concerning external objects, and observing:

Nature has . . . doubtless esteem'd it an affair of too great importance to be trusted to our uncertain reasonings and speculations (T 187).

But what is such regulation of feeling by feeling like, and, if it cannot be reconstructed as an argument, how can it constitute justification? It seems we will need to supplement the normative "force of argument" in epistemology with something like a normative "force of feeling," if we are to resuscitate epistemic discrimination or even self-discernment. How can feeling be appropriately discerning to possess epistemic authority? To have some idea of how this might go, we will turn to another work of Hume's – on discerning, knowing, appreciative feelings.

NORMATIVE AUTHORITY AND APPRECIATION

We encounter a structurally similar problem – of how to find the resources necessary to support a domain of appropriate discrimination in judgment – in Hume's late essay, "Of the Standard of Taste," which apparently is a survival of a systematic project he had undertaken on the nature of "criticism," to include morality as well.[10] After observing that we cannot ground aesthetic distinctions on "reasonings *a priori*" (ST 231), he begins to consider the possible contribution of sentiment. Yet he quickly finds that mere *acquiescence* in sentiment would equally leave aesthetic distinctions groundless:

> There is a species of philosophy, which cuts off all hopes of success in such an attempt, and represents the impossibility of ever attaining any standard of taste. The difference, it is said, is very wide between judgment and sentiment. All sentiment is right; because sentiment has a reference to nothing beyond itself. . . . [E]very individual [therefore] ought to acquiesce in his own sentiment, without pretending to regulate those of others. . . . [And thus it is] fruitless to dispute concerning tastes (ST 230).

This species of philosophy has the wholly "skeptical" result that we cannot even say that Milton is better than Ogilby, and any such philosophy effectively undermines the discrimination upon which taste must be based. Agreeable as this "levelling" sort of skepticism may be to some strands of common sense, common sense on the whole, Hume notes, does not really take it to heart:

> Whoever would assert an equality of genius and elegance between OGILBY and MILTON, or BUNYAN and ADDISON, would be thought to defend no less an extravagance, than if we had maintained a mole-hill to be as high as TENERIFE, or a pond as extensive as the ocean. Though there may be found persons, who give preference to the former authors; no one pays attention to such a taste; and we pronounce without scruple the sentiment of these pretended critics to be absurd and ridiculous (ST 230–1).

Hume isn't personally threatened by a "species of philosophy" that would force us to give up aesthetic distinctions. "The principle of natural equality of tastes," he believes, can hold sway only in disputatious or esoteric settings where we are not actively relying upon taste to guide us. In ordinary life, it is "totally forgot" (ST 231). Unlike the younger Hume, who wrestled nearly to the point of exhaustion with reason's normative force, worrying aloud "For my part, I know not what ought to be done" (T 268), the older Hume who wrote "Of the Standard of Taste" seems confident that he knows reason's place and is unafraid of the world of normative discrimination tumbling into ruin around him. Any aesthetician – rationalist or sentimentalist – who cannot find a basis for distinguishing a Milton from an Ogilby will simply find himself without authority in Hume's eyes, or ours.

To whose taste, then, *do* we actually pay some attention, that is, attribute some normative force, and why would this count as authority about *beauty*? Hume identifies two sources of authority, convergence of "expert opinion" among those with relevant knowledge and sensory discriminative capacities, and convergence of general, experienced opinion in the "test of time." In both cases, we are seen to accord some authority to these sources, beyond our own simple likings. After all, we know that our own simple likings, convincing though they may be as feelings of attraction, may nonetheless be attributable to our own partiality, ignorance, fashion, novelty, lack of sensory discrimination, or distaste for (or perverse fascination with) the odd or déclassé. Why should this matter – isn't it up to us what we like? Yes, but when we judge beauty, we attribute something to an object or event, not merely to ourselves; and we accord ourselves authority concerning it. Partiality, fashion, lack of sensory discrimination, and so forth are all ways in which the pleasure one takes in the experience of a landscape or of a work of art might simply be unrelated to the "beauties" (in Hume's terminology) it possesses – since we do not think self-interest, fashion, and the like are, or "make for," genuine beauty.

Well then, what sorts of features do we uncontroversially take to have a constitutive role in beauty making, in both natural and man-made objects? Where do we expect to find the "beauties"? Surely, if there is anything at all to our notion of beauty, then among these features are form, proportion, color, texture, composition, melody, harmony, rhythm, progression, and the like. When these features of an object are of a kind that our sensory and cognitive engagement with them seems reliably to yield experiences we find intrinsically enjoyable, we seem to have (to that extent) a candidate for beauty. That such features do figure in our assessments of beauty is reflected in ways we typically attribute lesser or greater aesthetic authority to our own likings or the likings of others. For example, I do not take my likings concerning Middle Eastern music to have much authority – I am inexperienced with it; unable to discern its shades of tonality, structures, progressions, or variety (the different pieces sound too much alike to me); and I don't claim to be exercising taste or discernment when I express sporadic likes and dislikes of what I happen to hear. And I certainly claim no authority over others. By contrast, there are those whose likings in Middle Eastern music I find much more authoritative than mine, and whom I would consult for guidance. Now someone I take to be expert could lose some standing in my eyes if I came to learn that he plays favorites, judges music by its ideological content, lacks sensory discernment, or cannot find other individuals seriously engaged in making or judging such music who take his judgment seriously. Our practices – including our patterns of normative deference – reveal that we do have some idea of what it would be for a feeling (an appreciative delight) to be more or less attuned to objective, beauty-making features of objects, even though this attunement is effected in part through careful cultivation of, and attention to, subjective feelings or sensations.

A degree of deference to experts who possess demonstrable skills of discernment, greater knowledge of genre or context, wider experience, and so on, enables me to extend my "critical" power in detecting beauty-making features – they help me form a better idea of what I'd find delightful were I to gain greater experience. As a result, they help attune me to the "beauties" of objects, features that can be rich and lasting sources of sensorily based, cognitively engaging delight. Hume puts it thus:

> Those finer emotions of the mind are of a very tender and delicate nature, and require the concurrence of many favourable circumstances to make them play with facility and exactness, according to their general and established principles. The least exterior hindrance to such small springs, or the least internal disorder... and we shall be unable to judge of the catholic and universal beauty. The relation, which nature has placed between the form and the sentiment, will at least be more obscure; and it will require greater accuracy to trace and discern it (ST 232–3).

A similar sort of authority, also related to an authority we already accord ourselves, attaches to the "test of time." Hume writes, concerning the relation "nature has put between form and sentiment" that underlies beauty:

> We shall be able to ascertain its influence not so much from the operation of each particular beauty, as from the durable admiration, which attends those works, that have survived all the caprices of mode and fashion, all the mistakes of ignorance and envy.
>
> The same HOMER, who pleased at ATHENS and ROME two thousand years ago, is still admired at PARIS and at LONDON. All the changes of climate, government, religion, and language, have not been able to obscure his glory (ST 233).

Long exposure, developed sensibilities, the authority of countless experiences on the part of different individuals – how far we are from my inexperienced self overhearing a snatch of Middle Eastern music at lunch and saying "Hmm, don't care much for that." It is natural to see this as a difference in attunement to musical value.

Over the course of a life, we participate in a complex critical and appreciative practice, attributing some authority to our own growing experience ("In the end, the proof of the pudding..."), making recommendations and seeking confirmation in the opinions of others ("Try it, you'll see for yourself"), and also showing some deference to various external sources of authority ("After what I've heard about it, I'm eager to try this place"). Situated within such a practice, which extends across societies and times and is held together both by our fundamental human sensory and cognitive similarities and by our reciprocal deferences, my judgments of beauty have at least a chance to be "normed by" the sources of aesthetic value, and words like 'beautiful' in my mouth have a chance of expressing genuinely aesthetic evaluations, even when I get things wrong.[11] We manage, that is, to have a domain of real distinctions concerning beauty, a domain of genuine taste, even though "subjective feelings" play an essential role in its shape.

Kant was also concerned to underwrite the possibility of objectivity in the domain of taste. Like Hume, he worried about various ways in which appreciation might be attuned or disattuned to genuine value. Kant writes:

> ... everyone says: Hunger is the best sauce; [but] to people with a healthy appetite anything is tasty provided it is edible. Hence if people have a liking of this sort, that does not prove that they are selecting by taste. Only when their need has been satisfied can we tell who in a multitude of people has taste and who does not (CJ 210).

Hunger makes our likings unreliable. But when, for Kant, could a subjective condition such as liking be a reliable guide to a purportedly objective matter, such as aesthetic value?

Kant could not pursue Hume's solution, of looking to the refinement and qualification of empirical faculties and sentiments. Hume's psychology attributes to "the internal frame and constitution of the mind" appetites and passions that are *directly* aimed at features of the world independent of the self, and are "antecedent" to self-interest or happiness (Inq 113–19). But in Kant's empirical psychology, by contrast, appetites and passions are always guided at base by one's own pleasure:

> All the inclinations together (which can be brought into a tolerable system and the satisfaction of which is then called one's happiness) constitute regard for oneself (*solipsismus*) (CPrR m 73).[12]

Within such a psychology, to become ever more delicately attuned to nuance in one's empirical feelings would simply be to become ever more attentive to promoting personal pleasure, regardless of how the pleasure

335

is produced, whether any appreciative or cognitive faculties are engaged, and whatever the nature of the cause of the pleasure. Pleasure and affect are in this sense "blind" for Kant (CJ 272), since "if our sole aim were enjoyment, it would be foolish to be scrupulous about the means of getting it" (CJ 208). An Oriental massage in which the joints and muscles are agreeably "squeezed and bent" would be lumped together with a stirring Greek tragedy (CJ 274).

In aesthetics, we must focus not on which phenomena produce the greatest or most intense pleasure, but rather on the "presentation" of objects to the senses: we must be able to see the object "as poets do," and "must base our judgment regarding it merely on how we see it" (CJ 270), that is, on the genuinely beauty-making characteristics. Self-oriented and pleasure seeking, our empirical sentiments are careless as to modality. Kant thus foretold the fate that awaited aesthetics in the hands of that redoubtably thorough going proponent of egoistic hedonism, Bentham: the only ground of discrimination would be *quantity*, the "mass of agreeable sensation" (CJ 266) – and pushpin (or Oriental massage) would indeed be deemed as good as poetry.

Moreover, Kant joined Hume in insisting that aesthetic judgments purport to be "non-personal" and communicable to others – in the sense not only of *informing* others concerning what we like, but of *recommending*, where each of us purports to have potential authority for others. "But," Kant argues,

if we suppose that our liking for the object consists merely in the object's gratifying us through charm or emotion, then we also must not require anyone *else* to assent to an aesthetic judgment *we* make; for that sort of liking each person rightly consults only his private sense (CJ 278).

For similar reasons, Kant insists that in order to ensure that our account is "concerned solely with aesthetic judgments," "we must not take for our examples such beautiful or sublime objects of nature as presuppose the concept of a purpose" (CJ 269–70). To the extent that the force of an example can be attributed to purpose (e.g., self-interest), the judgment will not be aesthetically attuned – we might substitute for the object of appreciation anything that would bring about the sought-after result equally well.

... the purposiveness would be either teleological, and hence not aesthetic, or else be based on mere sensations of an object (gratification or pain) and hence not merely formal (CJ 270).

Therefore:

It seems, then, that we must not regard a judgment of taste as *egoistic*... we must acknowledge it to be a judgment that is entitled to a claim that everyone else ought also to agree with it. But if that is so, then it must be based on some a priori principle (whether objective or subjective).... [J]udgments of taste presuppose such a command, because they insist that our liking be connected *directly* with a presentation (CJ 278).

If our judgment is to be attuned to the sources of aesthetic value by a "liking" that is "connected *directly* with a presentation," but empirical likings cannot do this, where then is taste's infrastructure, where to turn for regulation of our feeling of appreciation – for Kant insists that appreciation, even of the beautiful and the good, is a *liking*, a feeling (CJ 210)?

Kant looks to reason. The seeming peculiarity of Kant's aesthetic, that it sees aesthetic judgments as "demands of reason," can be understood in this light. But we must be careful, for such demands of reason are *not* demands based upon argument, rule, or conceptual demonstration:

... the beautiful must not be estimated according to concepts, but by the final mode in which the imagination is attuned so as to accord with the faculty of concepts generally; and so rule and precept are incapable of serving as the requisite subjective standard for that aesthetic and unconditioned finality in fine art which has to make a warranted claim to being bound to please. Rather must such a standard be sought in the element of mere nature of the Subject, which cannot be comprehended under rules or concepts, that is to say, the supersensible substrate of all the Subject's faculties (unattainable by any concept of understanding) ... (CJm 344).

Here, then, we have Kant's version of the subjective attunement that affords reliable guidance concerning the beauty-making features of the world: the pleasure afforded by activity on the part of the self's supersensible substrate, when directly engaging the sensory "presentation" of the object. This substrate, shared as it is by all rational humanity, helps supply the needed infrastructure for a domain of objective taste. Now an invocation of a supersensible substrate may sound like hocus-pocus, but Kant deserves credit for refusing to be false to the non-personal compellingness of the experience of aesthetic appreciation, in order to satisfy an allegedly scientific egoistic, hedonist psychology. Not hiding its "unfathomableness," Kant gives the best explanation he can: only the rational self has the requisite formal, disinterested, "non-personal," and universal character to be the source of such a pleasure.

But Kant's rational self is not simply a *reasoning* self. Beauty is a "way of presenting" that requires concepts, yet Kant recognizes that aesthetic appreciation is not simply a matter of being "brought to concepts" (CJ 266). If we were nothing but "pure intelligences," "we would not present in this way" and could not see beauty (CJ 270). Nor is the rational self the whole infrastructure. According to Kant, beauty "holds" – presumably, is capable of "norming" judgment through feelings of appreciation and the practice of taste – only for "beings who are animal and yet rational, though it is not enough that they be rational" (CJ 210).[13]

Despite the indispensable role of reason, then, in attuning us to the beautiful, the normative force of judgments of beauty, even for a rationalist aesthetic such as Kant's, is not the force of argument. We therefore cannot expect that we could *reconstruct* aesthetic justification in propositional terms. As in the case of *de se* attitudes, an attitude (in this case, aesthetic appreciation) may stand in a justified relationship to its proper object even though this relationship is not mirrored in an argumentative relationship among propositions.

In appreciation we find the right mix of force and freedom for normative guidance. On the one hand, "the liking involved in our taste for the beautiful is disinterested and *free*" (CJ 210). On the other hand, we all know the *compelling* character of aesthetic appreciation and good criticism: we find in our first-personal experience of the object, as informed by the contributions of the critic, something both likeable and convincing. "Ah, *now* I see it," we think, thereby feeling the force of aesthetic authority: a force of credible influence from the critic ("He helped me see it"), of convincing experience from our own case ("Now I get it"), of a compelling work ("There was a lot more in it than I thought"), and of a discovery of value that we can share with others ("You must try this" or "You must read his essay, it'll change how you look at Miró").

Wittgenstein, in his "Lectures on Aesthetics," gives as his model of aesthetic appreciation an example of this process, drawn from his own case:[14]

Take the question: "How should poetry be read? What is the correct way of reading it?" ... I had an experience with the 18th-century poet Klopstock. I found that the way to read him was to stress his metre abnormally. Klopstock put ∪–∪ (etc.) in front of his poems. When I read his poems in this new way, I said, "Ah-ha, now I know why he did this." What had happened? I had read this kind of stuff before and had been moderately bored, but when I read it in this particular way, intensely, I smiled, said "This is *grand*," etc. But I might not have said anything. The important fact is that I read it again and again ... that I read the poems entirely differently, more intensely, and said to others: "Look! This is how they should be read" (LA 4–5).

Kant and Hume agree with Wittgenstein that, underlying aesthetic evaluation, there must be some form of "liking" or "enjoyment." Moreover, the liking in question must be sensorily based, cognitively engaging, discerning, disinterested, and *communicable*. If Hume is right, our essentially similar "internal fabric" – our empirical psychology and sentiments – can afford much of the ground for such a liking, since many of our appetites and passions take external conditions or sensory "forms or qualities" as their immediate objects and are disinterested in character, even though satisfying them will also yield pleasure. Thanks to additional qualification of feeling by the influence of reason, understanding, and the commerce of opinion, we can develop on this psychological "common ground" a domain of discernment and knowledge, where we can recognize and possess authority, and 'beauty' can have its true meaning – apart from fashionableness, novelty, endearing schlock, ponderous "importance," snobbish overrefinement, and so on. In Hume's account, as in Kant's, what possesses ultimate aesthetic authority is a *qualified appreciative attitude* and not a mere liking. In Hume's account, as in Kant's, much of the qualification of attitude is supplied by reason. And in Hume's account, as in Kant's, it seems we could not reconstruct aesthetic justification in terms of the force of argument.[15]

## THE NORMATIVE AUTHORITY OF MORAL RULES

Perhaps no one is really tempted by the idea that the normative force of aesthetic appreciation rests upon argument. But things might be different in the moral case, where the supremacy of reasoning and rules is often invoked. Perhaps in morality at least we will find it possible to account for normative force in terms of the force of argument.

Let us set aside for now a very general worry about this line of thought, briefly touched on in the introduction: any appeal to rules as a foundation for justification runs the risk of regress or circularity unless we can appeal to a super-rule of a mysterious kind. For now let us cheerfully assume that we don't mind mystery, as long as its name is *rationality*.

Kant's moral philosophy is often taken to be the *locus classicus* for the idea that normativity resides in rationality itself, and the moral law it prescribes. Perhaps this is indeed how we should understand his view: there is a super-rule, and it commands our obedience as a rational obligation. But is it obvious that this is how *he* understands his own most basic approach to normativity? We are told to have respect (*reverentia*) for the moral law, but Kant observes:

Respect (*reverentia*) is, again, something subjective, a feeling of a special kind, not a judgment about an object that it would be a duty to bring about or promote. For, such a duty, regarded as a duty, could be represented to us only through the *respect* we have for it. A duty to have respect would thus amount to being put under obligation to duties ... (MM 402–3).

So it seems we must look for "a feeling of a special kind," not obligation, at the bottom of moral duty. What is this feeling like? Here is an example of the sort of reverential appreciative feeling Kant appears to have in mind:

... to a humble, plain man, in whom I perceive righteousness in a higher degree than I am conscious of in myself, *my mind bows* whether I choose or not, however high I carry my head that he may not forget my superior position. ... Respect is a tribute we cannot refuse to pay to merit whether we will or not; we can indeed outwardly withhold it, but we cannot help feeling it inwardly (CPrR 76–7; compare G 454).

What we perceive in this individual is not simply more severe dutifulness than our own. We are all familiar with individuals who turn sensible everyday rules into severe duties that rise above all inclination, but our mind does not bow to that.[16] What we perceive, according to Kant, is greater *righteousness*, dutifulness that "includes" a good will (G 397).

In our appreciative encounter with it, we once again encounter the mixture of force and freedom characteristic of normative force. On the one hand, the respect is "freely paid" – for Kant, nothing in our experience suggests that any self-interested incentive or external coercion lies behind our appreciation. On the other hand, the respect is in a way compelled, it is something "we cannot help feeling," even when it comes in the face of interest. Kant writes:

*Duty*! Thou sublime and mighty name that dost embrace nothing charming or insinuating but requirest submission and yet seekest not to move the will by threatening aught that would arouse natural aversion or terror which of itself finds entrance into the mind and yet gains reluctant reverence ... (CPrR 86).

Now this impressive paean might suggest an *intrinsic* evaluation of duty. But, as Paul Guyer reminds us,[17] Kant continues, still addressing "Duty":

... what origin is there worthy of thee, and where is to be found the root of thy noble descent which proudly rejects all kinship with the inclinations and from which to be descended is the indispensable condition of the only worth which men can give themselves?

It cannot be less than something which elevates man above himself as a part of the world of sense, something which connects him with an order of things which only the understanding can think and which has under it the whole system of all ends which alone is suitable to such unconditional practical laws as the moral (CPrR 86–7).

Notice that the practical laws of morality, and even duty itself, are not self-subsistent sources of unconditional worth – their worth arises from their "descent," which does secure the noble standing of morality.[18]

At the bottom of morality's normative authority, then, Kant speaks not of an analytic demand of consistency nor a willful exercise of our capacity to govern ourselves by rules, but of the experience of a synthetic demand and a free acknowledgment, the subjective expression of which is a feeling more aesthetic in character, akin to the demand upon us that the appreciation for the sublime in nature involves:

It is in fact difficult to think of a feeling for the sublime in nature without connecting it with a mental attunement similar to that for moral feeling (CJ 128).

For Kant, as we saw in the aesthetic case, human inclination and appetite cannot attune us to *this* sort of demand, because they are by nature self-interested ("*solipsismus*," CPrR 73) rather than non-personal and disinterested, and thus "human nature does not of itself harmonize with the good" (CJ 271). Kant therefore must find a faculty internal to us, capable of evincing or guiding a special sort of liking, a "moral feeling," that is attuned to the moral-value–making features of the world, the sources of moral *worth*. We can, he writes, be attuned to the good "only through the dominance that reason exerts over sensibility" (CJ 271). So, as in aesthetics, to underwrite a rational demand as grounded in the right sort of attunement, we must have recourse to a "supersensible substrate," a noumenal self. Moral judgments are akin to aesthetic judgments of sublimity – judgments of beauty draw in part upon our "animal" nature; for the moral and the sublime, reason alone, the "supersensible substrate," suffices.

Now for Hume, the "substrate" for moral and aesthetic judgment can be our empirical psychology, since it contains sentiments of a suitably "impersonal" and non-self-interested nature. For example,

We are certain, that sympathy is a very powerful principle in human nature. We are also certain, that it has a great influence on the sense of beauty, when we regard external objects, as well as when we judge of morals. We find, that it has force sufficient to give us the strongest sentiments of approbation ... (T 618).[19]

Thanks to sympathy, among other sentiments, our sentiment of direct approval can be attuned to the ends of others as such, and to the general interest, even when we have no personal interest at stake: reading ancient history, we wince at a tyrant's cruelty, and root for the hero to save the populace from him. And much aesthetic judgment, likewise, depends upon a capacity to feel the feelings of others. If well-developed, well-informed, and attentively listened to, such "impersonal" sentiments can attune us to – "harmonize" us with – the good and the beautiful.

We may observe, that all the circumstances requisite for [sympathy's] operation are found in most of the virtues; which have, for the most part, a tendency to the good of society, or to that of the person possess'd of them (T 618).

Sympathy can of course be misled, and may lead us astray. It may fail to be engaged in unfamiliar or misunderstood surroundings. Or it may immediately attune us to the evident pain of an animal undergoing an emergency veterinary procedure, making us wish fervently that the procedure would stop, even though this operation is necessary for the animal's survival. Sympathy – like aesthetic admiration – therefore must be assisted and qualified by knowledge, understanding of cause and effect, and reason. Sympathy needs attunement by participation in social relations in which our personal responses and judgments can be developed, challenged, and improved. This can occur if we are disposed to defer to some degree to the responses and judgments of others, and to social practices hammered into shape over generations. Thus – once again, as in the aesthetic case – our feelings can develop greater freedom from prejudice, finer discrimination, and closer attunement to genuine moral distinctions.

By contrast Kant, as an egoistic hedonist in psychology but a universal humanist in morality, could no more entrust moral attunement to "solipsistic" empirical sentiment (cf. CPrR 73) than he could aesthetic attunement.[20] And thus we arrive at Kant's answer to the question why nature attached reason to will (which is, for Kant, also a *liking*; CJ 209): without the "substrate" of reason to ground impersonal feelings, we would arrive only at a personalistic willfulness, not a good (i.e., general) will. Hume gave us a story as to how the empirical, psychological "substrate" we share as humans generates likings that can be attuned to beauty and the general good. What mechanism does Kant give to explain how a "supersensible substrate" can function similarly? Here Kant is, as befits his penetration as a philosopher, entirely frank: he has no positive idea – the matter involves an "unfathomable depth of [a] supersensible power" (CJ 270; cf. G 462–3).

Note, however, that Kant is also clear that reason cannot operate here by argument alone:

... when in intuiting nature we expand our empirical power of presentation (mathematically or dynamically [a "might over the mind"]), then reason, the ability to [think] an independent and absolute totality, never fails to step in and arouse the mind to an effort, although a futile one.... [W]e are compelled to subjectively *think* nature itself in its totality as the exhibition of something supersensible, without our being able to bring this exhibition about *objectively*.

...We cannot determine this idea of the supersensible any further, and hence cannot *cognize* but can only *think* nature as an exhibition of it.... This judging strains the imagination because it is based on a feeling that the mind has a vocation that wholly transcends the domain of nature (namely, moral feeling), and it is with regard to this feeling that we judge the presentation of the object subjectively purposive [CJ 268].

Our mind, in its "supersensible vocation," is here functioning in a way Hume would have recognized despite the heavily Kantian language: feeling and imagination are regulating judgment, beyond the scope of cognition and argument alone. Within this scheme, as within Hume's, we may *use* arguments to help us attain or correct a moral feeling or sentiment. For Kant, the "contradiction in conception" and "contradiction in will" tests of our practical maxims can place a purportedly good will face-to-face with its potential own limitations, deflating or affirming its self-representation as perfectly general. For Hume, understanding and general rules help to extend or correct untutored sympathy.

If reason's functioning as a supersensible substrate for feeling remains for Kant something of which he cannot give a positive account, he nonetheless believes we can convince ourselves of its possibility: we know from firsthand experience the "striking down" of our pretenses and humiliating acknowledgment of our own limitations, and we also know that reason alone among our faculties possesses the qualities necessary for such experience – it alone can furnish guidance that is impersonal. There is no mystery about this when we confront the sublime in nature or morality. The peculiar awe we experience when we come upon "a mountain whose snow-covered peak rises above the clouds" (OBS 47) or when we observe an act of genuine duty performed in spite of conditions of extreme "subjective limitation," has extraordinary power to move us, yet cannot be attributed to empirical sentiment. We find our own self-conceit "humiliated" or "struck down" (CPrR 73) in the presence of the sublime. Fortunately, we are not merely flattened. Instead, we are awakened to a value "beyond price," carried beyond ourselves for the moment to sense a "direct liking," a liking even of that which strikes at the very heart of our own prideful self-interest. Thus it recruits our fundamental allegiance, despite any personal interest to the contrary.

To behold virtue in her proper shape is nothing other than to show morality stripped of all admixture with the sensuous and of all the spurious adornments of reward or self-love. How much she then casts into the shade all else that appears attractive to the inclinations can be readily perceived by every man if he will exert his reason in the slightest . . . (G 61–62n).

No wonder such a "presentation" moves us, and yields not the "cold and lifeless approval, without any moving force or emotion" (CJ 273, 274) that we would otherwise expect from any merely un-self-interested presentation. Confronted with the sublime, we are not tempted to think, "Yeah, but what's it to *me*?" No wonder such a "presentation" is regulative for our wills when we are rational, that is, attuned thanks to our "supersensible substrate."

This has an important implication for our normative life together: since it owes nothing to personal interest, our sense of the sublime in nature and in conduct should be "subjectively" confirmable by other rational beings in their own experience. Others, too, Kant is confident, will stand in awe before the Alps during a storm or find that their mind bows when observing a humble person doing his duty in the face of great temptation. Our moral understanding, like our aesthetic understanding, will be communicable to others in the form of a recommendation, and it will afford a compelling ground for life together that conflicting individual interests do not. The compulsion here is not at bottom that of will, or law, or rule, or consistency. Instead, it is a kind of liking that is free but not simply chosen, and that is regulative for action. It is, then, *our* attitude when we are "mentally attuned" by reason, and no mere submission – even though we precisely recognize that it is not simply up to us what we make of it. This is the experience of normative authority.

## THE RULE-BREAKING CONSIDERATIONS

Duty belongs to a family of rule- or consistency-based notions. And indeed we typically assume that morally good conduct will follow rules and exhibit consistency. But if Kant is right, then behind these rules – exceptionless, in his system – lies something quite different: a kind of direct liking akin to the experience of the sublime. We do not have rules "all the way down," but must instead encounter a substantive appreciation of value and associated feelings.

Hume was acutely aware of the potential this affords for conflict. If following "the rules of reason" led always to conclusions that substantive evaluation and feeling also embraced, we'd have no difficulty. But at least in epistemology, Hume finds that following the strictest epistemic duties, to accord epistemic respect ("rational credence," we might say) only to conclusions justifiable by reason alone, leads him to an epistemic condition that he cannot find stably credible or genuinely compelling in the guidance of his overall epistemic life. Might the same be true in the moral case?

Consider Kant's discussion of obedience to a tyrannical ruler.

... a people has a duty to put up with even what is held to be an unbearable abuse of supreme authority [since] its resistance to the highest legislation can never be regarded as other than contrary to law. . . . For a people to be authorized to resist, there would have to be a public law permitting it to resist, that is, the highest legislation would have to contain a provision that is not the highest and that makes the people, as subject, by one and the same judgment sovereign over him to whom it is subject. This is self-contradictory . . . (MM 320).[21]

Here Kant appeals to a consideration of consistency to ground a claim of duty. And he has an excellent point, emphasized earlier and in a characteristically different way by Hobbes: a sovereign can benefit us by solving the problem of potentially unending social conflict only if our agreement to obey does not contain a clause reserving to each the right to decide on his own authority when to obey.

Hume, likewise, is aware that "the *advantage* we reap from government" will be imperiled if each allows himself to regulate his own obedience in accord with his own ideas of what is just or beneficial. The result could only be "endless confusion, and render all government, in a great measure, ineffectual" (T 555). "We must, therefore, proceed by general rules and regulate ourselves by general interests" (T 555). But how is it possible for advantage-based duty to take on a life of its own?

... there is a principle of human nature, which we have frequently taken notice of, that men are mightily addicted to *general rules*, and that we often carry our maxims beyond those reasons, which first adduc'd us to establish them. . . . It may, therefore, be thought, that in the case of allegiance our moral obligation of duty will not cease, even tho' the natural obligation of interest, which is its cause, has ceas'd . . . (T 551).

Hume, political conservative that he was, has here a golden opportunity to embrace a Kant-like principle of passive obedience, and even continues

"It may be thought that . . . men may be bound by *conscience* to submit to a tyrannical government" (T 551). But he shrinks from this conclusion:

Those who took up arms against *Dionysus* or *Nero*, or *Philip the second*, have the favour of every reader in the perusal of their history; and nothing but the most violent perversion of common sense can ever lead us to condemn them. 'Tis certain, therefore, that in all our notions of morals we never entertain such an absurdity as that of passive obedience, but make allowances for resistance in the more flagrant instances of tyranny and oppression (T 552).

How, then, does Hume block the unwanted conclusion of passive obedience? What general rule or practical maxim does he formulate for the citizen to follow to replace the rule of passive obedience? He offers none, only a general suggestion that "the obligation to obedience must cease" when it sufficiently loses its point, that is, "whenever the [common] interest ceases, in any great degree, and in a considerable number of instances" (T 553).

How is this to work? "The common rule requires submission," but "grievous tyranny and oppression" allows individuals to make "exceptions" (T 554). Here we have a discontinuous change, a departure from our conscientious dispositions to obey which "bind us down," as we rise up in active resistance to government. It looks as if the chief mechanism that awakens us from our "addiction" to general rules is a sympathetic sense of the violation of the general interest. Indeed, sympathy is strong enough that, however much we dislike mayhem and disorder, our approval is excited by rebellions against tyranny of which we hear only in histories or fiction. A morality that would put a people at the mercy of its rulers will not win our wholehearted admiration or esteem. Here we follow no maxim or rule, but a developed sentiment.

It is important to see, however, that the sentiment *is* developed. Self-love and sympathy alone do not yield any comprehension of when a complex political system is abusive or when such abuses have become too considerable. Justly and unjustly inflicted punishment alike look and feel painful; just and unjust war alike are costly and terrifying. An attunement to the general interest calls for complex awareness of cause and effect, and of long- versus short-term, as well as sympathy for victims. Nonetheless, Hume's account is, in the Kantian sense, heteronomous, since it gives sentiments an essential role, and moreover it yields no strict maxim that individuals could legislate for themselves.[22]

But, stepping back from a model of autonomy as maxim-based self-legislation, if we reflect upon Hume's position on passive obedience versus Kant's, which of the two, in fact, seems to provide greater practical or political autonomy? Which affords us, as citizens or as moral agents, greater scope to deploy and act on the full range of our human critical faculties?

Suppose Kant were to abandon his egoistic hedonism about human psychology and accept instead the Humean view that sentiments can help attune us to be attuned to legitimate grounds for moral, aesthetic, or epistemic evaluation. Would he still insist that our only hope for genuinely moral, aesthetic, or epistemic conduct – or autonomy – lies in imposing over sentiment a regime of exceptionless rules?

Of course, I cannot answer on Kant's behalf, but I can attempt this: apply Kant's own test of *fundamental* normative authority, and see where it might lead. How is this possible? Kant's test, recall, involves a special sort of first-personal confirmation: when (for example) we confront the humble man who insists on being honest despite personal costs that we realize would likely overwhelm us, "the mind bows"; when we attend perceptually to sublime scenes in nature, we cannot help but be awed.

Return now to the tyrannical ruler and the obedient citizenry, who accept without resistance all forms of abuse and humiliation. Does "ordinary reason" (G 394) find passive obedience to tyranny sublime – does the mind indeed bow?

I'm willing to bet with Hume that in this case it does not. Impressive as the spectacle may be of passive obedience in the face of great abuse, and powerful as the will must be to restrain an individual feeling the tugs of inclination to strike back at the tyrant, does our mind really bow before this sight? Suppose that the peculiar abuse by government is an order to inform on our friends, to reveal their location to an authority whose plan is to eliminate or torture dissidents or religious minorities. It seems, perhaps, that we know Kant's answer: obey authority; never lie, even to conceal a friend (cf. SRL). And this is the sort of example that has often enough been used by critics of Kant as a *reductio* of his conception of the ground of morality.

But Kant deserves better treatment. Those of us who find in Kant's writings a deep insight into the authority of moral experience should not betray this insight by allowing critics to focus instead on his attempts to apply a multi-layered theory in practice, mediated by a defective empirical psychology. His application may go wrong in cases like "passive obedience," but the fundamentals may yet be sound.

At the fundamental level, I suspect, our mind simply does not bow at the spectacle of the citizen who, despite strong ties of family and friendship, reveals their location to a tyrannical authority. Such an act of will may be monumental, but it is not majestic, and even seems to us peculiarly self-contained or blind. Can we attribute this response on our part to self-interest? No, the response seems to be the same even when we consider a case from history or fiction. Is it then merely an unconsidered reflex? No, Hume is right that our initial reaction to disobedience is usually discomfort. But we reflect further. The deep normative distress we feel when Germany's greatest moral philosopher defends the unalterable necessity of obedience to the state, and the exceptionless duty never to lie to conceal the location of a friend, is an impersonal and historical shudder. It arises from the full range of Humean faculties, developed through experience: reason, imagination, sense, sympathy, memory, and a feeling for one's place in history.

How different our reaction when we learn that Kant failed on one notable occasion to keep to his habit of regular afternoon walks – the afternoon he received Rousseau's *Emile*, and would not put it down. We might be less impressed by the iron will of Kant upon hearing this story, but we are more impressed by the man and his mind.

Let us conclude with a thought experiment using Kant's own division of the "three different relations that presentations have to the feeling of pleasure," namely, the *agreeable*, the *beautiful*, and the *good*, to understand our reactions and their normative force (CJ 210).

Suppose we had learned that Kant missed his afternoon walk only once, but not to read *Emile* – rather, to avoid a pesky visitor to town whom he knew to be lurking in wait for him with an embarrassing question he preferred not to answer. As a result we might like Kant better – he would be more amiable for showing this human tendency to indulge a desire to avoid an uncomfortable truth. But our self-conceit would not be struck down by this realization – instead, we would find it gratifying to our sense of ourselves that even Kant could be self-indulgent when it comes to allowing oneself to sidestep an awkward truth. This we would find *agreeable*, but not in an altogether admiring way. Especially, the critic who finds Kantian moral rigorism excessive would smile inwardly, with perhaps a touch of condescension.

Suppose instead we had learned that he missed his afternoon walk on that one occasion in order to avoid spoiling the end of lovely afternoon tea with a visitor whom Kant rarely saw but personally admired. Then we would like the act, and also Kant, yet better. Moreover, we would like him and his act impersonally as well as personally – for someone to break from routine or personal resolution for such a reason shows a kind of gracefulness or *beauty* of gesture. Even those Kantian critics who find it gratifying to view him as a cold, "clockwork" Prussian would be taken a bit aback, and find a bit of appreciation of Kant creeping in.

But when we learn that in fact Kant missed his afternoon walk but once, in order to continue reading Rousseau's *Emile* – Rousseau! whose unruly mind, scandalous conduct, and colorfully inconsistent prose contrast so sharply with Kant's, but whose insights we know nonetheless reached to the core of Kant's thinking – we like this because it possesses something of the sublime. And we like Kant better, impersonally as well as personally, for showing in a concrete but dramatically appropriate way just how attuned he was to the insights that awaited him in Rousseau, how capable he was of being displaced from the ruts the mind is wont to settle into. We here find in both Kant and his mind something *good*, something estimable in its own right. That afternoon's display of "mental attunement" is much more impressive than would be the strength of will, consistency, or resistance to inclination that Kant would have exhibited had he instead overcome the desire to continue reading *Emile* and maintained above all a resolve to take an afternoon walk each day, exactly at the same time. Thus does Kant's omission strike a bit at the self-conceit of critics who might attempt to look upon him with intellectual condescension as hermetic, narrowly moralistic, trapped within his own technical language and scheme of categories. For when we appreciate this story, we cannot help but feel, freely, a kind of admiration for Kant as an intellect. And thus does the experience of normativity combine force and freedom.[23]

NOTES

*Ratio (new series)*, XII, No. 4 (December 1999).

1. Moreover, we have an equally concrete way of illustrating part of what Kant had in mind in insisting that the normative is *a priori*. A *norma* (or *regulus*) has its form "before the fact," giving the builder a "standard of correctness" for the cut, but not staking a claim as to how the cut will in fact be made. His subsequent cutting performance is "guided" but not "predicted" by it, so actual failure on his part to conform to the *norma* does not impugn or discredit the *norma a posteriori*. For further discussion of these examples, and their relation to the *a priori* status of norms and rules, see P. Railton, "*A Priori* Rules: Wittgenstein on the Normativity of Logic," in Paul Boghossian and Christopher Peacocke, eds., *New Essays on the* A Priori (Oxford: Clarendon, 2000).

2. Herein I will use the following abbreviations in citing work of Immanuel Kant: CJ = *Critique of Judgment*, Werner S. Pluhar, trans. (Indianapolis: Hackett, 1987); CJm = *Critique of Judgment*, James Creed Meredith, trans. (Oxford: Clarendon,

1952); CPrR = *Critique of Practical Reason*, Lewis White Beck, trans. (Indianapolis: Bobbs-Merrill, 1956); CPrRm = *Critique of Practical Reason*, Mary Gregor, trans. (Cambridge: Cambridge University Press, 1996); G = *Groundwork of the Metaphysics of Morals*, H. J. Paton, trans., 3rd ed. (New York: Harper & Row, 1956); LoE = *Lectures on Ethics*, P. Heath and J. B. Schneewind, eds., P. Heath, trans. (Cambridge: Cambridge University Press, 1997); MM = *Metaphysics of Morals*, Mary Gregor, ed. and trans. (Cambridge: Cambridge University Press, 1996); OBS = *Observations on the Feeling of the Beautiful and Sublime*, John T. Goldthwait, trans. (Berkeley: University of California Press, 1960); SRL = "On a Supposed Right to Lie from Philanthropy," in *Immanuel Kant: Practical Philosophy*, Mary J. Gregor, trans. (Cambridge: Cambridge University Press, 1996). All page numbers are to the Academy edition; Academy volume numbers are given only for the *Lectures on Ethics*.

3. Jean-Jacques Rousseau, *The Social Contract*, Maurice Cranston, trans. (Baltimore: Penguin, 1968), bk. I, ch. 3, p. 53.

4. Perhaps *judgments* concerning these attitudes are more directly within the scope of will, but it is one thing to form a belief or feel an emotion, and another to form a judgment of it. Although our judgment is supposed to guide our belief, our beliefs might in fact prove recalcitrant. Thus we say: judgment is *normative for* attitudes like belief or feelings like appreciation. For a seminal discussion of evaluation as normative for attitudes, see Elizabeth Anderson, *Value in Ethics and Economics* (Cambridge: Harvard University Press, 1993) ch. 2.

5. I am grateful to Peter Vranas for bringing to my attention this discussion in Kant of *reverentia* vs. *observantia*.

6. For discussion, see David Velleman, "The Guise of the Good," *Noûs* 26 (1992), 3–26, and "On the Possibility of Practical Reason," *Ethics* 106 (1996), 694–726; also, P. Railton, "On the Hypothetical and Non-Hypothetical in Reasoning about Belief and Action," in G. Cullity and B. Gaut, eds., *Ethics and Practical Reason* (Oxford: Clarendon, 1997). Reprinted here as Chapter 10.

7. See David Lewis, "Attitudes *De Dicto* and *De Se*," in his *Philosophical Papers*, vol. I (New York: Oxford University Press, 1983).

8. There is some experimental evidence in the literature on autism that autistic individuals may experience deficits in developing a feeling for the self, much as individuals can experience color deficits in ordinary perception. Autistic individuals, for example, experience difficulty with first- versus third-person asymmetries in so-called "false belief tasks," and are known to lose track of first- and second-personal pronouns in conversations, as in the phenomenon of "echo-locution." After reviewing a description of a cognitively very high-functioning autistic individual, Temple Grandin, who herself professes finding ordinary social language and exchange baffling, but technical or scientific language much clearer, Simon Baron-Cohen writes:

And her own explanation . . . ? "She surmises that her mind is lacking in some of the 'subjectivity,' the inwardness, that others seem to have.
From *Mindblindness* (Cambridge: MIT Press, 1995) 142–3.

9. Here are the abbreviations used in the text for Hume's writings: Inq = *Inquiry Concerning the Principles of Morals*, C. W. Hendel, ed. (Indianapolis: Bobbs-Merrill,

1957); T = *Treatise of Human Nature*, L. A. Selby-Bigge, ed. (Oxford: Oxford University Press, 1888); ST = "Of the Standard of Taste," in *Of the Standard of Taste and Other Essays by David Hume*, John W. Lenz, ed. (Indianapolis: Bobbs-Merrill, 1965).

10. See David Fate Norton, "Introduction to Hume's Thought," in his edited collection, *The Cambridge Companion to Hume* (Cambridge: Cambridge University Press, 1993) 27.

11. A common standard of time and shared conventions about when to arrive for (say) a noon engagement make it possible for me to be *on time*, but also *late*. In the case of good – and bad – taste, something more than this conventional infrastructure is required, for example, Hume's account of *beauties* to be attuned to.

12. We can see an analogy with the case of theoretical reason. If we thought that all *inclination to believe* was essentially self-regarding (*solipsismus*), and attuned to gratification rather than objective conditions, truth, or evidence, then we would find genuine "epistemic worth" only in a dutiful capacity to resist epistemic inclination and regulate belief by epistemic principle alone. This would not make "epistemic dutifulness" into the "highest end" of epistemic activity – that would remain the marriage of justified belief with truth that constitutes knowledge – but into an indispensable condition of it.

13. According to Kant, an appreciation of the *sublime* also depends upon a "way of presenting," and so is not available to a pure intelligence (CJ 270). However, he also believes that our capacity to appreciate the sublime does not depend upon our animal nature. More on the sublime in the following text.

14. Ludwig Wittgenstein, "Lectures on Aesthetics," in Cyrill Barrett, ed., *L. Wittgenstein: Lectures and Conversations* (Berkeley: University of California Press, 1966). Hereinafter, LA.

15. For further discussion of Hume's aesthetic theory, see P. Railton, "Aesthetic Value, Moral Value, and the Ambitions of Naturalism," in Jerrold Levinson, ed., *Aesthetics and Ethics* (Cambridge: Cambridge University Press, 1997). Reprinted here as Chapter 4.

16. For a description of dutifulness of this kind, see David Schapiro, *Autonomy and Rigid Character* (New York: Basic Books, 1981) 83–6.

17. See Paul Guyer, "Kant's Morality of Law and Morality of Freedom," in R. M. Dancy, ed., *Kant and Critique* (Dordrecht: Kluwer, 1993) 70.

18. Guyer emphasizes the consistency with which Kant, over the course of his philosophical career, recognized that all evaluation presupposes some values-in-their-own-right. The value Guyer identifies is the special *freedom* Kant attributes to human agents. See his "Kant's Morality of Law and Morality of Freedom."

19. A more contemporary psychological account would notice that Hume's sympathy involves two elements: empathy (a direct internal simulation of the circumstances and mental states of others) and sympathy (a direct positive concern for their well-being).

20. Contemporary empirical psychology on emotion, motivation, and moral development tends to favor a more Humean view. See for example, J. H. Barkow, L. Cosmides, and J. Tooby, eds., *The Adapted Mind* (New York: Oxford University Press, 1992); Baron-Cohen, *Mindblindness*; Antonio Damasio, *Descartes' Error* (New York: Putnam, 1994); N. Eisenberg and J. Strayer, eds., *Empathy and Its*

351

*Development* (Cambridge: Cambridge University Press, 1987); N. Eisenberg and P. Mussen, eds., *The Roots of Prosocial Behavior in Children* (Cambridge: Cambridge University Press, 1989); Joseph LeDoux, *The Emotional Brain* (New York: Simon & Schuster, 1996); L. May, M. Friedman, and A. Clark, eds., *Mind and Morals* (Cambridge: MIT Press, 1996); and David G. Myers, *The Pursuit of Happiness* (New York: William Morrow, 1992). Empathy has been credited in some historical cases with greater efficacy than principles in inhibiting compliance with cruelty commanded by authority. See Roy F. Baumeister, *Evil: Inside Human Violence and Cruelty* (New York: W.H. Freeman, 1997).

21. I am grateful to Tamar Schapiro for bringing this passage to my attention.

22. The difficulty of formulating a decision rule to be used by individuals here may be a difficulty *in principle*. Whether it makes sense for you to disobey a tyrant, for example, depends upon whether others will disobey, and their reasoning has a similar dependence upon yours. Problems such as this may admit of general criteria for evaluation (such as a standard of the general interest), but no decision rule or maxim that individuals can self-legislate that would satisfy those criteria. For discussion, see Donald Regan, *Utilitarianism and Cooperation* (Oxford: Clarendon, 1980). More generally, significant limitations of decidability and computability arise for any attempt to give individuals non-self-defeating maxims to guide their conduct in collective settings requiring coordination "autonomously" (in the literal sense – each following his or her own rule).

23. Many colleagues and friends have helped me in developing ideas contained in this essay. Special thanks are due to Elizabeth Anderson, Paul Boghossian, Nomy Arpaly, Stephen Darwall, Allan Gibbard, David Hills, Mark Johnston, David Lewis, Donald Regan, Gideon Rosen, Michael Smith, David Velleman, and Kendall Walton, all of whom have tried hard on a number of occasions to straighten out my thinking about normativity. I owe a particular debt to writings on normativity of Allan Gibbard and Christine Korsgaard, who have set out, from their own perspectives, much of the terrain I wander here. A long time ago, Nicholas Sturgeon made me realize I had to rethink Hume. And David Hills and Stephen Darwall deserve special thanks for patience in helping me to engage (insofar as I have!) with Kant's thought. Paul Guyer's writings and correspondence helped me find relevant passages in Kant. Jonathan Dancy gave me very useful comments on an earlier draft, and he and John Cottingham have been exceptionally considerate editors.

# 12

## Morality, Ideology, and Reflection; or, The Duck Sits Yet

I

Should we see morality as an ideology? And, if so, what are we to conclude?

Morality *does* make an almost irresistible target, a sitting duck, for *Ideologiekritik*. For it presents itself as a set of evaluations and commands of lofty impartiality or universal validity; yet a glance at history shows instead a succession of norms – all at one point or other widely viewed as moral – that have sanctioned slavery, the subjugation of women, and a host of other purported rights and duties that seem to us in retrospect to correspond more closely to the prevailing distribution of power, privilege, and interests than to conditions of absolute value or universal reason.

Nonetheless, we seem to have a soft spot for morality and moral theorizing. Professional philosophers and historians not excepted, we by and large continue to think of our own morality as something possessing considerable authority (with allowance for the usual slippage between what we practice and what we preach). This social and cultural deference has inspired some of our most incisive intellects – Marx and Nietzsche, to take an interesting pair – to critique morality mercilessly.

"The ideas of the ruling class are in every epoch the ruling ideas," Marx wrote, and are "nothing more than the 'ideal expression' of the dominant material relationships."[1] Every ruling class will "represent its interest as the common interest" and "give its ideas the form of universality, and represent them as the only rational, universally valid ones" (GI 65–6). As soon as Marx makes a distinction between "theoretical" and "philosophical" communists, we know which ones to take seriously on the subject of morality:

Theoretical communists, the only ones who have time to devote to the study of history, are distinguished precisely because they alone have *discovered* that through-out history the "general interest" is created by individuals who are defined as "private persons." They know that this contradiction is only a *seeming* one be-cause one side of it, the so-called "general," is constantly being produced by the other side, private interest . . . (GI 105).

Philosophical communists, by contrast,

innocently take on trust the illusion . . . that they are concerned with the "most reasonable" social order instead of the needs of a particular class and time. . . . With perfect consistency they transform the relations of these particular individuals into relations of "Man"; they interpret the thoughts of these particular individ-uals concerning their own relations as thoughts about "Man." In so doing, they have abandoned the realm of real history and returned to the realm of ideology (GI 104, 109).

Theoretical communists "do not preach *morality* at all" (GI 104).

Nietzsche, for his part, did not doubt that interests far from universal underlie existing morality, though he hardly thought of them as élite interests. In morality "high and independent spirituality, the will to stand alone, even a powerful reason are experienced as dangers; everything that elevates an individual above the herd and intimidates the neighbor is henceforth called *evil*; and the fair, modest, conforming mentality, the *mediocrity* of desires attains moral designations and honors."[2]

Many elements of the full critiques Marx and Nietzsche have lodged against morality are uncomfortably convincing. Even the seeming contra-dictions to be found between their accounts do not evidently disqualify the key insights of either, or both. Morality is not one phenomenon, homogeneous across time and place. What we experience every day as morality has diverse roots and a continuing dynamic; Marx and Nietzsche might well be credited with picking out contradictory elements within morality itself.[3]

Even shot full of holes, however, the duck sits yet. What are we to make of this situation? I will venture the suggestion that this situation is, in a sense, as it should be. But I do so with some awareness of the paradox this appears to involve. As Rousseau once said concerning humankind "living in chains," in his own characteristically paradoxical way: "How did this situation come about? That I will not say. What could make it legitimate? That I will."[4]

But why try to defend or legitimize morality's continued standing (or sitting)? Why not think it an unfortunate but predictable fact of life, like the continued standing of many popular conceptions – religious, pseudo-scientific, and so on – that flourish despite devastating critiques? Morality, it seems to me, is remarkable for the number of people who are *not* the sorts attracted to Old Time Religion or New Age Spirituality, but who tacitly or explicitly affirm it. Perhaps they know something?

II

Morality certainly does seem to possess many of the symptoms of an ideology. Indeed, these often become more acute the further we go up the scale of philosophizing about morality – even (perhaps especially?) when the philosophy in question calls itself 'critical philosophy.'

The man (or woman) in the street would almost certainly say "yes" if asked whether morality should be an important factor in life. Perhaps he'd simply be embarrassed to say anything else, but more likely he'd sincerely be of the opinion that he wants to see more rather than less of it in the world at large. But how many pedestrians would readily assent to the philosophical opinion that moral thought and action are *rationally mandatory*, and those who act against the requirements of morality are *ipso facto* irrational? Popular reification of morality may be rampant, but the question whether there might in a given situation be reasons that outweigh moral considerations seems hardly to be strictly *unintelligible* to the average person.

I, for one, was brought up in a very moralistic household, but without the intrusion of professional philosophy. In that household, it could be a source of pride that one would get one's head cracked for acting on a principle of justice. But you could have knocked me over with a feather when I first heard – in graduate school, as it turned out – that the very principles that seemed to require so costly a transformation of one's life to take fully to heart were actually requirements I would simply be *irrational* to evade or ignore. Either the world contains a surprising amount of irrationality even in its most sensible and successful corners, I thought, or morality must be a lot happier with the present state of the world than any morality worth its salt could be.

Perhaps, though, the very moralism of my household distorted my perspective by giving me too elevated a notion of what morality asks of us. How then can I pretend to speak from firsthand experience of morality in general? In asking about morality and ideology, it would

355

perhaps be better for us not to start off with anyone's full-fledged moral concepts or experiences, but to attempt instead to identify some relatively central and uncontroversial elements in moral discourse and practice. In doing this, we will focus largely on moral *discourse* and especially the moral discourse of philosophers. This is somewhat regrettable. However, it is the philosophers who have been most explicit about what they take morality to be. Moreover, they are (if anyone is) the intellectual cadres of secular ethics. If their moral conceptions can be seen as ideological, then we will have made a good start on the way to a general ideological critique.

III

In recent years the term *ideology* has once again acquired currency. Though it has always borne a range of senses, the range appears to be shifting in some ways that I certainly wish I better understood. For present purposes, a conception of ideology along fairly classical lines as laid out within the Marxist – or *marxisant* – tradition seems best able to express the concerns about morality I hope to explore. In any event, this conception continues to inform much contemporary discussion.

An ideology is in the first instance a set of beliefs or values held by individuals or groups,[5] not a set of propositions considered in itself. The same descriptive or evaluative proposition could be held for quite diverse reasons,[6] and this points us to a key element: whether a belief or value (as held by someone) is ideological will depend upon the nature of the explanation of why he or she has it.

A given set of descriptive or evaluative propositions as held by a certain individual or group might be more or less questionable, but it will count as ideological only if there is an explanation of these beliefs and other attitudes according to which their prevalence is attributed (to a significant degree) to the fact that holding them serves certain nonepistemic interests – especially, perhaps, interests in *legitimation*. The interests in question need not be the interests of all of those holding the beliefs. They may, for example, be the interests of the socially or culturally dominant class. An *ideological diagnosis* (as we might call it) of why certain attitudes are held typically involves showing that they serve a legitimizing function because they represent particular institutions, practices, or norms as good – or as obligatory, natural, universal, or necessary. Equally, they may represent alternative institutions, practices, or norms as bad – or as unnatural, impermissible, foreign, or, especially, impossible.

\* \* \*

Although this diagnostic notion of ideology is at root explanatory in ambition, it has a potential normative relevance that has been salient throughout its career. For example, to attribute the currency of a belief chiefly to *non*epistemic interests is hardly a form of epistemic endorsement. As Pascal's wager illustrated, it is evident that beliefs can satisfy various sorts of interests without being true or well warranted – indeed, in certain contexts true or well-warranted belief might be antithetical to an individual's or group's strongest interests.

Now it cannot be the whole of ideological critique to claim that there is a contrariety between a belief's functioning ideologically and the belief's truth or warrant. For there are many cases in which epistemic and nonepistemic interests point in the same direction: often our nonepistemic interests will be advanced more effectively by true belief or reliable belief-forming practices than by error or arbitrariness. A belief's truth or a belief-forming mechanism's reliability can be part of an explanation of why I get so much out of it, and it sometimes seems quite possible for me to "see through" a largely nonepistemic explanation of my belief to an epistemically vindicatory picture of why that nonepistemic story works.[7]

However, we also find cases in which the attempt to "see through" to the nonepistemic explanation is naturally destabilizing of belief. Suppose that, like most automobile drivers, I consider myself well above average (on a 0 to 10 scale, I have heard it said, drivers on average rate themselves about 7.5). This belief not only feeds my vanity and legitimizes my conduct – it also gives me the nerve to venture out on the roads, to trust my children to my hands, and so on. Let us suppose that I could be shown rather quickly that this belief of mine really stems almost entirely from these nonepistemic interests – for example, that I have been grossly selective in my attention to evidence and highly biased toward my own case in interpreting what evidence I do notice. Can I "see through" this nonepistemic explanation of my belief to an "epistemic explanation" that would provide reasonable warrant? No. Neither can I attribute the effectiveness of the belief in advancing my interests to its truth. (The main contribution of the belief is to enhance my mobility and confidence. Even as a below-average driver I may well benefit on the whole from this.) This sort of nonepistemic explanation invokes a mechanism that depends to some extent on its lack of transparency. The belief is therefore more likely to be destabilized than reinforced on reflection.[8]

This destabilization itself calls for a bit of explanation, lest it seem to be simply a psychological quirk without normative relevance. For example, certain beliefs might not survive two weeks of fasting and chanting, but that need not be relevant to their epistemic status. We need to have some picture of how destabilizing effected by an *accurate reflective awareness of the causal explanation of one's beliefs* could even be a candidate for special normative epistemic relevance.

Belief that *p*, as a propositional attitude distinct from pretending or supposing or merely accepting that *p*, is distinguished in part because it not only represents *p* as true, but it represents *itself* as an attitude responsive or accountable to *p*'s truth.[9] This representational claim need not be understood as a claim about a conscious mental act. It can be understood counterfactually: a believer that *p* who is confronted with contrary evidence will feel "cognitive pressure" either to weaken (qualify, hedge) that belief or to undermine or dismiss the evidence.[10] Reflective awareness that a belief of mine is to be explained ideologically tends by the nature of its content to exert this sort of pressure, even if the belief in question remains attractive to me.

We might note, for example, the special place in our mental economy for what we call 'belief *in*' – "Though I can see only too well that the reasons why I believe in God are not evidential, I will nonetheless continue to believe in God [or in my driving, or in my child's innocence, or in the possibility of universal brotherhood]." 'Belief in' often marks locations of a kind of *structural tension* or *incompatibility* within the domain of our beliefs. Not outright mutual exclusion – it is not *impossible* for us simultaneously to believe that *p* and believe that the explanation of this is ideological. Indeed, we seem quite capable of believing both that *p* and that not-*p*, so long as they aren't presented to us in the same way at the same time. But we are imagining a context of full, reflective awareness, and there the claim of incompatibility is more credible: to sustain genuine belief that *p* (rather than a hopeful 'belief in *p*') requires somehow undermining, supplementing, or detoxifying the nonvindicating explanation.

IV

Thus far we have been speaking primarily of belief in general. What, then, of *morality*?[11]

To begin, we need to re-emphasize that the interests a given ideology serves need not be interests of all those who hold the ideology. The "ruling ideas" of which Marx spoke, for example, are held by ruler and ruled alike. And Nietzsche held that potentially great individuals were being kept back in their development in part by their own assimilation of ideas that express the standpoint of the "herd."

Nor need the interests served by an ideology be the interests of particular individuals. Ideological analysis is not to be confused with the sort of cynicism that attributes everything to self-interest. On the contrary, ideological analyses have often focused on structural interests, interests belonging to individuals only *qua* members of groups, classes, or institutions. Individuals may acquire or lose these interests as their roles change, since the interests in the first instance attach to the roles themselves – to the conditions favorable to the preservation or strengthening of a given role, say, rather than to the conditions favorable to the preservation or strengthening of the particular set of individuals who happen to occupy that role at a given time. Thus the bourgeois entrepreneur ardently champions the market, even though increased competition may mean *his* elimination from the role of bourgeois. A patriotic German father of three joins the army in the Great War, even though he and his progeny would probably benefit more if he could contrive to stay at home and leave the fighting to others. Yet he willingly shoulders his Mauser and marches off to the front to defend the Fatherland, his head full of grand and dangerous ideas.

How can we identify *moral* convictions within the welter of convictions that help constitute a society – assuming, as we will, that this is a reasonable thing to attempt to do? Just as the term 'ideology' has a descriptive and a normative sense, so does the term 'morality.' We speak of morality descriptively when we try to give an empirically accurate account of certain norms and notions current within a given society, the extent to which they are observed, the ways they are taught and sanctioned, etc. We speak of morality normatively when we ask whether actions, practices, and so on are indeed right or wrong, better or worse, appropriate or inappropriate.

Should we use 'morality' in the normative sense to delineate which of the convictions abroad within society are the moral ones? That would seem to be the wrong approach for present purposes, since it would deem a widespread conviction a moral one only if it really would pass muster with us evaluatively. But if only legitimate norms and convictions will be counted for our purposes here as moral ones, then we have a quick, entirely definitional answer to the question whether ideological criticism can delegitimize morality. Better for our purposes to adopt a less normative approach to distinguishing morality, based upon some relatively uncontroversial ways in which our culture itself identifies the distinctively moral, and leaving open at the outset whether these prevalent norms and convictions will be judged by us to be appropriate at the end of the day.

It would be too ambitious empirically and too problematic philosophically to attempt to answer the question, What are the criteria of 'the moral' as found in our traditions of discourse and practice? Let us try for something more modest, which will still be ambitious enough. Avoiding the problematic term 'criteria,' and restricting our focus to the mainstream philosophical traditions, can we identify certain core elements that serve to distinguish moral evaluation from other species? We can then ask whether these elements might be vulnerable to critique as ideological.

Here, then, are some central truisms of various philosophically self-aware traditions within modern thought. Moral evaluation is:

(a) *impartial* (or, as I would prefer to say, non-partial) – it takes into account all those potentially affected;
(b) *universal* (or, as I would prefer to say, non-indexical) – it claims a legitimacy and scope of application that goes beyond any particular set of social boundaries or conventions;[12]
(c) *beneficent* – it assigns *prima facie* positive deliberative weight to the well-being of those potentially affected, negative deliberative weight to their suffering.

I said "traditions" within modern moral philosophy, but have I just written a recipe for utilitarianism? The utilitarian does think that (a)–(c) – fully fleshed out – suffice for the essential framework of morality. But numerous others think of (a)–(c) as expressing necessary conditions of moral thought.[13] Thus, on a fairly orthodox Kantian conception, morality is unquestionably impartial and universal, and, moreover, a precondition of the rational acceptability of moral demands is that following them will in the end be compatible with the well-being of the individuals and communities who do so. And Rawls's less orthodox Kantianism, which has its own forms of non-partiality and non-indexicality, also involves an underlying beneficence, as a concern for one's index of social goods is combined with ignorance of one's particular place or prospects in society.

There is, however, another truistic aspect of morality, which (a)–(c) do not capture, and which has figured most prominently in nonutilitarian thought. Elements (a)–(c) are in effect constraints on third-personal moral *evaluations* of states of affairs – how things look from a moral point of view. But this standpoint is not the whole core of moral thought or the point of view of the moral agent in choosing. Just as an alchemist might identify both a *passive* and an *active* essence in any given substance, so must we notice an active element in moral thought. This active element is reflected in a truism:

(d) Morality is *practical* – it purports to provide answers to the agent's questions "What ought I to do?" or "How best to live?"

How this fourth truism is to be understood in any detail is highly contested, and no one interpretation could answer to our need to identify relatively consensual elements of philosophically minded moral thought. Arguably, it is as much by their answers to the question "What is the practical nature of morality?" as anything else that moral philosophers differentiate themselves from one another. For here we find disputes over internalism versus externalism, the priority of the right over the good, the priority of action versus character, the relationship of morality to practical rationality, the overridingness of moral judgments, the conditions of moral agency, and so on.

What does seem to be elemental in (d) is the notion that moral discourse affords some first-personal directive content for agents deliberating about what to do. Such *directive*[14] judgments might be expressed as recommendations, commands, or permissions, but they are in any event thought of as *non-hypothetical* in form and *non-optional* in scope. To say they are non-hypothetical is not to claim that they are commands of pure reason, but only that they are not conditional upon the particular desires or preferences an individual happens to have at the moment. Thus they have the form 'You should . . .' rather than 'If you happen to go in for this sort of thing, you should. . . .' Many sorts of directives are non-hypothetical, from the laws of the state of Michigan to the rules of cricket. But unlike these directives, moral directives are also thought to be "non-optional" for normal adult human agents. That is, I can (as various unsavory but wealthy individuals do) remove myself from the scope of the laws of Michigan by moving to a country that has no extradition treaty with it and is not a signatory to certain international accords, and I can keep myself out of the reach of the rules of cricket by the simple expedient of never venturing to play it (thus in using a notebook computer at the moment, I am not either in violation of, or compliance with, the rules of cricket prohibiting electromechanical assistance). Moral directives leave us no such way out. Were I to decide to have done with life, and to end my normal human adulthood in suicide, this decision itself would be within the scope of moral norms, and would remain forever so even if I succeeded in wholly annihilating myself a moment afterward. These features of non-hypotheticality and non-optionality characterize moral directives, but do not suffice in themselves to define morality. For epistemic directives, prudential directives, aesthetic directives, rational directives, and so forth also seem to have these characteristics. They differ from morality more in substance – as given in the moral case by (a)–(c) – than in form.

I have spoken of 'normal human adult agents' rather than, say, 'rational agents as such.' Even as we had to be careful not to ally elements (a)–(c) too closely to utilitarianism, we must be careful not to ally (d) too much with Kantianism. A utilitarian or perfectionist who asserts "the right follows the good" is making a directive judgment, despite the priority being assigned to an evaluative standard. She is claiming that acts are to be guided by the ends they might embody or bring about, and she is doing so in a way that is both non-hypothetical and non-optional. For there is nothing in the utilitarian's or perfectionist's claim to restrict its application only to those who happen to want to follow it, or to permit normal adult humans to opt out through the exercise of choice. Even virtue ethics, which in some cases dispenses with the notion of *moral obligation*, is hard to imagine without directive judgments – for example the wise instruction to follow the path of developing, sustaining, or heeding virtues in our lives, rather than be distracted into other directions of personal development and decision. Virtue theories may do this – indeed, may have elaborate accounts of proper moral instruction and education – without grounding the enterprise in the motivational scheme of conscientiousness and guilt that seems characteristic of (and perhaps problematic about) moral obligation. More likely, they will ground it in ideals of a good life, "fit" for normal adult humans. We may require instruction and education to appreciate these ideals – their normative bearing in guiding our lives need not be hypothetical upon whether we now are attracted to them. If we claim somehow to have decided to opt out of their scope, we will have accomplished no more than to deceive ourselves about our real nature – just as we can continue to deceive ourselves about the nature of the world in general, without thereby changing anything about how things are or should be. So directing choice non-hypothetically and non-optionally is common ground across major moral theories.

But how does a non-hypothetical, non-optional directive judgment in accord with (a)–(c) actually engage us, and "guide action"? An early printing of Mackie's *Ethics* had on its cover an image of an immense hand descending from heaven, pointing the way to a traveler at a crossroads. This sort of device may caricature certain aspects of popular thinking about morality, but surely it cannot be what Mackie had in mind when he claimed that morality, if genuine, would have to possess "objective prescriptivity."[15] For even if the other heavenly hand (the one not seen on the book cover) holds a mighty thunderbolt, poised to be hurled at the traveler the moment he disobeys, and even if the puzzled traveler at the crossroads knows this, the tableau remains one of external rather than moral guidance or directive force. Things would be no different if the unseen hand held a golden reward for travelers who comply. In either case the reason the traveler has been given to comply is powerful, but not in itself a moral one.[16]

If genuine moral direction cannot simply be a matter of coercion or reward, what is to be the force that directs agents or guides moral action? The time-honored Aristotelian and Kantian answer is to say "the force of reason," but there is also the time-honored Humean answer that reason itself could possess no such force, and it must instead come from certain reasons in conjunction with certain distinctive sentiments, for example sympathy. Clearly we cannot say that there is an uncontroversial common ground on the question of "moral motivation," beyond the consensus that it cannot come down to mere coercion or reward – even if well disguised. Yet this is nonetheless enough for us to carry on our discussion of morality and ideology, since an ideological critique of morality often takes the form of attributing what a populace calls "moral motivation" precisely to structures of power and interest, of coercion and reward – albeit well hidden from direct view by "false consciousness," which talks of Reason, proper function, human nature, duty, impartiality, universality, sympathy, supersensible selves, and the like. If the critics are right that purportedly moral motivation can be given a fundamental "unmasking explanation" of this kind, revealing the discourse of moral motivation to be superficial and naïve, that would be sufficient to place Aristotelian, Kantian, and Humean moral traditions alike in a most uncomfortable spot.

V

We will come back to morality shortly, but first let us pick up the thread of our discussion of ideology and belief. We had briefly discussed how a philosophical explanation of the destabilization of belief under reflection might go: in the relevant cases, reflection on the ideological origins of belief will be destabilizing not merely by some quirk, but because belief by its nature "aims at" truth. The fact of destabilization thus seems to possess a kind of normative relevance *internal* to epistemology, even if it is not in itself normatively determinative (it is, after all, just a fact). Might there be an analogue on the moral side, such that if ideological criticism in fact tends to undermine moral commitment, this is more than a mere curiosity but rather possesses internal normative relevance to morality?

To be sure, ordinary, "descriptive" belief has a central place in moral thought and practice. It is easy to say *a priori* that moral evaluation "floats free" of descriptive belief, so that people could have all the same descriptive beliefs yet differ arbitrarily much in their moral evaluations, but in fact this is seldom or never the case. Historically, beliefs about the nature of action, the psychology of motivation, the likely causes and outcomes of acts and practices, the teleological structure (or lack of it) of the world, the distribution of human differences and similarities, and so on, tend to be found clustered with particular moral points of view, rather than distributed arbitrarily across the moral landscape. Arguably, some of the most profound historical changes in moral opinion have been precipitated precisely by changes – seemingly very "normatively relevant," if not "logically compelling" – in underlying descriptive beliefs about the existence of natural hierarchies, human variability, cosmological origins, and so on. And much of ideological critique is focused directly on these areas of belief, from Feuerbach's criticism of religion to contemporary feminist criticism of the naturalizing of gender distinctions.

To grasp the nettle, however, we need to ask explicitly whether the effect of the "reflection test" in changing moral opinion can be underwritten in a way *normatively internal* to morality. After all, some quite humane values might as a matter of fact fail to survive a ruthless preoccupation with personal failings or with the loss of national prestige suffered as a colonial empire crumbles. How would this tend to disqualify these values morally?

We need, then, to locate a path of disqualification that is relevant according to distinctively moral standards of relevance. We began in the case of belief with the *attitude* of belief, and the norms said to be "internal" to it. Let us proceed similarly with the attitude of valuing, and moral valuing in particular.

The attitude of valuing typically involves some sort of desiring, it seems, but is distinct from *mere* desiring, much as believing that *p* typically involves some sort of "finding oneself drawn to believe that *p*," but also involves something more. Belief that *p* characteristically involves various commitments and claims of authority, usually tacit: one accords *p* a degree of confidence in one's actions and interactions; one gives *p* a certain weight in assessing one's own beliefs, new evidence, or the beliefs of others; one seeks to render *p*, and one's commitment to it, consistent with one's other beliefs; one is inclined to feel defensive about one's attitude toward $p$ and to be disquieted by learning that the explanation of why one believes that $p$ is not truth related – that one's belief that $p$ cannot be seen as *attuned to* evidence for $p$. At this point one may freely recognize that one still is drawn as strongly as ever to believe that $p$, but one's attitudes of epistemic commitment to $p$ and claimed authority regarding $p$ will not comfortably remain undiminished. Putting things the other way around, one might find that one is not much "drawn to believe" this uncomfortable explanation of one's belief that $p$, but that, given the evidence, one is nonetheless inclined to accord it epistemic authority.

Similarly, I can desire $A$ without the sorts of commitments or claims of authority that valuing $A$ characteristically – and, again, usually tacitly – involves. When I value $A$, other things equal: I am inclined to accord $A$ some weight in regulating my deliberation and choice, and also my judgments of others and recommendations to them; I seek to reconcile my plans, goals, and ends with $A$; I am inclined to invoke $A$ to justify or defend myself, and to treat it as in turn justified and defensible; thus I typically feel uneasy when I perceive $A$ to be threatened, and defensive when I take $A$ to be challenged. One way in which $A$ might be challenged is by an explanation of my valuing $A$ that removes any element that I would count as an appropriate ground of value, such that my valuing could not be seen as an *attunement* to relevant value-making features. In the absence of any other backing for $A$, I could still acknowledge that my desire for $A$ is undiminished, even as I will no longer be easy in according $A$ the same regulative role in running my life or judging myself and others. Put the other way around, I may come to see the taking of not-$A$ as an end as appropriate – as attuned to value-making features – even though I do not now much desire not-$A$ at all.

An example of this "internal" purport of the attitude of valuing might help, and for our purposes the relevant domain of evaluation is the moral. Given the amount of content in conditions (a)–(c), and the regulative practical role (d), we can see how moral evaluation cannot "float free" of other attitudes and beliefs. Consider someone brought up in a racial or caste system, who initially deemed it morally appropriate to keep "higher" and "lower" groups from mixing. Were he ever to be attracted to a member of a "lower" group, this individual would likely find that attraction "unclean," "intrinsically degrading" – an appropriate source of guilt, and not to be permitted to regulate his choice of social relations. Were he to learn that his sister had formed a romantic relationship with a "lower" group member, he would think her "disgraced" and "for ever stained," and be very ashamed for himself and his family. Suppose now that this individual learns that the supposed historical and biological basis of the caste or racial distinctions is bogus: the groups are virtually indistinguishable genetically and the actual origin of the subordination-superordination relationship is a brutal conquest unrelated to any moral concerns. This individual might well continue irresistibly to *feel* that there is something in itself "off" or "shameful" when members of the different castes or races intermix, but would be unlikely to think that moral righteousness lies in reinforcing this feeling to prevent any intercaste or interracial attraction from having a regulative role in action. He might still find himself acutely uncomfortable when his sister presents her new spouse, but he would feel quite differently about whether or why she now should be driven from the family.

Moral evaluation, then, finds its place in a complex constellation of non-moral beliefs and attitudes, and indeed *supervenes* upon them, yielding the final element of the moral point of view to be mentioned here:

(e) one is committed to defend one's moral evaluations by citing non-moral but morally relevant value-making features.

This sort of supervenience has been seen by moral philosophers of all stripes as a conceptual, *a priori*, or otherwise fundamental truth about valuation – one would simply not grasp the idea of value if one thought that values could simply be "added" to a state of affairs or "pasted" to them (such that two states of affairs could be identical in all non-moral characteristics, yet, properly, receive different moral evaluations). When allied with elements (a)–(d), the result is that moral evaluation hardly "floats free" of our best account of how the world works, why we believe what we do, and so on. Thus, while these various constraints are logically consistent with the persistence of moral disagreement in the face of many factual agreements, factual agreements that concern matters within the scope of (a)–(e) – such as learning that there is no difference between the races and castes of a given society that could affect characteristics relevant to well-being, capacity for rational action, and so forth – impinge forcibly on moral opinion, not as a psychological curiosity, but by the nature of the moral attitude itself.

Of course, even in the presence of an explanation indicating that the only reason I value *A* is one that counts as morally irrelevant under (a)–(e), I could insist that there must be *some* morally relevant ground for *A*, and I could be right. Nonetheless, lacking any defense of *A*, and with a favorable attitude toward it already explained in a non-justificatory way,

I may have difficulty impressing anyone with my authority in continuing to urge $A$ in moral decisions. I am likely to appear more dogmatic than upright, closer kin to an unquestioning "believer in $p$" than to a responsible "believer that $p$" whose attitude is to be accorded some normative authority.

And that alternative attitude is often resorted to in just such circumstances. Absent any further ground for valuing $A$ than, say, learning that I picked it up from my family's traditions, I could continue to make it a fundamental matter of faith that I "believe in $A$," and will conduct myself accordingly. What is likely to drop away in humane individuals is the conviction that those from different family environments, with different evaluative traditions, are in a *morally indefensible* position when they disagree with me about $A$. One can, that is, retreat from the domain of mutual moral condemnation and affirm one's conviction only on behalf of a personal, familial, or cultural ideal or preference.

Reducing reflective disequilibrium can take yet other forms: I might on further reflection reject the non-justificatory explanation as lacking sufficient credibility; I might arrive at an independent justification for $A$ (one that does not depend upon how I acquired the value); or I might simply live in a certain bad faith – not clearly rejecting the explanation, not clearly repudiating the value, trying not to dwell on the tension between the two, bluffing my way through until I myself am no longer much troubled, buffering my self-esteem with the usual rationalizations. Being in bad faith makes one vulnerable in certain ways, but it is a very familiar sort of vulnerability.

VI

We now are in a position to begin to apply our characterization of what (at least in part) makes a set of views an ideology to our account of what (at least in part) makes a set of views a morality. It is already easy to see why it is so tempting to apply an ideological critique to morality. But spelling this out a bit will help us to say something about a quite general question, "What is the nature of ideological critique itself?" It will also enable us to pose a more particular question, "Does the weight of ideological critique, such as it is, fall uniformly upon moral notions, or are there some elements that are much more vulnerable than others?"

Marx spoke of ideologies as standing things on their heads: representing the particular as general, the local as universal, the contingent as necessary, the profane as sacred, the effect as cause. Although he diagnoses ideologies as in fact expressing a particular standpoint in a contingent and historically evolving world, he insists that they do not – indeed, cannot – represent themselves as such. A given class (for example) will "represent its interest as the common interest" and "give its ideas the form of universality, and represent them as the only rational, universally valid ones."[17] It is essential to a functional ideology that those holding it and passing it along to others by and large take it to heart. That is, if (say) partial, conventional, contingent norms are to be reified as disinterested, natural, and necessary, then this reification must have a deep grip on the ideologues themselves. That is what entitles us to take the rather grandiose but typically sincere philosophical conception of ethics as manifest in (a)–(e) as paradigmatic.

We have identified both passive and active elements in our philosophical understanding of morality. Each is at risk, in its own way, from ideological criticism. But to the same degree?

Shared risks first. The passive, evaluative component (comprising (a)–(c) and (e)) claims to perceive things comprehensively and coherently, from a point of view that is not merely descriptive, and yet is not the point of view of anyone or any time in particular – no individual, group, or society. This seems not only grandiose, but also potentially nonsensical. Points of view do not need to be perfectly coherent, but surely they cannot be as incoherent as the jumble that would result from simply aggregating individuals and their ends across time and space. A point of view is by its nature selective, offering a perspective on the landscape rather than the landscape as such. The moral point of view *is* supposed to be selective, glimpsing only that which is relevant to moral evaluation – typically, philosophers have spoken of the general interest and the intrinsically good. Yet Marx and Nietzsche each argued in his own way that actual societies are scenes of conflicting interests, and that actual goods have their value not inherently, but in virtue of their relation to subjects. Without subjects, nothing would be of value. Not because there would be no one to see or appreciate it, but because, without subjects, there would be nothing that could *constitute* value. Absolute or non-relational value, value that stands apart from subjects and calls forth their pursuit, is a *fetish*.

One can, of course, readily see the legitimizing function of a claim made on behalf of a particular standpoint that it is universal, impartial, attuned to objective, intrinsic value-making features. Such a claim privileges a particular standpoint, and privileging is the secular equivalent of canonization. Yet it is altogether too easy in retrospect to see past claims of universal validity as unwarranted projections of the local and particular into the eternal and sacred, and thus supposedly beyond question or challenge. Philosophical conceptions of the good, too, seem in retrospect expressive of their context. Not much imagination is required to see in the Aristotelian notion of proper function a reflection of the Greek caste system. Or to see in medieval notions of noble and base, or honor, the reflection of an aristocratic warrior society. Or to see in the utilitarian ideas of happiness as individual desire-satisfaction and of a universal metric of value the reflection of modern bourgeois commodification and market society.

The issue here is not, or at any rate not yet, whether this constitutes a telling reason for rejecting these notions. And it would take an altogether different level of engagement with history to say anything about the credibility of these claims. But at the moment our concern is merely hypothetical: since previous conceptions of the good bear some of the superficial marks of ideologies, we should ask whether and to what extent this diagnosis, if borne out, would disqualify them. Before investigating further, we need to have a similarly preliminary look at the active element in morality's alchemy.

The active side of morality has characteristically found expression during the modern period[18] in the notion of *obligation*, which in turn has been voiced in two terminologies. First, a terminology familiar from emergent civil society: rights, laws, duties, requirements, contracts. Of course, however much they resemble civil notions, moral rights and laws are, according to this conception, natural or rational rather than conventional. We understand the "force" of these notions in civil society to lie in their civil embodiment: mechanisms for verifying and enforcing contracts, advantages of mutual trust, the institutionalization of property, and so forth. As natural or rational notions, we must see these as owing their force to something else, such as the abstract notion of respect for others, reasonableness, or fairness.

Second, we find a terminology of religious and, ultimately, I suppose, familial origin: a language of commands and imperatives issued from some authoritative source. This language we understand tolerably well if attached to an actual (presumptively authoritative) issuing subject using the imperative voice. And we can grasp its "action-guiding" force if we imagine that the issuer is someone we wish, or are constrained by some interest or incentive, to please. But moral commands or categorical imperatives are supposed not to be issued by a lesser force than Reason itself, or rather, that part of each of us that embodies Reason.

It is, again, not difficult to see the potential contribution to legitimation of such "denatured" notions of obligation or imperative. Yet as philosophers since Hobbes and Hume have urged, it is problematic whether these notions can really have application apart from a background of actual institutions, sanctions, and so forth. Kant's critical philosophy sought to move from a metaphysical conception of the ground of obligation to a "practical" one, but even for him a background teleology of reward and sanction remained in place as a necessary postulate of practical reason. Historical perspective may well convince us that what is in fact going on is less an expression of divine teleology than of local social circumstances. The distinctive notion of natural property rights as individual entitlements that demand respect, which gains ascendancy in early modern moral philosophy, seems to have a great deal to do with the emergent forms and conflicts of modern civil society, but it hardly affords the *only* or *natural* condition under which humans have lived together with some semblance of peace and flourishing, or mutual respect.

So has the mainstream moral philosophy of Hobbes and Hume already done the work of ideological critique for it? Not the whole job, surely. For the philosophical critique of "naturalizing" obligation and property has made use of its own "naturalizing," which Marx and others have deemed to be equally dubious: a theory not of Reason but of Human Nature (and allied theories of "natural appetites" or "sentiments"). Hobbes of course offered his conception, and asked contemporaries who might doubt it simply to look into their own hearts. There they might indeed find that which Hobbes describes, Marx could assert, but this introspective device cuts off inquiry or insight into the social and historical origins of that "human nature." If the anthropologist Karl Polanyi is right, however, never has a conception less faithful to the history of mankind been more prophetic of its future.[19] Hume, for his part, spoke confidently of origins, and of natural versus artificial sentiments, but for the most part innocently of any anthropological or evolutionary evidence. Indeed, his quasi-anthropological remarks are the clearest cases of his uncritically projecting the attitudes of a metropolitan culture, and thus among the most acute sources of embarrassment for his contemporary admirers.

The philosophical critique of natural law, brilliant as it was, did not in Marx's eyes bring an end to ideology in ethics, but rather ushered in a new ideology, of "human nature" or "natural sentiments" as an exogenous constraint on human history and practice, rather than a (partial) product thereof. Claims of human nature or natural sentiment afforded a fixed point of criticism that was itself beyond criticism, and afforded the basic vocabulary that determined all that could – or could not – be achieved socially or collectively in the name of morality. But who knows how much human practice (e.g., the history of sexual selection) has shaped our evolution, or will continue to shape it (now that genetic engineering is a possibility)? Marx chided Feuerback for taking the cherry tree outside his study window as a recurring image of "nature" in his writings, without seeing the extent to which that very tree was the product of generations of human hybridizing practice.

Although often placed in a realm apart from reason and argument, sentiment has been seen by its champions as not without force in justifying morality. Indeed, it holds out the prospect for a compact account of the "action-guiding" character of morality – 'ought' implying 'can,' as it does – since sentiment *drives* action. One can view a theory of sentiments as telling us where, if anywhere, the motivational infrastructure requisite for justification is to be found. A theory of sentiments is well suited to play this "limit" role in setting the horizons for the modern imagination, for is not contemporary society the expression *par excellence* of the priority of private sentiment, of the elevation of personal preference to the point where it seems more authoritative for the individual than some Platonic Form or something called the Laws of Reason?[20] At any rate, this is how a Marxist diagnosis might go.

We are obviously moving absurdly briskly here, but the goal is only illustration. On the surface at least, modern moral philosophy – even modern critical moral philosophy – is grist to the mill of ideological analysis. The particular character or content of the reifications involved varies between passive and active elements in morality, and with the evolution of the various schools of moral thought. But in general it is possible to begin to tell a story in which the particular is being taken as universal, the conditioned or relational as absolute, the contingent as necessary, and the socially and historically local as natural. And in all cases we can see how these stories could have a legitimizing function, at the least by turning back certain challenges to legitimacy.

VII

But what are we to do with these bald claims? Let us simply suppose for the moment that something like them is true.

Ideological (self-)criticism is normally understood to involve posing to ourselves the question: Can our commitment to particular views and practices be (sincerely, and with awareness) sustained in light of a full social-historical understanding of where those views, practices, and commitments come from, how they operate within us (e.g., their

371

psychological or psychodynamic mechanism), and what their actual or likely consequences are (e.g., which interests they effectively promote or hinder)?

At the outset I mentioned the remarkable degree to which even philosophers critical of past moral theorizing or practice have defended continuing commitment to morality.[21] One usually has to look outside mainstream philosophy – to Marx or Nietzsche, say – to find attitudes more openly dismissive of the core of conventional morality.[22] Suppose, as I just did, that the ideological diagnosis is largely true. Which response – the skeptical or the defensive – seems more appropriate?

Asking this question seems, however, to be stepping outside the framework of ideological critique. For it suggests that we have a *second* sort of test in mind. In the first test we ask whether or to what extent our convictions do in fact survive critical self-awareness. In the second test we ask what to make of that – whether this response on our part is or is not appropriate. When put this way, it seems as if the second test is the locus of all the *epistemic* action – the first test is just one more piece of empirical psychology, which might figure in the second as a kind of evidence but that lacks normative standing in its own right.

Or is the "second test" really separate? Deeming one's responses *appropriate* appears to be just one more normative conviction. Are we now asking whether this conviction itself will in fact be retained when we are fully aware? Yet ordinarily we distinguish questions of the appropriateness of a response from questions of whether in fact we have it under such-and-such conditions. Perhaps we can clarify this as follows. Consider the following "second-order" ideological argument.

You say we should reflect on our commitments by asking whether they would survive in the harsh light of historical and social self-understanding. Fine. But where did the commitment *that* expresses come from? It has all the trappings of an Enlightenment ideal of a transparent self and of psychologically frictionless belief-acquisition. It shows a touching faith in the curative or therapeutic power of knowledge and self-awareness, and in the *psychological* unity of knowledge – genuine knowledge can always sit comfortably beside other knowledge. Though adding knowledge may have some dramatic and unwanted noncognitive effects on us (reducing self-esteem, say), it is supposed not to be destructive of existing knowledge. Moreover, this seeming Enlightenment ideal also shows a deference to the notion of *historical fact* and the context of *third-party explanation* rather than (say) *social construction* and *self-narration*. The ideal invests authority in a "bird's (God's?)-eye view" of ourselves, our history, and our psychology. And is it to be imagined to be a genuine possibility that we actually take this perspective? We are being asked to accord normative standing to our responses in this notional condition. But why should we not distrust this conceit, too, and the deference it involves? Perhaps this transition cannot be negotiated, and we can only replace one self-narrative by another, still grander in ambition and still further from the situatedness that gives at least some genuine content to our thought and activities. One might hope that the transition could be attempted in good faith, and yield some genuine gains in knowledge. But mightn't it have more or less severe epistemic costs at the same time? Mightn't it also be destructive of some epistemic value?

How might we make sense of this last possibility?

Bernard Williams, in his influential book *Ethics and the Limits of Philosophy*, raises what I take to be a similar concern about the easy supposition that a distanced perspective destroys prejudice but nothing of real epistemic value.[23] This looks like a normative issue, for it requires us to ask not "What is *altered* by reflection?" but "What *of epistemic value* is at peril?" or "What do we have *epistemic reason* to make of this alteration?" It begins to look, therefore, as if we can normatively problematize ideological critique itself by a reflective process that asks where our confidence in the authority of changes wrought by such critique might come from.

Are we trading here upon mysterious claims? Consider then the following very mundane story. Somewhere in the depths of the medieval English countryside is a village huddled around a large clocktower. The clock's mechanism was the work of an itinerant clockmaker, Cruikshank, who built many clocks that stand in towers across the broad countryside in those parts. Unfortunately, Cruikshank was more a master of building impressive-looking clocks that could enhance the self-esteem of a village than of the delicate business of gears and escapements. So his clocks keep very poor time and are so often in some state of disrepair that one can seldom form a reliable judgment about the time by glancing up at the clocktower. However, in our little village, which we'll call Wrell, an accidental feature of the way the clock's weights were suspended has had the surprising effect of making a Cruikshank timepiece run like clockwork. Residents of this village can form reliable judgments of the time by consulting this clock, and often do. They have come to rely on this clock, and have done so successfully over the years. Although they have not formulated elaborate reflective beliefs about "the reliability of this sort of mechanism," they do count on their Cruikshank clock in a way that villages elsewhere do not, and that they themselves would not were the clock typically inaccurate. It seems to me pretty clear that the residents of Wrell can know it's noon from observing the single, ornate hand at twelve.

A traveler who has visited the other towns where Cruikshank had traveled and left clocks in his wake is well acquainted with both their singular appearance and their unreliability. When he arrives in Wrell, he, too, sees the clock's hand at twelve. But he does not thereby acquire the knowledge that it is noon, for he recognizes the clock to be a Cruikshank. The villagers can learn that it is noon from looking at the clock, but he can't. He knows too much.

Might there be a model here for moral lore and practices, with a similar possibility of being "wised up" in a way that cuts one off from certain genuine ways of knowing? We might think of ourselves in the contemporary world as akin to travelers who've become aware of the wide historical and geographic diversity in certain norms, of the particular contingencies so many seem to reflect, and of the ways in which they typically garner the support of their communities as natural and evident – however arbitrary in content they may seem to us. We're struck by the disparity between the cosmic purport of these normative systems and the particularity of the forces that shape and sustain them.

It is unsurprising that the first great wave of anthropological fieldwork in the late nineteenth and early twentieth centuries precipitated many relativist thoughts and sentiments. The possibility thus arises that in our home society we have a working moral "clock" that nonetheless is to a significant degree the result of historical accident. That is, our morality does indeed permit mutually beneficial social coordination, promote individual flourishing, and reasonably allocate benefits and burdens. Yet perhaps we have come by exposure to a wider world to "know too much" about the real origins of moralities to be able to know (as perhaps we did before) that an act is good or fair by knowing it to be in accord with our established practices.

Suppose, moreover, that part of the very way the practices in our home society have made so many good lives together possible is that the worm of reflection has not (at least, until recently) begun to gnaw at our hearts. Perhaps one setting (maybe one of the few) in which a moral life is compatible with moral knowledge has been lost to us. If moral lives and moral knowledge are endangered species, we have not done much to promote their survival by removing one of their few habitats! This does not look like much of an advertisement for the normative authority of reflective self-awareness or ideological critique. After all, part of the explanation of why, in the pre-anthropological home society, people held the moral beliefs they did *is* that they did not problematize their moral assumptions, by insisting on prying into questions of origin, and becoming as a result disequilibrated by an awareness of the role of morally irrelevant or unsavory factors in the history of their moral opinions.

We can, however, give this argument – and these two examples – one more twist. Return first to Wrell. Not all explanations are debunking. Despite our initial, justified skepticism, we as travelers *could* acquire confidence in the clocktower that would permit us to learn from it after all. When we enter the town we know too much to learn the time from the Wrell Cruikshank – but also not enough.

If we knew more, we would know that it is in fact reliable. Perhaps we could observe its coordination with another timepiece we know to be accurate, or with the movement of the sun. This coordination would, however, remain a mystery for us in a way that it is not for the Wrellians – for we know the faultiness of Cruikshankian handiwork. To whatever extent they may have reflected on the question of the reliability of clocks of this type – which need not be much, I would think – they have had no reason to think that it is otherwise than part of the order of nature that clocks like this would be reliable. Does this lack of reflection upon reliability or insight into mechanism impugn their claim to be able to know the time by looking at the clock? That would be a severe judgment. We daily gather knowledge from countless indicators in our environment that are indeed reliable, even if we have not formed reflective beliefs on their reliability or on how it might be brought about.

Our own situation with regard to Cruikshank clocks is, however, different. The reliability of such clocks has been explicitly *problematized* for us – and not in a gratuitous or generically skeptical way. Forming judgments based upon the reading of the Wrell clock strikes us as a perilous business, needing justification. At the outset we can only regard it as a happy coincidence if the clock's hand is at twelve when the sun is directly overhead. Why should we expect the clock's agreement with local solar time to be robust or enduring – this is after all a Cruikshank clock – before we at least have some more extensive experience with it and are aware of the possibility of an explanation in which accidental features of a clock's installation or idiosyncrasies of its location can (for example) offset built-in characteristics of its mechanism? This is a contingent, relational kind of reliability, of course, but it is nonetheless a kind of reliability. We see what a poor proxy for "arbitrary" the notion of "contingent" really is. And we see how poor a word 'relativistic' (which suggests observer dependence) is for 'relational' (which suggests contextual dependence). Whatever the source of the Wrell clock's reliability, my initially skeptical frame of mind only made *me* unable to rely upon it rather than making *it* unreliable in any way.

Now let us return to the other imaginary example, in which we suppose that existing moral practices in our home country are highly appropriate from a moral point of view, but we have become uneasy about relying upon them owing to reflective awareness of their arbitrary origins and of the extent to which social practices in general are variable or arbitrary. Can our pre-anthropological moral knowledge be rewon? Moral inquiry can no longer for us take the form of asking with great care, "Is tradition being followed?", even if this question did occupy the center of prean-thropological debates over a practice's wisdom or fairness. We must be able to see established moral practices as yielding certain regular outcomes – contingently, relationally – in our evolving context. And we perhaps must also have some idea of how it could be that practices of arbitrary origin whose surface appearance or formal features do not as such distinguish them from other, morally unreliable practices might nonetheless, in a given social and historical setting, be robustly dependable morally. Of course, our participation in any such reflective, vindicatory process may now have tainted us or our society: we have lost the innocence that was a key ingredient or a saving grace, and an ideally full self-understanding that would overcome this could be forever out of reach in practice. But even this unfortunate result need not preclude our knowing that the pre-anthropological practices were good. So normative moral knowl-edge perhaps need not be an altogether closed book to the cosmopolitan mind.

We are working here with the idea of a *vindicatory explanation* of a prac-tice, as opposed to a debunking explanation. Vindication may take many forms. The explanation can be "direct": we might show that, though the origins are arbitrary in various ways, the practice (or artifact, phe-nomenon, etc.) has certain features that, in its context, make it robustly reliable in particular respects. Or, the explanation can be "indirect": the practice (artifact, etc.) exists as it does and where it does (or plays the role in people's lives that it does) because of a *selection mechanism* that favors reliability of the relevant sort. The explanation can also combine the two, as our story of Wrell does: a direct explanation of the clock's reliability along with an indirect explanation of why people in Wrell pay attention to what its hand says (unlike residents of other villages with other Cruikshanks). Direct explanations are often of the "existentially quantified" form: we have reason to think there is *something* about this practice (or artifact, etc.) in this setting that yields reliability. Indirect explanations are often highly speculative: we have reason to think this practice (or artifact, etc.) wouldn't continue to be used if it didn't play such-and-such a role at least as well as salient, available competitors.

Not much is clear about *how much* vindicatory explanation one must possess once a practice (artifact, etc.) has become as deeply problematized as talk of objective moral knowledge has been for us moderns. No doubt the answer is pragmatic in the sense that how much vindication we need depends upon the centrality of a practice (artifact, etc.) to our lives and the seriousness and specificity of the problematization.[24] What perhaps does seem clearer is that Wrellians themselves need not (at least, not before they hear about the other clocks) possess a vindicatory explanation of their Cruikshank's reliability in order to know the time from looking at it, but that *our* need for such an explanation is greater. It is one of the burdens of knowledge.

We might think that telling time is of little direct relevance to the moral case because of the existence of objective indicators to check correlations independently. And we might also think that, in the story of the pre-anthropological home society, the real issue for moral epistemology has just been assumed away – the practices are described as if they unproblematically bore identifiably moral properties. This, too, would yield the possibility of objective indicators and independent ways of checking, but only because we have fixed the moral criteria. What if our concern – what has been problematized by the ideological critique of a Marx or a Nietzsche – is with the criteria themselves, or their very possibility? Where then is the objective indicator or independent check?

IX

To move further along in answering such questions we need to be more self-aware in thinking about the critical reflection test itself. How well does *it* survive critical reflection? First, we must ask, what does it (at least, in its classic form) seem to presuppose? Here is a partial listing:

(1) There exists a relatively determinate causal history of our beliefs and values.
(2) There exist real needs and interests, capable of shaping behavior on the individual and social level in the manner ideological explanations require, and also such that we can make sense of the claim that a purported general interest is in fact not so.

377

(3) We are capable of acquiring reasonably warranted beliefs about (1) and (2), despite our own particular interests and historical and social situatedness.

(4) The failure of certain beliefs and values to survive reflective exposure to these warranted beliefs constitutes some degree of warrant for rejecting or revising them, whereas survival constitutes some degree of warrant for continued acceptance.[25]

Don't (1)–(4) themselves run afoul of the critique of objectivity and of the reification or fetishization of value?

What sorts of ambition must a theory of belief or value have in order to underwrite talk of warrant or objectivity? These are very large and contentious questions, and we will have to content ourselves with looking only at one aspect: how *rationalistic* must the ambition be? Hume famously argued at the end of Part I of the *Treatise of Human Nature* that a strict rationalistic project failed even in its own terms: "Understanding, when it acts alone, and according to its most general principles, entirely subverts itself, and leaves not the lowest degree of evidence in any proposition, either in philosophy or in common life."[26] Kant, coming along behind Hume, attempted to rescue rationalism by rendering it *critical* rather than dogmatic, grounding claims of objectivity and warrant in *postulated* synthetic *a priori* conditions of thought and action rather than *rationally demonstrable* metaphysical necessities inherent in the world. Many in the tradition of *Ideologiekritik* can be thought of as pressing this critical rationalist project beyond Kant, situating it socially and historically. But that would appear to sustain after all a commitment to the attainability of objectivity and warrant through an operation of reflective understanding – as exemplified in (4). In a word, a *faith* in *reason*.[27]

The critical reflection test does not belong to any particular philosophical tradition, and is just as important to Hume as it is to Kant. For by the end of Part III of the *Treatise* Hume summarizes his "accurate proof of this system of ethics" in just these terms:

It requires but very little knowledge of human affairs to perceive, that a sense of morals is a principle inherent in the soul, and one of the most powerful that enters into the [human] composition. But this sense must certainly acquire new force, when reflecting on itself, it approves of those principles, from whence it is deriv'd, and finds nothing but what is great and good in its rise and origin. Those who resolve the sense of morals into original instincts of the human mind, may defend the cause of virtue with sufficient authority; but want the advantage, which those possess, who account for that sense by an extensive sympathy with mankind. According to the latter system [i.e., Hume's sort of system], not only

378

virtue must be approv'd, but also the sense of virtue: And not only that sense, but also the principles, from whence it is deriv'd. So that nothing is presented on any side, but what is laudable and good (*Treatise* 619).

Descending from Hume we have a compatibilist conception of freedom, a relational conception of value, and a contingent conception of the operation of human motivation and understanding. A de-escalated version of the Kantian synthetic *a priori* regulative principles of thought and action results. Hume argues, against outright skepticism, that we cannot even begin to think – even to think skeptical thoughts – without attributing some *prima facie* warrant to reasoning and experience, and that we cannot even begin to act – even to act on skeptical thoughts – without attributing some *prima facie* commending force to what we aim at. But, much as a Bayesian claims that epistemic rationality consists not in starting from demonstrable truth or certainty, but in starting from one's existing beliefs (one's *priors* for both propositions and new evidence), and proceeding to condition them in a potentially self-correcting way upon new experience, which may lead us arbitrarily far from our original starting point, Hume does not assume that *prima facie* warrant and commending force is tantamount to *a priori necessary* or *unrevisable* warrant or commending force. Indeed, for Hume, even "*general rules*" of justice know some limits, as sentiments of sympathy and credibility (and "a serious good-humour'd disposition") continually act as countervailing forces, capable of undermining a rigid compliance with rules and bringing us back to our senses (*Treatise* 551).

Reification seems inessential in any of this, though it is always a danger. Hume may strike us as overly complacent, but it is important to record that he thought skepticism should never be wholly set aside (*Treatise* 270).

In any event, the crucial step lies in repudiating such thoughts as those equating subjectivity or contingency with arbitrariness. Subjects are parts of the world, possessing at a given time more or less definite properties, as well as the capacity to remake themselves in various ways. Sentiments as well as reasoning are products of a long-term interaction between organism and the natural and social world, and both sentiment and reasoning may be more or less impartial and object-oriented. When critical reflection brings them together, it may accomplish something neither could accomplish on its own. If we call that which relates to subjects *subjectual* – as we now call that which relates to objects *objectual* – we can see at once how misleading the equation of subjectual with arbitrary can be. Ideological criticism draws upon this very thought: while the subjectual cannot simply be reified as merely objectual – subjects have ways of seeing themselves that then contribute to the explanation of how they behave – subjects nonetheless are implicated in the world and interactive with it in ways that may make them more or less capable of seeing themselves or the world as things are. We might call this *objective subjectuality*, a condition that requires effort and good fortune, to shake the complacency of our ordinary self-conceptions, but is in no way incoherent. Ideological analyses contribute to the shaking of our complacency by indicating how deeply things might not be as they seem.

There is a remarkable similarity between the critical machinery of ideological analysis, Hume's "accurate proof" of his ethics, and Rawls's notion of (wide) reflective equilibrium as a form of justification.[28] All three operate with the thought that we concede normative authority to conclusions that show a certain kind of stability in the light of fuller information, greater sensitivity and awareness, and movement away from various kinds of parochialism. Such a picture presents the appearance of illicit movement, from an 'is' (that which in fact is stable) to an 'ought' (that which we should believe or value) – from brute fact to normative authority. But the fact isn't very brute (it is reflective, critical) and the authority isn't absolute (it is provisional, and dependent upon rationally optional natures and purposes).

We do of course start off with what we believe and value, and where we end up may depend more or less heavily upon that. But rationality in belief – as philosophers of science have long emphasized – must be a matter of *where one goes from here*. For surely neither alternative is rational: to go nowhere (because one cannot start anywhere) or to start from where we aren't (with what we *don't* believe).

If morality, the sitting duck for ideological critique, is still afloat, that is because we have been able both to criticize and to rebuild it – as we have rebuilt scientific belief – from normatively available materials to meet the empirical onslaught of experience. Moral thought itself furnished the essential ingredients to give rise to challenges of partiality, false factual assumptions, or parochialism about the good life. These have been recognized grounds of criticism within moral practice, stemming from its objective purport. But moral thought has also evolved under these criticisms, becoming less partial, less factually benighted, less parochial. As criticisms have become normatively intelligible (e.g., charges of parochialism of various kinds), so has a morality rebuilt in response to them.

We ask a lot of morality for it to be in good standing because we grant moral assessment a good deal of authority. Perhaps this will be vindicated over time to a significant degree. Further knowledge and reflection do seem unlikely to unsettle altogether such ideas as these: that lives can go better or worse for those who will live them; that institutions and attitudes can be less or more partial; and that practices can be more or less widely, reciprocally, or equally beneficial to those affected by them. Perhaps the reluctance of philosophers in the modern epoch to consign morality to the depths where notions of honor, divine order, and natural teleology now repose reflects their sense that morality has proven remarkably adaptive, remarkably effective at co-opting its critics. A sitting duck, morality is also Neurath's duck.[29]

NOTES

*Morality and Ideology*, Edward Harcourt, ed. (Oxford: Oxford University Press, 2000).

1. K. Marx and F. Engels, *The German Ideology*, W. Lough, trans., C. J. Arthur, ed. and abridged (New York: International Publishers, 1970) 64. Hereinafter GI in parenthetic page references in the text.

2. Friedreich Nietzsche. *Beyond Good and Evil*, Walter Kaufmann, trans. and ed. (New York: Random House, 1966) 201.

3. And there might in fact be less tension between Marx's and Nietzsche's critiques than these few passages might suggest, since the two appear to use the term with a different scope – the "morality" Nietzsche most famously stigmatized is more specific historically.

4. Translated freely from Jean-Jacques Rousseau, *Du contrat social*, François Bouchardy, ed. (Paris: Egloff, 1946) 42. It seems to me plausible to depart from the more standard translation of *ignorer* as "do not know," since in his Second Discourse Rousseau offers a theory of just how our situation came about. It seems more apt to see Rousseau as announcing that he does not see the doctrine of social contract itself as a form of *historical explanation* of man's social bondedness (and so he wishes to set aside at the outset such questions of explanation), but rather sees it as a way in which social bondedness *might*, under certain conditions, be legitimized.

5. That a group can properly be said to have a belief that is not simply the collected beliefs of its members has been nicely shown by Margaret Gilbert, *On Social Facts* (London: Routledge, 1989).

6. I mean to use 'proposition' fairly neutrally here. No commitment to cognitivism about value is presupposed, only the admissibility of the following sort of dialogue:

> *Bill.* Shortening the work day is a good thing. It will make people more well-rounded.

> *Joe.* I agree with your first proposition, but not your second. I doubt people will become any more well-rounded in their spare time than they already are, but I do think it will help reduce unemployment.

Whatever is expressed by 'Shortening the work day is a good thing,' and that which Joe is claiming to be of one mind with Bill about, is what I will call an 'evaluative proposition.'

7. A situation of this kind seems to exist in Bayesian "Dutch Book" justifications for conforming to the probability calculus in one's subjective credence assignments. This argument has been seen as a way to *defend* Bayesian epistemology as such.

8. This raises, however, a delicate question for ideological critique to which we will return: What if, as a psychological matter, the belief for which no vindicating explanation is found nonetheless seems to remain stable on reflection (as typically seems to be the case when it comes to self-ascriptions of driving skill)? Is the issue in ideological critique whether a belief *is* destabilized, or *should be*?

   A more realistic psychological portrait of the situation would allow for higher-order beliefs. A belief in the above-average quality of one's own driving may indeed be very robust under all manner of reflective exposure to evidence, but one can more readily shed certain second-order beliefs in the light of this evidence. For example, does one take one's firm first-order opinion that one is an above-average driver with a grain of salt when deciding how much insurance to buy, or whether one's family would be safer in marginal driving conditions with oneself at the wheel, or someone more experienced?

9. This sort of thought has been emphasized by Bernard Williams, "Deciding to Believe," in Williams, *Problems of the Self* (Cambridge: Cambridge University Press, 1973). David Velleman gives a seminal account of the ways in which this self-representation distinguishes belief as a propositional attitude in "The Guise of the Good," *Noûs* 26 (1992), 3–26.

10. This is something that can properly be said to be understood – for example, by a young child – before a "self-representation of one's beliefs" becomes self-consciously available.

11. As before, we are assuming that we can speak of 'moral belief' or 'belief in moral statements or propositions' innocently, without thereby presupposing a cognitivist moral metatheory.

12. Universality in this sense must be distinguished from *non-relationalness*. The particular principles, motivations, virtues, etc. that are morally appropriate in a given social or historical context might be quite diverse, and might make a place for a number of essentially *individual* variables – for example one's spouse, one's children, one's friends, etc. But this does not morally privilege particular individuals as such (i.e., is non-indexical). I may have special moral obligations to my children, but *your* special moral obligations are to yours.

13. Recently, there has been an emerging critique of (a) and (b) in particular as essential to moral thought. Partial and particularist conceptions have been defended as (nonetheless) morally principled. One might, in the present context, see this critique as attempting to remove some of the *pretense* of morality that leaves it so vulnerable to ideological criticism.

14. I owe this term to David Wiggins; see his "Truth, Invention, and the Meaning of Life," rev. in Wiggins, *Needs, Values, Truth*, 3rd ed. (Oxford: Clarendon Press, 1998).

15. See J. L. Mackie, *Ethics: Inventing Right and Wrong* (Harmondsworth: Penguin, 1977).
16. Mackie's own view on this matter is not entirely clear. At one point he suggests that, if God were to exist, then so could "objective prescriptivity." But though God might provide an *external incentive* to act in accord with moral requirements, or might afford an awe-inspiring spectacle of command, there is no suggestion in Mackie's text as to how God or God's commands might actually ground *moral* authority.
17. In a sense, Rousseau pioneered this sort of understanding, when he argued that every group with a distinctive set of interests tends to develop a *moi commun* – a collective "me" – that purports to speak on behalf of the good of the whole. His remedy is to fight ideology with ideology, recommending the inculcation in the populace of a "civil religion" of deference to civil authority, and recommending to lawgivers that they purport to have received the laws from a divine source (Rousseau, *Du contrat social*).
18. It would enrich our discussion to be able to consider more teleological conceptions of the active side, such as those found among the Greeks. But, apart from noticing in passing the interesting legitimizing relationships among organic conceptions of proper function and hierarchy in society, the body, and the soul alike, we will leave these questions aside.
19. K. Polanyi, *The Great Transformation* (New York: Rinehart, 1994).
20. Cf. the paradigmatic "modern" response to attempts at the objective justification of morality, "So what?"
21. Even Mackie, who finds morality to be based upon a fundamental error, offers a reconstruction of moral practice.
22. Hobbes and Hume remain distrustful of social innovation, and come to the rescue of established property and hierarchical relations – urging citizens strongly (if not, in Hume's case, exceptionlessly) to have respect for private property, contractual obligations, and political authorities.
23. B. Williams, *Ethics and the Limits of Philosophy* (Cambridge: Harvard University Press, 1985). He gives special attention to "confidence" in an ethical outlook.
24. Some have thought that philosophical skepticism of the "the world might have been created five minutes ago to look just like this" sort doesn't need much of an answer, because it so unspecific in its problematization and because its practical implications are slight. I am grateful to David Lewis and Jim Joyce for reminding me of this.
25. On at least some accounts, a further, important presupposition is also present:

    (5) Beliefs and values that survive reflection are not only warranted, but also are such that holding them and acting upon them tends to promote genuine, usually general or "emancipatory," interests.

    For further discussion, see Raymond Geuss, *The Idea of a Critical Theory* (Cambridge: Cambridge University Press, 1981).
26. David Hume, *A Treatise of Human Nature*, L. A. Selby-Bigge, ed. (Oxford: Clarendon Press, 1888) 267–8; hereafter *Treatise* in parenthetic page references in the text.

27. And, of course, in the case of (5) (see note 25), in the power of reason to set us free.
28. See John Rawls, *A Theory of Justice* (Cambridge: Harvard University Press, 1971).
29. With special thanks to David Hills and James Joyce for helpful comments and conversations. Thanks, too, to Edward Harcourt for organizing the conference at which this paper was presented, and for his thoughtful and patient editing of this volume. A fellowship from the National Endowment for the Humanities helped support the writing of this paper (Grant FA-35357-99).

# Index

(Occurrences of names and subjects in endnotes and acknowledgements are not indexed.)

Lockean philosophy: and rights to private property, 187–90; and pollution and boundary crossing, 190–2, 218–20; and dispositional harms and risk, 192–4; and common property, 194–9; and risk and responsibility, 200–3

Mackie, J. L., 362–3
Marx, Karl: and critique of morality, 353–4, 367–8, 372
meaning: normativity of, 75–6; in factualism, 76–81. *See also* functional role versus concept; noncognitivism; nonfactualism
means/ends reasoning, 315–18
Mill, John Stuart, xiv, 118
Moore, G. E., xiv, 87, 100
moral ideal: compared to duty, 272–3
morality: in Gibbard, 79–80; reducing alienation in, 162–8; normative authority of, 339–44; ideological critique of, 355–6, 358–9, 369–71; characterized, 359–73; as contingent and relational, 375–7; and reliability of critical reflection on, 377–81
moral realism: characterized, xiii–xv, 4–5; and dilemma, 282–3. *See also* determinateness; explanation, moral; fact/value distinction
moral remainder or residue, 278–80
moral rightness, 22–3; evaluating naturalistic accounts of, 32–5
moral theory, 282–5; and contemporary ethics, 249–52; and pluralism, 252–60, 264–8; and moral dilemmas, 260–8; and expressive aspects of moral dilemmas, 268–82; critiques of, 353–5
moral values and norms, xvii, 117–20; characterized, 18, 21, 360–3; nonhypotheticalness of, 120–1, 122–3; and aesthetic value, 123–6; and regidification, 141–2, 143; and valoric utilitarianism, 240–5; and desire, 364–7. *See also* normative moral theory; intrinsic value
motivation: link between non-moral value and, 12–14; and instrumental rationality, 21; and instrumentalism, 47; and internalism, 48; and judgment of permissibility or obligatoriness, 120–2; benevolence as, 254–8. *See also* intrinsic motivation

naturalism, 62–6; characterized, 3–4; and moral realism, 4; and moral facts, 9; and aesthetic value, 114
natural rights. *See* Lockean philosophy: and rights to private property
necessity: in constitutive argument, 309–11
Neitzche, Friedrich: and critique of morality, 353–4, 372
noncognitivism: characterized, 70
nonfactualism: costs, 70–6; and factualist alternatives, 76–81
non-hypothetical reasons: defined, 293
non-moral goodness, 10–17; theories of, 32–5; and fact/value distinction, 43
normative facts, 69
normative judgment: appropriateness of, 45
normative moral theory, xv–xvii; realism, 17–29
normativity, 74–6; characterized, xvii–xviii, 322–4; and normative authority, 324–6, 348–9; and reason, 326–31; for belief; 327–31; and appreciation, 331–9; of moral rules, 339–44; and rule breaking, 344–9; of ideological critique of morality, 371–5
norms: of practical reasoning, 300–2
Nowell-Smith, P. H., 117
Nozick, Robert, 176

objectified subjective interest, 11–13; as supervenient upon facts, 16–17
objectivity: of morals and ethics, xi; and moral realism, 4, 5; versus subjectivity, 55–6; of subjects, 89–91; of aesthetic value, 91–3, 100; vertical and horizontal, 115; of moral evaluation, 131–3, 141–3. *See also* value: objectivity of

Parfit, Derek, 314
pluralism: in consequentialist accounts of the good, 162–3; in Kantian philosophy, 252–60; in utilitarianism, 264–8
pollution. *See* Lockean philosophy; Lockeanism, revisionist
practical reasoning, 293; and action, 300–9; constitutive argument in, 309–11
property rights. *See* Lockean philosophy: and rights to private property

psychological theory: and value, 52–3, 56, 61–2

queerness: facticity of values and argument from, 44, 55–6

Ramsey, F. P., 77, 80
rationality: instrumental conception of, 6; social versus individual, 22–9; and determinability in defense of fact/value distinction, 43, 44–5; and agency in Gibbard, 71–2; natural-factual meaning of, 77–81; and rational choice defined, 326–7
Rawls, John, 141, 155, 175; and definition of morality, 360
reasoning. See theoretical reasoning; practical reasoning
reductionism and reducibility, 17: and moral realism, 4, 5; and subjective interests, 10, 11, 12
reflective equilibrium, 301–2
Regan, Donald, 262
relationalism, 48; and goodness, 16, 48–9; and aesthetic value, 126; and intrinsic value, 138–40, 142, 143; and morality, relational, 375–7
relativism: and moral realism, 5; distinguished from relationalism, 49; of moral evaluation, 142; of morality, 373–5
rights to private property. See Lockean philosophy: and rights to private property
risk: pure, 193–4, 198, 203; acceptable, 206–11
Ross, W. D., 266
Russell, Bertrand, 88, 241

Scheffler, Samuel, 173
secondary qualities: and value, 10, 131–44
sentiment: and aesthetic value, 91–2
Shoemaker, Sidney, 132, 138, 139
Smith, Michael, 307
social rationality: and moral rightness, 22–3; and feedback, 24–6; and evolution of social norms, 26–9; limitations on theory of, 30–2

subjective interests, 10–11
supervenience: 10, 16–17; and aesthetic value, 114. See also explanation
sympathy: in Hume versus Kant, 341–2; versus obedience to rules, 346–8

theoretical reasoning, 293; and beliefs, 294–9
truth and truth values: theories of and moral realism, 4, 5. See also noncognitivism; nonfactualism

universality: and moral realism, 5; of moral maxims, 262–3
utilitarianism, 226–7, 250, 251; and alienation, 162–3; rule utilitarianism, 227–8; motive utilitarianism, 228–31; act utilitarianism, 230, 241; character and act utilitarianism, 231–3; character versus act utilitarianism, 234–9; valoric
utilitarianism, 240–5; and pluralism and dilemma, 264–8; and indirect-utilitarian theories, 265–6; and definition of morality, 360, 362

valence, 56
value, 45–7; realism about, xiii–xv, 9–17; absolutism, 47; as relational, 48; judgments, 49; facticity of, 53–7; and determinateness, 57–62; and naturalism, 62–3; objectivity of, 85–7, 89–93; subjectivity of, 88–9; and value-based explanations, 106–9. See also aesthetic value; moral value; intrinsic value; fact/value distinction; non-moral goodness. See also moral evaluation and value
Velleman, David, 293–4

wants/interests mechanism: and desire formation, 14–17, 20, 49–52. See also desires: and beliefs
Williams, Bernard, 161, 167, 171, 173, 373
Wittgenstein, Ludwig Josef Johan, xviii, 120, 121, 123; on aesthetic appreciation, 338–9